THE COMPLETE INTERDICTION AND SURVIVAL STRATEGIES

Criminal Interdiction / Tactical Survival / Behavior Analysis and Interviewing Techniques / Statement Analysis all with Expanded Material / and S.T.E.Ps – Stress, Training, and Empirical Perspectives

STEVEN VARNELL

"It will be your life or your death depending on how well you train."

Criminal Interdiction
Steven Varnell

To those brave souls that have suffered the ultimate sacrifice for the rest of us, whether we were deserving of such sacrifice or not. Still you stepped into the streets and gave it all.

<u>Also by Steven Varnell</u>

Criminal Interdiction
Tactical Survival
Behavior Analysis and Interviewing Techniques (BAIT)
Statement Analysis – An ISS Workbook

CONTENTS

Criminal Interdiction

Tactical Survival

S.T.EP's

Behavior Analysis and Interviewing Techniques

Statement Analysis

"There is a destiny that makes us brothers, none goes his way alone. All that we send into the lives of others comes back into our own."

William Jennings Bryan

THE TRUTH OF THE STREET - 1

Every year approximately 150 police officers are killed in the line of duty within the United States. On average, one police officer will be killed every other day. Were all of these deaths caused by felonious attacks upon the officers? No, but about half of their deaths will be the result of some type of personal assault. According to statistics maintained by the FBI, nearly 60,000 officers are assaulted each year. These assaults resulted in nearly 16,000 injuries. The number is staggering. I believe, without a doubt that these numbers can and should be reduced. An act of God can never be stopped, but an act of man can.

During the course of my duties as a State Trooper, I come across other officers every day. I watch as they go through their "routine" on a stop or encounter. All of us are taught the basics in the police academies; somehow, over time we lose much of what we have learned. We have all heard about complacency. It exists at all levels of everyday life. In the profession of law enforcement, it can result in dire consequences. I do not say this to criticize other officers, but simply to make observations of their actions. I have studied and understand why many of the things we do can lead to additional dangers upon ourselves. I know we can do better. Our lives and those lives of people around us depend on us honing certain skills. My hope is to change the habits of at least one officer by the reading of these pages. As I will tell you at the end, we will all feel that self-satisfaction, at the end of the shift.

Throughout these chapters, we will cover items as basic as a traffic stop to the more difficult task (not really) of identifying a criminal. We will go through the clues they give us during an encounter that we so often miss. They tell us the things we need, but we do not listen. They show us everything required to alert ourselves, but we fail to watch. Some of the topics may seem basic to a few of you, but I believe everyone will learn something. One of the many things lacking in all police departments is training. Some outsiders believe that the training officers receive is intense and never ending. The truth of the matter is that much of it is based on tradition and not reality. The intensive training is in the beginning at the academy level. It is designed heavily to see who can take the rigors of discipline and who cannot. You only begin to learn the job once you are on the streets. Once you are on the street, budget restraints and personnel shortages usually prevent proper field training from taking place.

Firearms' training is one of the most important areas of instruction. Most agencies only qualify their personnel once or twice a year. There are many among us who can barely shoot. Every time we are on the range these same people are unable to properly load their weapon, have jams, which they cannot clear, or simply fail to qualify. We will see in the upcoming chapters just how important it is to be proficient in all of the high liability areas. It is frightening to me that these same people will be my backup to purportedly drag my ass out of trouble if I ever need help. We have them in every agency, therefore the burden falls upon us to train even harder to overcome and adapt.

We are all told after a day on the range that you should get ammunition and practice on your own time. This unstructured, self-teaching time on the range, can be just as important as any formalized training you will ever receive. The agencies simply cannot afford to continually provide all of your training; therefore, the onus falls to you. I am writing this with the sole purpose of trying to share almost three decades of law enforcement, which includes 27 years as a full time criminal interdiction officer. There are always those people who will find fault with everything. Many may disagree with the ideas I present. That criticism, if well founded, is all right with me. I am not here to tell you what the definitive answers are, but to share what I have learned along the way. I still learn new things all of the time. The officer who is locked into a single path to get to the other side will always fail if there is an obstacle on the trail. You have to always have an alternate route in order to understand the landscape. I have taught many of these ideas in classroom settings and some of you may have been in one of my classes. The result of this book has been a compilation of teaching and learning from officers throughout the country. I took this knowledge

2

into a world of self-experimentation and practical use in the field. My father spent nearly four decades in law enforcement and my son is now with us as well. Getting it right means a lot to me because I will still have assets in the field long after I am gone.

Cops will always be cops. They act tough and mean sometimes, but it is a necessary part of the occupation. They are also the softest, easiest, most kind, and giving people in the world. Other than firefighters or our soldiers, who else is willing to put their life on the line for a total stranger? Until tragedy strikes in someone's life, they will only see the tough side of a police officer. Remember, the most common interactions that anyone will ever have with the police is when something has gone wrong in their life.

But with an open mind, new or old, experienced or brand new, I think you will find something in these pages that can make you a better officer. More important to me is the possibility that you change a current habit which saves your life. This sometimes occurs without anyone's knowledge, but at the end of the day, you know you did a good job. What nobler profession exists than one which protects people's property and lives? After taking care of everyone else, you complete the most important task of each day. You go home safe to your families.

WHY ARE WE THERE? - 2

The first city police services to be established in the United States was in Philadelphia in 1751, followed by Richmond, Virginia in 1807, Boston in 1838, and then New York in 1845. Many people feel that justice should be handled independently by the masses without the need for an organized police force. They feel as though the police have too many powers over their everyday lives. The community itself could better serve Justice. All those brave liberals could ban together against the evil hordes. In fact, many will tell you that it is the police themselves which are at the root of so much of the violence in today's society. Many people living in their utopias cannot tell the difference between the cops and the crooks. They believe that if you saw a problem in your neighborhood, you would organize the neighborhood against the problem. What a great idea, which so many free thinkers actually believe. Now let's face the truth! How many people have ever wanted to get involved in even the smallest of issues? How many none-gun owners are there who are physically stepping into the fight for this country? They certainly know how to call upon others to do the hard work. They are swift to write in their blogs about all of the evils perceived in society. The question is which one among them is willing to step up to the plate. Take a swing out of crime. Do more than run your mouth. Actions talk and the words run away to hide so they can blog another day.

There has always been and always will be a percentage of the population who do wrong against others. There will always be predators among us looking for their prey. There have always been a few people with the abilities required to take a stand against this type of person. Most people's life is just too busy doing other things that usually leaves us with just one option. That option has never included the above-mentioned utopia. The option, which we are speaking about, is that we pay others to do the work for us. Community and business people have always had other desires in mind. However, they have always understood that these predators had to be dealt with. As many officers will tell you, they themselves are not always the most admired people. We have to dirty ourselves for them, but they often will have disdain towards us. They know it will be the cop who will direct them on how to conduct their own behaviors. What a shock! There are people who do not know how to conduct themselves civilly in society. It is the sheep herd mentality. All of the sheep hate having the sheep dog around overlooking their every move. The dog requires them to do things beyond their utopist freewill. That is until the wolves appear on the hill. Then the stay huddled together, finally willing to obey every rule and wait for the dog to finish their fight.

Have you ever thought about the reason why there really are police officers? There are many academics who can give you the textbook versions why, but for me it is just two words; Asshole Confrontation. I heard it said once in a Matt Braun novel about the great Oklahoma lawman Bill Tilghman. He said, "The good intentioned men of the world are quick to recruit others in the name of justice. But, they were wary of dirtying their own hands and easily frightened. The moralists in life are seldom fighters." Well said, Mr. Braun.

Most people do not have the combination of senses, integrity, and courage that are all required to be a cop. Most people cannot do this job that is a fact. It is a job for a special person. Just as before, most people do not want to get their hands dirty. They do not want to face down those who need to be faced. It is a unique profession where you are given weapons. You have the requirement to make life and death, freedom or detention decisions. Any one of these decisions can affect a person's life forever. You are given a certain amount of power that no one else possesses. Yet as we all know, make one mistake and there can be hell to pay.

What other job has an internal affairs division? What other job exist where the instantaneous decisions you make can lead to your own termination, civil lawsuits, or even criminal charges? Who else do you know has to go to work each day and wear a bulletproof vest because in the course of the job someone may want to shoot you? How many people go to work and strap on guns, knives, radios, pepper gas, Tasers, a baton, and handcuffs as the defensive tools of their trade. Without them, many more of us would never come home. The average person goes to work with their computers, aprons, pens, cell phones, and other common tools of their trades. They are not sure if they like you and are often afraid of your authority. I know this sounds like them versus us mentality. Nothing could be further from the truth. There are far more supporters of the police than there have ever been of detractors. Unfortunately, in our day-to-day dealings with the others, we do not always get to see or hear our supporters.

Many people in law enforcement have no business being in the job. So many people in the public wish they were doing our job, but for a multitude of issues are not. A very fulfilling job continues to professionalize itself more every year. Many thousands of people apply to the various agencies. Very few applicants will ever complete the process and have a career in law enforcement. Fewer yet will ever retire from the profession.

To most people, you are the cop who pulled them over for speeding or running a red light. "But I am late officer." You are the cop who only turns on their emergency lights to go through traffic lights because you are late for lunch. On the other hand, you are the jerk who arrested my friend over a little weed. The moment they need help, who are they going to call? Will it be their friends, family, or others? No, it is 911. Now it becomes, thank God you are here officer. By the next morning, all has returned to normal. When they are pulled over for something else, it will be, "But officer I was just going with the flow of traffic." All cops are on a power trip, right? The attitude that we face from the people we encounter each day takes a toll on you. Cynicism develops and grows inside of you. I find this topic to be so important that I will talk about it in the last chapter. You will hear the following sentence again. The job entails more than most realize and produces a brotherhood that few understand.

Many start the profession with good intentions, but the vast majority discover, for a variety of reasons that law enforcement is not for them. You have to be hard, yet soft. You have to be a strong talker and a good listener. You have to be able to think on your feet and make split second decisions. You have to be very visual in your perceptions for the common things and still notice the faint clues. You have to be aggressive, yet patient. You have to be willing to tolerate what few people would throughout your career. You have to be willing to work when everyone else you know is off. You work shift work, days, evenings, relief, midnights and holidays. You have to keep yourself physically fit and mentally intact. Most people believe that cops are uneducated thugs, but actually, they are well educated. All officers today have completed high school, almost all with some college education, many with 2 and 4-year degrees, and some with masters or doctorate degrees. While in the profession, you will be required to complete courses of various types throughout your entire career. The learning can never stop.

It is a profession with no equals. The ranks of the agencies are filled with every type of person. There are ex-military, college graduates, and recruits who are very young to middle aged. They decided that they wanted to do something in an effort to help their communities. The training academies are very difficult. Most will last as long as 6 months. Most people will tell you that they would rather go through boot camp again than to go through a police academy. There is a reason for this. More police officers will be injured each year than American soldiers in the Afghan/Iraq war will. The streets can be a battle zone and it is where we work every single day. The truth of the matter is you never can tell who will make a good cop. It is worth repeating that it entails more than most realize and produces a brotherhood that few understand.

In the end, after all of the discussions, arguments, and lectures, the conclusion remains the same. Our primary responsibility is Asshole Confrontation. The size of the asshole varies, but we are the only ones willing and ready to confront them. It is the thin blue line. It is the brotherhood. It is our job.

THE UNIFORMED OFFICER - 3

The one event where citizens interact with the police most often is the traffic stop. We reach out and touch more people each day, across the country, with the traffic stop than with any other action. For this reason alone I can tell you, the uniformed officer is the single most effective weapon that exists for fighting crime. Everyone talks about becoming an undercover officer, a detective, or any position other than working the street in uniform. I have listened as investigators talk about going back on patrol in uniform as a negative action or a punishment.

The street cop will arrest most criminals. A street cop arrested most serial killers in the history of America. There is one fact that has never changed in the last century. After nearly every crime, the criminal will get into a car and drive away. That same criminal is guaranteed to be the driver or passenger in a vehicle at some point after every crime. We live in a mobile society. No longer, do most people live, grow old, and die in the same neighborhood. We are all going to drive. When trying to solve a crime we always try to find the vulnerable spot. There is always the proverbial weak link in a chain. For the criminal element it is the moment they enter a car.

Look at some of the more notorious serial killers. There was Ted Bundy, pulled over for a broken tail light. Dennis Rader, the BTK Killer, captured after a traffic stop. David Berkowitz, the "Son of Sam," was initially picked up for loitering. William Suff killed over 12 prostitutes. He was arrested after a routine traffic stop. The list goes on and on. This does not take into account the non-serial killers who have just committed a homicide. When the criminal travels to commit a crime, they carry the tools of their trade with them. When they finish their crimes, they will travel with the tools and with the elements of the crime itself. A sharp uniformed street cop will stop this person. The cop goes past the stop based on the actions of the criminal and an arrest is made. The daily news is full of wanted fugitives arrested by police after a traffic stop. They are involved in criminal interdictions.

From the Bureau of Justice Statistics, the most common reason for contact with the police is some form of traffic stop or traffic related incident. In 2005, 41% of all face-to-face contacts with police involved traffic stops and 12% involved traffic accidents. About half of all traffic stops resulted in a traffic ticket. Police searched approximately 5% of all stopped drivers during a traffic stop. Of the 43.5 million persons who had contact with police in 2005, an estimated 1.6% had force used or threatened against them during their most recent contact. To some people this is taken out of context to show the injustices committed against people. What this actually indicates is that we are out there doing our job. Despite what some people try to claim, the statistic that only 5% of the drivers stopped in this 2005 study were searched is very telling. Some try to claim they are stopped and searched everywhere they go. As a person who has been pulled over by the police and you have done nothing criminally wrong, have you been searched? No, probably not. There are always exceptions to the rules, but we do a very hard job very well. We have to distinguish between the innocent and the guilty during a short encounter. They both tell us everything during the stop. I hope to show you how to recognize these nuisances in the chapters to come.

What about potential terrorist? Look at some of the arrest.

February 2002 – I-70 in Utah, a deputy seizes $300,000.00 from an undocumented Jordanian believed to have ties to Al Qaeda.
February 2002 – I-80 in Omaha, a police officer stops a car with two Jordanian's. The information obtained leads to breaking up a money laundering operation funneling drug proceeds to the Middle East.

April 1995 – An Oklahoma State Trooper stops Timothy McVeigh and arrest him for driving with a suspended license and carrying a concealed weapon. He was fleeing Oklahoma City after bombing the Alfred P. Murrah building.

May 2002 – Nevada State Troopers stop Lucas Helder who was identified as the mailbox pipe bomb terrorist.

August 2007 - Arrest of two University of South Florida Middle Eastern students with pipe bombs in their trunk.

These are just a few of the countless encounters and criminal interdictions being accomplished each day. Let's not forget the great cops we have on our waterways and points of entry into the United States. There are the water cops who have interdicted several possible terrorist events in and around MacDill Air Force Base, the home of Central Command for our military. There are the uniformed Customs Inspectors who stopped the Algerian man who planned to bomb Los Angeles International Airport. There was the Customs Inspector who stopped Mohammed al Kahtani in the Orlando airport. He was to be the 20th terrorist on Flight 93 on 9-11. Flight 93 was the plane that crashed into the empty field near Shanksville, Pennsylvania after the passengers courageously tried to take the plane back over. This plane was destined for The Capitol Building or The White House. With the terrorist short one comrade, who knows what the outcome would have been.

In earlier times and in other countries the uniformed patrol officer is called the "Preventive Police." It designates the police, which patrol and respond to emergencies. The name preventive police says it all in that the first line of protection for the general public is our mere presence. Everyone tries to behave when the cops come around. We will soon learn that this change in behavior will identify the person who has excessive nervous behaviors when encountering the police.

The interdiction of criminals, fugitives, kidnappers, murders, human traffickers, gun smugglers and drug traffickers occur every day on the streets of this country. Most of us never hear of the vast majority of these events. Many will only hear about those that occur in their local area of news coverage. The average person, crook and even cop never thinks about how safe our communities are because of the uniformed officer. Many criminal activities are prevented simply by their presence. These preventions are never seen or recognized, but they do exist. If there was some way to account for these preventions we would all be amazed by what is accomplished just by having a marked patrol car driving in an area. There are programs around the country where the local police will park a marked unit at a location and leave it. The crime in that location generally goes down even though there is no officer in the car. Just the presence of the patrol car alone deters criminals. Many people owe their lives to the street cop who just happened to be in a certain place at a certain time. Their presence prevented property from being taken, personal harm from occurring or even homicide. However, because these events never took place, it is not possible to account for them. Every cop out there knows that they have saved lives by simply driving down a street.

Everyone loves statistics, so let us use them for a moment. How many times has a cop been told after a traffic stop, "Don't you have anything better to do than to stop me for …?" Fill in the blank. We have all heard it at least a million times for every violation somewhere. A scene from the Kevin Costner movie "The Untouchables" always brings the question clear to me. There is a scene on a bridge in the front part of the movie where Costner is leaning on the rail of a bridge. Sean Connery walks by as a beat cop and sees Costner throw a piece of paper into the water. When Connery questions Costner of his actions, Costner says the same thing.

Connery - You want to throw garbage. Throw it in the goddamn trash basket.

Costner - Don't you have more important things to do?

Connery - Yeah. But I'm not doing them right now. Do we understand each other?

If you would like another answer to the question, you can always provide them with the statistics from the National Highway Traffic Safety Administration. There are over 6 million traffic crashes each year. Approximately 40,000 people will die in the U.S. from traffic crashes alone. Almost 3 million people will be injured with a financial cost of about $230 billion dollars. Yearly, there are fewer than 10,000 murders. Statistics now show numerically which one is about four times more important. However, to the victim and their families, the loss is the same. You cannot devalue one over the other. A loss is a loss. But to everyone, cops included, it is the homicide investigator receives all the accolades while the uniform cop just does his job. Though one can see that I am bias when it comes to this issue, I can still honestly tell you I have nothing but respect for the investigators. They are doing a tough job, but everyone forgets where they first learned the tricks of the trade. It was as a uniformed patrol officer working the streets. It is like the offensive linemen of the NFL. Most of us know very little about them, but can tell you everything about the touchdown makers. Few touchdowns would ever be made without a good offensive line. The uniformed patrol officer is the best source of everything that is happening on the street. They can tell you who is doing what, where, and with whom. They are the criminal interdiction officers.

PROACTIVE PATROL - 4

There are many definitions for a good cop. In my opinion, a good cop is aggressive. They seek out their activity. They are proactive. They do not sit and wait for someone else to radio them their next assignment. You are on patrol and observe someone waving to get your attention. You stop to see if you can help the person. This person tells you that people in the area are driving too fast and are not stopping for the stop signs. They then proceed to explain your plan of enforcement to deal with this activity. They instruct you to park in an adjacent driveway and enforce the aforementioned violations. Is this actually going to happen? I think not! We sarcastically laugh at the thought of this scenario. However, by the same account, waiting for a civilian dispatcher to tell you what your next assignment will be is exactly the same thing. Go on patrol and stay aggressive. The dispatch center should be interfering with your proactive patrol.

While on patrol, a felony call comes out. Everyone is breaking their necks to get there. At the same time while on patrol, you see a person leaning into a car. The two exchange something. The person then drives away and the other person walks off looking around suspiciously. In all probability you just witnessed a felony drug purchase! Most uniformed officers drive by and know what is happening, but fail to react. Why? There certainly are enough reasonable suspicions to conduct an investigative interview. Besides, the pedestrian is probably going to run when you approach. The driver is going to be very nervous if you pull him over. These actions are some of the responses that we will be watching for. Their actions will add more to substantiate your observations.

My first partner and I would collect information where the most crimes had occurred. Working at night, we knew where the drug holes were located. We would go to these areas and park on a dark side street. Using binoculars, we would stand at the edge of the street and watch, as cars would stop at the end of the block. When they finished, the car would drive past our location. The drivers would not be able to see our marked patrol cars in the dark. We would follow them out of the area and conduct a traffic stop. Only one time was the driver or passenger not holding drugs. On this occasion, the driver had a $20.00 dollar bill in between his legs. He just had not yet decided to buy the drugs, but he would have on the next approach. We would then watch to see where the dealers were going to pick up their drugs at the time of the sale. Some people call it their "bomb." It is the larger stash that dealers will keep nearby. When a sale has transpired, they will remove from the stash the amount of drugs sold. In this manner, they may not be caught with drugs on their person. We would then drive to their location and stop. Of course everyone would run. Some of them were caught and arrested. Most would slip away in the night. We would then go and seize their stashes. The intelligence gathered would be given to street crimes units. We made a lot of arrest and were always in uniform with marked units. An aggressive patrol officer can seize more drugs than most narcotics detectives have ever dreamed of getting.

You must know the laws of your state. You must seek out the simplest of violations. Some may call them petty, but their enforcement is your job. You do not write the laws, you enforce them. This knowledge of the law gives you more abilities to reach out and touch. It opens additional avenues to conduct a stop. The more quality stops you have, the more arrest you will make. Remember, Ted Bundy the serial killer, was arrested over a tail light.

There are so many factors of safety, especially with a new officer. In addition, it takes a new officer time to comprehend everything. With time comes the experience. The problems arise from the type of academic and field training each officer receives. I know there are field-training officers who are inexperienced. They are training new recruits with only 2 or 3 years of experience themselves. Are these the veterans we need to train our recruits? How much experience can possibly be shown to the new recruit? How much information is retained and what is lost without repetitive actions. We are all taught many good techniques, but then we forget them without regular use. Every stop should be performed as if it could be the best stop of your life. It certainly could be the most dangerous. There are so many factors to consider each day. It is impossible to stay completely focused on the job during your shift. Every officer has to have that mental sharpness each day to stay focused. I have always gone back to the fatal errors made by police officers to help keep myself focused. Here they are for you to use as your daily guide:

a. Your attitude – The failure to keep your mind on the job. We each have different circumstances taking place in our personal lives. There are illnesses, divorces, financial issues, problems with children, etc. If you are not maintaining your attention on the job, you must do something about it. Take a sick day or an annual day off. Make sure you discuss issues that can affect your performance with your zone partner. Some will think that these issues are no one else's business. However, you depend on each other for personal safety. When someone else's well-being can be determined by how you react, it is their business. Withholding your problems is fine for an office job. On the streets, you can get someone hurt. They can watch over you more closely. This is something most of us forget. We are completely dependent on one another.

b. Tombstone Courage – Yeah all right, we all know you are a tough guy. Do not hesitate to wait for back up. When I first came on, I was told you do not call for backup unless you were already in a life or death situation. What a stupid philosophy. Call as soon as you believe backup should be there. That extra sense we possess is usually right on the money. When the hair on your neck stands up, the radio is pressed.

c. Rest – We all have been guilty of this. Our bodies need rest. Any fitness trainer will tell you the big three issues for health are exercise, nutrition, and rest. All are equally important. Your mind and reactions are not as sharp when they are tired. In today's world of overtime and off duty, remember which job comes first. Most agencies have maximum hours allowed requirements for on duty and off duty employment. How many of us see officers work a shift all day and then have to be on duty all night. They are dangerously tired. They become inattentive and in no hurry to do anything, but sleep. They may have made a couple of dollars to put in their pocket, but at what cost.

d. Bad Positioning – This applies to everything from the placement of your car to your personal placement. Our positioning in various situations will be discussed later. But, remember, if possible, your car should be well off the road. You should always maintain a lot of distance from the violator.

Make a passenger's side approach and keep everyone in the vehicle.

e. Recognizing Danger – This will also be discussed later in detail. We mentioned earlier that we do not always hear and see what has been said and done. We are good at seeing the large issues, but usually we will miss the small clues. Brake lights or turn signals are still on after the stop, breathing, behaviors, etc. You will find this fault frequently in officers because they are moving too fast. Motor cops are notorious for having activity requirements. If you want to stay on the squad, you will produce activity. All this produces are unsafe practices and sometimes leads to excessive punishment to many drivers. How many tickets are you giving each person? You have to slow the pace of the stop down to recognize what is happening.

f. Hands – The two things that will usually lead to us being injured or killed are the hands. Watch a person's hands. You do not have to stare at them, but always be aware of them. The hands are the weapon that is going to strike you, push you, or draw a gun. We will see later through scientific studies how attention to the hands produces a faster response to danger. Watch the hands because they also indicate a person's level of nervousness. When the adrenaline begins to pump, the hands will shake.

g. Relaxing Too Soon – Never completely relax in any type of encounter. Unless you have stopped your mom, the person is a complete stranger in every way. Their history, their temperament, or their intentions are unknown. I know you have to relax during your shift. This can occur while on patrol. By paying attention to yourself and your surroundings, you will discover how quickly you elevate or deescalate your senses.

h. Handcuffing – All too often, we do not handcuff a person that should be secured. It is all right, go ahead, and handcuff to detain. Do you have a reasonable suspicion that the person has or is going to commit a crime? If yes, then handcuff them. If it is later determined the person is not going to be arrested, you can take them off. Remember (f) above. You are much safer having the one thing that can cause you the greatest harm secured. In a profile of officers killed, as examined by the FBI, other officers stated they would have reacted sooner than the victim officer had. This is a lesson that many newer officers fail to comprehend. Hesitations can cause you harm.

i. Search – A bad search is no search. Always search a person well. Always search a vehicle thoroughly. Pat downs are different. Can you ask to pat down anyone? Yes, you can. Can they refuse? Yes, they can. Should your internal alarms be going off if they do? Yes, they should. Do not forget to crotch a person if you are searching them. Make sure if you do, it is a person of the same gender. Only 4%-8% of offenders questioned ever felt they were thoroughly searched. 70% said they had never had their groin area searched; therefore, the groin area is their preferred place to conceal a gun or contraband. With the opposite sex, you can use the back of your hand to complete the pat down.

j   Equipment – Goes without saying. Keep your equipment clean. Test daily those things that are supposed to be tested i.e. Tasers, handcuffs. I like an old Navy SEAL saying that one is none and two is one. If your gun jams, you have none unless you carry a backup. The same goes for two knives, handcuffs, and several handcuff keys.

We could probably all add to this list. Creating anything to this list, which has a safety focus, is a bonus. Thinking ahead and always studying the situation is critical. Once you have determined that you know all there is to know about law enforcement, you have committed a grievous error.

We should all be in some type of physical fitness program. You do not have to be Charles Atlas, or maybe more of you would recognize Arnold, but get out and do something. If you do not like to run, do some type of strength training, walking, swimming, or biking. Look at the Officer Down Memorial Page website and you will see several officers each year who die from on duty heart attacks. It is about taking a proactive approach to the job. Your personal appearance can have consequences or benefits. Outside of probably living longer, a sharp, well-kept officer displays a greater air of authority. I am not talking about arrogance, but attentiveness to the job. We all know those arrogant self-centered officers. We never want to try to immolate them. Examining several cases where officers were assaulted and murdered, the criminal stated they felt that they could overtake the officer. Sometimes the criminal stated the officer did not respect them. They were too easy going. All predators in life seek out the weakest prey by appearance. If they had to choose to attack an officer, who would they attack. The officer, who is overweight, has a sloppy appearance, and their equipment is dirty. They have missing equipment on the belts and stains all over their uniforms. What do I mean by missing equipment? I know you have seen the officer who does not wear their radio outside of the car. The officer who has forgotten their flashlight during a low light traffic stop. Or do you think the predator is going to go after the officer who is physically fit, well-groomed, sharp equipment, good stance and posturing. Sometimes none of it will matter, but many times it will. It goes back to the one word I have used for my family, friends, and opponents. Choice; we all have choices in everything we do. Some will refer to it as freewill. Only you can choose which choice you wish to pursue.

Keeping the list of fatal errors in mind, let's take a look at the FBI's study on Law Enforcement deaths. Their studies show that the mistakes made by law enforcement that contributed to their demise was:

- Failure to wait for back-up
- The failure to draw their weapon when the time was appropriate
- Tunnel vision when dealing with more than one individual
- Failure to keep people in their car
- Their vehicle placement after the stop
- Failure to immediately control a known suspect
- Mental planning of different scenarios

We see these issues and refer back to the fatal errors. We will see all of these repeatedly in the pages that follow. We can examine each of these topics. We can discuss them, think about them, and see what we can do to avoid them. What can I do to make myself a more safety conscience and efficient officer? When you see your partner make these mistakes, bring them up to them tactfully. Remember, there are very few sheep in this profession. Sometimes you will do better by diplomatically talking things out with them rather than by being blunt. But, it needs to be talked about. This officer may be your back up one day. You will not want them to make the same mistake when your back is turned and your life could be on the line. We have all been guilty of the mental errors and tactical mistakes. It is inevitable and unavoidable. But, any reduction in the number of these mistakes that we make can save lives.

THE TRAFFIC STOP - 5

One area is rarely practiced once we have left the training academy. It is the practice of various tactics for a traffic stop. I know you have made thousands of them and believe there is no need to review the strategy of a traffic stop. I say you are dangerously wrong. We have made so many traffic stops; I believe most of us have become complacent. We try not to use the terminology; however, most officers view them as routine. I see so many errors committed each day by officers in traffic stops. Most of the agencies will study the causes of patrol car crashes. After collecting the data, they always review what can be done to avoid them. We always discuss the dangers of guns, yet rarely talk about the dangers of cars. I like to put it this way. You are in a regular sized room when you are given a choice. The event will happen and you must stay in the room. You can lie down or seek cover behind the tables, but it is your choice. Option A is someone on the outside will fire a gun at the window of the building and into your room. Option B is someone will drive a car at 70mph into your room. Given these mandatory options, we would all accept Option A and probably be left unscathed. Options B will in all likelihood, lead to us being injured or killed. A motor vehicle is the true deadliest force. We constantly practice to defend ourselves against the persons in the cars we have stopped. Rarely do we practice tactics to protect ourselves from the cars going past the stops.

We are on patrol on any road system of America in a marked patrol car. You see a violation ahead and you decide to take action. We have always known that one of the most dangerous situations for law enforcement is the traffic stop. There exist dangers as you pull out into traffic to make a stop. There are the additional dangers inherent with the overtaking of the targeted vehicle. Then there are the dangers that exist after the traffic stop. With time and repetition, all of these actions seem to fade in importance. Because there are problems at every level of the stop, they should always be in the back of your mind. Not to frighten you, but to keep you from becoming complacent. Because of the speeds involved, an interstate system is by far the most dangerous place to work. There is good reason why pedestrians are forbidden and there are minimum speed limits on an interstate roadway. How many people are actually driving the speed limit of 70 mph? We can say the actual number is rather low. Most people are driving much faster. At 70 mph, you are traveling at approximately 105 feet per second. The standard perception-reaction time is 1.5 seconds. Therefore, by the time you react, you have already traveled over 157 feet. You will travel almost half the distance of a football field before your brake response to avoid a collision has begun.

You are working patrol and decide to conduct a traffic stop. Just prior to the stop you enter the tag number into your in car computer, if you have one. You start watching the occupants in the car. You are taking note of their activities. Has anything about their behaviors changed? Are there passengers in the vehicle? Are the passengers looking back at you? Is the driver changing his driving patterns or committing any additional traffic violations? Is the driver watching you obsessively in the rearview or side view mirrors? I have always preached to anyone who would listen. Never just, race up to a car and immediately stop them. Give it a moment to see how they are going to react as you are driving behind or near them. This is the start of your encounter.

You should already be taking a mental inventory of what you see such as: bumper stickers, air fresheners, or maybe a rental decal in the side rear window. They will place bumper stickers such as police or firefighter unions, American flags, or patriotic symbols on their cars. They want you to believe that they are on your side so you will not stop them. Excessive air fresheners should attract your attention. Have you ever placed a dozen air fresheners in your car? We have also seen cards of Jesus Malverde, "El Rey Guei de Sinaloa." He is the patron saint of smugglers. Even as common today as Malverde will be Santa Muerte, the saint of death. If you are not familiar with either of these characters, you should be. They are very visible in the smuggling trade as both tattoos and figurines.

When the car pulls off the road, what happens? It sounds simple enough, but a lot of additional information can be obtained at this point. How long does it take them to stop? Are they using the turn signals? Do all of the lights on the vehicle work? Are there any changes in the occupant's behaviors? We ask ourselves this question again because the behaviors may not change until they are actually pulled over? Often times you will see a passenger fake being asleep. Should your level of awareness be increasing? Yes.

The violator moves to the right side of the road and stops. For the safety of everyone involved, be sure that the location is right. When I say right I mean is it as safe as it can be. Is there plenty of shoulder or is it next to a ditch, guardrail, or some other obstacle. If it is not a good location, then it is your responsibility to move the stop to a better location. You have to choose the location for the stop, not the violator. How many times have you seen a police officer talking with a violator against a wall? It sounds so simple, but the "routine" is overriding their common sense. How often, while working on the interstate, have you heard the sound of a vehicle hitting the rumble strip on the shoulder? That vibrating tire sound always draws your attention, especially if it is behind you. You always curse the driver in your mind because that could have easily been on top of you. Get off the road. Get all the way into the grass if you can. Have the other driver do the same if possible. Remember, the vast majority of people you pull over have only committed a traffic offense. You brought them to where they are; therefore, it is up to you to keep them safe until you have completed the stop.

This last paragraph carries a special meaning for me. On 9 June 1989, my field-training officer Lt. Benedict J. Thomas was walking back to his patrol car. He had stopped to check on an abandoned car on I-75. As he reached his driver's door, another driver accidentally drove off the road and onto the emergency shoulder. I lost a friend that day I will never forget. It is for "BJ" I can tell you to get your car completely off the road. Handle your business as far from traffic as is possible.

The stop takes place and it turns out to be a bad spot. Give the violator instructions via your PA system or approach partway to explain where you want them to move too. Tell them "I need you to drive past the guardrail and pull completely onto the grass." "I need you to drive to the next parking lot on your right and stop inside of the lot." Be specific, otherwise they will use their own judgment, which is why you are having them move in the first place. They are only responding to the lights in their mirror. They are not giving any thought as to where the best place to pull over will be. Many people have never or rarely ever been pulled over. The safety factors of the stop are up to you to determine. Do not pull up alongside of them and talk to them out of your window. Some of you chuckle because you have done this or have seen this performed many times.

What about your positioning in the car? At the time of the stop are you still wearing your seatbelt? Do the policies or specific training requirements of your agency dictate when you can take off your seatbelt? In my opinion, your seatbelt should have come off at the time your emergency lights were activated. By the time the cars come to a stop it is too late. If someone intends to do you harm you now have immediate avenues of escape. If the person suddenly speeds away after the stop, all you have to do is put the seatbelt back on. How many times have you tried to get out of your car and you were still wearing the seatbelt? How many times has the seatbelt been caught on a piece of equipment on your utility belt? What if you are not wearing your seatbelt and the person you are stopping suddenly brakes hard? You must maintain plenty of distance. The discussion of distant is forthcoming; however, your car should be just far enough away that they still know you are pulling them over. I know of a specific case where the officer had tried to pull over a known killer, but positioned his patrol car very close behind the subject. The criminal saw this action and slammed on his brakes. The patrol car actually crashed into the rear of the bad guy's car. The killer immediately exited and killed the officer as he sat in his car. The officer, stunned by the action, was never able to respond.

Another important aspect of the stop will be the brake lights and turn signals of the violator's car. Are they still on after the stop? I mentioned this before, but they can be a very telling action. If they are still on, ask yourself why? Who would sit in their car with the turn signal continuously clicking? Why would they sit in the car with their foot on the brake? Most people would place their car into park. Did you see the backup lights flash as the car was placed into park? These are all very important questions because it shows the occupants are preoccupied. We will see this again later when it comes to the all-important statements about audio occlusion and mental preoccupation. The driver stops the car and it is at a good location. You pull up behind them and stop. Most officers will stop somewhere between a few feet to one quarter of a cars length back. I do not understand why this is such a standard practice for officers across the country. The distance should be at a minimum of two cars length and preferably more. I have seen where after the stop, you would have to back the patrol car in order to read the tag. You will know the distance is appropriate when you have to hike in order to reach the violators car. Most officers stop very close so they do not have to walk so far. It is so hot outside. It is so cold outside. I am so tired. We all know about excuses. I try to teach that even at a traffic light you should stop about a cars length or more away from the traffic in front of you. In the event that you need to pull out quickly, you can. In addition, if you are struck from behind, you may not have to suffer the second impact with the car in front of you. This is a habit I practice even in my personal car. You never want to be trapped in a position with no options. There are no negatives to the distance you place between the cars. Stopping very close to other traffic has no positives. We are practicing safety, so let's take a look at it.

Think of it as being on the firing range. The closer you are the better shooter you become. The more distance created, the longer you need to set up to be accurate. How many times have you stopped a car only to have the driver immediately exit the car? How surprised were you? How vulnerable were you? Had you even taken your seat belt off? Think of the complete disadvantage you had while sitting in the car if the driver you pulled over had the intentions of doing you harm. Think back to the true scenario I described that cost an officer his life. If you stopped too close to them, they only had to walk 15 – 20 feet to shoot you at point blank range. Even if they walked half way or 7-10 feet, how hard of a shot was this going to be? Even for an untrained shooter, you will probably be shot.

Most police involved shootings occur no further than 21 feet (81%). 58.8% of all police shooting occurred from 0 to 5 feet. In fact, the FBI's "Law Enforcement Officers Feloniously Killed in the Line of Duty" research from 1994 to 2006 showed that law enforcement officers failed to hit their assailants 69.4% of the time. When I first started at the academy, our last 6 rounds of a fifty round course, was from the 50-yard line. This was not a practical shooting course. Over time and with the examinations of police involved shootings, the course was modified to a distance not greater than the 25-yard line. Still nearly half of our qualifying shooting is performed from the 15-yard line or greater. There is no reality in these distances. Most police shootings will occur in less than 3 seconds with multiple shots required to bring down a suspect.

Instinctive shooting is a style of shooting that needs to become a required practice with every department. If your department will not allow it, then you will have to practice on your own time. There will be no sight picture, sight alignment, breathe, trigger squeeze in this training. You must draw and fire as fast as possible. It must be done safely and with accuracy. You must teach yourself to hit where you are looking. You must have the target sighted in without taking the time to look at your sights. You start the technique slowly. You must teach yourself the motor movements involved which are required to begin placing the action into memory. Slow and easy while gaining speed with practice. We all know the one area of the body that when hit, turns out the light instantly, is a head shot. As it was once taught to me, a shot placed between the upper lip and eyebrow will sever the stem producing an instant kill. Of course, the shot does not have to be placed exactly in a person's face. Practicing to hit a tighter group with this technique will assure you a faster hit than your opponent will. If you ever have to use your gun, then it is a life or death situation. It will be your life or your death depending on how well you train. I already know the thinking behind most agencies. They will say "have you seen the way that many of our people shoot? There is no way we can teach this in the field without taking the risk of someone being hurt." The answers are easy. As a firearms instructor, I say stick to your own rules. If someone cannot learn to properly handle a weapon, then fire them. If not, then let them be someone else's backup. I do not want to be hurt because there is someone who is incompetent watching my back. What other profession that faces life and death decisions, keeps incompetent people? Most others will be washed out.

Force Science Research Institute describes itself as; "studying the science & human dynamics behind deadly force encounters." They have a very interesting site that you can go to on line and read their articles. They will also provide you, free of charge, with emails to show you where some of their research is currently. In Transmission #134, they conducted a fascinating study entitled: How your eyes can cast your fate in a gunfight. They experimented with both elite seasoned officers and new officers. The experiment was conducted where an officer was advised they were going to encounter a possible deadly threat. The test was to see where the officers were looking at the first sign of the threat and how fast they responded. It was found that an officer's performance could be impaired or enhanced by where their eyes and attention are focused in the midst of a deadly encounter.

The study began when a subject became irate in a lobby area. After a moment, he spins towards the officer, usually drawing a handgun. Sometimes he would spin and have a cell phone. They provided the officers with special equipment to determine at all times where their gaze was focused upon. Here are some of their findings:

First, the elite officer spent significantly less time assessing the situation before drawing their gun. On whole, they drew "well before the assailant began his pivot." Most drew early and "held [their gun] at chest level before aiming." The rookies tended to delay drawing until about a second after the subjects turn.

The elite officer shot before the assailant got his round off 92.5% of the time, beating him by an average of nearly 180 milliseconds (ms). The rookies shot first only about 42% of the time and on average lagged behind the attacker by more than 13 milliseconds. Responding "very poorly," the study says, the rookies essentially "reacted to his attack, rather than being ahead of him as were the elite officers during every phase of the encounter." The rookie's final saccade or rapid eye movement, especially among those who missed when they fired, "occurred at the same time they tried to fixate the target and aim," the study reveals. At that critical moment in the last 500 milliseconds, the rookies in a staggering 82% of their tests took their eyes off the assailant and attempted to look at their own gun, trying to find or confirm sight alignment as they aimed. "This pulled them out of the gunfight for what turned out to be a significant period of time." Also noted was "On a high percentage of their shots, the rookies did not see the assailant as they fired," contributing to inaccurate shooting and the misjudgment of the cell phone as a threat.

The researchers pose the possibility that the rookies' training may have contributed to their poor performance. They were taught pistol craft "similar to how most police officers first learn to shoot a handgun: to focus first on the rear sight, then on the front sight, and finally on the target, aligning all three before pulling the trigger." Somewhere across their training, practice, and experience, the successful elite officers had learned what essentially is a reverse process: Their immediate and predominate focus is on the weapon carried by their attacker. With their gaze concentrated there, they bring their gun up to their line of sight and catch their sights only in their peripheral vision, a subtle sight glimpse.

This study says in terms that are more technical than what I was saying a moment ago. The standard practice of sight picture, sight alignment, is taught initially to recruits for the basics of shooting. The real shooting lessons should be taught up close and without the use of sights. Military elite forces are taught this technique while law enforcement never trains in the methodology. Maybe you can see why we lose most of the gun battles with the bad guys. We miss nearly 70% of our shots against an assailant. Because the shootings happen so close and so fast, there is no time for aiming. Most police officers are not prepared for this type of confrontation. Instinctive style shooting is the answer to this problem.

Edged weapons or even any blunt weapon, when possessed by an offender, deserves the same attention as a gun. The old standby rule we were all taught was the 21-foot rule. Stay at least 21 feet away from a person who has picked up an edged or blunt weapon. You should be able to draw and fire your weapon before being struck by the assailant. Studies have shown they were wrong. In a new study, one researcher found that an individual can cross 30 feet in 2 seconds and suggested that the person could travel 70 yards before succumbing to injuries created by an officer's firearm. According to the FBI, "There is sufficient oxygen within the brain to support full, voluntary action for 10 to 15 seconds after the heart has been destroyed." Can you draw and fire in this period? You had better give it some thought if you cannot. Do you ever try to fast draw your weapon? Practice this at home with an empty and safe weapon. If you have not drawn your gun when someone is squaring off against you with any type of weapon, you should re-evaluate your tactics. Remember the fatal errors from above include not drawing your weapon when danger is recognized. On this note, I know officers who will not pull their gun out in situations when others would. The why to this statement can be varying. Many supervisors are very confused in their interpretation of use of force. Too many people see the drawing of their weapon as a use of force. It is only a use of force if you have to pull the trigger. Prior to that moment, it is a show of force. The other reason is the officers become hesitant over the fear of lawsuit, arrest, or the loss of job. It is pounded into their head that if you do this or that, you will be held liable. It causes many officers to hesitate instead of reacting. You cannot afford to hesitate when confronting a potential life-threatening situation. Agencies have to pull away from worrying about financial responsibilities versus their personnel's own welfare.

Have you ever practiced drawing your gun from the front seat of your cruiser? Because of the various styles of holsters today, you may not be able to get your gun out. Try it with both the seatbelt on and off. Also, think about the placement of other weapons you may carry on duty. Are they locked up in the trunk? Are they locked in a gun rack in the passenger's compartment? Are you wearing a back-up weapon? Have you ever tried to draw the backup weapon while sitting in your patrol car? What about having another accessible weapon in your car? Take advantage of them only if it is allowed by your agency. As you can tell, I believe strongly in the preparations to every event which I may be faced with. Fatal errors tell us all about lack of mental preparations. Even though the actual practice could appear to be physical, you are playing the situation out in your mind.

Many officers are killed or seriously injured each year during foot pursuits. I know we want to catch the bad guys. How many times you have heard on the news about an officer ambushed by the subject they were chasing. There is no reason for you to leave your car and the subject's vehicle to run after someone alone on foot. Again, cover needs to be provided by back up officers. You will find that the subject will sprint away from the scene, but quickly runs out of steam. When their adrenaline rush ends, their tank will be empty. Slow your pace down and be methodical. You can still overtake the suspect because you will be able to move over greater distances without exhaustion with a slower pace. In addition, you can change positions with other officers who are fresher. If the call allows for the utilization of a K-9, you will not want to have people running all over the place and contaminating the scene. Just in my area alone, over the last few years I have been to two funerals for officers involved in foot pursuits. You always have to think about your own safety versus catching a petty criminal who will get caught anyway. Wait for the backup, establish a reasonable perimeter, and let's take these thugs into custody safely. Let us also remember to be sure to pay close attention to the subject who runs from you. How many times have you had someone flee from a scene; however, moments later there is very little physical descriptive information given to other officers. If the subject is dangerous, by not slowing down and following safe procedures, you have made it even more dangerous for the responding officers. Instead of instantly recognizing the perpetrator, they will have to investigate people who could be the suspect.

Remember earlier when we spoke about mental planning? It is part of the seven deadly mistakes by officers. It also falls under the 10 fatal errors category. This is a good time to discuss what we mean by mental planning? I am on patrol and stop at a traffic signal. I look over and see the front of a convenience store. I imagine in my mind what I would do if I saw someone run from the store with a weapon. I just witnessed a robbery. What will I do next? Do I have to think about it or do I just react. If you have played this scenario out in your mind a hundred times, you will react. If you have never thought about it, you will hesitate. You will have to think about each action you take. The same goes for traffic stops. I make mental plans for various situations that can occur in each stop. As the car is stopping, I will watch and think about various possible scenarios. If this happens, what would I do? If that happens, what would I do? Mental planning is a rarely used tool in our profession. It carries with it as much value as the physical training. What do you think the bad guys are doing all day? If they are in jail, they are mentally planning. If they are at home devising some criminal act, they are mentally planning the occurrence and so should you. When I am out on a stop, if it has come to a point where I have the driver out of the car, I am mentally planning. We will discuss when the driver should be out of the car later. However, I am standing there watching the subject and planning my reactions to various possibilities. If this guy breaks bad on me what would I do? I usually picture a throat strike or other action I know will incapacitate the subject quickly. Another axiom that is taught to military Special Forces is the best defense against a physical attack is to avoid it if possible. If a confrontation becomes physical, strike as hard as possible, with whatever force is needed and back away. Separate yourself from the attacker and give yourself the chance to take a stronger defensive action with one of your weapons. But, if the opportunity does not present itself, you strike as if your life depends on it. Anytime a subject physically attacks an officer, it has to be perceived as a life-threatening event. Not all of the defensive tactics practice in the world will prepare you for the real thing. If you have been in a real fight and not when a subject is just trying to get away from you, the violence will shock you. Practice deadly response tactics to defend your life.

The same is true with situational awareness. Be aware of your surroundings at all times. I already know that this not completely possible all of the time. However, just like your traffic stops, everywhere you stop should be considered. As you pull into a parking lot or an abandoned area to work on reports, be aware of the area. When walking into restaurants or convenience stores, do you survey what is going on inside before entering? Do you sit at a restaurant in a place of advantage or disadvantage? Wild Bill Hickok was killed while sitting at a table with his back to a door. Recently in Washington State, four police officers were shot to death while sitting at a table and working on their computers at a coffee shop. Situational awareness is everywhere you go on or off duty. You should park in an area where you can leave easily and it is well lit. The area where you park should have a clear view all around. This is so you will not be surprised if someone approaches you. Remember, with the technologies that exist today in a patrol car, like in car computers, it causes us to stare at the technology all of the time. Be aware of your surroundings at all times.

THE INTERDICTION STOP - 6

It is true that the more stops you make the more opportunities are presented to you to make an arrest. However, contrary to the thoughts of many, there are different qualities of stops. What do I mean by quality? Within the first minute of the stop, you should recognize whether to send them on their way or take the stop further. The signs will appear to you almost instantly. You have to stop a variety of vehicles, but you also have to play the odds. Let's assume you are operating stationary radar. You see an elderly couple that you clock speeding. Behind the vehicle is a rental car with two younger males who are also speeding. To play the better odds you would stop the car with the two younger males. Does this mean that the elderly couple has not committed a crime? No, but the odds are greater that the two younger guys have. Additionally, you should never try to stop more than one car at a time for safety reasons. We see multiple car stops all the time by officers who are solely stat driven. Some will argue that this is a pretextual stop. We will cover pretextual stops later. However, it does not matter what was in your mind before the stop of a vehicle as long as that vehicle has committed a traffic violation. They were both violating the traffic code and are each equally susceptible to being stopped.

If all you do during your shift each day is work speed enforcement, then you are eliminating most criminals from your stops. There are a percentage of criminals that will speed all of the time, but most will not during their criminal activity. The stops must be for a variety of reasons. Again knowing your traffic laws is critical. Many stops are for what some will call BS stops. Remember that you are paid to enforce the laws of your state and community. I have never looked up a violation in a law book under the chapter of "BS violations." What you need for a vehicle stop is probable cause. If there is none, you leave it alone. I have always said to throw it a seed. It will grow and come back another day. Never put your reputation on the line with any gray area stops. Make it a good stop for a violation that you can articulate and you will always be fine. I know there are officers that will follow a car, mile after mile trying to find any reason to stop them. When you first observed the car there was no probable cause for a stop. You caught up to the car to look at it and the occupants closer. You run the tag and everything appears all right. Turn around and find another car to stop. Many cars with different types of criminals are driving by your location all day long.

You are sitting in the median or the shoulder of any roadway USA. Are you hiding or out in the open? Many of us will hide so we can surprise traffic offenders. The target vehicles approach and you clock them at the last second before they have a chance to slow down. You want to see them before they see you so they cannot stop what it is they are doing until it is too late. This can be a great strategy if all you want are traffic violators. I say the interdiction officer should be out in the open most of the time. This allows numerous things to happen. First, if you are hiding on the opposite side of an overpass monitoring traffic, almost all of the traffic that comes over the crest will react to you. They will break, grab the steering wheel, change lanes, etc. When you are out in the open, generally only certain ones will change their behavior. When people are traveling down the highway, they will have tunnel vision. All they are going to notice is the area just in front of the car. On the interstate systems, most people just stare at the car in front of them or the lane they are traveling within. The furthest down range people will watch is about a quarter mile. Cops always want to hide in order to catch traffic violators when they could do just as well by not hiding. You are looking for the clues that appear from people who are not doing anything very wrong. You have to look twice at a car that is driving at or below the speed limit, but slows when the driver sees you.

Criminals always know they are criminals. Criminals always react to cops. It is up to you to recognize them and their actions. They know you are there to catch them. When they are committing, have committed, or are about to commit a crime, no matter how large or small, seeing you causes a reaction in them. These reactions are what we seek. It takes a little practice and patience, but it will pay off. In the open you are watching traffic approach. You see their actions before they see you. What you want to see is their actions when they do see you. You will know when you see them. Speed may start to decrease or the front of the car will take a nosedive if they brake too hard, regardless of whether or not they are speeding. If you are in the median and they are in the inside lane, they may move to the outside lane. They may or may not signal the lane change. Subconsciously, they want to move further away from you. What was once a relaxed driving position becomes an intense one. They will grip the steering wheel with both hands. They may not look at you when they drive past. If there are two people in the car, do they look relaxed, or have the thousand mile stare as they drive by you? Some may look away from you, others may rub their head, face, or play with their hair. These are the same nervous reactions seen in an interview. It will be reactionary, subconscious, and without thought. There are many different reactions from people. Not all of these people are criminals when they do react to your presence. Some people are nervous by nature. Others could have gotten into trouble recently, no matter how minor and have a reaction to the sight of the police. This is very important later on. In the minds of those people who are guilty of something, they are looked at or stopped by you for the worse thing they have ever done. They are not thinking about their speed, faulty equipment, or any other traffic violation. In their mind, it is because they stole the clothes from the store at the mall or some other criminal act.

A car approaches your location and slows down. They activate their turn signal and change lanes to the lane furthest from your car. They drive by you and are sitting straight. You noticed as they approached that they were leaning over on the center console. They go by you and grab the steering wheel with two hands. When you first recognized them, they had their left wrist lying across the top of the steering wheel in a very relaxed position. They now look tense. If they are concerned about you, they will be watching you after they have passed your location. They will want to see what your reaction to them will be. They will be watching their side view mirrors and/or rearview mirrors. They will not be paying attention to their driving. The cruise control will not be set because they braked a moment ago and their speed may continue to fall. They may drive outside their lane of travel, tail gate another car, or suddenly create distance to the other traffic directly in front of them. A good location for performing this type of patrol observation is just before any type of curve. You can really see how worried they are after passing you as they try to negotiate the curve. It does not have to be a sharp curve. A shallow curve will highlight their inability to stay in the lane. But, there will be a change in behavior. You have to be alert and watching the entire series of events. You may recognize some of the events and miss other parts. It is only important for you to see some of these behaviors that drew attention to the driver.

To better explain the last section to you, let me provide an actual case summary to you. While working one night on US27 (a four lane highway) in Polk County, Florida, my partner and I watched as two cars approached. They were driving under the posted speed limit. They were the only two cars in sight. The second car was tail gating the first. As they approached us, the driver of the first car hit the brakes. The driver of the second car had to brake hard to keep from hitting the first car. This tells me that the first driver saw us in the median and braked. The second driver was doing what most drivers will do. They had tunnel vision on the rear of the first vehicle. A young man and woman occupied the first car. They were in a new car and it appeared to be a rental. The second vehicle was older and occupied by two males. We could see this because when working at night, we will sit in the median perpendicular to the roadway. Our lights are on and shining across the lanes of traffic. You will want to do this so you can see the occupants in the car as they travel past you. They will react to you the same, but without the lights, you will not see it. Be sure the lights are not shining down the lane of traffic because the drivers could be temporarily blinded. We are stopped in the open on a long stretch of road.

As the two cars drove past our location, we already had probable cause to stop the second car for following too close. My partner and I were in two separate marked patrol cars. The second car continued to slow down until they were separated by several hundred feet. As we proceeded north, I saw the first car drive completely off the road and onto the outside-unpaved shoulder. This occurred at a small curve. Why did this happen? Because the driver of the first car was watching us in his rear view mirrors instead of the road. As the grass, dirt, and rocks flew into the air, I proceeded forward to the first car. My partner stayed with the second car. Why? Because they were the only two cars in sight on the road; therefore, you should be questioning yourself why the second car did not just pass the first car. Remember we are on a four-lane road and they are traveling under the speed limit. We both believed now that they were traveling together. But, why would they be in separate cars, especially a rental car if they were in fact traveling together?

We coordinated between ourselves quickly. I told my partner to stop the second car when he saw the emergency lights of my car behind the first vehicle. I told him if his targeted car stops away from my stop location, he was to move the stop to a position behind mine.

At least in this fashion, we could provide immediate backup to each other. I activated my emergency lights and stopped the rental car. I watched as my partner activated his emergency equipment and stopped the second vehicle. The second vehicle, by this time, had slowed so much that there was now at least a quarter of a mile between us. I exited my car, but waited to approach as I watched my partner's actions. A moment later, I watched the second car and my partner drive directly behind my car. I now approached the car I had stopped.

My vehicle stop had a young male driver and young right front passenger female. I saw in the back seat a fast food bag with food boxes in the rear floorboard. I also saw that there was a single red rose in one of those plastic containers on the rear seat. You would get the type from a convenience store. I asked for the driver's license and registration to the car. He produced both. The driver explained they were going home from Miami, Florida. He stated that he was trying to spend some "quality time" with his girlfriend so he thought he would take her to Miami for the day. I then heard my partner yell "gun! Let me see your hands!" I looked back and saw my partner with his weapon drawn and pointing it into the car. I told the driver of my car to give me the car keys and he complied. I ran back to cover my partner. We removed, handcuffed, and secured the two occupants of the car he had stopped. The passenger had reached for a handgun in the glove box as the driver was trying to get the registration. He immediately released it as my partner drew down on him.

Why did I take the ignition keys from their car? It was my belief that they were traveling together. If they tried to escape or chose to run us over, he could not without the keys. We removed the gun and I saw a fast food bag with food boxes. They were from the same restaurant as the bag in the first car. I do not believe strongly in coincidences. I returned to the first car carefully. I asked if they knew the people in the car behind them. They said no. We utilized a K-9 on the exterior of the rental and he alerted positive to the trunk area. A search of the trunk produced a couple of kilos of cocaine. A satchel was found in the second car with money and cocaine residues. The couple from the first car was arrested for trafficking in cocaine. The guys in the second car were arrested for conspiracy to traffic in cocaine. We followed the route they had traveled and found the fast food restaurant where the food had been purchased. The fast food employees identified all of the persons involved. They stated how the four of them had ordered all of the food together. However, the employees had to place two of the four meals into separate bags because they were in separate cars. The outcome for everyone involved was guilty in state court. The two subjects from the second car were tried additionally and later in federal court.

Can you see how it all comes together? What if I had been alone that night? I do know which car I would have stopped. I probably would have chosen the rental. If they were traveling together and had anything illegal, it would be in the car that none of them own. We will talk about rentals later. I can assure you I would not have stopped both of them. I also would have been extremely careful about the stop if I had felt that they were traveling together. If the second car would have stopped, I would have ordered him to wait down the road at the next business. No search would have taken place without backup.

What quick points were noticed about the first car before the arrest? First were their nerves. Then you think about the story. Does it make sense to you? The drive to Miami is 6 hours one way from their home. There are no clothes in sight and they are eating fast food on the go. There is nothing romantic about a cheap convenience store flower. They bought the flower to try to add credence to their story if they were stopped. All of that was gathered in the 30 seconds I had with them before the events in the other car occurred.

Their physical actions while driving may not be probable cause to stop them, but the results of their inattention to driving will be. Failure to drive in a single lane, following too close, speed, driving too slow, and failure to signal a lane change, could be a result of their carelessness which you could use. If there are no clear violations, leave it alone and wait for the next one. You pull out to look at a car that has driven by you. You do not have enough information to conduct a stop; you just want to take another look at the car. There was something about the car or its occupants that did not seem right. Maybe you had a funny feeling, so you pulled out after them. Trust in those feelings. Your body responded to something it recognized that you just couldn't explain. I have found many younger officers who will ask; "Can I do that?" Sure you can. You just want to look at the vehicle. You are not going out to stop the vehicle on a hunch. You are trying to confirm or deny the feeling you had. Keep all of your activity on high moral ground and no one will ever be able to harm your profession.

We were discussing earlier about pretextual stops. It used to be that a pretextual stop was illegal. However, the Whren decision from the United States Supreme Court states that pretext is no longer a negative factor. The only decision made is if there was a legal reason to stop the car. I remember in the past, a stop had to be for a reason that you would commonly stop people. I have seen good cases thrown out because of the violation committed was minor, but it was a violation just the same. Unfortunately, the officer had rarely used the particular violation. Defense attorneys would claim you stopped their client because of this or that reason and only used the traffic violation as an excuse. In other words, a pretextual traffic stops.

Now you can think whatever you want before the stop as long as the reason for the stop is a legitimate violation. You were somehow not supposed to have any fore thought about the vehicle you were stopping. No one cared about your educated hunches based on years of training and experience. To summarize the Whren decision it says; that when a police officer observes a traffic violation, they automatically have probable cause to stop the offending vehicle and to issue a citation or a warning to its driver. With probable cause thus established, any incriminating evidence of the traffic violation or any other criminal activity found by an officer in plain view within the stopped vehicle could legally be seized and used as evidence in court. The Court also rejected the argument that traffic stops used as a pretext for obtaining other evidence should be abolished, noting that such pretext would be impossible to ascertain. In the final analysis, the Court ruled that as long as a traffic stop was made following an actual traffic infraction it was reasonable by definition.

I think this is a good place to bring up racial profiling. Briefly is about all I think this subject deserves. Simply put, if you have not heard it too often already, do not do it. Crime is an equal opportunity occupation. If one was to only choose one race to enforce the law upon, you would be missing out on the greatest majority of crime. Officers, regardless of their own race, have been accused of some type of racial profiling. I am sure it has occurred at times somewhere in this country, but I have never witnessed it. It is an extremely rare occurrence, but a very regular complaint. I had a fellow officer who once told me he had a racial profiling complaint filed against him. The officer, who is white, said the defendant, who had cocaine on his person, stated the only reason he was stopped was that he is Russian. Everyone has a beef with someone and some have more beefs than others do. Don't do the crime if you cannot do the time. The very accusation of this in order to muddy the water in a clean well has always disgusted me. It is usually in an effort to get off from a crime you have committed. Punish those who violate the rules and leave everyone else alone. It is the typical excuse of all excuses, which tries to damage a proud profession. There are groups of people in each race that are more prone to do different crimes. The Mexican drug trafficking organizations control the vast majority of drug transportation into the country. Is this a negative statement towards Mexicans? No, it is simply the facts. Transportation around the country may be by any race once it travels from its storage hubs that are close to the border. Blacks predominately distribute crack cocaine. Are all crack dealers and users black? No, they are not. Whites predominately carry out the prescription drug trade. Are whites the only distributor of the illegal prescription drug trade? No, but more importantly do you see the common thread? All drugs are transported, distributed, and abused by all people and across the entire color spectrum. The population of the area in which you work can cause one group to be predominating over the others in the makeup of your stops. We will see this later on when we discuss marijuana grow operations in Florida. However, never is any one race solely responsible for any of the many drugs that plague this country. It has nothing to do with driving while black, brown, yellow or green. It is just another desperate attempt to escape taking personal responsibility for your actions. It is simply a crutch to lean against so you can pass the blame. I know I was transporting 10 kilos of cocaine, but the only reason I got caught was because I am .... It is always the same crap, but it is just from a different asshole. The fact of their color did not cause them to be arrested. It does have everything to do with the fact you are an asshole on society. We did what we were supposed to do and confronted the asshole. Remember, it is why we are here.

I see it all of the time. A car drives by with tinted windows. The window is lowered slightly and you cannot see inside. Because the window is lowered, you know they are ventilating. But, ventilating what? The weather is bad it is raining. Maybe it is cold or very hot. A person drives by you with a newer car and their window is down. You have to ask yourself why? Can you justify a reason why you would drive like that? Always put yourself in the car you are observing and determine if what you see makes sense. Does this guarantee that something is wrong? Of course it doesn't. Not everyone behaves the same, but for most of us, it is very similar.

You are working on a section of highway and a car drives by. The driver exhibits many of the things we have talked about thus far. He approaches you and changes his behavior in the vehicle. He drives past you and commits a minor violation. All of his behaviors have attracted you to him. Because of the traffic violation, you conduct a traffic stop. Is this person a criminal? Not necessarily, but it is time to find out. Usually they are not criminals. Most of the time there will be no reason to even search the car after the stop. So why did they behave like that? It could be any of a number of things. Maybe they are just nervous around the police. Maybe they had gotten into trouble in the past, but still fear doing anything else wrong. Maybe they have a bad driving record and know that if they get just one more ticket it will cost them their license. Many times, I have found it was a person driving with a suspended license. Other times they had warrants for their arrest. Sometimes they had drugs or guns. The point of the matter is just because they exhibit all the signs of a guilty person, there may still be nothing to the stop. Unless it is a known criminal you are stopping, you must still be professional and courteous until their actions call for adjustments by you. Their behavior will dictate your actions.

While patrolling on side streets, we have all seen a driver react in some way which has attracted our attention. You will see people at a stop sign waiting to pull out, but then they see you drive by in the direction they had intended to travel. How do you know they were? Their blinker is on or it comes on when they see you. They have their tires turned slightly in the intended direction. They have every opportunity to pull out, but they do not. You have to be saying to yourself; "Why not?" You are watching them in your rearview mirrors after you drive past. You begin to slow, but they suddenly turn and go in the other direction. Have they committed a crime or violation? Not unless the turn was prohibited. They have done enough though to cause you to be turning around quickly. Does your quick action cause them to take any additional reactions that appear evasive? You must remember, maybe they were not from the area and confused. Maybe they changed their mind as to where they were going. But maybe they wanted to stay away from you.

If they suddenly drive into a parking lot, but still have not committed a violation, go to an area where you can stop to watch them. If there is not an immediate area that you can travel to, then go down the road and position yourself where you can watch their exit back to the road. If they do not come out for a while, drive by again and see what they are doing. If they have exited and walked into somewhere, do not spend any more time on them. Often times, they will travel back out to the road and in the other direction once they believe you are gone. If they do, see if they have changed drivers or see if there is any reason to stop them. If there are none, move on to the next person. This is all proactive patrol. We spoke of this earlier about being aggressive in your patrol. The more often we can remove a criminal from our roadways, the better off our society will be.

Inclement weather, be it rain or snow, leads to some additional dangers. I will not make regular traffic stops in the rain. Other drivers cannot drive very well when the weather is good. When it rains or snows, the dangers of out of control vehicles greatly increase. Why take the additional risk? My advice to you is if you feel that a stop in these conditions are necessary, due so with extreme caution. But be sure it is absolutely necessary. I learned my own lesson one day while working overtime. It was a bad place to be stopped and it had just finished raining. We were required to have a certain amount of activity while working overtime. I had to approach the driver's side because of a ditch. While standing there, I was grazed in the back with a side view mirror from a passing vehicle. There I was, standing on the driver's side, the roads are wet, and traffic is traveling past me from about 3 feet away. One of the cars was watching me instead of the road. He drifted towards me and traveled past at about 1 foot of distance. I went home and said never again. In addition, I have never again put myself in that predicament.

One more bit of information on inclement weather. Uniformed Immigration and Customs officials usually man the border checkpoints. The Border Patrol checkpoints on the United States border with Mexico are going to be inland. Generally, you will find the checkpoints about 60 miles inland. Because of their nexus with the border, all of the roadways leading away from the border will be covered. As illegal persons and contraband make it across our porous borders, they will soon thereafter, be transported by vehicle. Sounds familiar from earlier and you will hear it again. All criminals enter into a motor vehicle and are therefore subject to our scrutiny. When it rains in the border areas, because of the traffic hazards involving motor vehicles and wet roads, the Border Patrol will often close the checkpoints. No traffic will be stopped and inspected. The smugglers know this too. They will make a dash for the heartland of America as soon as the rains come. As an interdiction officer, you watch the daily weather reports from the border areas. Determine how long of a drive it is to your area and for how long has it been raining in the border area. For instance, when I see it is raining in the Texas Valley, I know it will be about a 26-hour drive for the smugglers to reach Tampa. If it rains for 2 hours, I will give and take a little time. I will definitely want to be looking for vehicles from this area in the next 24 through 30 hours. The vehicles may not be Texas plated, but I will pay attention to people with the appearance of driving nonstop around the clock. This strategy will pay off with due diligence and patience.

Rental cars have always been the vehicle of choice. As we mentioned earlier, if a person is arrested in a rental car he will not lose the vehicle through the forfeiture seizure laws. The occupants using the car for nefarious reasons will often not be on the rental agreement. It will be a third party rental. They will use a third party or a stolen credit card in order to rent the car. Sometimes, they will have their own associates working at the rental car company. They are often late on their returns or have someone continuing the lease. The car will not belong to them, but they will do things to personalize it. Why would you do things at your own expense to a rental car? Things like apply window tint, attach a club to the steering wheel, and personalize the key chain. You have your own car, but you pay hundreds of dollars a week for a rental and continue renewing the contract. Again, would you ever do this? Would you rent a car for someone else and put the risk on your credit card? 99.9% of the population will say no.

If you stop a rental car and the driver is not on the rental agreement, you have several options. Be sure to examine the rental agreement for the "due in" date. Check the mileage of the car and compare it to the mileage on the agreement at the time of the rental. Is the mileage excessive? Was the car due in days ago? Call the rental company and verify that the rental agreement was continued. Are there damages to the car by the third party with actions you would not do to your own property? Call the rental car company and explain there is a non-contractual driver in the car. The person who rented the car is not present and you have the following things taking place with their property. The rental car company will often times advise you they are sending a tow company out for their car. You can then advise the occupants to exit the car and find an alternative form of transportation. Again, you have to ask what you would do in a similar situation. If the totality of the circumstances does not make sense to you, then you must take the stop further.

THE APPROACH - 7

The passenger's sides approach is without question the best approach for your safety. How many times have you walked up to a car on the passenger's side and scared the driver? They are watching their side view mirror for your approach on the driver side. Everyone expects you to walk up on the driver's side. For this reason alone you should not go there. Never act in a way they would expect of you. Keep them a little off guard and do the unexpected. Again, you need to control every aspect of the stop. There are more dangers for the officer at a traffic stop than in almost any other action you can take. Standing on the passenger's side, your car and its distance provides a barrier from oncoming traffic. The violator's car gives you some more protection from a direct impact. From the driver's side of the car, you are limited on what you can see. To observe the inside of the car, you have to move beside the driver or in front of them by the A frame. Neither of these places is at all safe. Not even having the experience of being a police officer, how much confidence do you have in the other drivers around you? There is a reason why we have always been taught to drive defensively. How many distractions take place in today's technological society? When you stand at the driver's side of a car, consider the fact that the traffic is going past you from about 3 feet away. Do you really believe you are invincible? I have almost been a victim of this position and refuse, unless no other options are available, to be there again. People's eyes are attracted to the bright emergency lights and want to see what you are doing. The same philosophy applies to a bug zapper. They will always have a tendency to steer their car in the direction of the lights, all be it unconsciously. Is this really, where you want to be standing?

From the passenger's side you can see the front seat and the complete right side of the driver. When they retrieve paperwork from the glove box, you can see inside of it. I have found people who will still hide contraband in a glove box, but deliberately place it on the left side. They expected you to be on the driver's side of the car where you cannot see the left side of the glove box. The entire box comes into view and from a much closer position when standing on the passenger's side.

Usually if a driver intends to do you harm, he will have a handgun. Even if he is left handed, the gun will probably be in or near his right hand. If he expects you to approach on the driver's side, he will turn to shoot you. You will have nowhere to go from the driver's side approach. If you move away from the vehicle, you will be in traffic. If you stay in place, you could be shot. Turn to run, you can be shot and run over. To shoot you is nearly impossible utilizing his left hand because of how far he will have to twist. From the passenger's side, you can see the action hand in advance. Staying behind the side doorpost, means the driver has to reach up and over the seat to shoot at you. It will be a difficult maneuver for anyone to do successfully. As we have already seen, having your focus on the hands gives you an advantage if you are prepared. It has always been said that if they really want to kill you they will. They know what they want to do and you do not. Good tactics and mental preparations gives the advantage back to you or at least puts you on a level playing field.

Here is some good data provided in an FBI Study. Offenders' carry a weapon with them when?

- At work 30% of the time
- At home 42%
- Just out traveling around 56%
- Traveling with a destination 62%
- Involved in a criminal activity 74%

This shows if you stop a criminal, the odds they will have a weapon are high. If it is a gun, most will have it on their person followed by under the seat and on the seat next to them. Considering the locations that they will most likely carry a weapon, you can observe all of them from the passenger's side of the car.

Contrary to what has been set in our mind, the greatest dangers are traveling towards you from behind. Driver distractions mean death and injury to the patrol officer. We always think and prepare for the criminal element in the car we stop. If you look at your actions taken at the stop, many are for everyone's protection from other driver's. Having the cars drive completely off the road or into a parking lot. Stopping your vehicle, several car lengths back. A passenger's side approach. These are some of the actions that you took to protect everyone, including yourself, from the next approaching car. More officers will be killed or injured from other drivers at the scene of a stop than will be assaulted or killed from the occupants inside the car in an average year.

You make the traffic stop and the violator pulls over in a good spot. They stay in the car as you stop at least two car lengths back. You have already run the vehicle tag and it shows a valid registration. The driver appears to match the description of the registered owner. Your seatbelt has been removed and you immediately open your driver's door. You turn on your handheld, exit and approach on foot. Some will tell you that you should go backwards behind your car and circle around to the passenger's side. Others tell you to go forward from this point. The reasons vary. Some say you should never stand in between the cars. This is true. But, we are not going out to stand around we are simply passing through. It is also dependent on whether it is daylight or night. If it is at night, we have several additional steps to make at the stop. One will be to turn on your spotlight and shine it into the passenger's compartment. The other is to have your flashlight ready. The flashlight is another piece of equipment that falls into the one is none two is one category. Few of us ever think about it until you are working at night and your flashlight quits working. I like my large, vehicle charged, Department issued flashlight. It serves not only as a light source, but also as a weapon. "But you have never been trained in the use of a flashlight as a weapon!" I hear you already. If you are about to get your ass beat and the flashlight is the first weapon in your hand, defend yourself! I also carry an additional light on my utility belt. This is the light I am going to use to search a car if the circumstances arise.

In my opinion, if the stop is made in the daylight, I am going to approach the passenger's side of the car straight on. I will exit and move forward before moving over to the passenger's side. This is where I want to conduct my business. If the stop is made at night, I will exit and pass around the rear of my vehicle and approach the passenger's side.

In the daylight they can see you through their rearview mirrors. There is not as much surprise if they see what you are doing. There is no need to walk the extra distance involved. They will often still be caught off guard. You will see them roll down the driver's window and start to look for their driver's license. Also during the day, I may approach as if I was going to the front driver's door, but turn at the trunk to the passenger's side. At night, once the spotlight has been positioned on the vehicle, the occupants cannot see you or your approach. If you pass between the cars, they will see your shadow as you break the beam of light. Therefore, you can take the extra steps required to walk around the back of your vehicle. They will never be able to see if you are approaching the drivers or passenger's side. But the approach will always be on the passenger's side.

As you complete your initial approach to the vehicle, you turn and walk back to your car. As you do, every couple of steps, you should look back over your shoulder to make sure all is the same with the occupants of the car. You get back to your car and initiate whatever action you intend for this driver.

In today's modern patrol car, there can be so many distractions. Technologies change constantly. I remember not having a handheld radio and hand cranked windows. You would roll down the passenger's window and hang the microphone out the window. Then you would turn on your outside speaker so you and the violator could hear all of the radio communications. Added to that was the cross draw holster and drop pouches for ammunition. There was a manual choke in my first Chrysler patrol car so I could idle the engine at a higher speed when I was out on a call. You rarely heard anyone call for assistance. But if you did, you knew that trooper really needed help. The actions that we would take against people who resisted was also different than today. I would hear the old timers say that they would never take crap from anyone. Back then, rest assured they did not. But today things are different. That philosophy of no back up was as stupid then as it is now. Sometimes when I think back, I am amazed we were not all killed. People are different. The respect for the uniform is not what it once was.

More safety issues arise once you are back at your vehicle. More than likely you have a computer in the car. If it is possible, you can stand at the passenger's door and complete your work. Most of us will climb back into the driver's seat. The new computers in many units are not very adjustable to allow a 180-degree rotation to work on both sides of the car. Remember situational awareness. Be aware of your surroundings all of the time. Do not just sit there with your head down in the computer. Stay alert and cognizant of the actions of the vehicle's occupants. If they are fidgety, stop and give them your full attention. Again staying at least two car lengths back gives you the added distance and time to react. I will regularly look behind me as well. You never know when someone will stop behind you even if it is to ask a question. I do not like surprises. Whenever someone on the road surprises you, you should use the experience as educational. Think about how it happened and what you could adjust so it would not happen again. Just imagine if the someone you never saw or heard was with the person you have stopped and they intended you harm.

There are always situations that occur that cause for a change in plans. What if the driver pulls into the median? Am I still going to make a passenger's side approach? No, but I will pull further than the violators car into the median. This will still give me some tactical advantages by having my unit between us and several car lengths back. I will then have to approach the driver's window. Remember the greatest threat to you is approaching from behind. At least with the driver's side approach from the median you have eliminated one of the threats to you. A passengers approach now is too dangerous.

What if the vehicle has nontransparent tint? I can tell you a large percentage of your arrest will involve window tint. Criminals like to stay hidden. They feel a sense of security behind the tint. They can easily see out, but you cannot see in. Everyone remembers the DC Sniper case involving John Allen Muhammad and Lee Malvo. The first thing they did to prepare their vehicle for the assaults was to tint the windows.

In Florida, there is a window tint law. It requires a minimal visible light transmittance for the side and rear windows. There is no tint allowed on the front windshield. The only exception is the small strip at the top of the window above the AS1 mark. This is a federal standard mark on windshields found at the bottom of the natural tint line.

There is an additional statement in the law that gives the specific ratings (In Florida the law states 28% on the sides next to and adjacent to the driver and 15% for the rear windows) and states "or makes the windows nontransparent." I have used this one word, nontransparent, before in court when I did not have a tint meter available. I have also used the word nontransparent to describe the window tint on the vehicle which I observed which led to me to conduct a traffic stop. I have had defense attorneys ask me if I thought, it was subjective on my part to say the windows were nontransparent. My answer is always no. Either you can see into the car or you cannot. This is the meaning of nontransparent. One person will not see any more than another will if you cannot see into the interior of the car. I have never lost the argument in court. I will also utilize a tint meter. It is the one piece of equipment I use many times daily. If you see a rental car with window tint, it was not done by the rental agency. Rental car companies will tell you that they will charge a person's credit card to have it removed from their vehicle. It is the person inside seeking a false sense of security. Many people will now use the disposable tint. It is very dark, but will peel right off the window without leaving any residue. Each state will have an approved list of acceptable tint meter devices. I encourage everyone to get one any way they can. As you will see it will pay for itself quickly. Again know the laws in your state.

There are several ways to approach these vehicles. Approaching a vehicle with window tint carries its own set of challenges. As you exit and approach the car, the driver will usually roll down his window. You can now see the driver in his side view mirror. If not, request the driver to do so by using a hand motion of manually rolling down a window. Speak loudly and request the driver to roll down all of his windows if you cannot see into the car. Because the front window should be clear, before conducting a stop on a tinted car, you can try to see through the back window. You will only be looking through a single tinted window as the light from the front silhouettes everyone inside. From the side, if you try to look directly into the vehicle, you are trying to see the area between the driver and passenger windows to the opposite side that are both tinted. You may not be able to see anything. Always try to observe from the side and at an angle from back to front. This way you are again using the clear windshield to make out silhouettes. Sometimes a driver may tell you his windows will not roll down. Have the driver open the doors. Once you can see all is clear inside the car, take up your position on the passenger's side.

The next thing you will want to do is have the driver close all of the windows except for the front passenger's window. If for uncontrolled reasons you are on the driver's side, have them keep that window down. The reasons for this will be clear later on.

THE INITIAL CONTACT - 8

We have identified the violation and conducted a traffic stop in a safe location. We exit our patrol car and approach the vehicle. It is now time for our initial contact. Now is the time to utilize our entire God given senses. There is a lot to do for the officer at the initial contact. Take your time. Go through the steps slowly. Allow yourself the opportunities to complete the contact. You make contact with the driver and explain the reason for the stop. Already we are going to work in many areas seeking any reason why this stop should be expanded or released. We make a quick observation of the vehicle interior and the driver. If there are passengers in the car, we also want to visually examine them for any signs of nervousness. Do we see anything illegal or unusual? Is there residue on the clothing of any of the occupants? Remember they will often times fill the bowl of a pipe, roll a joint, or make a blunt while driving. When they do, they will always spill part of the contents somewhere.

Explain the reason for the stop and request the drivers required information according to the laws of your state. I like to explain the reason for the stop as soon as possible. Several things can occur in the beginning. Remember earlier we talked about this and now are where it can help. In the mind of the person being stopped, they are being stopped for the worse thing they have ever done. In your mind, you are pulling them over for a simple infraction. Your guard may not be as high as it needs to be. He knows he just robbed a convenience store. You have no idea about the robbery. By explaining why you stopped them immediately will let them know why they are being pulled over. It helps to clear the doubt in their mind. Initially you may even see them relax a little. At this time, they may even become friendly or apologetic with you.

If the person really is up to a criminal act, you can pretend to be the naïve traffic cop. They put their guard down a little and yours becomes heightened. You have recognized some small actions or behaviors that have put you on alert, thus giving you a little bit of extra time in the event something happens. You are mentally prepared with situational awareness. I will usually tell them at this time I will just be giving them a warning and sending them on their way. "You all will be out of here in a moment" is something else I will commonly tell them. They may not want to take any actions against you if they believe you will release them in a moment. The second advantage is if a person is a member of the criminal elements, they will not as often argue with you over minor things like a light out, window tint, or speed. You represent authority or the enemy in their eyes. They do not want to be in your company any longer than they have too.

In addition, when I first approach a vehicle, I like to immediately look at the steering column and keys. Is the steering column busted or is there a single key in the ignition? Maybe the steering column is covered with a towel. Any of these things can be significant. Of course, we know if the column is broken, the car may be stolen. If there is a towel over the column, they may be hiding the fact that it is stolen. If there is a single key in the ignition, why don't they have any additional keys? Everyone carries a set of keys for their home, cars, etc. It may not mean anything or it could mean that the car is not theirs and they were only given the ignition key. The key to open the glove box and trunk is somewhere else. This should draw your suspicions. Many officers have let stolen cars leave because they are only focused on getting their activity. Slow the progression of the stop down.

While the driver is looking for their license and vehicle paperwork, watch everything closely. Continue to look around and watch for bulges or other items under any of the occupants clothing. If there are any passengers in the car, what is their behavior? Are they engaging with you, helping the driver locate some of his required documents, or staring straight ahead? Look into their face at their breathing rhythm to see if it is normal or fast and short. Can you see their carotid artery pumping blood rapidly? Can you see the front of their shirt jumping because of their pulse? Watch the suprasternal notch, which is the soft indention at the base of the throat. When they are nervous, an adrenalin release increases the heart rate. Their insides are preparing for the flight or fight syndrome. This increased heart rate will cause the suprasternal notch to pulse. All of these are very important factors in determining your next steps.

I once had a car stopped for speed and following too close. I had the driver at the side of my patrol car. I knew I wanted to search the car after noticing he was a little nervous and his trip plan did not make any sense. His car had the appearance he was living in it. But most interestingly was the fact that his spare tire was lying in the back seat. I had asked him to step out of the car after my backup units had arrived. I was watching him closely as I got to the question of why his spare tire was in the back seat. You could clearly see every beat of his heart via his suprasternal notch pulsing. His nervous system was starting to go into overdrive. He said he had too much luggage in the trunk to keep the spare tire there. Does this sound about right guys? I know how we like to pack heavy for a week trip by ourselves.

I said he had an unnatural trip plan. He told us he was going to Colorado for a week from Miami, Florida. He stated he was going on vacation. He is wearing a wedding band and traveling alone. Even with a girlfriend and not a wife, how many significant others would like to see you go across the country on a vacation alone. In and of itself, is this anything? Not much, but added to other indicators and it will be. How long would it take to drive there and back again? Does he have enough time to complete what he has told me? Would you not just put your excessive luggage in the back seat and leave the spare tire in the trunk? Do you see how it all adds up? Is this similar to any of your vacations? If it does not make sense to you than it probably is not correct. He had 513 pounds of marijuana in the trunk.

While you look at the passengers, watch their movements and listen to the statements of the driver. Is he nervous? Are his hands shaking? This is very visible as he gives the documents to you. Are his behaviors normal when compared to everyone you have made contact with in the past? Is he too talkative, has a nervous laugh, too friendly, aggressive, talks to himself, or angers quickly? Together with other issues, any of these actions could be an indicator of guilt. If the driver cannot find his paperwork, but never opens the glove box or center console, make a mental note of it. When he says; "I must have left it at home or in my other car". Ask him if the paperwork could be in the glove box or center console? See if there are any changes to his behavior when you ask the question. Is there a hesitation that indicates thought or an instant direct answer? Ask him if he would mind looking in the glove box or center console. They are required to have this paperwork in the vehicle when operating a motor vehicle. They usually will go ahead, open these areas, and look for the paperwork. This will give you the opportunity to see inside. If there really is nothing there, you just satisfied your curiosity.

Familiarize yourself with marijuana and other drugs. I know this sounds simplistic. I can hear you saying, "What are you talking about? I know what marijuana is!" I am talking about studying the plants to understand all of the various differences. Learn how to grow marijuana and you will learn things about sexing the plants, the items one needs to grow marijuana, and the fact it has seeds and stems that will not look like any other plant. The chemical makeup of cocaine HCL and how to convert it to crack cocaine. The chemicals needed to make methamphetamine. What each of the drugs looks like because of these changes is based upon the cooking process. Include in your studies all of the various types of paraphernalia. When you see a gun you will know it is a gun. However, will you recognize some of the components of a bomb? Do you see why it can be important to understand all of these categories? Study all of these subjects and become a better interdiction officer. It is not always drugs that we seek, or even find. You have to be prepared to discover anything.

A case comes to my mind about being too focused on a single target. I stopped a pickup truck with a white Hispanic male driver. It was a large Chevrolet 2500 HD 4x4 truck. The stop was for window tint. There was a galvanized toolbox in the truck bed positioned up next to the cab. After the stop, I walked up to the cab. I saw the entire bed of the truck was enclosed with a plastic snap on cover. The driver was very nervous and had a confusing trip plan. This led to a search of the truck. Two small bags of cocaine were found in the ashtray. The cover in the bed was pulled back. This exposed a huge homemade steel tank, which encompassed three quarters of the truck bed. I lifted the toolbox cover and found it to be just the upper shell of the original item. It disguised an electric pump and hoses. Wiring was traced up to the engine compartment and was found to be attached to the battery. The driver refused to talk. We knew we had seized a large quantity of drugs. This oversized, homemade gas tank was going to be filled with drugs and we had to find the trap door. We towed the vehicle to the station and began searching it again. Discovered behind the plastic cosmetic wall covering on the back interior cab wall, we found a stack of hotel room key cards. After many hours of searching, this was all we had found. Then we realized the actual crime. He was stealing diesel fuel! The tank could hold 200 gallons. He was filling it at different fuel stations with the hotel room keys. They have a magnetic strip on the back just like a credit card. Credit card information was being stolen and placed on these cards. The driver would go to a fuel station and buy the diesel with the stolen information. He would then travel back to Miami and sell the diesel at half the cost to other truckers. We were so focused on finding drugs that we overlooked the actual criminal act. We could not see the forest through the trees.

The seed of a marijuana plant is unlike any other seed in nature. Also, marijuana stems are different as well. Look for the dried seeds or stems anywhere in the car that is visible from the outside. At night you can utilize your flashlight to look around at the vehicles interior while standing outside. I say this because it has been an issue brought up by defense attorneys in the past. They have unsuccessfully tried to claim that since you had to use a flashlight; it was not in plain view. In Florida and in most states, it is against the law to be in possession of any part of a marijuana plant. Know the laws of your state. If any of these items are visible in the car, you now have probable cause to search the vehicle. If you suspect someone has been smoking a pipe in order to ingest drugs, you may find copper Brillo pads. Using your flashlight, you can shine the flashlight at a low angle just above the carpet. Have the beam of light sweeping across the floors. If anyone has been using the copper Brillo pads, there will be small pieces of it reflecting in your light on the carpet. This is because they will tear off pieces of the Brillo pad to stuff into the drug pipes. It is also common to use an aluminum drink can as a pipe. Examine them closely for crushed sides. There will be holes punched into the top for the pipe bowl and a hole underneath for the carburetor. The drinking area is used to inhale.

Another thing I watch for are burn marks in the seats. These can be simple cigarette burns which are generally more elongated in shape. When a person smokes marijuana, the seeds will heat up and often times fall out. When they hit the seat material, they will burn a perfectly round and small hole in the seat. See if the person smokes cigarettes. If they say they do not, have them explain the burn marks. Do not indicate your suspicions to them unless there is another unit with you. This will be covered in more detail later. By itself it may not be enough, but added to other discovered factors may indicate you should continue the stop.

What about the ashtray? Is it open or closed? Is there a bottle of Visine? Do you see things like a lighter? If you do, ask them if they smoke? They may say yes or no. They may answer you with a question like "cigarettes?" This tells you they have more than one thing on their mind that they could smoke. If they say no, keep these statements in mind. Why would you have a lighter in plain view if you do not smoke? Are lighters illegal? No, they are not, but the items we use the most are usually laid nearby and in the open for easy access. Otherwise, they would be in the bottom of the glove box or center console.

We all know what Visine is used for. It takes the red out of your eyes. Unless you have sensitive eyes, how many people do you know carry one or more bottles of Visine with them? The sight of a bottle should also be tucked away in your mind as the list grows. When you start to notice enough small indicators, suspicion builds that could lead to you seeking consent to search. This of course is after another officer arrives.

I refer to it as shake. Some just call it tobacco. It is simply the cigar tobacco removed from a cigar when making a "blunt." They will take a razor blade, split the cigar down the side, and remove the tobacco. Usually they put the tobacco into store bags, garbage bags, food bags, or just dump it on the floor. You will see remnants of tobacco all over the floorboards. Most of you have seen a blunt, but have you ever thought about how one is made? The internet is an incredible source for all things. As an officer, you should be visiting various web sites about drug use. Here are the instructions from one site on how to make a blunt:

Needed: Cigar, weed, knife or scissors, grinder (optional), lighter

Lick your blunt until it is moist. Take a blade and cut a straight line lengthwise from butt to tip. Stick your thumb into the opened blunt and slide the insides (known as "guts") out. Do not try to push them all out at once because you can tear the blunt up that way.

At this point you can tear or cut off the rounded end of the blunt, or leave it there. I prefer to remove it because sometimes it causes you to roll the blunt shut. In this tutorial, we'll remove the end. Using only the inner layer will cut down on the amount of nicotine.

Now that you've got a nice rectangular blunt wrap, lick the edges to seal up any tears. Then, take the wrap and fold it in the center like you would for a joint.

Spread the weed evenly down the length of the blunt. (If you don't use enough weed to support the size of the wrap it will collapse in on itself while you're trying to smoke.)

Give your blunt its shape by carefully folding and rolling it up. Tuck the shorter side of the wrap around the weed, and then continue to roll it all the way. Be careful not to pinch the ends shut or roll it too tight as this will cause you to pass out from sucking too hard.

Lick the last half inch of paper lengthwise. Then, press the rest carefully down to the blunt. (Blunt type is really important here, since some blunts are stickier than others.) Do not taper the ends too much as this can cause the blunt to end up with a hole too small to pull from.

Take a lighter and run it up and down the length of the blunt while spinning it. This will dry out the moisture and give it a good bake, which makes the blunt firmer. Don't let the fire linger in one spot too long or it will burn. Bake the blunt just long enough to make it firm and a little darker in color

Hold the fire at the very tip of the blunt. Spin the blunt around to evenly distribute the flame and minimize the possibility of developing runs. (Runs can be remedied by smearing saliva on the longer side of the cherry.)

Do you see the care that goes into it? Knowledge is power. How many times have you searched a car and found a razor blade. How many of us keep a razor blade in the ashtray? None of us I'm sure. They keep them to cut the side of the cigar open to make a blunt. Learn all you can about marijuana, cocaine, crack, meth, ecstasy, heroin, and stay abreast of current events. An officer who knows about criminals habits will recognize things in a vehicle or on a person that an untrained officer will not. Most of us have never been exposed to this world prior to taking the job. You are not usually hired as a police officer if you have been a drug addict, have a criminal background, or with gang activities. Again your agency can only teach you so much. We are hunters. As any hunter will tell you, you must be well indoctrinated to the life of your prey if you want to be successful with its capture.

Smell is the other sense that is in full swing as I approach a vehicle. Everyone knows the potent odor of marijuana. Whenever a person smokes marijuana, the odor absorbs into everything. Earlier I stated when I first walk up to a car, I ask the driver to roll up all of the windows except for the one where I am standing. What does this do? First of all I can hear what is being said by the occupants without being drowned out by passing traffic. Next, because this is the only open window, all of the odors in the car are escaping out of the window past me. If anyone is or has been smoking anything in the vehicle, I will smell it. We are looking for plain view items, contraband, and residues. We smell for the trace odors of contraband. Once you have smelled the strong chemical odor of cocaine, it can be recognized coming from inside a car. That is if they have some quantity of cocaine and it has been enclosed in the car for long enough.

Generally, you can tell if something is wrong with the occupants of the vehicle by this time in the encounter. Even though we have mentioned many things, this all took place in a very short period. If you do not see, smell or sense anything, complete the contact so you can find the next one. If anything has drawn your attention, do not indicate this to the vehicle's occupants. I know I have already said this, but I cannot stress this enough to you. Return to your patrol car and radio for another unit. Be observant of the vehicle until your backup arrives at the scene. Tell the assisting unit what you suspect and what actions you plan to take. Coordinate the game plan together and remove the driver alone.

BEHAVIORS - 9

Police officers are generally visual people. Everyone is either visually, auditory, or emotionally oriented. We respond best to stimuli via one of these pathways. They are known as Representational System Channels. Everyone responds or learns best through the Channel that is dominate with them. The average person is about 60% visual, 30% auditory or hearing, and 10% emotional or internal feelings. Most of us comprehend a subject better when we are given visuals during an explanation. Other people are able to understand better by listening to someone or something without the visuals. Some college students discover they have to attend each class. They have to watch their professor say and illustrate everything in order to understand. If the professor just talks without the added visuals, many students will come away with the feeling they are terrible instructors. You will hear them complain; "I did not learn anything in the class." Other students can walk into a class and record the lecture. They will sit there writing notes and absorbing most of what is said. They can listen to the tapes later and fill in many of the areas that were lost in the lecture. The visual students may take a ton of notes and never absorb any of the content. They were too busy writing and never actually listened to the lecture. Most people can only function within one Representational Channel at a time. For instance, you are talking on the phone and watching television. You can do one or the other well, but not both. One of the Channels must be turned off. You see people who are talking on the phone, but where are they looking? They will be looking down at the ground. It is a way for us to not see, so we can listen. If they fail to do this, their visuals will overtake their audios. They will have to ask the person on the phone to repeat themselves.

The same understanding applies to written statements and recordings. A written statement represents only 7% of the information that it is intended to give. For this reason alone, I hate texting. How many misunderstood messages are flying around in cyber space? With a tape recording of a person's statement, you can comprehend 45% of the intended message. You are now receiving the spoken word and tone of voice. Only a video recording will add the body language and give you 100% of the intended statement.

Police officers learn from the beginning of their careers to watch. You always have to be watching. Our job is based on the things that we see. Is the car speeding? Did that driver run the red light? Did I see a bulge under the person's shirt? Did you see that? The person in that car, was that so and so? We are taught to look, watch, and see. Forget about the concept of look, listen, and feel. That implies too much information to comprehend. If the average person is 60% visual, 30% auditory and 10% internal feelings, think about a police officer. Our channels of communication alter. We are on average 87% visual, 7% auditory, 6% internal feelings. This is great! We learn to see things better. We are great at recognizing the big things, but we easily miss the small things. However, the small things are just as important as the large ones. In a study of people's behavior, before attacking someone, it is commonplace to wipe your hands on the front of your pants. You are drying them off in preparation to use them. It is wise of you to recognize this in advance. If you see someone wipe their hands on their pants roadside, does it mean you are going to be attacked? No, but the fact that you recognized it could save your life. You were paying close enough attention to see this action. Now you combine it with all of the other signals this person has shown and you have a greater chance of protecting yourself. If there were no other signs or behaviors then it could have been a simple act of drying their hands. Combined with several other things and this could indicate their fight or flight signals are going off. The stress of the encounter with you has caused their hands to sweat. How many times have you watched a video where an officer has been caught completely off guard? They will say in an interview if they are lucky enough to narrate the video, "I never saw it coming!" Never has an action been taken where the subject gave you no prior indications. We just failed to recognize them. Being able to recognize actions better than the average person makes us great for the profession we have undertaken, right? Yes and no.

We see the big picture better than most, but we have reduced our listening skills less than others have. What is it that cops do all day every day? We interview people all day long. Did you know you were going that fast? Is there a reason for the speed? Tell me what happened here today. Interviews are what we do all day, but they require good listening skills. Cops can make terrible listeners. We like to be in control. We like to tell you what you saw or did. "Where are you going, to Miami?" Answer; "Yeah officer, that's right Miami." Who is in the car with you, is that your brother?" "Ah, yeah he is my brother." We have all seen and heard it before. The officer already has all of your answers ready for you.

We have to write everything down for our reports, but rarely pay close attention. Ask your friend's, especially the non-officers or your family how good of a listener you are. Usually they have just become used to the way you are or stopped trying to change you. There is a difference between listening and hearing. When you hear something, it means there are sounds created that you may recognize. When you listen, it means you understand the meaning of those sounds. Just think of it as Charlie Brown's schoolteacher. The only thing any of us ever heard was blah, blah, blah.

Here is a test to try tonight with your significant other. Ask them how their day went, but give them you're complete, and I mean complete attention. Do not lose eye contact with them. Be the most attentive person you can be. Lean forward as they talk because this shows you are interested. See how deeply it affects them. They may ask you, "What is wrong with you." "Is there something going on?" You're complete attention is strange to them. We all know someone who is a great listener. Think about why they are good listeners. They pay attention to you. They will stop whatever they are doing and give you their time. We also know people who are terrible listeners. They constantly interrupt you or walk away while you are in mid-sentence. You will notice them looking around at other things while you are trying to talk to them. It is something you will remember about the person and can even cause you to dislike them.

To be a safe officer you have to really work at being both a good observer and listener. We all know the person who works like a machine. He writes more tickets and reports than anyone else does. Looking further, you will notice they have fewer actual arrests than anyone else. If you are stopped by them you will hear; "License, registration, and insurance. I stopped you because of this." They leave and return a moment later with your tickets that you sign and accept. They walk away and leave. You are left there thinking what a jerk that cop was to me. To the statistically oriented brass in many agencies, this officer is the best. He will receive the accolades for his high activity. If we could adjust him slightly to spend more time on the stop and ask more questions, then you would see the arrest go up. Everybody has their own cup of chowder. Everybody prefers to do different things. Some people like working DUI's while others do not. Some hate speed enforcement while others love it. Some may not like to do interdiction. But interdiction is an absolute part of every officer's job. It is involved in every aspect of patrol. Do it as safe as possible and with attention to detail. Remember, every criminal will drive at some point after nearly every crime. If the only thing you care about is tickets, then you are only doing part of your job. This may come as a blow to some people, but traffic safety can be achieved with a warning too. There are times when a driver's action requires a citation, but not always.

We all know certain things about body language. We just don't always realize how much we know. Through our normal interactions with others while growing up, we learn to recognize things. They are never taught, but they are learned. One of the best places to see this is in the mall. Have you ever sat around and watched people walk past you? You can see the young couple in love holding hands, walking slow, stopping to window shop and not recognizing anyone else around them. There is the couple that has been together for a while. They no longer have to give their significant other their full attention. They will start together, but then split off into different directions. They may not even notice that their other half has stopped and they are walking alone. Then there is the one who thinks he is a tuff guy and struts around with a swagger. The woman who thinks she is a runway model as she walks with one foot placed directly in front of the other causing an exaggerated hip swing. Then there is the geek who has little arm movement and walks faster than the average person's walk. Then there are the ones who are walking with confidence. They have good posture and their head is high. The one who is less confident, poor posture, and unable to look around or make eye contact. These are all small things yet they speak volumes about the person. Think back to the Seinfeld Show and how well they used different people's body language and actions to make us laugh. The reason we laughed is because we could relate to the comedy.

Men go into a public restroom where there are urinals on the wall. If for instance there are three, side by side. You are the first guy to go into the bathroom, which one will you use. Everyone knows it will be one of the end urinals. Why is this? Because if you took the center one and another guy comes in, he will have to stand next to you. Men are uncomfortable having their privates out around other men even to go to the bathroom. This is why so many men's rooms today have newspapers on the wall for them to read as well as divider walls. It is like the window tint of the car. We get that false sense of security standing next to that small divider wall. It helps them to relax. Do our parents teach us this? No, it is just something that is learned. We also do not like to have conversations in the bathroom. The man's bathroom motto is, Go in, be quite, stay away from me, and leave.

Women have no issues going into restrooms. Unlike men who prefer to be alone, women prefer to go in platoons. How often have you heard several women at a table say "I have to go to the ladies room, would you all like to go?" Every woman at the table gets up and goes. They may not have to go to the bathroom, but their going with you anyway. They almost appear excited about it. They will go in, sit around, and talk to each other. Total strangers! How? Can you imagine the look on the face of the guys if one of them was to stand and ask if the other guys wanted to go to the bathroom with him? Self-taught behaviors.

There are many types of behavior for people. We have often seen the actions of people who get nervous or are shy. People in traffic stops who are afraid or have something to hide will often display various behaviors. Some may not be able to stand still, while others have to constantly lean against something. Some may get out of a car and start what I call the felony stretch. Their arms stretch high, arching back, and appearing to have just gotten out of bed. It is the body's way of releasing stress. Others may be talkative while others will yawn. Are there any set patterns that will appear with everyone? Everyone is different and will respond to stimuli in various ways.

A person who feels guilty and confronted by the police will begin having increased nervous feelings. Some are able to hide these feelings pretty well while others cannot. They will not all be apparent, but they all will be visible if you are watching for them. Once you are confident something is wrong, it is time to go after the person's internal feeling. This is the third of the three representational channels. It is the stimulus applied to expose their feelings. They are the physical and psychological reactions to stress. You use this by adding stimulus to a person so you can observe their behavior. This is known as kinesics. Communications are expressed through body language, tone of voice, and spoken words. It will be the same as we discussed earlier with written statements. The amount of information we receive from someone through spoken words is only 7%. You can change the meaning of the spoken words with tone of voice, which accounts for another 38% of information. Generally, a person's volume and pitch increases with stress. Anger can increase the speed. We have all seen angry people talk and it is rarely slow and deliberate. A person's body language provides us with 55% of the information we are to receive.

We are watching for the information to spill from a person in clusters. A single action may not indicate deception. When you notice a person's heart rate increase, skin blush, and their eyes dart around, this can be indicative of stress. The cluster of things says something is wrong. Watching a person's eyes can tell you things about what they are saying.

Most people when asked a question can tell you the truth without thought. When the information is removed from an internal file, aka memory, they will generally move their eyes high and to the left. This is not true for the entire population, but it is similar to assuming everyone is right handed. The chances are they will be except for about 10% who will be lefties. For this generalization of eye assessment, we will play the odds. You would have to ask a person numerous base line questions of known facts to determine how a person retrieves the information. You can gather much of the information from their pedigree questions. Now you have their basic known information, you can have them expound on the facts. If with these base questions they move their eyes high left, then they are seeking the information, as would most people. If you asked for a person's family birth dates, they may have to think about it. You will see them look high and left as they "look" at the numbers. They may initially go high right and then go to the left. That is ok because they are trying to find the file that the information is stored within. Now as you ask someone questions and they vary their eye movements drastically, the chances are they are being creative. It may not mean they are lying to you, but maybe they are not telling the whole truth. If it is current events such as where are you coming from or where are you going, little to no thought should be necessary. Very little eye movement should take place. Little if any hesitation should occur. It is not much different than asking someone their name. They should be able to easily tell you.

Always keep in mind that there are cultural differences. Eye movements is an involuntary action that can work based on your observations of their eyes with simple questions. There are cultures where people do not make good eye contact. They look down all of the time, especially when speaking to a police officer or other authority figure. Many people who have recently arrived in the U.S. from Central or South America will be very passive and none confrontational with authority. Many who come from countries controlled by oppressive governments see all authority the same. Keep these issues in mind when watching the eyes.

When you are talking to someone and you ask a question that should stir an emotional response, they should look down. Something that is very close or harmful to them will cause them to look down and to the right. With the eyes down, this is an emotional response. If you are interviewing someone and they begin to look down, you will need to mirror them. Stay on an emotional line of questioning. By this I mean with questions and statements like "I can only imagine how you feel" "What are you feeling right now?" or "How do you think that makes them feel?" It is also a good time to move into their personal zone. Move within 3 feet of them if you feel it is safe. They are in their internal emotion channel.

For a more comprehensive study on the subject, every police officer should take as many kinesics courses as possible. They should even re-take classes they have had in the past to refresh their knowledge. Dealing with people is our job. Understanding body language is critical to us in performing our job safely.

When asking someone a yes or no question, the only acceptable answer is a yes or no answer. When a simple direct question is asked of a person, they should be able to answer it simply and directly. When they start hesitating or repeating the question back to you, they are trying to buy time to figure out the best answer. It may be the truth, but they had to decide whether to give it to you.

Once the stop has taken place, you become suspicious of the occupants. You call for another unit to back you up. There is a driver and right front seat passenger. The backup unit arrives and you explain to your partner your suspicions. Explain what it is you are going to do and what you want from them. Not everyone is going to have the same experience and you do want to have to explain everything in the middle of something going wrong. Be sure to use good approach and cover techniques. Do not walk up to the same side of the car side by side. You are presenting yourselves as easy multiple targets to the occupants inside. The cover officer can stay at the rear of the vehicle or to the outside of the approaching officer. No matter the number of occupants in the car, whether or not you have the driver exit, the approaching officer has cover from the other officer. If you have the driver exit the car, the rear cover officer can watch and direct the driver out of the car. The approach officer watches the passengers in the car. You remove the driver, pat him down and move to the passenger's side of your car. From here you have the drivers back turned to his car and you are facing it. This serves several functions. First, the driver and the passengers cannot communicate with one another. Second, it places the driver between you and the car. You can see if anything is happening past the driver. The cover officer should be continuing their observation of the car. If someone starts to get out of the car, you can both react quickly.

This is a good place to talk about video cameras. A video camera has its pro's and con's. All too often, I see officers playing everything up for the camera. They know it is there and recording everything. Often times, they will not act naturally because they know the camera is on. This distraction can also interfere with what you are trying to accomplish with the subjects in the car. You no longer have complete concentration on the situation. So often, I see officers who have the violator place their hands on the hood of their car to be patted down and handcuffed. It is an all right method to use, but they are doing it from the front of their own car. They are doing it for the sake of the camera. They have their backs turned to the violator's car that creates additional dangers to them. A passenger in the violator's car can come out before you have time to react. We have all seen it happen on video. What would happen if their patrol car is struck from behind? Both the officer and the violator will be killed or seriously injured.

You approach the passenger's side and ask the driver to exit the car and bring the keys. This prevents the passenger from sliding over and driving away. It also makes it harder for the driver to re-enter the car to leave. One of the first things I will do is ask if I can pat them down for weapons. They are now outside the car and on a level playing field with you. It is the time to clear them of any weapons they may have. I will remove any weapons including pocketknives and cell phones from them. What did you say? A cell phone can be used as a weapon. It can conceal a weapon and contraband. I have seen people wearing several cell phones. Be sure check the battery area and the inside of the phone if they are wearing one that does not work. With the battery out, it can hold a small amount of contraband. But more importantly, do not let people talk on their cell phones while you are with them. They could easily call someone else to tell them where they are and what is happening with them. If the violator intends you harm, they could have their own backup arrive in moments.

I know some officers will teach and swear by the method of having the drivers always exit their car. It is in my opinion a bad idea. It places them on equal ground to you. You always want the upper hand. When the subjects are out on foot and they draw a weapon, they will have the same options as you. They can attempt their actions at their own discretion. There is a reason why more officers are assaulted while attempting to arrest someone. It is because they are for that moment your equal. If you traded places with the bad guy and said in your mind you had to take this officer out, when would you do it? You would initiate your assault when you were out of the car. This is when the officer is closest and most vulnerable to you. We have seen and heard about it forever. Inmates in prison are constantly practicing various techniques to overcome you as you arrest them. They can advance on you, take cover from you, or attack you and run. We learned earlier that if they had a weapon, we would need more than 30 feet to protect ourselves by using a weapon from our utility belt. How close is the average person to you at a traffic stop? Usually just outside of our personal space of 2-3 feet.

If they are restricted to the confines of the car, their options are limited. If they start to exit their car, you will give them the verbal commands to stop and re-enter the car. If you have to tell them more than once you should see the danger flags. As we will soon see, if you have to repeat your commands, their minds are preoccupied. This person could be dangerous. You had better start doing something which could include drawing your weapon. See what their response is now. Are they still not listening to your commands? You had better be calling for backup. Are they unarmed from what you can see, but not advancing yet still not listening to you? Keep your distance, maintain cover, and wait for the backup. Are they advancing on you? What secondary weaponry are you trained with and have available. What is their physical size compared to you? There are many factors to consider in a split second. Just remember, despite what some people believe you are not paid to get injured or killed. You take the immediate action required to stop the threat.

Another study from Force Science News, Transmission # 155, involves what some are calling The Fatigue Threshold. Remember when I said that it was good to know various fighting techniques, but the best defense to a fight is in avoiding one. All fights eventually end on the ground. This is why so many agencies are now practicing ground fighting techniques. Break away and separate as fast as possible in a fight. Here is what this study tells us about an all-out fight for your life. "Certain muscles can be affected after approximately 30 seconds of maximum-intensity exercise. While "roughly" 1 to 5 minutes might seem a likely "normal" range, don't figure on most people being able to hold out for more than 2 minutes or so. You don't have much time to get a suspect under control before you're going to be in trouble. The suspect may not tire as quickly as you because it's a lot easier to resist than to overcome resistance. The exact point can be influenced not only by the officer's fitness level but also by such factors as the intensity of the altercation, the number of suspects and officers involved, the suspect's physical condition, environmental influences (heat, humidity, cold), the officer's equipment (20-lb. belt, motion-restricting ballistic vest, heat-retaining wool uniform) and the combatants' will to overcome and survive. Your recovery may take as long as a quarter-hour. Once an officer hits the wall, all gains are lost and all advantages evaporate. The reasonable officer understands that any suspect who is willing to fight the police with such intensity that he can bring the officer to the limits of his strength is dangerous and cannot be allowed to control the outcome. In most cases you can tell when you are about to reach your physical limit, although you may still be surprised at how rapidly you can fade, especially where upper-body strength is concerned. When you sense you're nearing your threshold, you must act quickly and decisively to control the suspect."

From the car, the only time they have to assault you with a firearm is in your approach. Again, if you will follow the rules as we have discussed, you will still have many advantages. We know how to physically approach the car; our disadvantage is usually going to be in our mental planning. Is your head in the right place to deal with this problem now? When you are at home, you leave the stress of the job at the job. When you are at work, you leave the stress of your personal life at home. Never should the two intermingle for very long. I know you cannot just turn off a switch. If you cannot concentrate on what you are doing, especially when interacting with someone, you should take a day off.

An example of keeping someone in the car is an event that occurred in Louisiana involving the traffic stop of a van occupied by two males. As it was reported in the news is the following:
The trooper exited his vehicle and asked the driver to do the same. As the driver stepped out of his vehicle, he immediately turned towards the trooper and began firing several shots at the trooper with a handgun. As the trooper took cover behind his patrol car, twice bullets from the driver's gun struck him. They then fled the scene westbound on Interstate 20.

There is the case of the Texas Trooper who stops the pickup truck. He suspects the driver of DUI. The driver has made him nervous enough where several times he has grabbed the handle of his service weapon and blades his weapon away from the driver. I believe he plays up many things for the camera. He turns his back on the occupants to bring a bottle of liquor to set on his hood after having the driver exit the vehicle. The driver is wearing a long trench coat and there is a passenger in the truck. He has to repeat his commands several times to the driver. He decides to arrest the driver for DUI next to the truck and the passenger. The passenger exits, distracts him, and they each pull guns firing over 20 rounds at the trooper. Only by the grace of God did he survive. It is easy to be a Monday morning armchair quarterback. All that I want to stress is with a few simple changes to our strategy, I know we can not only survive more encounters, but prevent them as well. We all watch these events unfold and say I would never do it that way. But I know we all have many times over. We just have to try harder not to do them again.

Now you are separating the occupants. Even if there is only the driver in the car with no passengers, you will ask them to exit the car. Tell them to bring the keys after another unit is with you. If you have enough suspicions about the driver which causes you to have him exit the car, then you will want another unit with you. If there was nothing about the stop that created your increasing interest, then they should have stayed in the car. You should release them as soon as you complete your enforcement actions.

The purpose of separating the driver from the passengers is because you suspected they were up to something wrong. If they are not, when questioned with a few basic questions, their answers will be identical. However, if they are up to no good, there will be discrepancies. Two people traveling around together can easily tell you about the events which started their time together to the present. There are people who have done nothing wrong now, but feel compelled to lie to you. It is hard to put together a lie and have several people explain it the same way. Because it is not tucked away in their memory file, they have to try and remember what they did. They can even practice their story, which they never do, and still not get it right. If you direct enough various questions toward them, it will fall apart.

Can you lie to them if you suspect them of wrongdoing? The answer is yes. They are easily played against one another because they are criminals together. They know they can never fully trust one another. Those long pauses they presented are causing stress. The brain takes more time to create a lie than it does to tell the truth. The statements a person makes have to match their body language. People like to talk with their hands, but there are times when a guilty person may not. A point they try to stress appears wrong. You will recognize it if you are paying attention.

Stress causes confusion and confusion causes stress. This stress will cause change and the change initiates the leaking of clusters. I have watched a man who became so nervous he fainted roadside. The stress just reached a point that his brain said "that's enough let's say good night." Another time I watched as a guy was talking to us roadside and chewing gum. He became so nervous that he quit producing saliva and the gum started to stick all over his lips. The first guy had a small bag of cocaine and a little weed. The second guy had 500 pounds of marijuana.

Another clue to a person's behavior is in their listening abilities. Once the stress increases, a condition known as audio occlusion kicks in. They will no longer hear or understand you. They are on a mission in their mind. Be very careful if you notice this person.

Often times they will do no more than mumble, but not while they are looking at you. They are very stressed and trying to determine their best options. If you have ever been in a high stress event, you may not remember any sounds. Your body is in overdrive to save itself.

I spent a lot of time examining the video tapes of police officers who were assaulted and sometimes murdered. At the time I was teaching police departments around the country a course in highway interdiction techniques. My goal then, as it is now, was officer safety. I wanted to see if I could find any verbal or physical actions of people before they attacked. It did not take long before I realized I had. I do not know if I am the only one to recognize it, but I do know I have tried to teach it to as many officers as will listen. You can look back at almost any video of an officer being assaulted and there was always one common denominator. The officer had to repeat their commands to the subject several times just before the attack took place. I do not care how old a video is, it still teaches us a lesson. I have shown videos of officers and been asked if I had something newer. We have been killed the same way since the beginning of law enforcement. It does not matter what was used or when they died. What does matter is the how it occurred. Watch all of the videos, regardless of their age and you can learn something that may save you later.

There is the video of a Texas constable who conducts a traffic stop. Three subjects who will later assault and kill him occupy the car. We watch as he gets the driver out car and back by the trunk of their car. He returns to the driver's window and begins to talk to the subjects inside. You can watch the driver stretch. It is the felony stretch. The officer asks about the trunk and the front right passenger exits. The constable tells him to "stay in the car, I'll get it." He repeats himself several more times before not saying it again. The passenger was already on a mission. The passenger knew there was marijuana in the trunk and they were not going to be arrested. Many people have mentioned that the passenger also takes his hat off as he gets out of the car. It is a good observation. Explain why you would wear a hat in the car and take it off when you exit. Some even say it would be normal to take off your hat before a fight. Once they are standing at the rear of the car the constable is standing at the trunk. The driver is behind him and the right front passenger is to his right. The constable is asking whose bag is whose and the passenger just quits listening. He mumbles a couple times and even the constable does not understand him. His mind is preoccupied as he instructs the driver in Spanish to get the officer. The constable was killed with his own gun. The constable had to repeat himself so many times, but he never sees this as a danger to himself. He never asks for back up. I do not know this for sure, but I question if a lot of his actions were performed for the camera. He had to know what was in the trunk, yet he kept pushing them. They snapped and he paid the ultimate sacrifice.

There is the video of the female officer in Texas who smells marijuana in the car and the driver is on probation. She instructs him out of the car and tells him to put his hands on the hood of her car. She has to keep repeating herself as he turns and punches her. He beats her into a coma roadside and unsuccessfully tries to remove her handgun.

There is also the video of the Georgia deputy who stops a subject believed to be involved in an armed robbery. The car stops and the driver exits. The deputy asked him for his license as the subject reaches into the car. The deputy tries repeatedly to verbally stop him as he moved closer. The subject comes around with a gun and kills him. As with the other videos, the officers repeated their commands and did what most cops do. When you do not listen to me I am going to get closer to you. When you recognize they are not listening to you create distance and wait. Just like earlier when we spoke about Representational Channels, when their mental or internal feelings are on full speed ahead, their visuals, and audios will be turned off. Only one Channel will play at a time.

Watch other videos as the officer's actions repeat themselves. They will reiterate their commands to the subjects who will ignore them. The officers fail to wait on back up and the officers get closer instead of backing away. Remember our shooting ally known as distance? We have to maintain our distance. When you are commanding someone to do something and they are moving to an area you can not see, back away. Do not be afraid to draw your weapon if you need to. Take the offensive by becoming defensive and live. Television has gotten many officers killed. You see the person you are dealing with has a gun, and you yell, "Drop the gun!" Your action should have been sight picture, sight alignment, breath, trigger squeeze. This is stated as an example only, but your actions had better be swift. Do not forget your instinctive shooting techniques. You do not wait for them to shoot first. You do not give them any additional advantages to kill you. If they have a weapon and you hesitate, the outcome may be fatal to you.

I will describe an event that occurred and finished on a positive note. A trooper is parked watching traffic. A pickup truck speeds by. The driver, upon seeing the trooper, brakes and actually turns around in his seat to watch what the trooper will do. The driver's window is half way down. The trooper sees the unusual reaction of the driver (remember these behavioral reactions from earlier as they realize they see the police) and attempts a traffic stop for unlawful speed. The driver of the vehicle travels a short distance before they begin to slow down. They move to the outside shoulder and travel slowly about one half mile before stopping. This can be a significant event. You have to have red flags going up in your mind. Why would someone not immediately stop for the police? The windows are tinted and it is unknown how many occupants there are in the vehicle. What was the driver doing inside the vehicle while it traveled slowly down the shoulder? The trooper maintains a lot of distance between his vehicle and their car while they were driving slowly. The driver could stop suddenly and exit which puts you in a bad position. The trooper has removed his seatbelt and has called in his location. A backup unit is already enroute to him. The vehicle finally stops. The trooper positions his unit almost three cars length back and completely off the road at an angle. The trooper opens his door and steps out, but stays behind his opened door. He has also already drawn his service weapon and holds it down to his side. The driver still has the window partially down. The driver of the vehicle keeps looking back at the trooper through his side view mirror. The trooper sees that the brake lights are still on and he does not attempt to walk up to the car. The trooper stays in his position of cover and sees his backup approaching. The trooper calls for the driver to exit the vehicle, but the driver does not comply. The trooper calls repeatedly for the driver to exit, but he still fails to comply. The driver eventually puts the car into park and exits the vehicle. The trooper brings his gun up and orders the driver to the ground. Now the driver complies with the orders. The backup unit has arrived and he deploys a shotgun. The passenger is removed from the vehicle. Both are handcuffed and secured.

Remember that not all situations are the same. This quit being just another traffic stop when the driver of the vehicle began to act suspiciously. The trooper called for another unit to be en route to his location early. The driver failed to obey commands and the trooper had to repeat himself. He had already positioned himself some distance back and behind cover. His gun was pulled and at a low ready position. What were their reasons for this erratic behavior? There were drugs, warrants for the driver's arrest, and a gun.

Do you see the deadly mistakes made in the earlier cases as compared to the last one? There was the officer's failure to wait for backup before proceeding with a confrontation. Once danger should have been recognized, there was a hesitation to react properly and with enough force to control the situation. When you suspect criminal activity, do not let suspects know what you are thinking. I even like to cut it off short if I know something is wrong. Tell them you will be right back, I am only going to write you a warning and send you on your way. Another will be "You will be on your way in a moment." I know the tactic works because after they are arrested or detained, they are placed into the rear of a patrol car. They are recorded and on the tape recordings, you will hear them telling each other. "Why didn't you do this or that?" The driver will say "you heard him; he was going to let us go." You can even see their behaviors go from tense and nervous to a more relaxed state. This topic will be touched on in the next chapter. The one that makes me cringe is when there is single officer at a traffic stop and they smell marijuana inside the car. The officer will say, "Do I smell marijuana in your car?" or "Is that marijuana I smell?" or "I smell something in your car. What is it?" I know we think of most potheads as easygoing stoners, but the fact of the matter is they kill many of us every year. Almost all criminals smoke pot. Smoking pot in most states is a crime. What do they care if they are caught with a little pot? Never let them know what you know. Keep the advantage over them at all times. You do not know what this person has done prior to your encounter.

Everyone has little things that work for them. When you have the opportunity to work with different agencies, try to go along. Watch how they work and try to find methods that they employ. You will find that many of these can be incorporated into your own tactics. I have patrolled with the United States Border Patrol in El Paso and worked many checkpoints with them in Texas and New Mexico. I patrolled with the Texas DPS in the Valley for several weeks. I rode along with the Mississippi Highway Patrol. I have watched and learned from everyone. I was on I-10 one night at the Sierra Blanca checkpoint east of El Paso watching the Border Patrol at work. As cars drive up, the agent will either wave them through or over to a secondary inspection. Agents have their own behaviors, car types, and other things that interest them. Some say the people just look out of the ordinary. When you stand there all day, watching cars slow and drive by, you get a feeling for ordinary. Some are too friendly, too talkative, too tense, or just look afraid. I cannot tell you exactly what to look for because everyone is different. What is important is to start paying attention to your own stops and the stops of others. Learn to slow things down and watch for unusual behaviors. They will stand out like a beacon. You will see them and start developing your own set of criminal behaviors that work best for you.

Behaviors are applied to the identification of terrorist as well. I had a former Israeli intelligence officer tell me even though a terrorist is on jihad; it is still not a simple task for them to commit suicidal homicide. They could usually see a terrorist in public because of his behavior. He may think he's going to heaven with a bunch of virgins, but their handlers always have to give them barbiturates to help calm them down before the journey. They would sweat profusely and not respond to verbal commands. They are on a mission with a lot on their mind. Sound familiar? Their mind is on a set task. This person is dangerous. They are operating in their internal Channel.

The FBI, stated in the September 2005 Law Enforcement Bulletin;

"Patrol officers need to know, for example, that suicide bombers may wear clothing out of sync with the weather, their location, or their social positions; carry heavy luggage, bags, or backpacks; repeatedly and nervously pat their upper bodies with their hands; display hyper-vigilant stares; or fail to respond to voice commands."

It all sounds familiar because the behaviors of the criminal will be the same as the terrorist. They are both filled with nervous feelings. Someone walking with a gun on the street will repeatedly check that it is secure by touching it. They may check with their hands or with their arms, but their actions will be noticeable.

I was assigned to our Dignitary Protection Detail for several years. We were trained in advance preparations and security measures of the protectee. In our case it was the Lieutenant Governor of Florida. He was the Lt. Governor under Jeb Bush, the president's brother. It was post 9-11 and we worked hard to cover the basics with the manpower which was available. In our training sessions, we were always taught to watch for people behaving differently and watch the hands. When you are working a crowd line, you are always watching the hands that are presented. Some of us would be watching ahead to where we were walking. Others are working the back of the crowd. Still others would be behind the protectee watching the behaviors and facial expressions of the people in the crowd. But you were always looking for the person who appeared different. Maybe it was with their smile. Bad guys know we are looking for their behavioral changes. Everyone there is smiling except one guy. Maybe that guy smiles, but you can see it is a fake smile. Look at yourself in a mirror and see how many muscles are moved in your face when you actually smile. Then fake a smile and see how many fewer muscles are used. They will usually give themselves away. It was a great experience and I learned a lot about people's behaviors.

I can never stress to you just how important this last chapter has been to me and should be to you. We need to constantly practice and watch people's behaviors. We need to listen closely to the words they speak. We need to pay very close attention to the behaviors of people in order to determine what is normal and what is dangerous. Practice and training in the area of body language interpretations can give you the skills that may allow you to recognize danger seconds before it happens. These seconds are exactly what we need to act before having to react to a situation.

THE CULMINATION OF TACTICS - 10

We need to be asking many types of questions. If the violator can answer our questions in a way that satisfies your curiosity, good keep moving. There is nothing to see here. If not, keep asking questions until they can satisfy you. If they cannot satisfy you then it is time to find out why. I have had people complain over the years because I asked if they had ever been arrested or was on probation. There is nothing wrong with this question. The information of a person's arrest record can be critical to your safety. How many of your best friends and family have an extensive arrest record. The number will be low because we will not associate with them. Criminals have criminals as friends and associates. Only 3% of offenders interviewed for and by the FBI in regards to attacks on officers stated they had no prior criminal history. This was only from a random group of 50 violators. (19) Therefore, 97% of the random group did have prior arrest. Do you understand its importance now? They should be asked the question near the beginning of an encounter.

Why am I asking them so many questions? The answer is easy, because I want too. There is no limit on what you ask as long as the encounter remains consensual. If I feel there is a need for it, I will ask as many questions as I can. It is my job. We are supposed to be inquisitive.

No single answer from a subject will give you everything you need, but it will lead to more questions. Where are you going? Where are you coming from? These two questions start to establish the bases for the remainder of the stop. If they say from work, then ask, "What kind of work?" After they answer you, ask yourself if their appearance matches their stated work? They do not appear to have any nervous behaviors and they can easily present all of their documents. Take the appropriate actions for the violation and move on. Often I watch as officers spend entirely too much time with simple stops. Do not try to make something out of nothing. Do not let your drive cause you to waste time. Find and stop the next violation.

You ask the same questions to someone else and they say they are traveling from Houston, Texas to Tampa, Florida. You already see they have a Florida driver's license and they are by themselves. Their address is in Tampa and you can see no luggage in the passenger's compartment. The registration shows a third party owns the car. Is there enough information to ask for consent already? Yes and no. More information is needed to establish a higher probability of criminal activity. Consent can be asked of anyone at any time. There is no need to waste everyone's time if there are no substantiating facts. It goes back to trying too hard to make something out of nothing. How does this person look? Have they been sleeping in the car? How well kept and rested do they appear? Are there fast food bags and caffeine items visible? Was this trip for business or pleasure? You ask them, "When did you travel there and when did you leave to return?" These are all viable questions in order to obtain additional information. How well can they answer these questions? Does the line of questioning create additional nervous reactions? Can you see them becoming more nervous or starting to get angry? Sometimes they will ask you questions. "Why are you asking me these questions?" I have heard this response more than once. The tension they are experiencing is causing them stress. Remember, stress causes confusion and confusion cause stress. They may start asking you questions in an effort to delay or divert you. Stay on task and in control. Another spontaneous statement you will hear is; "Do you want to search my car? Go ahead I don't have anything in there." But while they are saying this they are unable to stand still. What their body language is telling you is, "I hope you do not search the car because I am so friendly and co-operative." Often times they are looking everywhere or staring at the car. People still believe that if they tell you all is ok, you should believe them. When they offer you this opportunity, take it. Ask them, "Is it ok if I search your car?"

Based on the circumstances which you are confronted with, there are many things you can ask. They just need to be relevant with the information you received which caused you to start asking the questions. If there is more than one person in the car, be sure to separate them before asking questions. Before you separate them, be sure to have backup. I will repeat this again because it is so important, but do a pat down for weapons.

Ask them; what is your name? What is the name of the other person in the car with you? What time did you start out together? What is the exact location you are traveling to today? How many times have you stopped someone on a trip and they do not know where they are going? When you ask them, how are you going to get there? They will tell you that they are going to call someone when they get close. Ask them for the number they are supposed to call. Ask them from where are they to call? What exit are you supposed to take? If they are not related, ask them how are they dividing the cost of the trip? Did they stay anywhere along the way? If yes, then where? When did you last eat and where? Simple questions any two people can answer if they are on a trip together. The problem will exist when they are not sure about what the other one is answering. Lie to them if you think they are lying to you. When they give you an answer ask them, "Why would the other person tell me this or that?" For example, the passenger tells you that they are going to Miami. You ask him if they are supposed to stop anywhere else. They will answer "not that I am aware of." Then you ask why would the driver say you are going somewhere else if you say you are not? This really puts the pressure on them. When they are very nervous a great question to ask is, "Why would someone call the police today to say you have drugs in your car?" Now just think about the question a moment. You are a drug smuggler and a police officer asked you that question. In your mind you are thinking who would have snitched on me. Now you know the body language would be pouring out in clusters at this point.

You have to look at the answers people give you and see if they make sense. Would you possibly do anything this person did? If not, you need to keep digging. In the end, things may still not make any sense to you. However, at least you can say you exhausted all of your options to figure out why. Some people have never made sense at anything they have ever done. You have to accept it and move on. Incredibly, there are still many judges in the system who cannot believe the evil people do. I recently had a judge explain in court that he finds it hard to believe anyone who has ever been in the system would give the police consent to search. Verbal consents have always sufficed for consent in the jurisdiction that I work. Whenever I ask for consent, I will make sure my partner is present to witness the consent.

When asking someone if you can search their car, ask them if you can search their car. Yes, I did repeat myself. This may sound strange, but there are many officers who ask if we can look in your car. In many areas this means that you can stand on the outside and look inside. We want to search your car and all of the contents in the car. Another good question at this point is to ask if there is anything in the vehicle that does not belong to you. Give them a chance to distance themselves from anything illegal. One other good question is to ask if there is anything illegal in the car. You or I can instantly answer the question; they will have to think about it. Another standard answer to the question is, "not that I know of."

There is always new case law arriving from the courts overseeing the rules for your jurisdiction. Follow those rules closely. Do not allow a good case to fall to the wayside over a small misstep on your part. It will happen inevitably, but try to cross all of your T's and dot your I's. In some areas, it is required that you get consent to search forms signed. In other areas, it is ok to ask for everything verbally. Do what your prosecutors and department want you to do. I also have a K-9 present with me all of the time. His nose and the free air sniff on the exterior of the car is my probable cause. A K-9 alert in Florida is probable cause to search the vehicle. I know in other areas of the country it is not.

I encourage everyone to read about the drug trade. Where and how are drugs manufactured? How are they coming into the areas you work? With this small amount of information, you can interdict drugs. Not just the street level nickel bag people, but smugglers. Make contact with the local narcotics investigators and DEA. Talk to them and let them know what you are trying to do. Let them know you will give them any information on any arrest you make. You will be surprised how many cases will tie into many of their cases. Ask them what kind of cases they are currently working and how are they moving the drugs into the area? Where do they think the drugs are coming from? Look at a map and find the most direct roadway that leads to your area. Ask them about the couriers they have seen and if there is any intelligence they could give to you to watch for. Do they recognize any trends? Are the mules normally single or double males? Maybe they like to use females. If so, are they usually traveling alone? Do they use counter surveillance techniques like chase cars?

Currently there are many trends in the drug business. They are not surprising trends either. Some are frightening. They were all received from the DEA current trends information on their website. For instance, most of the MDMA, which enters the country, arrives from Canada. Overall, there really has not been a change in the use of MDMA. It is neither higher nor lower in consumption. The manufacturers of the substance in Canada have decided to try and change that. How is the shocking part. They are spiking the MDMA tablets with methamphetamine. This is much more addictive and will cause all of the party crowds to become very addicted, very fast.

The Mexican DTO's (Drug Trafficking Organizations) are having some success in the transportation and distribution of Heroin into the northeast. No other region of the country has a heroin problem as large as this region. Why not make it worse! The Mexican heroin production is not only up, but it is producing white heroin. Mexican heroin has traditionally been brown or black tar.

Shipments of ephedrine and pseudo ephedrine are easily diverted from the ports of Mexico. They are not controlled as they are here in the U.S. What this means is an increase in meth production in Mexico and transportation into the U.S. The greatest drug threat across the nation is still cocaine. It is followed by methamphetamine. If you make an arrest or have probable cause to detain people, you place them into the rear of your patrol car. This is where one of our greatest tools exists, the concealed audio recorder and microphone system. You have to find out what is allowed in your state, but in Florida, no one has any rights to an expectation of privacy while in a patrol car. We will often place covert microphones in the rear passenger compartments of our vehicles. There are as many people in prison from their taped patrol car statements as most other investigative tools. They talk about the drugs, where it is, and who put it there when they were pulled over. They tell us if there are hidden guns and numerous time, we have had to take female defendants to the hospital because it was discovered they had placed drugs inside a body cavity.

In the 1970's and 1980's, almost all of the drugs entering the United States came into South Florida. It had become the second home to nearly every South American drug lord. It was a financial Mecca. Drugs left through Florida and money returned. This is where I started in the interdiction business.

No one in the 1970's and few in the early 1980's were involved with interdiction. The State of Florida tasked the FHP with creating a K-9 corps to combat the drugs as they left Miami. President Reagan had sent Vice President George Bush to south Florida to lead the war on drugs. In July 1984, I was asked to assist a K-9 trooper with his interdiction duties. It was to be a pilot program to determine how effective we could be as a team. It turned out to be very effective. Few if any officers in the country were working full time interdiction. We had no one to train us because there was no one involved in interdiction. We read the news and were aware that Miami was home to all of the drug trafficking organizations. We took out a map and said if we were going to transport drugs from Miami, what route would we take? Of those routes, which ones seemed to encompass our area of patrol? That location was where we went to look for drug smugglers. We started out only working late at night. We learned over time it did not matter what time of day you worked. The drugs were going to travel day and night. We learned on our own what people liked, what the transportation trends were, and more importantly how quickly they would change. They will use a method of transportation until it is no longer effective. The cartels have an expectation of loss to law enforcement. The majority of the product will get through. If this method worked that month, but then was discovered by law enforcement, the method would be changed.

The smugglers rarely attempted to hide anything. We would stop cars with hundreds of pounds of marijuana in the back seat. We seized over 900 pounds of cocaine from the bed of a pickup truck and over 700 pounds of cocaine sitting in the passenger compartment of a van. Over the years, as more and more law enforcement people became involved, their tactics started to change. Because of the heavy police presence in South Florida and the Caribbean, the Columbian cartels started to move their product through Mexico. They arranged for Mexico and some of its early cartels to transport the drugs over the border. It is still flowing across the border today. The country of Mexico is for the most part a narco state. The drug trade supports the bulk of its economy. Mexico has always suffered with its ruling class. You are in either the upper class or the lower class. There is nothing in between. There is no middle class. Anyone who has ever worked in any facet of government will tell you Mexico is very corrupt. A few have everything while most have nothing. Economics is the driving force of everything. I once had a high ranking member with the National Security Advisors Office tell me the reason why we do not close down our border with Mexico is because of socio-economics'. If we were to shut the border down tight, the economy of Mexico would collapse. The massive rush to the United States would be overwhelming. Can we stop the illegal drug flow into the U.S.? Yes, we can, but we choose not too. The State Department is far more important than the Justice Department. Drugs still arrive into south Florida, but with nowhere near the volume it had in the 1980's.

If you stop someone and they tell you they are coming from a source area, it is a good start. Check out the rest of the story and see if it makes sense. Does the interior of the car match the trip plan in regards to visible items? Do not be placed into a false sense of security when it comes to families. My partner and I stopped a van once with luggage on the roof. The driver said he was going to his cousin's house. The female passenger stated the driver was her husband and they were taking their three children to Disney World. The driver was asked what the cousin's address was. He did not know the address, but he was to call him when he got to the exit. We said give us the number and we will call to get the address for you. Then the story changed again. He said he lost the number, but he knew how to get there. Ok, we said how do you get there? He stared down the road at the large golden arches sign and said, "I am supposed to turn at the McDonalds." The location of the stop was 20 miles south of the interstate to go to Orlando. The female passenger said they were going to Disney World and did not know anything about the visit to the cousin's house. The driver described the passenger as his girlfriend. We asked him why she thinks she is married to him and he thought a moment and said, "Because we have been together a long time." There was something about the vehicle that did not make sense. We ran the K-9 around the van. The dog would move away from the vehicle and then track back. It was a definite change in behavior, but different. Then it hit us. Why would you travel in a van, even with three children, and put your luggage out in the weather. There was more than enough room in the rear of the van to hold the luggage. Inside of the luggage on the roof was over 300 pounds of marijuana. The woman was paid to travel with the driver. When the trip was over to deliver the drugs, he would take her and the children to Disney World. It was a rental family added to the load vehicle to try to give legitimacy to the appearance. The driver could not control his behaviors as he approached and passed us. The K-9 was detecting the odor of marijuana that due to the wind was passing over the van. He was wind scenting away from the van and then trying to follow the odor back to the van. Due to the height of the vehicle and the cross winds, there was a void area of odor when you got close to the side of the van.

I will give you another case scenario to bring everything together. We stopped a guy in a pickup truck. He is traveling alone. He says he is going home to Gainesville, Florida, from Key West. He states he had gone on vacation for a few days and his girlfriend stayed at home because he was going to go SCUBA diving. All of his equipment was in the back of the truck. What do we have so far? He is nervous, but this could be just because he was pulled over by the police. He has gone on vacation alone for a few days even though he has a girlfriend. Still this could be plausible, except that it will take you 10-12 hours to drive there one way. There is one day travel in each direction. He only went down for a couple of days. He points out his equipment is in the back of the truck. I look and see fins, mask, snorkel, and an old air tank. I do not see any other equipment. Being a SCUBA diver myself I know what he has is equipment to go snorkeling. There is not a regulator or bouncy compensator. Guess where the drugs are? That's right; it was in the air tank. When you pulled the plastic boot off the bottom of the tank, there was actually a screwed down plate. He had 10 pounds of marijuana.

The strategy behind interdiction is simple. Take your time and be observant. Be cautious and stay with it when you are suspicious. Do not be fooled by the presence of families or women. Women are actually very much preferred in smuggling because the DTO's think we are less likely to stop females. Ask the questions to see if the answers match their behaviors and the appearance of the vehicle. Does everything look the way it should, based upon the statements they have made to you?

Another topic, which is very prevalent today, is human trafficking. Most of us never realize to what degree this is taking place around the country. Many of the same DTO's around the world are involved in the human trade as well. It can be just as lucrative financially, yet it does not carry the same stiff penalties as drug violations. Most police officers, if they were to stop a human smuggling vehicle would never know it. There are differences with the people and the vehicle that can give them away. Just as before with drugs and other crimes, a police officer who takes their time will notice the differences. You have to pay attention.

All of the human traffickers I have encountered have been of Mexican descent. That is because Florida has an enormous agricultural economy. Florida has long growing seasons because of the climate. There is a large demand for temporary field workers. They will travel along the same routes as the drug traffickers. The driver or the "coyote" will load their cargo often in vans. The cargo is of course people. Traffickers will often refer to them as "pollos" or chickens. They will be from all parts of Central and South America. Vans are the most common means of transportation and the reason is simple. You can load more people into a single place. They are paid per person. The windows of the van behind the driver often times are very dark tinted. The driver will sometimes have another assistant who will help drive. How will you know if they are the "coyote" or the cargo? By the way they are dressed. You will see a distinct difference in the appearances in the two groups. You can see how the cargo will be dressed in much older clothes and shoes. Their luggage will most often be paper or plastic bags. They will often times appear dirty and tired. Usually they have traveled far to cross the border on foot. Once they have made it to a certain location, they will be picked up for the drive across the country. The driver is well dressed with nice clothes, shoes, or boots. They will look very different from their cargo. All they have done is drive. The passengers have spent days or weeks trying to get across the border. They are immediately loaded into vans and driven for several days straight through. With this description in mind, you can get a mental picture of how different they each will appear.

To find out if the vehicle is a human smuggling vehicle, look at the rear springs. The vans would normally squat in the rear because of the weight of the people. They will put much larger and stiffer springs in the rear to prevent this. If you will go under the rear of the van, you will see the added springs. Often times they are not professionally attached. You will see them with simple nuts, bolts, and clamps. The car will be cluttered with soda cans and other snack trash. Generally, the odor in the van will be strong. In many locations across the border, trying to buy a minivan is very hard. These smuggling groups will buy every one of them at auction to use.

They will charge up to $2000.00 dollars per person to transport them from the border to cities in Florida. This payment is usually made at the end of the trip. The person is turned over to their sponsor once the payment has been made. Several times we have caught the coyotes traveling north with a large bundle of cash. This would be the transportation payments to the smugglers from the sponsors. The entire group is turned over to the U.S. Border Patrol who will seize the persons, vehicle, and cash. As with most things in the business, after the organizations lost money several times, they quit transporting the cash. Instead, the coyotes will make regular stops and have the cash wired back to their organizations via companies like Western Union. Several times, we have caught human smuggling vehicles northbound with South American passengers. We later found out these people had lost their sponsors and were returning back to the border. Another time in a southbound smuggling vehicle, we discovered numerous females. This turned out to be part of a prostitution smuggling ring. They will pick up the young girls and take them to migrant camps throughout the state. They are originally told they are being taken for regular work. However, when they arrive to the location there will not be a sponsor. The girls are then taken to pay off their transportation debt as prostitutes. They will often earn less than $5.00 per "trick" in order to pay off their $2,000.00 cost. The Border Patrol is very aggressive with these people. The coyotes will be arrested and charged. We have many of them receiving 3-5 year federal prison terms. The passengers themselves are usually very reluctant to talk. They may want to try again to travel later or have family somewhere, which can be jeopardized.

It helps to have some basic understanding of the language of the foreign nationals you may encounter. We have taken courses in Spanish for law enforcement to help us converse better. Florida is a melting pot of cultures. Cubans who come here do not speak any English. Then there are Haitians with Creole and other Islanders who speak Patois. Patois is a combination of languages from English and African. It all depends on the various cultures you may have in your area. It pays off in huge dividends if you are an officer in the community and you practice their language. You never have to be fluent, but it helps to understand as much as you can. The people themselves are more likely to help you with problems when they see you trying to understand them and their cultures. In many parts of central and south Florida, people can go throughout their entire life without having to understand English. The communities are very tight knit and the various cultures stay together.

LABS AND THE DANGERS TO THE PATROL OFFICER - 11

I wanted a chapter to talk about labs because we need to plan about the possibilities of mobile labs. Clandestine labs possess a huge threat to us all in so many ways. There are many officers injured and disabled by this threat every month despite the controls on precursors for methamphetamine manufacture. As a patrol officer, especially in a rural area, the likely hood of encountering a lab is relatively high. Even though there are not as many lab operations in the U.S. as there once were, they are still prevalent. With new methods of cooking, the rise of the lab is returning. Most of the meth which is utilized in the United States is transported here from south of the border. Meth produces its own set of dangers to the patrol officer. In many areas of the country, methamphetamine is one of the most common drugs.

Many of these labs are mobile. Many others are broken down labs which are being transported to a different location. There are current processes of one-pot methods where people can drive around while the chemicals are processing in the vehicle. The entire cooking method takes less than hour. It is crucial for the officer to recognize a possible lab in a vehicle. Many officers around the country are injured by inhaling and touching chemicals they thought was something else. Common household containers are used to transport the chemicals to the lab. Many of these containers will then be taken to a location to be dumped. It is during these movements that the patrol officer commonly encounters this criminal.

In Florida, there are still many rural areas where the production of meth is practiced. This newer method like the one pot method, also called the shake and bake, is being produced because of the ease of production. The process is quite simple. Everything is placed into a single container and shaken. The pressure, which builds within the container, presents explosive dangers. The containers, which can be Coleman fuel cans or 2-liter soda bottles, were never designed for withstanding the amount of pressure these mixtures produce. Some of the items you will see in this type of cooking method are:

- Ammonium Nitrate or Ammonium Sulfate
- Common fertilizers
- Anhydrous ammonia
- Instant cold packs
- Lithium – from batteries
- Pseudo ephedrine or ephedrine pills
- Ether – Starter fluid
- Sodium Hydroxide – usually drain cleaner

The items that you may find in a standard lab can include the items below which was obtained from the Portland Oregon Police include:

Acetone	Alcohol (isopropyl or rubbing)
Anhydrous ammonia and ammonium sulfate (fertilizer)	Battery acid (sulfuric acid)
	Coleman fuel
Bleach	
Drain cleaner (sulfuric acid or caustic soda)	Drain openers such as Red Devil lye
Heet and Iso-Heet, gasoline additives (methanol/alcohol)	
Iodine (both crystal and liquid)	Lithium batteries
Matches (red phosphorous)	Mineral Spirits

Muriatic acid

OTC cold pills containing ephedrine or pseudoephedrine

Salt (table or rock)

Sodium and Lithium metal

Starting Fluid (organic ether)

Toluene

Trichloroethane (gun cleaning solvent)

Hydrogen peroxide

Aluminum foil

Bed sheets

Blenders

Bottles; such as pop, water and milk bottles

Chemistry glassware

Camp stoves

Cheesecloth

Coffee filters

Cotton balls

Duct tape

Electric portable hot plates, single and double

Funnels

Garden spray jugs

Gas cans

Jugs

Paper towels

pH test strips

Plastic tubing

Pressure cookers

Propane tanks and thermos

Pyrex dishes

Rags

Rubber and latex gloves

Strainers

Swimming pool chemicals

Thermometers

Turkey basting wands

These are some of the items you may come across at a mobile lab. This is a list of items you may find in a dump site, trash can, or public trash disposal. You may also come across these items if you were to stop a vehicle that was enroute to dump them:

- Rags with red and/or yellow stains
- Large number of pill blister packaging from over-the-counter cold, diet or allergy remedies
- Empty containers from white gas, ether, starting fluids, lye or drain openers, paint thinner, acetone, or alcohol Compressed gas cylinders, or camp stove (Coleman) fuel containers
- Packaging from Epsom salts or rock salt
- Propane tanks or coolers containing strong ammonia odors
- Pyrex/glass/Corning containers, with dried chemical deposits remaining
- Bottles or containers connected with rubber hosing and duct tape
- Coolers, thermos bottles, or other cold storage containers
- Respiratory masks and filters or dust masks
- Funnels, hosing and clamps
- Discarded rubber or latex gloves
- Coffee filters, pillow cases or bed sheets stained red (used to filter red phosphorous), or containing a white powdery residue

As you can see, it may look like someone's kitchen pantry in the vehicle. You are on a traffic crash investigation and the car was left abandoned. The standard policy for most agencies will be to inventory the car and tow it for safekeeping. You open the door and there is a chemical odor coming from inside. You need to get out and move away up wind from the vehicle as fast as possible. Just inhaling small particles from some of the chemicals involved can cause lung damage. Cops are curious by nature. You see a glass mason jar in a car with a clear liquid in it; you automatically think it is alcohol. Many will open and smell the item. Do not open and smell any item you are not absolutely sure about. This could cause a lifetime of misery. Remember, in the beginning of these labs, law enforcement did not know the dangers involved with these chemicals and their byproducts. There is many federal, state, county, and city officers who were tasked back in the early days to raid and break down these labs. They did not wear the Tyvek disposable suits and self-contained breathing apparatuses or SCBA's used today. Hundreds of these officers have since died or are completely disabled. They are suffering from complications of lung damage to rare brain cancers.

If you have a vehicle you suspect contains lab materials, as was said before, get away and move up wind. Do not let anyone near the vehicle. If your agency has a clandestine lab team, have them respond to the scene. Cordon off the area to protect anyone from getting near the vehicle. If fire rescue or other personnel arrive, be sure to notify them of the possible lab. Many fire departments have never had any training nor have experience around meth labs. Let them know that if they must approach the vehicle, SCBA's have to be worn. In most instances, because of the cost involved to clean up and dispose of a site, contact the DEA. They will have the personnel and resources to handle the situation. Also, remember if a subject is arrested from the vehicle, their clothes can contain dangerous chemical compounds that need to be addressed before placing them into a closed patrol car. You may have to have them strip out of their clothes before securing them in your car. A Tyvek suit or a medical gown from the medical services will suffice. Also, if your own clothes become contaminated, consider disposal of the uniform in a biohazard bag. Be sure your supervisor writes a first report of injury report for any exposures you may have had. Exposure to a chemical could have repercussions later in life. The first report of injury report will be necessary to protect you if you need assistance later on with complications to the exposure,

While we are on the topic of labs, one type has become very commonplace. In Florida, there are literally thousands of indoor marijuana grows. All parts of the state have been affected. A house in almost any neighborhood can be a grow operation. Most people see these as out in the middle of nowhere grow operations. We have served warrants on multiple homes in the same neighborhood and at the same time. Not just once or twice, but all of the time.

In Florida, the indoor marijuana grow operations are mostly controlled by Cubans. Cuban criminal organizations in South Florida will purchase or rent homes throughout the state. They will then bring in Cuban immigrants and place them in the homes. They do not speak English and require little in the ways of furnishings. They are promised everything from money, cars, and even the home after they produce a certain number of crops. Sometimes they will live in the house, but usually will stay somewhere else. Generally if they live in the same house, they will seal off the area of the grow operation. Often times the grow area will be in the garage. The garage door area will be boarded off and it is common to cover it with plastic sheeting. The door to the house is often sealed off to cut back on the odor of the fresh marijuana.

There are many hazards in a grow operation. The atmosphere itself is usually lower oxygen and higher carbon dioxide. Some try to filter outgoing exhaust with carbon filters. Others will use ozone generators in the air ducts to clear the exhaust of odor. The ozone generators produce ozone which is dangerous to inhale. It is often pumped into the attic to help dissipate the odors through the top of the roof. This will also make it more difficult for the neighbors to smell the illegal crop. Add to these items mold and chemicals throughout the house and you have a formula for disaster. The officers who have to enter this location are in an unsafe work environment. If you are in a grow house, a good gas mask should be worn with Tyvek suits. Do not forget the maze of electrical alterations in the home. It is without question that many of these homes are a fire hazard. The electrical is bypassed before the meter. This was their answer to law enforcement tracking electrical consumption. There will be no change to their electric bill. The additional lines are strung all over the place in order to operate all of the equipment. Care is necessary and the local power company should be called in to secure the power.

Growing 1 pound of marijuana per plant about every three months, a single house can produce about $1 million a year. Grow houses ship about 100 pounds each every three months to Miami and it is then distributed in the northeastern United States, at up to $4,500 a pound.

Criminal organizations have always taken advantage of the downtrodden. In 2008, Florida led the nation in grow house bust with 1022. A spreadsheet on every grow house bust in Polk County Florida since 2005 shows that 142 of 172 suspects, or 84 percent, caught tending marijuana grow houses have identified their place of birth as Cuba. In south Florida, the percentage rate is 85-95 percent. This not a disparaging statement towards Cubans, it is just the facts. Especially in south Florida, many areas are primarily Cuban. Statistically, for the overall Cuban population it is low. Again, it is an issue of taking advantage of Cuban refugees who are recent arrivals. Is it a Cuban issue alone, absolutely not. Again drugs are an equal opportunity employer. Because it is the worlds most abused illegal substance, anyone can grow it anywhere. A 200 plant grow operation was discovered in a second floor storeroom at the Mall of America in 2008 in Miami. The operators had tied into the malls power source to run the equipment. (23)

Many of these homes are discovered because of a traffic stop. So often, you can smell the strong odor of raw marijuana from inside the car. The odor of the plant permeates everything the person has in their possession. Their clothes and everything in the car will smell like raw marijuana. After a traffic stop you may see things like:

Plastic plant containers, barrels, electrical wire, rolls of string, construction material, a/c duct work, electrical ballast, timers, fans, 1000 watt sodium vapor lights, rolls of plastic, fertilizers and other planting chemicals. Each light is going to need its own, igniter, capacitor, and transformers. These are a few, but not all things found at a grow operation. The possessions of these items are not against the law. However, the proper investigative authority according to your own standard operating procedures should follow up the collection of the intelligence upon.

THE SEARCH - 12

You have the car stopped and there are numerous things about the subjects, which attracts your suspicions. Now you want to search the car. You have removed the occupants after your backup arrives. If there are plain view items, and the laws of your state permit, you can search the car. There is nothing in plain view, but you have enough indicators to believe you should search the car. You ask for consent to search. If the owner is not present, it is generally accepted the driver can give consent. While the subjects wait outside with your back up units, you conduct the search. Just as mentioned before, I like to pat everyone for weapons. Do not let anyone use a cell phone. Remove and set aside any knives. Even if there is probable cause to search the car, I will still at times ask for consent. It gives me additional courses to conduct the search. Is it necessary to ask? No, it is just something I like to do to see what a person's reaction will be. If they say no, I explain I do not need their permission because of this or that. You will need to follow the rules of search and seizure in your state and your departmental rules.

If I have probable cause to search, I will not allow the subjects to stand around outside and watch. They are detained and need to be secured. Even if it is a completely consensual search, at times based on the number of people or weather conditions, I will have them sit in the rear of a patrol car. The windows will be rolled down and the patrol car placed closer. This accomplishes several things. First and foremost, is officer safety. No one in the group can cause us any harm. The second is if they decide to withdraw the consent, they can. We are in a position we can communicate with each other. Thirdly, they are being recorded.

If we are suspicious enough to search you, then we need to record you to see if you can confirm anything.

When the search of the vehicle is initiated, I have always conducted the search systematically. First make sure the car is pulled completely off the road. Pull it even further off the road if it is possible. Start at the same point each time. Be sure to wear a good set of search gloves. Clear the passenger's compartment first. I will usually start at the right front passenger's door. This is the location I walk to on most stops so it is a natural position to start the search.

Open the door to examine the handles and lower door pocket. See if there appears to be any tampering with the inside panels or speakers. Look at all of the screws and plastic panel rivets for any signs of tampering. If there are power windows and locks, see if these switches are on a panel in the armrest. These panels can be lifted out easily, which exposes a generous void. Examine the rocker panel. Have the screws been tampered with and examine the dirt line. The dirt and dust lines are important. It shows if anything has recently been moved. If the panel has been moved, then it will be cleaner and obviously different than other areas. If the seat has an aftermarket seat cover, be sure to check under them. Always look at the bolts holding the seats for indications that a tool has been used on them. As you search the car and examine these locations, think to yourself. When was the last time I took the seats out of my car? Did you actually unbolt them from the floor? I will say it again that everything has to make sense based on your own personal experiences. False compartments in the floor below the seats are popular. In front of the hinge for the front door, there can be foam insulation, which you can push out of the way to look forward into the front fender on both sides. You may have to use a probe or baton to move it. Once these areas are cleared, I will sit in the front passenger's seat.

Open the glove box and examine the contents. Another item we are looking for is receipts. The receipts can help confirm or discount a subject's travel itinerary. If there are any garbage or food bags on the floorboard try to locate the receipt. If it has been a long trip you will see where and when they have been. Does the trip itinerary as it was told to you match the receipts? Remove the latching system on the sides of the glove box and let it fold down. Examine the area behind the glove box and up towards the air bag. Make sure the bag is in place. You can also look a little to the left and see behind the stereo system in the dash. In this area there can be an inside air filter for the air conditioning system. Be sure to open it and look inside past the filter. If all of this is clear, check the headliner above you especially along the front edge above the windshield. It is just cardboard and you can run your fingers across the passenger's side. If there is a sun or moon roof, be sure to examine the area around it and the cover that closes it off. We have found many personal stashes in these areas. Look at the air conditioning ducts to see if there is anything visible inside. Often times you can remove the vent covers and see better inside the vents.

Look at the area of the center console. Open the console and remove all of the contents. Make sure that the plastic inside liner is secured or has it ever been removed. If there is a gearshift with a plastic or vinyl wrapped base, lift it up. Check around it and down into the console. If there are cup holders, be sure to pull these out if they are not secured. They will usually reveal a large void under the front part of the console. On the larger SUV's, the area under the center console is a very popular location to hide contraband. The console is raised because of the size of the vehicle. Generally, the entire plastic interior liner comes out and the cup holders will pull out as well. The size of the void in this area can be surprising. Stepping out of the car and kneeling down, utilize your flashlight under the seat and dash. If there is a center console you can run your fingers under the bottom edge that covers the transmission hump. At the front edge of the console, under the dash, be sure to search this area well. There is a large void at this location and you can reach around to feel the space easily. It is a quick location for someone to stash contraband. Be sure to examine the plastic shield covering the bottom of the dash. In many models, there are simple clips for the easy removal of this plate. If you feel the search of this area is complete, move on to the next location.

Next, I will walk around to the driver's side and do the same examination from the open door as I did on the passenger's side. On the side of the dash is generally the fuse box cover that will remove. The horn and/or air bag cover on the steering wheel should be carefully examined. On many older models, this cover will pop off and can be a popular personal stash hiding area. Be sure to examine the driver's side floors, seat, and side of the center console. Examine the plastic cover under the dash. We have found a handgun in this location before. Just like on the passenger's side, there may be clips for the quick opening and closing of the panel. Any pockets on the dash or above in the roof should be looked at and removed if needed. Be sure to complete the sweep of the headliner along the windshield on the driver's side. If you are satisfied, move to the driver's side rear door or pull the seat forward if it is a two door.

If it is a four door, again check the door areas from the outside. Lift up the bottom of the rear seat and clear this area. If someone else is assisting you, have them help you remove the seat.

Look at the seat belts and see if they are passing through the slits in the seat. If not, then the seat has been removed. Once the seat has been removed, lift up the insulating padding that is covering the metal floor. See if anything appears to have been tampered with. Often times the fuel pump is located here and needs to be examined for signs of tampering. Also, examine the metal on the side-to-side hump at the front edge of the rear seat for any type of tampering. Often there will be small rubber caps in this area that can be removed. You can examine the void in the metal under these caps. If clear move into the seat. Lift up and check the headrests that are in front of you. Feel and check the back of the driver's seat. If it is a two door, check the side panel on your left closely. Also, examine the vertical plastic cover in between the driver's seat and the frame. The shoulder strap for the driver's seat belt is attached here. The molding pulls off and the area is hollow. Once you are satisfied with the search, next I will move to the trunk.

Open the trunk and examine the contents. Look to see if anything appears out of the ordinary. Is the spare tire in the proper location or is it just lying there? Remember there is a tire well or other locations for the proper tie down of the spare tire. If you do not see it, go beneath the trunk and see where it should be. There could be a false floor in the trunk. Look up at the underneath or inside portion of the trunk lid. Few people actually will look up. There are voids in the area for concealment and it usually has a carpet like covering. You should be able to tell if it has been tampered with. Look now along the edge of the trunk by the lock and see if the molding there has been removed. You can easily remove it and snap it back into place when satisfied. I will move to the sides of the trunk if it is empty. The side carpet moldings will easily pull out so you can check all of the voids leading forward above the side tire wells. If there is a lot of stuff, bags, or luggage, remove them one item at a time for examination. If there are several people in the vehicle ask them which items belong to whom. Sometimes you will have an article that no one will claim. Can you guess why? Search each item thoroughly. If it is luggage with clothes be sure to handle every piece of clothing. People love to put their drugs and paraphernalia in the socks. Be sure to examine the sidewalls of the luggage itself. If all is clear, move to the front of the trunk. If the rear seats fold down, be sure to search this area with the seats folded forward. You will discover a natural cavity between the fold of the seat back and the trunk floor. A piece of carpet will cover it that can be lifted out of the way. Closely examine the speaker area beneath the hat rack. Many new upper end vehicles will have a plastic covering over the speakers. This can be removed so the area beneath the hat rack can be examined. If they have the large speaker box in the trunk, remove the face of the speakers after taking out the screws. Once you are satisfied with the trunk, move to the passenger's rear seat area.

Be sure to examine all of the areas as you had done on the driver's rear side. Examine the door area before going inside. As before, examine the headrest, back of the seats and sides. These include the armrest and the rear of the right front passenger's seat. Once you have completed this area, you can now move to the engine compartment.

After opening the hood, look around the engine for anything different. Watch for areas that have been touched which will leave a clean area or fingerprint. Look at the firewall for signs of tampering. Check all of the void areas in the radiator and grill. Look along the fenders on each side to make sure it appears normal. At the base of the windshield, there is a plastic molding. Most of this molding is removable with a rather large void beneath. On many models of cars, you will find the inside air conditioning filter on the passenger's side above the firewall. There will be a void beneath it. On many models, the air conditioning fan can be removed with a large void in this area. It will be obvious based on the prints left from taking the cover or screws off. Be sure to check the windshield washer reservoir. If still nothing is found, you can examine the tire wells and bumpers for any signs of tampering. Most people have never had their engine compartment thoroughly searched. The firewall has become a very popular location for the transportation of firearms. When you are finished with the engine, look at the tires for excessive tire weights. Look at all of the tubes and bolts that run down to the gas tank. If you will go under the car, look for areas that do not match. By not matching, I mean there will be tool marks, scratches, bolts with tool marks, under spray, or clean areas.

On different styles of vehicles, there can be other areas. Vans and mini vans will have more sidewalls to examine. Be sure to examine all of the side walls covered in plastic molding. They remove easily and have large voids behind. SUV's are notorious for having their hidden compartments in the floor from the back seat to the rear door. If you fold the rear seat forward, you will see where the floor comes up and runs toward the back at the same height. This entire area needs to be examined. Smell for the odors of glue, bondo, and paint. Check the carpets for any indications of being glued down. Carpets in any location of any vehicle should not be glued. The bad guys will glue it down to keep us from lifting it up. On the SUV's, be sure to check the molding that holds down the carpet in the cargo area. Again, check the dirt line on the edge of the molding.

Pickup trucks are not very different. The area behind and beside the rear seat in the cab walls have always been very popular locations. Check the bed floor and front wall for thickness. A false front wall of the bed can be easily concealed with any type of topper. Put your hand on one side of the wall and tap the other side. You should be able to feel it. The front wall compartment will usually be through the top of the rail. The bed of the truck can have a double floor. This is recognized by looking through the side of the bed above the rear tire to the other side. You should be able to see the frame, springs, and out the other side. A false floor will cover this area. At the tailgate, lower it and be sure to check the locking mechanism plate. In most trucks there will be a panel across the top of the inside tailgate. This can be taken off by removing the screws. It is supposed to be used to replace the lock, but it is a rather large cavity across the width of the gate. Look at the taillights because once removed, many will expose the inside of the sidewalls of the bed. The federal brake light high on the cab can be removed exposing a nice void along the roof. If there is a mounted toolbox in the bed of the truck, examine it closely. Be sure that the exterior dimensions of the box match the interior.

Is this a completed list of search locations? Of course not, but it is a good start. Let your search be guided by your intuitions. Think about where you would hide something and search it. Every vehicle will be different. Everyone has their idea of a great place to hide contraband. It is up to the imagination of the person to determine where to hide contraband. It is up to you to be just as creative and think of any type of anomaly or natural void, which can be utilized.

Below is a list of locations that street users and dealers say themselves are the best places. The following list was from a marijuana user's site.

- Inside Food
- Diversion Safe – this is a common product with a false bottom like a can of flat tire fix or soda can. We have seen them as liter soda bottles or plastic water bottles. The compartment will be behind the label. Turning the bottle back and forth will reveal a bubble for the top half and one for the bottom.
- Secret Compartment – any area in the car that can be opened
- Very Messy Trunk – This is to intimidate you to not want to look through it. The worse the better. Old food and opened condoms spread around is used to deter a search.
- Gas Tank Compartment - the gas filler door.

This was found on another site for heroin abusers:

"If you are trying to conceal a small quantity of drugs, you may use your mouth, nose, or ears. The mouth has the same issues we already discussed. The nose and ears have the advantage that they are not common hiding places. They have the disadvantage that if a cop decides to search in these places, there is nothing that you can do. The nose is less likely to be noticed, but it is possible to accidentally blow it out of its hiding place should you sneeze or just breath hard. It could also just fall out due to gravity. In using the ears, you must make sure that you can still hear or this will call attention to the ears. "

"For those smuggling large amounts of drugs, the anus is the typical location. There is no reason that it cannot be used for smaller amounts on a day-to-day basis. The reason is that in order to do a cavity search, the officer must take you into custody. This means that under normal circumstances, the anus is a very safe place to hide drugs for a short period of time. "

"Women have the advantage that they can use their vagina as a hiding place. For the purposes of this discussion, the vagina and the anus are equivalent. In either case, the drugs should be placed inside of a condom. A lubricated condom not only protects the drugs, it also makes sticking it inside yourself easier and less painful. If the package is small, the condom also "bulks it up" and makes it less likely to get lost inside of you (this is surprisingly easy to do)."

On yet another site they are trying to teach each other what we are doing:

"This is the greatest piece of advice I have heard here yet in my short amount of time at this forum. Don't act sketchy, don't dress like a thug, practice talking to cops in situations where you can't get arrested, do plate checks on you. Failure to plan is planning to fail, and the way you dress and present yourself is the difference between a speeding ticket and "go about your business sir" and a flashing neon sign saying "search me, I have dope in the car officer!"

Finally here is a bunch of meth abusers and their family members telling each other where they have or can hide drugs:

I would often rollup the baggie and put it in the cap of a Bic pen.

My addict boyfriend always told me (when sober) that most addicts will carry their drugs on them or have them close by.

Light fixtures under the bulbs (not screwed in all the way) to where you think the light is just burnt out. In the plastic toilet paper roll holder (you know, with the spring in it). Taped behind picture frames and mirrors. In the spine of books. Fuse box in the car. Tape deck in the car. "Stick ups"...thought they just quit smelling? No, they've been emptied and is now a hiding place. Bottom of the Q-Tip box. Inside of an ink pen (very common place) Cigarette pack (very common place) Breath mint tin, like Altoids (very common place). Top of mini blinds Under batteries in the TV Remote Little coin pocket of jeans hanging in the closet

As you can see there are as many places to hide drugs and contraband as there are people. The more imaginative they are, the better the hides. Be imaginative when you are doing your search. Think like they would as you are sitting there looking at the car. Pace yourself and move slowly. Be systematic so you do not overlook anything. If someone else wants to search the car behind you, do not be offended. They will have a different set of eyes and a different imagination. You may be surprised by what they will find that you missed.

TRACTOR TRAILERS - 13

Tractor-trailers carry a unique set of possibilities as they travel down the road. You as the interdiction officer have to look closely at all trucks. They have the potential to carry enormous amounts of all types of contraband. Just like with cars you have to consider many factors. There are thousands of tractor-trailers on the road all day every day. You have to try to select the vehicles that statistically carry the greatest possibilities for you to make an arrest. You must concentrate your attention to the owner operators. Does this mean the large companies do not transport contraband? No, of course not, they do every day. It is more likely the large companies have a dirty driver rather than the company. A trucking company can get into trouble and the next day shut the company down. They will then reopen the company under a different name. The difference will be their DOT numbers. If they are interstate carriers, they will be traveling across state lines. When they change names, they are required to change the number. That number will be higher as new companies are created everyday across the country. What is the difference between interstate and intrastate carriers? Interstate carriers operate vehicles that are authorized to operate in multiple state jurisdictions, which include U.S. and Mexican states and Canadian provinces. Intrastate carriers operate entirely within a single state jurisdiction. Based on the above definition, with the knowledge of where contraband comes and goes to, whom should you be attempting to locate? If an interstate carrier can travel across state and national borders, this is where the contraband will be. When they change the company name and USDOT numbers, you can usually see the shadowing that is left behind. It can be an indicator to keep in mind at the beginning of the stop. If more things arise during the stop, it can change the course of the stop to a search.

Currently, in 2010, there are over 2,060,000 DOT numbers issued to truck companies. When you are working and see a tractor-trailer, look at the DOT number. How high the number is will tell you how new the company is. You can go to Safer web-company snapshot on any online system and get instant free information on truck companies. If you have access to the web from your patrol car, you can get instant truck company information from the USDOT numbers on the truck. Remember, the truck has to be lettered before the number with USDOT and not just DOT. Tint is another great tool for probable cause to stop trucks because they cannot have any according to Federal DOT regulations based on the high 70% visible light transmittance. The factory windows will fulfill the requirement. If you have never worked the big trucks in your area, be sure to study up on the state and federal rules and regulations. Just like with cars, the more you know what you can do, the more you will be able to do.

My tactics for the stop of a tractor-trailer is different. Because of the size of the vehicles, I do not like the standard parking position of our vehicles. Whenever I stop a tractor-trailer, I like to follow them to the shoulder of the road just like a car. Once we are on the shoulder, I will drive along the side of the truck. I will stop in a position to the right and a little ahead of the truck and trailer. This is not possible if there is not enough area on the shoulder to drive on. If there is not enough shoulder to drive on, I may drive around and stop ahead of the truck. From this vantage point, I will immediately exit my unit so I can observe the actions of the driver. A Texas DPS Trooper taught me this tactic. If you make it a standard stop for a tractor-trailer, you will pull to the shoulder at the rear of the trailer. From the back, you cannot see anything. You exit and move to the driver's side of the truck. You stand next to the traffic and wave at the driver to come back to you. The driver gets out and walks along the side of his truck back to you. While walking the 50 feet or so, the driver has traffic going past him at the roadways speed. You can stand next to the road to watch him or you can move back to the passenger's side and wait for them. As they come around the end of the trailer, you encounter him for the first time. Can you see all of the disadvantages to this tactic? It is simply terrible for both you and the driver. Remember, just as if with a car, you brought him to the stop. It is now your responsibility to get him back on the road safely. If he is a bad guy, it would be easy for him to cause you harm as he comes around the trailer. Some may say the same is true from the position in front of the truck. That is correct with several exceptions. From the front, I can see the actions of the driver.

He cannot just step out and be on ground level with me. They will have to climb out and down from the truck against traffic. You have many opportunities to maintain visual observations on the driver.

- We pull up just past the right of the tractor and stop. You immediately exit and are now looking at the driver. You can also see into the cab if the curtains are open. If there is a co-driver or passenger, you have the best chance to see them now. You can also see if the driver is trying to do something different like reaching around or writing. He could be trying to hide something or change his logbook. Many of you are not DOT certified and are not comfortable with the big trucks. That's alright; you can still do your job. Truck drivers know when they are pulled over whether or not a police officer is familiar with their trade. Several things you can do from the beginning to establish yourself are to always refer to the driver as "driver." Do not look at his driver's license and call him Mr. or Mrs. so and so. It should always be "driver." It is the language they understand and respond best too. Ask them for their driver's license, registration, and medical card. They will usually get their license and medical card out of their wallet. They will generally have some type of notebook that contains the paperwork for the truck. If they are from a different state or traveling more than 100 air miles radius across the state, ask them for their logbook. 100 air-mile radius from your work reporting location can be figured as 115.08 statute or "roadmap," miles from your reporting location. It is ok if you do not understand all of the time entries in the logbook. The reason you want the logbook is to see where they have been and when they were there. Ask them for their bill of lading if they are loaded. This will be their cargo manifest. Is it generally professionally printed by computer and not hand written. Most companies today operate with a computer system. Hand written bills are not as common as they once were. Some questions you may want to ask with a suspect driver are:
- Who owns the truck and trailer?
- How long have you driven for them?

- What is your load today?
- Did you watch them load it?
- Who sealed the trailer?

Why are these questions pertinent? Bad companies and drivers go in and out of business. Bad drivers are always changing companies. If there are drugs in the load, they will not want to tell you that they watched it being loaded. A legitimate driver knows all there is to know about his load. His arrival on time and with a load in good condition is how they are paid. Just look at the logbook. A good driver lies about his sleep time. A bad driver lies about their driving time. Real drivers are going to drive and go over their time if they can in order to get there. Bag guys are going to be stopping with down time to get drugs loaded or off loaded. A real driver is not paid unless the wheels are rolling. A bag guy does not care about the load. His money will be made doing something else. Remember the cost of operating a tractor-trailer. The cost can be about $0.50 per mile. They will earn about $1.00 per mile. Check the load and determine its value. Is the driver making money? If it does not make sense to you then it is probably wrong.

After a few moments have passed, it is a good time to talk to the driver about the load. He has told you that he was not there when it was loaded. There is a seal on the door. Ask if the load is on pallets, 1 or 2 stacks high, and are the locks in place. The driver answers these questions definitively; how would he know this information if he had not seen the load. The load locks will be the metal bars with rubber feet that are stretched across the sidewalls and locked in place. They keep the load from shifting back when the truck accelerates.

There are many questions to ask. These are just a few you can talk to the drivers about. Most of the drivers will be legitimate. You will know when you have a dirty driver. Spend some time stopping big trucks and get accustomed to them. Get used to talking with the drivers and one day that criminal driver will stand out to you. Their behaviors will be the same as the car drivers.

Tractor-trailers remain daunting to many of us. They really are nothing more than very big cars. An entire course can be made into the search of a tractor-trailer. Let's keep it as simple as possible. Some will say that most of the cases made from a tractor-trailer are from a discovery in the cab. In fact, I was on the border one night with the Border Patrol at the Sierra Blanca checkpoint on I-10. I spoke to the agents who told me that 85% of their seizures from tractor-trailers would be from the cab. I do not know what the national average for the concealment of drugs in a tractor-trailer is, but the cab is a good starting point. Again, no search should begin without enough back up present.

With the driver under control, step up to the passengers door. First, examine the side storage boxes, which are used as steps. With the door open, you can quickly assess the floor and under the passenger's seat. Again, look for receipts to confirm his stated trip plans and log book. Be sure to look at the usual places on the dash like the glove box and ashtray. Be sure to look behind the ashtray and glove box. Both will pull out and you can see inside the dash. Enter the truck and be systematic. Examine the headliner and overhead pockets. Be sure to check behind the padding on the walls in the overhead storage areas that will circle the front and sides above. On the driver's side, they will often have their personal use stash in the dash or behind the horn on the steering wheel. It will usually be within arm's length of the seat. Check the closets and drawers behind the seats. Check the underneath storage of the bunk. Often times you will see a suitcase or bag in the center storage area below the bunk. Lift the bunk up and check the storage area which runs the entire width of the cab. Watch for rolls of shrink-wrap. This could indicate that they are trying to re-wrap parts of their loads. Look at the walls, light fixtures, and air vents for signs of tampering. You will find the interior wall lining in the corners is rounded with a void behind them. Look at the headliner for any signs of tampering or tool marks on the screws.

Moving outside again, if there is an air dam, carefully climb up and examine it. You can pull the hood forward and it will lock out. To do this, you will have to disconnect the rubber straps located on each side of the hood. There will be a foot hole in the center of the front bumper. Reach up to the center of the hood and you will find a handgrip. Pulling back on the hood with your foot in the front bumper will bring the hood forward. It will stop once it is opened and you can examine the engine compartment. Check the areas on the inside of the hood. Be sure to check the air breather. See if you can find anything that has been touched. Again, it will stand out just like a car's engine. Look at the frame under the cab and you will see a wide-open area for concealment. The battery cover can be removed and examine the batteries. There are many fake batteries on the market and I know of several cases of cocaine found in the false bottoms of batteries. Generally, you will find two batteries. At times, they will have three or four. Remember that everything cost money. The more you spend the less you make. When you see the trucks with all of the chrome stacks, bumpers, and rims you should be questioning how all of the extras can be afforded. According to current reports, the average driver makes

$0.30 to $0.50 cents per mile. Can anyone imagine spending that much money on unnecessary equipment like chrome?

In the trailer, examine the load the best you can. If it is hot outside and you are inside a reefer unit, you will want to take along a flashlight. Have your partner close the door behind you. He does not have to lock you in, but the extreme temperature change will create a fog inside which will limit your visibility. As a safety precaution, you can place the lock through the locking plate on the driver's side door. This door will not be open during your investigation. If there is a seal on the door, do not let this prevent you from going inside. If you need to break the seal, write a note on the bill of lading that you removed it. Write seal broken by, your name, date, and the department's phone number. If you replaced the seal, write the new seal number on the papers.

Once you are inside, look to see how the load is stacked. By this I mean is it on palates, or on the deck. A good legitimate load will be palletized for ease of loading and unloading. Try to look over the top of the boxes and watch for signs that someone else had walked over them. Footprints or crush areas can mean someone crawled across the load. Only two types of people will do that, cops or crooks. See if nothing in the box stacks seems the same as all of the other stacks of cargo. Are there different types of boxes at any location or is not anything wrapped the same? Are there any high or low areas where there is something in the stack that is not like the others? Check the front wall for signs of tampering. The front wall is a very common place to conceal contraband.

You have a tractor-trailer pulled over and you work a K9 around the vehicle. The K9 alerts to the trailer. In most areas around the country you now have probable cause to search. You do not have a K9 available so you are examining the load. It is apparent to you there is something very wrong with the load. Now what are you going to do. In either case, the load should be removed and examined more closely. Trying to plan for this eventual event can save you a lot of trouble. If you are planning to start searching big trucks, find a location where you can unload cargo if you need too. One location that has always helped law enforcement is Walmart. Speak to the managers and explain what it is you would like to do. See if you can have access to their loading dock. They have always been very cooperative. They will even have some of their dock personnel unload the trailer for you. If you do not have a convenient Walmart, go to your local grocery stores. Generally, all grocery stores are more than gracious in their assistance of law enforcement.

I know most of us will spend the majority of our time on cars, but do not overlook the trucks. Current statistics say that there are over 15 million trucks in the United States and over 2 million tractor-trailers. There are over 3.5 million truck drivers. There are another 500,000 trucks operating out of Canada. There are many trucks to decide from. Work the owner operators and one day you will hit a big one.

SCRIPTS - 14

A new drug business has flourished in Florida. Prescription drug addiction has reached new and frightening heights. I am certain it is the same in other areas of the country as well. We are stopping vehicles from Kentucky, Tennessee and other southeastern states coming and going to Florida. We call them "pillbillies." Either they will have money, prescriptions, or they will have bottles of the prescription drugs. It is a burgeoning problem in Florida because the state legislature has always refused to create tougher regulations by arguing patient privacy rights. Then the statistics continue to pour in as well as pressure from other states for Florida to toughen its laws. How do they get around the laws? Federal law states you cannot dispense prescriptions over the internet without at least one doctor office visit per year. They come to Florida where pain clinics have flourished. They visit the doctor who prescribes the medicine. There is your one visit per year. One never realizes how bad it is until you see it in black and white.

According to the Broward County Commission on Substance Abuse of 2008, in 2007 there was a daily average of 9 lethal overdose reports in the state of Florida that involved the non-medical or illegal use of prescription medications, total of 3,317 fatal overdose reports, a 19% increase over the 2,780 fatal overdoses from the previous year. According to DEA-ARCOS reports, Florida physicians dispense five times more oxycodone than the national average of dispensing physicians. (29)   There are 89 pain clinics in Broward County alone! With a phone call to these clinics, it is discovered it is a cash-only business and they do not accept insurance. Oh yeah, they are a legitimate business. Felons run many of these businesses.

If you are not sure whether you have a prescription fraud case, here is some information from DEA which has provided to pharmacies:

Types of Fraudulent Prescriptions

Pharmacists should be aware of the various kinds of fraudulent prescriptions which may be presented for dispensing.

- Legitimate prescription pads are stolen from physicians' offices and prescriptions are written for fictitious patients.
- Some patients, in an effort to obtain additional amounts of legitimately prescribed drugs, alter the physician's prescription.
- Some drug abusers will have prescription pads from a legitimate doctor printed with a different call back number that is answered by an accomplice to verify the prescription.
- Some drug abusers will call in their own prescriptions and give their own telephone number as a call back confirmation.
- Computers are often used to create prescriptions for nonexistent doctors or to copy legitimate doctors' prescriptions.

The following criteria **may** indicate that the purported prescription was not issued for a legitimate medical purpose.

- The prescriber writes significantly more prescriptions (or in larger quantities) compared to other practitioners in your area.
- The patient appears to be returning too frequently. A prescription, which should have lasted for a month in legitimate use, is refilled on a biweekly, weekly, or even a daily basis.
- The prescriber writes prescriptions for antagonistic drugs, such as depressants and stimulants, at the same time. Drug abusers often request prescriptions for "uppers and downers" at the same time.
- Patient appears presenting prescriptions written in the names of other people.
- A number of people appear simultaneously, or within a short time, all bearing similar prescriptions from the same physician.

- Numerous "strangers," people who are not regular patrons or residents of your community, suddenly show up with prescriptions from the same physician.

Characteristics of Forged Prescriptions

1. Prescription looks "too good"; the prescriber's handwriting is too legible;

2. Quantities, directions or dosages differ from usual medical usage;

3. Prescription does not comply with the acceptable standard abbreviations or appear to be textbook presentations;

4. Prescription appears to be photocopied;

5. Directions written in full with no abbreviations;

6. Prescription written in different color inks or written in different handwriting.

This is from the National Institute for Health:

An estimated 20 percent of people in the United States have used prescription drugs for nonmedical reasons. This is prescription drug abuse. It is a serious and growing problem.

Abusing some prescription drugs can lead to addiction. You can develop an addiction to:

- Narcotic painkillers
- Sedatives and tranquilizers
- Stimulants

Experts don't know exactly why this type of drug abuse is increasing. The availability of drugs is probably one reason. Doctors are prescribing more drugs for more health problems than ever before. Online pharmacies make it easy to get prescription drugs without a prescription, even for youngsters.

We will often stop a vehicle that has subjects from Kentucky or Tennessee. They will have one person driving and several people with various medical issues. They will tell you they were hurt in a car accident or a fall at work. They usually suffer from some type of neck or back injury. The person driving them will provide the cash they will need to take to the doctor. Often times they will have some documentation from their own doctors at home. These documents may include x-rays or MRI reports. They go to the pain management center and pay in cash. The doctor at the clinic will give them prescriptions for large amounts of the prescription drugs. This is usually oxycodone. The driver will then take the "patient" to a pharmacy and fill the prescription. They can then qualify to have prescriptions refilled via the internet. The pills bought legally cost about $5.00 to $10.00 dollars each. Taken home and sold illegally on the black market, the same pills can sell for $25.00 to $50.00 each for a 50mg tablet. There's the profit and there is your criminal.

Why should we care about this problem? My best answer is the one that hits us all in our pocket book. The diversion of controlled prescription drugs cost insurance companies up to $72.5 billion annually. Public insurers pay two thirds of this money. You and I pay out of our pockets for this fraudulent act.

EQUIPMENT - 15

I wanted to talk briefly about some of the tools of the trade. When I first started, we did not carry any tools. After a while, it was discovered that a basic toolbox would be needed. We bought our own beginning tools and as time passed, the department began authorizing tools to be purchased. We now carry with us an assortment of tools that we can use roadside such as:

- A basic tool box
- Regular and Phillips screwdrivers
- Standard and metric wrenches
- Socket set both metric and regular
- Cordless drill
- Allen wrenches
- Drill bits
- Brass headed hammer – for use on tapping around the tank without spark
- Regular hammer
- Portable air tank
- Pry bar or Crowbar
- Different sized probes

These are some of the tools that we use. In addition to these, we also have fiber optics, a laser-measuring device (You can quickly measure the inside of a tractor's trailer) and the best and most used piece of equipment, a density meter. The density meter is the single fastest way to clear various areas of a car. You can quickly sweep over the door panels, frame, side rails, and any other piece that could possibly have contraband. You can run it around the tires, over extra batteries, and anything else you may come across. Hollow items like doors and fenders will give you readings from the 20's to the 40's. Put a bundle of cash or a brick of dope inside the cavity and you will see the density measures into the 70's through the 90's. It is as simple as that. No one can completely search every cavity in a vehicle without one. Extra equipment will include an extension mirror and a camera. Photograph the scene completely from start to finish. When you know you have found contraband, photograph where it is and how you access the location. Sometimes this sounds so simplistic, yet so often it is not done. Another piece of equipment we carry in our vehicles is a fiberscope. This will give us access to view areas roadside that we may not have been able to check otherwise. You can scope out the interior of the gas tank or inside frame rails. Our newest piece of equipment is called Rapid ID. It is a very effective tool in identifying people. It is charged in our car and when needed, you can quickly scan the middle and index finger from one hand. The print is sent through the Automated Fingerprint Identification System (AFIS) for identification. If the subject has ever been fingerprinted, and the prints have been submitted, they will be identified. The identification information is returned to our laptop computers. This really cuts down on false information and the identification of fugitives. Much of this equipment is available through various grants to law enforcement.

Steven Varnell

TACTICAL SURVIVAL

Steven Varnell

"What you are is what you have been, what you will be is what you do now."

Gautama Buddha

INTRODUCTION

I started this book after hearing the news about another police officer gunned down in America. Sadly, it is now two. At the same time, I listen to what I consider "idiots" complaining about police brutality at the "occupy protest." Fortunately, they are the minority of the population. Some people will disagree with anything from the government regardless who is in charge, Republican or Democrat. A small disillusioned subculture exist which has lost all sense of reasonableness. There is no faction of government functioning properly unless it is to hand out entitlements according to this minority. Never mind the simple fact that the majority of our problems are a result of our own doing.

Personal responsibility and common sense are the key to solving most of our issues. The old adage of, "if it is too good to be true, then it probably is," would have prevented most financial problems. Stay on a true and tried course instead of a get rich quick scam. Everything turns out for the best when common sense and hard work are applied together to accomplish goals. On the other hand, we all know there are many among us who do not want to put forth the efforts. They do not want the true and tried course. They cheat the system and others to do the work for them. This apathy often guides them into a life of crime, violence, and an eventual confrontation with the police. It is now that we must be prepared to survive the encounter. I have developed an idea or mantra that I like to use; **Study Train Survive**. It is my way to remember and teach others about taking a multifaceted approach to resolve our problems. In most jobs, the philosophy is the same. You are required to become familiar with the companies inner workings before receiving the initial training for a specific job. The training will continue if it is a good and progressive company. Survival means to study and train hard. Otherwise, someone more dedicated comes along and your seeking another job.

For law enforcement, the basic premise is the same. Once hired, the studies initiate at the Academy followed by a training process. I refer to this as a training process and not a program because at some point, a program finishes. A process is a continuing learning endeavor which has no end. Training is nonstop as you are constantly striving to improve your skills. The difference lies in the result. Death and injury are the consequences for failing to partake in the task of **Study Train Survive** as a law enforcement officer.

The public walks around each day without observing any situational awareness. They are future victims. There are many predators on earth, and too many among the general populace are idealist without reasonable and realistic views of the world. They are the wandering sheep grazing on the beautiful green pastures, never cognizant of the fact that a wolf is always watching. Law enforcement does it best to protect us, and they do a good job. However, most police officers spend their days responding to the events that have already occurred.

Be proactive by not waiting for someone else for protection. How many times have you heard somebody say, "I cannot believe this has happened to me?" Generally, had people maintained some situational awareness, whatever occurred may have never happened. I will repeat it after every section because I want you to remember, **Study Train Survive**.

Use this book as a guide. It will cover the various topics having the greatest impact to the welfare of law enforcement. These are the essential areas where an officer may be injured in an encounter with an asshole. I want anyone who reads this to know that though I write from the perspective of a police officer, it also applies to civilian encounters. You do not have to be in law enforcement to follow these lessons because they are all about personal safety.

In *Criminal Interdiction*, I explained our primary responsibility as: "Have you ever thought about the reason why there really are police officers? There are many academics who can give you the text book versions why, but for me it is just two words; Asshole Confrontation." A year later, I still cannot find a better explanation for what we do. The problem is that so many officers continue to be injured and killed. By the end of the year 2011, the number of police officers killed in the line of duty by gunfire increased by 15% over the previous year and remains the number one cause of death. In Los Angeles, the number of incidents where officers have been shot at has increased by 29%. Crime will continue to maintain these levels and may increase. One can only surmise that so will the violence.

The current state of the economy will assist in dictating desperate people's actions. Everyone, civilians and officers alike, must be on a heightened sense of self- protection. I wish more people would read this book, *Criminal Interdiction,* and other titles dedicated to saving lives. For those who have studied these, you're thinking. It is the beginning phase of my adage; **Study Train Survive**. If only a single bit of information is retained, it may make a difference. Always thinking and concentrating at the task is a game changer. We already know how difficult it is to maintain this constant vigilance. I want you to remember the lessons learned, add to them if needed, change some if necessary, and adjust it to the job while insisting your partners do the same.

When working interdiction, three things must occur; the identification of the criminal, the seizure of the criminal and evidence, and a successful prosecution. If any of these factors are missing, the *Criminal Interdiction* was not successful. If the criminal is not recognized, the evidence and prosecution never takes place. If the criminal is identified, but the evidence is not found, there is no prosecution. If the criminal is identified and the evidence found, but the prosecution is not accomplished, then the interdiction was a failure. Sure the contraband was taken from the streets, however, the criminal was also returned to cause more harm. Do your job with diligence, safety, and completely within the laws of your jurisdiction. When completed, you are providing protection to your community.

This book is broken down into various topics by chapters. The situations are wide-ranging and are my opinion, based on nearly 30 years of law enforcement. It is all right to disagree with the ideas. As I have explained before, the goal is to get you to think. Read about the techniques that I have used successfully and tweak them for yourself. The basis for them all are solid, however, no two people are alike and prefer things done in a certain manner. My only warning is not to be so closed minded as to not at least try these techniques, because they can save your life. I know they have saved mine. Go out and seek the assholes while being fully prepared to deal with them. For those of you not in law enforcement, I say go out and seek them for your own protection. They are around all of the time. Watching and waiting for that opportunity to cause physical or emotional damages. Together we can make a difference. The wolves are stalking. The sheepdogs are watching. The sheep are always grazing with their heads in the grass.

Study Train Survive

Steven Varnell

TRAFFIC STOPS -16

It's amazing to me how we lose sight of the big picture with a single focus.

Traffic stops are the one activity that law enforcement conducts each day more than any other is. To coincide with this volume of contact, they are also one of the most dangerous and important crime-fighting tool in our arsenal. Every criminal before, during, or after every offense enters a motor vehicle. Our society is very mobile. This mobility affords criminals the opportunities to carry out and/or flee their crimes. Therefore, I will cover this event first.

In 2011, there were 26 police officers murdered by gunfire during a traffic event. Of these, four were by ambush while sitting in their car. Three occurred while the officers were not engaged in a specific law enforcement activity other than patrol. Additionally, nine officers were killed when they conducted pedestrian stops. In addition to these poor souls, another 59 police officers have been killed in 2011 because of some type of vehicle accident. Though gunfire has overtaken auto accidents as the primary cause of death, when you combine the vehicle accident aspect with the gunfire deaths during some type of traffic stop, the total becomes 85. According to the Officer Down Memorial Page (ODMP), the total number of officers killed in the line of duty during 2011 totals 166. Therefore, over 50% of all officers deaths are related to vehicles and traffic stops. It is the single most dangerous thing we do.

Many in law enforcement consider traffic stops as routine. We conduct them each day without any serious occurrence. According to the Bureau of Justice Statistics, only 1.6% of all traffic stops result in the occupants of the cars having force used against them. Each year there are over 43 million traffic stops conducted and only 5% are searched.

How often does your agency study and train for traffic stops? Because of the volume of work involved, we should train each year the safety aspects of a stop. Even though I spent years training other officers and worked the street right up to the day I retired, I never stopped training. Appendix I, at the end of this book is a list of training courses I received during my career. You can see which areas of law enforcement fascinated me as I saw each of these classes as a new experience. It was like seeing practical aspects of topics through other people's eyes.

Conducting a traffic stop involves a series or checklist of things to do. It all begins with the identification of the vehicle you want to stop. Most officers' race up to the targeted car with their emergency equipment activated. I am telling everyone now, slow down and approach with ease. Take these moments of approach and watch the behaviors of the occupants in the car. Watch everyone to see if they appear calm or nervous. Is the driver overly watching you in their rear and side view mirrors? Are the passengers behaving the same as they were when you first saw them? Notice the windows of the vehicle as they pass and again after you have caught up to the car. If they were up or partially down and now completely down, assume they are trying to air out the car.

Watch for bumper stickers, air fresheners, rental car information, and bibles on the dash or other religious gear. In and of themselves, they may not be important, but when applied with other items, they may be the beginning of a *Criminal Interdiction*. Take the time to study common items of paraphernalia, including gang signs of significance. Be cognizant of as much as possible and this extra effort will help you survive and make good arrest. Gang and certain types of religious symbolism's can have specific meanings of their intentions. Photos, statues, medallions, or tattoos of Jesus Malverde or Santa Muerte can indicate they are transporting contraband or have a connection with the business. Be aware of the gangs that are in the areas of your patrol zone. Their building tags, colors, and other articles can influence the stop.

Jesus Malverde   Santa Muerte

How long did it take the vehicle to stop after you activated your emergency equipment? Again, watch the behaviors of the vehicle occupants for changes now that they know they are being stopped. All of the vehicle's information should have already been radioed in or ran on your computer. Standing roadside with the violator is not the time to discover that the car is stolen or the subject of a Be On the Look Out (BOLO). Move the stop if the targeted vehicle stops in an unsafe location.

Remove your seat belt before coming to a complete stop to prevent tangling when exiting. Watch their brake lights and turn signals. If they left one or both on, use it as a warning that the driver of the car is nervous and is too focused on you. It is a form of audio occlusion.
Stop your vehicle as far as possible from the traveled portion of the road. The distance between your vehicle and the violators should be at least two car lengths. This provides you with some response time should the occupants take any offensive actions after the stop. If you park too close, they can be at the front of your car before you can react; an easy shot for most people. Distance is always our friend.

After the stop, you start the approach. Be sure everyone stays inside of the car. If someone exits without permission, order them back. Failure to comply with this order should definitely place you on alert. Maintain distance and observe while calling for assistance. Never be on equal grounds with anyone. Deploy whatever tools are necessary for the situation.

If possible, approach the car on the passengers' side. Not only is it a better tactical position from the vehicles occupants, it will also provide you some protection from approaching traffic. Remember that your vehicle is parked about two car lengths back. If another vehicle strikes it, it will absorb a lot of the energy from the impact. Additionally, you have the added protection of their car to deflect additional forces before being struck as a pedestrian.

From the passengers' side of their car, you can see most of the interior. When they open the glove box, the entire compartment is visible. Most people are right handed. Those who are left handed and intended to pull a gun, will hide it in their right hand because they expect you to walk to their driver's window. If you stop behind the "B" pillar or front door window frame, the driver would have to raise the gun above the seat and back to shoot at you. A few steps rearward and they will not have a shot, but you will. If there is a front seat passenger, the driver will have to sweep the gun over them to shoot. The passenger's side is unequivocally the best place to stand during a traffic stop because you have advantages over the occupants and approaching traffic. Several officers have been shot while on the passenger's side of the car. No position is perfect, however, the videos shows the officers are literally standing in the passengers window. They walk right up to the window and bend down to see inside. Start observing everyone as you walk up to the car, again nearing their rear side windows, and STOP before reaching the front passengers window. If the windows are tinted, have the occupants roll them all down before making the approach.

If you are pulling over a tractor-trailer, do not stop behind the vehicle. Drive to the front where you are in a position to watch the driver and see if there are any passengers. This can be done along the shoulder to a position forward and beside the tractor or passing and stopping at the same position in the front. You can observe the driver if they attempt to hide or do anything of a threat.

The standard practice of positioning your patrol car behind a tractor-trailer does not have any tactical advantages. You could be crushed against the trailer if any oncoming traffic leaves the road. How often do you see officers exit and stand around waiting for the driver to walk back? Often they will have to cover almost 60 feet to reach you. If they walk down the traffic side of the truck, passing traffic could strike them. Once they clear the back of the trailer, they are instantly in front of you. If they intend you harm, there is little time or space to prepare for it. In order to watch the driver walk back, you have to stand close to the passing traffic. Just drive along the side of the truck after it has stopped. Position your car at an angle to the side and front of the tractor. Now you can see everything occurring in the cab.

I have had several officers question this tactic. When they are standing around at the back of a truck, with no idea who is inside or what they are doing, and then waiting for them to walk back, you may change your mind. Every officer who has tried this tactic has adjusted the way they stop trucks. Once used, you will see exactly how effective and tactically sound it is compared to just standing at the back of a trailer. For a more detailed description of all of the above actions, please refer to chapter 5 and 13 in *Criminal Interdiction*. These are entire chapters dedicated to these actions.

Summary of Traffic Stops:

- Identify the vehicle you want to stop. Do not race up to the car with your emergency equipment activated. Ease up to the them to observe their behaviors.
- Begin taking a mental inventory of the things you see, e.g., bumper stickers, air fresheners, or rentals.
- Observe the actions of the driver when they pull off the road. Did they travel some distance or stop immediately?
- Be sure the area of the stop is safe when outside of your vehicle.
- Position your vehicle completely off the road if possible.
- Be sure you are already prepared to exit your vehicle at the time of the stop.
- Stop your vehicle about two cars lengths back. Remember, distance is for your benefit.
- Make sure everyone stays in the car.
- Watch for the brake lights and turn signals. Are they still own?
- Always approach on the passenger's side if possible.
- When stopping tractor-trailers, do not stop behind them as with cars. Drive to the front of the vehicle where you can observe the drivers actions.
- **Study Train Survive**

PEDESTRIAN ENCOUNTERS - 17

When things go wrong, simplify.

Olympic weightlifting coach Dan John – Never Let Go: A philosophy of Lifting

(Simplicity has always been the best approach to problem solving. We have a tendency to complicate.)

The last chapter mentioned that nine police officers were killed in the line of duty by gunfire from pedestrian encounters. This equates to one officer killed by a pedestrian every 1.7 months.

Similar to vehicle stops, pedestrian stops can have additional dangers. When stopping a vehicle, we know that we want the occupants to remain inside of the car. They are on equal footing when outside. You must always maintain a position of advantage. With the pedestrian, they are already outside and have the initial position of advantage. They can approach before you have the opportunity to exit your vehicle. Therefore, you must try to come up from behind and stop your car prior to passing. Your car should be parked at least two car lengths from the subject. This gives you time to exit before they can respond or provides the distance needed to react to any actions they take.

Sometimes it will help if you see the pedestrian that you want to encounter and drive past them. However, this tactic does remove the element of surprise. After driving past them, they may expose feelings of guilt upon seeing a police officer. Their behaviors may change or they could take evasive actions. Either way, this will tell you that the person is not your average citizen. Generally, people are not surprised or nervous by the sight of a police officer, unless they have done something wrong. Any person deserves your attention when there is a change in their behavior.

Do not immediately turn back around if you just drove past the subject. Drive a short distance and watch their conduct in your rear view mirrors. Observe and take note of all clothing, including hats, shirt, pants, shoes, jackets, and colors. Guess the subjects physical dimensions and watch for facial hair, tattoos, etc. The more information wrote down before the encounter the less you will have to take your eyes off the subject during the stop. Furthermore, should the suspect flee on foot or commit an assault; you will have a detailed description to report to responding officers. How often has someone fled and all we can give is a sketchy description at best? This is the time for you to observe their attire in relation to the weather. Is the person wearing a jacket on a warm day? Maybe they are wearing a heavy jacket on a cool day. Are their pants baggie? Can you see any bulges in their clothing? Are they wearing several pairs of pants? If so, this means they will have several layers of pockets that will have to be searched, if you arrest them.

Do they have a standard gait or is it exaggerated? Watch their hand and arm movements. When people are carrying illegal items under their attire, they have a tendency to touch them. A subject carrying a gun in their waistband will frequently brush against it with their arm or hand, which will show in the way they walk. The bad guy needs assurance that their weapon stays in place, especially when they see the police. Police officers have a tendency to not move their strong side arm as much as their weak. Sometimes, there will be more of an arc to their strong side arm. This allows the hand and arm to pass around your holstered weapon, which stands out from the side of your body. We get so used to this walk that when out of uniform, our strong-arm arcs around the hip.

An example of this behavior was conducted by a television show. They placed a sign on the sidewalk in Las Vegas that read, "Check your wallet." Nearly everyone who walked by the sign reached down with their hand and touched their billfold. What this actually provided was the exact location of their wallet. "Reformed" pickpocket artist were standing around the area and watching where they touched.

They could then use this information to steal from that exact spot on the person.

If you know you will be stopping this subject, be sure to take off the seat belt, turn on the hand held radio, and notify dispatch of your location. Therefore, the moment you stop, immediately exit the car with your full attention on the pedestrian. You can call out to the subject, but maintain distance. Be sure their hands are out of their pockets and remain in sight. Keep in mind it is the hands which will hurt you by striking, drawing a knife, a gun, or other weapon. Knowing exactly where their hands are the entire time is paramount to your safety.

Never drive up to any person on the streets, whether a pedestrian, a disabled vehicle, or any other type of event and stay in your car. You never want to place yourself in such a position of disadvantage. As an example of the dangers involved with this action, this is a quote taken from a New Jersey newspaper article at nbcnewyork.com:

"She said the officer was conducting "a routine stop" of the subject, chatting with him in a non-confrontational way for a few minutes, leading authorities to believe the two may have been acquainted with each other before the shooting. She said. "The individual stepped back and suddenly pulled out a handgun and shot the officer."

While talking to this pedestrian, the officer never got out of his patrol car, nor had an opportunity to draw his weapon. Unfortunately, this encounter resulted in the officer being shot in the head and killed. Never turn your back to a suspect, and always maintain a visual on them. Stay just out of arms reach, the further the better. As we have learned before, try to have another unit present if you intend to do a pat down. Keep the following informational statistics from the FBI in mind as we confront suspects.

- 38% of all officers killed in the United States occurred during a crime in progress.
- 60% of those officers were killed while attempting to make an arrest before their backup had arrived.
- 68% of those officers died at night.
- In a physical confrontation with a suspect, 86% of those officers ended up on the ground. 25% of those officers were seriously injured and 12% of that group was killed with their own weapon or secondary weapon.

Summary of Pedestrian Encounters:

- Pedestrian stops are similar to vehicle stops except the pedestrians position on foot gives them a temporary advantage.
- If possible, make an initial pass of the subject to observe their behaviors towards you. Your awareness should heighten if there are any behavioral changes.
- Try to write down or call in as much descriptive information about the subject before the encounter.
- Watch for bulges or the customary arm/hand touching of any item they are carrying.
- Approach from behind and have everything ready the moment your car stops so you can exit unimpeded.
- Even if you know the individuals, never sit in your car and talk to them. Under no circumstances should an officer sit in their car after approaching any person. This is a complete lack of situational awareness, for anyone could walk up to you from any direction. This includes disabled vehicles.
- Never turn your back on the subject(s).
- Always watch their hands and make sure they keep them where you can see them.
- If possible, never try to pat down a suspect until back up arrives.
- **Study Train Survive**

FOOT PURSUITS - 18

Strong in emotion, weak in tactics

From a Federal lawsuit against the Philadelphia Police Department in regards to police shootings after a foot pursuit.

There were five police officers shot and killed while engaged in foot pursuits in 2011. Countless others were injured while in pursuits or by the suspects, they were chasing. Most agencies have no policies at all, nor do they train their officers in the tactics of foot pursuits. Many never contemplate the inherent dangers associated with pursuits because they become overwhelmed with the adrenaline rush and the desire to arrest the bad guy. There are certain risk indicators that suggest it is important for law enforcement to manage these events. Faced with increasing pursuits and officer injuries, some agencies have sought outside assistance in understanding these dangers. One such study was conducted for the Los Angeles County Sheriff's Office in 2010.

      The University of South Carolina initiated the study entitled "A Descriptive Analysis of Foot Pursuits in the Los Angeles County Sheriff's Department." Information was collected on 100-foot pursuits. The researchers found that suspects threatened pursuing deputies with the use of a firearm or other weapon 15 times, or 5.7% of the incidents. Suspects assaulted the deputies in 42% of the occurrences and were armed 23% of the time. 73% of those pursued had a prior criminal arrest record. Because of enhanced prison time for repeat offenders, increased hazards to the officers exist due to the suspect's motivation to resist. Suspects were impaired with drugs, alcohol, or mental illness in 41% of the pursuits. Uses of force incidents are much higher than normal with 38% involving hand-to-hand tactics and 25% involving the use of impact weapons. 60% resulted in force-related injuries to the suspects and 17% of the deputies were injured.

There are definitive tactics for a foot pursuit. First, we must all overcome the appeal of an instant arrest. It is not a personal vendetta against you when a subject runs away from a traffic stop or other encounter. If you are alone during an encounter, and a subject sprints from the scene, does it make any sense to chase them while leaving your patrol car unattended? I have been in several scenarios of the officer returning from a foot chase to discover his patrol car had been stolen or burglarized.

There is not as much respect for law enforcement as in the past. In some areas, what greater neighborhood reverence would befall upon one who would steal a police car? Then there is the decision of whether this person has committed a crime that warrants a pursuit, or do you have proper identification to file charges? Additionally, if there are more subjects at the scene when one ran away, they cannot be expected to still be there when you return.

There are decisions that need to considerations before initiating a pursuit. Are you fit enough to conduct the chase? Is there available backup? Can you dispatch your exact location, suspect description, and direction of travel? What type of area are you in? If it is a crowded neighborhood or housing project, can you maintain a safe pursuit? Do you have a decisive plan of action once the suspect is caught?

Once you have decided to initiate the chase, try to keep your pace to a jog. The suspect will be sprinting and will soon run out of energy. Even if you are in great shape, the 20 plus pounds of extra equipment will exhaust you. Try to keep the suspect in sight and observe his behaviors. Watch his hands in case he reaches into his clothing for a weapon or contraband. Be cognizant of the available cover which is around in the event the suspect turns with a weapon. Watch the actions of the suspect as they run around corners. Does it appear they are trying to maintain their speed or are they trying to slow down? This can indicate their intentions of ambush. Once they are out of sight, you are no longer in control of this situation. Do not let adrenaline cause you to run blindly around the same corner. Many officers are killed or injured at corners around the country. Jogging keeps that over-reaction of your ego in check and allows for a clear thinking mind. Mental preparedness is half the fight.

Stay an arm's length off walls because you could be struck if the bullet strikes up to 20 feet away from your location. At a 5-degree angle, the bullet will be 18 inches off the wall at 20 feet. At 1 degree, the bullet will be at 4 inches.

You approach the corner where you lost sight of the suspect. It did not appear they slowed down. This is not self-evidence that the offender continued to run. You can try to "cut the pie" by keeping distance from the corner and slowly rounding the apex to view the other side in "slices." This action will equalize the situation if the suspect has set up an ambush. If you went past the corner, the advantage is 100% with the offender. By "cutting the pie," you will probably see each other at the same time. If there are cars and/or trees opposite the corner, a different option would be to swing wide and maintain cover behind those objects while observing the target area.

Another tactic is to stop at the corner, several feet from the wall. Do a quick peek with one eye around the corner. It has to be fast and expose only the portion of your face to see around the edge. If they are waiting in ambush, they will try to shoot at center mass. A simple peek will not afford them the opportunity for the trap. The downside to this method is taking in enough information during the quick peek to feel confident that the suspect is not waiting for you.

Keep your gun holstered during these pursuits. If you catch them or if they surrender, then draw your weapon. Think about being exhausted at the end of the chase and the suspect fights back. Your firearm can be taken away. Recently in California, a Riverside police officer was involved in a foot pursuit. During the chase, the officer was holding his service weapon when he tripped, fell, and the gun was knocked out of his grasp. The suspect saw this happen and ran back to the officer. He struck the officer multiple times with a pipe before grabbing the firearm and killing him.

What is your plan of action once you have caught the offender? There are issues to consider before faced with this situation. Will you maintain distance and hold them at gunpoint or a Taser? Will you attempt to handcuff them? Do backup units know your exact location and do you know theirs? Remember, the above study showed that the officers were assaulted in 42% of the cases and use of force is much higher in these adrenaline charged incidents. Mentally prepare with a response appropriate decision. If you know they are unarmed, deploy a secondary weapon. Always maintain a distinct advantage. Should they respond with any type of weapon, decide if the advantage is still yours with the weapon deployed or transition to your firearm. Planning will assist in a quick decision.

Often during a chase, the suspect jumps a fence. If it is a privacy fence and the subject cannot be seen, do not jump at the same location. Again, this is a perfect ambush location. They will expect you to cross where they choose. Move down and find a place to see the other side and then climb over if it is clear.

The first unit that arrives should be your backup unit. Direct the other units to initiate a tight perimeter to cause the offender to go into hiding. Containment is the best-case scenario for K9 and air services to quickly find them.

K9 will need the exact location where you last saw the suspect and their direction of travel. They will need the type of crime the subject is accused of and any information on weapons. In most jurisdictions, there are specific guidelines for the deployment of K9 and whether the handler can release the dog to bite.

Have another officer go to the original scene where the offender initially ran. If there is a vehicle or other information available, try to obtain identification and affiliation with the area that may provide intelligence as to where they are running. We are all creatures of habit and most people will try to go somewhere familiar. Have several units go to this location to see if the suspect is there or if anyone may know of their whereabouts.

Summary of Foot Pursuits:

- Foot pursuits should not be conducted alone.
- Very good radio communication is essential for both you and the responding units.
- If alone, initiate if you can keep the suspect in sight. Maintain surveillance of the subject while relaying accurate information to assisting units.
- Follow sound situational awareness ideas for areas which provide you cover.
- Never pursue a subject into a building or any area where you cannot maintain good visuals and have sufficient cover.
- Most subjects will try and hide once they have lost the initial officer. Be a great witness with a good physical description and wait for backup, K9, and air services.
- Try jogging instead of sprinting. Remember that we are wearing extra weight with our equipment. Let the suspect exhaust themselves with sprinting. Otherwise, you may not have the energy reserves to protect yourself. Know your own physical limitations.
- If the suspect goes around the edge of a building, this is a classic ambush point. NEVER run around that same corner. People anticipate you to follow the same path. Move out wide and slow down. This wide angle can give you a greater advantage. Cut the pie, try a quick peek, or swing out wide with available cover.
- Solid tactics and commitment to training can save lives.
- **Study Train Survive**

HANDS ON
COMBATIVES - 19

Simplicity is a powerful principle that allows us to channel our energy like a laser beam and avoid getting stuck in the rut of rigid thinking and acting.

Mark Devine – Sealfit

Some of the techniques I describe below can cause injury and possible death. Every aspect of safety in the practicing of these techniques requires strict adherence to safety. There is never a guarantee of outcome for any self-defense move in regards to injury to yourself or others.

I am not an expert in the field of hand-to-hand combat. However, I know that I have followed my personal philosophy for long enough to develop a certain understanding of defensive tactics. I have suffered through the hours of my own departments Defensive Tactics courses for almost three decades. I have studied the training and fighting philosophies of other disciplines such as MMA, karate, judo, and jujitsu. I participated in judo as a sport and I learned basic jujitsu once I became an officer. Having worked the street for almost 30 years, I have been involved in a number of fights. These always occurred as I was patting someone down, breaking up a fight, or trying to make an arrest.

I always noticed several things at the conclusion of the fights. They usually went to the ground and the tactics from all of the training I received, never worked well against a subject who was actually fighting back or resisting. I learned that something else has to be taught. I know my own agencies idea of Defensive Tactics training is to incorporate certain aspects of ground fighting. The premise is right, but the reality is wrong. The people who partake in sport's like MMA are mentally and physically tough. However, there are problems training like an MMA fighter to use on the streets and it exist in the rules:

(Taken from the UFC website) The following actions are banned:

1. Butting with the head.
2. Eye gouging of any kind.
3. Biting
4. Hair pulling.
5. Fish hooking.
6. Groin attacks of any kind.
7. Putting a finger into any orifice or into any cut or laceration on an opponent.
8. Small joint manipulation.
9. Striking to the spine or back of the head.
10. Striking downward using the point of the elbow.
11. Throat strikes of any kind without limitations and including grabbing the trachea.
12. Clawing or twisting the flesh.
13. Grabbing the clavicle.
14. Kicking the head of a grounded opponent.
15. Kneeing the head of a grounded opponent.
16. Kicking the kidney with the heel.
17. Spiking a opponent to the canvas on his head or neck.

When observed, you realize that MMA is still a sport. These are what you will want to do if involved in a fight. All tactics apply if a subject decides to pursue a physical confrontation with the police. You are not paid to get hurt, injured, or killed. You are paid to protect persons and property from assholes. The martial arts self-defenses taught are fine if you are in a competition. The entire purpose of the match is to place an opponent into a submission hold by following the rules that govern the sport. Training in real life to control or gain a submission hold on a subject that is fighting with officers, is exposing them to unnecessary dangers. Control and submissions are for subjects that are submissive or passively resisting, not grappling on the ground.

Remember the FBI statistics we spoke about before; 25% of officers who ended up fighting on the ground were injured.

Compare the MMA rules to the target areas preferred by Krav Maga, the CQB of the Israeli Defense Forces: hair, eyes, temples, base of the skull, nose, ears, mouth, chin, jaw, throat, all four sides of the neck, clavicles, ribs, solar plexus, kidneys, stomach, fingers, testicles, thighs, knees, shins, ankles, and top of feet. The majority of these areas are soft tissue. Always target these areas with strikes and kicks in an effort to inflict the greatest amount of pain or injury with minimal effort. After a couple of well-placed strikes, an officer will still have enough energy to maintain his security. More bang for your buck.

Follow through after these strikes with a transition to other weapons. You are not placed onto the ground with complicated grappling techniques. Never try to stay engaged in some type of arm bar, neck lock, or wrist bend. Again, these techniques apply if a subject is actively fighting.

I like to learn how the best train and find ways to incorporate that training into what we do. I am not talking about other police agencies, although many of them are quite good. The downsides to police training are the political correctness aspects that are incorporated for the legal defense of the department. The military does not worry about these issues in combat. I am talking about Special Forces Units. They train in CQB techniques or Close Quarter Battle tactics. They have spent decades studying the best ways to inflict injury and have had opportunities to develop these tactics in combat in the Middle East. One of the best things to come out of this type of training is the adjustments in battle tactics that give results.

Many of the units, which operate in small teams, like the SEALS, Delta, and Green Berets, train to strike hard, fast, and evade. These tactics are essential to their survival because they are not intended for a long sustained battle. Apply this mindset to a police officer on patrol. Most of the actions we take are when we are alone. We are often outnumbered and at a distinct disadvantage until our backup arrives. It is during these moments that I ask each of you to reexamine your practices. The job requires courage and calm nerves. Give your actions thought through mental preparations since fast reactions can save your life. Just as the Special Forces are required to train, so should we: strike hard, fast, and evade.

When has an agency ever required an officer to stand toe to toe with a suspect and fight it out, dragging each other to the ground in a test of strength, skill, or luck? This is why officers are given secondary weapons. Restraining a suspect who is passively resisting and then begins to actively resist requires officers to instantly adjust their mindset. This confrontation just became more serious because the subject can easily place you in a bad position on the ground. Get to your feet and deploy a weapon.

Most organizations initiated their training after the legendary Colonel Rex Applegate. Col. Applegate was tasked during World War II with training U.S. OSS agents. The OSS would later become the CIA. Applegate was to develop a system of fighting and training American agents during WWII. His techniques were found to be very effective.

Applegate had a few basic rules. He said that the training had to be fast, easy, and vicious. You cannot afford to spend years trying to perfect one of the martial arts. Besides, it is ineffective unless your opponent follows all of the rules of the sport. However, people who practice the martial arts understand the basics of striking and kicking. Another rule was to always keep your opponent at arm's length by using your hands and feet. It is always a superior tactic to use any type of blow or strike rather than wrestle or throw someone to the ground. Strikes are easier to teach than the complications of a wrestling hold. However, once you go to the ground, never stop moving. Your single purpose from the ground is to get back up on your feet. If you are unable to roll, pivot on your hips and shoulders while keeping the suspect away with your legs and feet.

If the subject goes to the ground, it is not necessary for you to follow. The outcome could go either way if you are wrestling and an even greater danger exists should anyone join in with the suspect. When you are on the ground in a fight, the first person who resorts to blows, bites, and gouges will come out on top. Always attack the areas of the body that are easiest to hurt. If someone is kept in pain, they are unable to take the offensive. Again to stress the FBI statistics: 86% of confrontations ended on the ground, 25% of these officers were seriously injured, 12% were killed with their own weapon.

Do not forget the lessons learned in the Force Science Fatigue Threshold studies. This study found that your body begins to fatigue within 30 seconds when you are in an all-out fight. In addition, you will exert more energy because of the extra equipment worn. You are wrestling on the ground with another subject who at first may be trying to escape. More energy is utilized trying to overcome than resisting. You begin to fatigue within 30 seconds and every second thereafter. Most people will experience almost total fatigue, especially in their upper-body strength after just two minutes. These times are dependent upon physical conditioning and were conducted with personnel who were in good shape. This should give everyone a reason to pursue a physical conditioning program. This also explains why 12% of injured officers were killed with their own weapon. Stay off the ground!

Let's assume you are in good shape as you sprint and tackle the fleeing driver from a traffic stop. You call out on the radio a quick "I'm in foot pursuit westbound towards … ." We have seen it repeatedly. It is a natural instinct for most of us. We allow our ego and tombstone courage to take over. Besides, how many times have we conducted this same scenario and always arrested the asshole.

Because of the instant burst of energy expended to chase and tackle the subject, you are approaching the 30-second threshold of losing energy. The subject is resisting, not fighting back. You are expending more energy than he is and starting to feel fatigued. What you do not realize is the passenger in the car has exited and is coming to the defense of his friend. There are drugs and a weapon in the car, and they both have served time in prison.

You are in serious trouble and your life is in their hands! This is not the way it was supposed to happen. You try to go on the defense, but there is another problem. Your energy reserves are almost depleted. In the distance, there is a siren of another unit enroute, but audio occlusion has occurred and you cannot hear them. If you try to draw a weapon, you will probably lose it. Several officers each year are killed with their own weapon while engaged in this type of confrontation.

We will never know how this scenario finished, however, it concluded at the discretion of the bad guys. Your survival occurred at their liberty. What is their physical description when they flee? Who will the responding officers watch for? Because of your initial over response and lack of good radio information, you have placed the backup units in jeopardy. There will be no way to know if the people they encounter are the suspect's. The bad guys do not know that a minimum of information about them was released. They believe that they are being stopped for the worse thing they have ever done; the attack of the officer. There is an excellent chance that their next encounter will be as violent, if not worse.

Avoid going to the ground at all cost. This does not include handcuffing of a subject who is obeying your commands. If you need to kneel down to handcuff a person in a prone position, do it. Just be prepared to back off if they start to resist.

When punching, a closed fist is one of the worse ways to hit someone. You can suffer hand injuries like broken bones or the infection of a tooth cut or other problems. There is a reason why boxers tape up their hands and wear gloves; to protect their hands. Most people fight the same way they have always fought. Breaking out of the closed fist technique is difficult without practice. If you must practice striking with your fist, strike with the fist perpendicular to the ground and the thumb side of the hand on top. This is performed by not turning the fist and is like driving a joystick. Another position is the rotation of the shoulder and arm where the top of the hand is facing up before impact. Without regular punching practice on a bag, hand and wrist injuries can easily occur. Our purpose is not to stand and box with someone; it is to strike quick and vicious to a vulnerable location. Remember what we said earlier. If you keep them in pain they cannot fight back. That applies to you as well. Imagine having a fractured strong side hand in a fight.

Remember the soft tissue areas discussed earlier? Open hands or hammer fist are the two accepted methods of striking. Most open palm strikes should be performed with your fingers extended and spread for palm rigidity. As for kicks, force is applied by using your entire foot while wearing shoes. Most people kick by striking only with the toe of the foot, which applies less force. Regardless of method, any strike or kick now needed is the best. Never become paralyzed with analysis. Strike the best way you can repeatedly and with as much violence as needed. Practice and mental preparedness will provide a plan of action in response to various situations.

In CQB training, the tactics taught are hit hard and evade. The initial strike has to be calculated. Most of what we do must be quick and instinctive, which is where simplicity comes into play. Touching the eyes is the one action that causes an immediate reflex response from someone. As soon as someone grabs or starts to assault you, the first action will be to jab, flick, or sweep your fingers into their eyes.

If they bend forward as a reaction to this action, elbow strike them in the side of their head or knee them in the face or crotch. The golden spots for a knockout are the chin, temple, behind the ears, and back of the head. Cause a shock to the brain and the person goes out. A hit to the soft spots of the head with a palm strike will put them down. Touch your own soft spots on the head. The temple, under the jaw, top of the jaw behind the ear, and the base of the skull around the hairline on either side.

If the person goes backwards with the eye flick, step forward with a knee spike to the groin or a kick to the knee. For the spike, be sure to point your foot and toes back as straight as possible. This allows the knee to move forward as an effective strike rather than just up. A full foot kick on the forward knee can cause a serious and painful injury.

Another effective defense if they move their head back is to palm strike them under the jaw around the chin with your fingers extended. If the chin is tucked, the nose or ears are also good targets.

The nose can be struck just as you would the chin and the ears can be hit with cupped hands to force excessive pressures into the eardrums. Always take the first target of opportunity as it is presented to you. These targets can also be utilized in the event that an assailant has brought you down to the ground. Remember that your primary goal if you are down is to get back onto your feet. To repeat myself, the first person who resorts to blows, bites, and gouges will come out on top.

Remember the target areas for Krav Maga if the person tries to tackle you. A common method is the ordinary football tackle. They will go for your legs to force you backwards. This is the same technique used against Texas Constable Lundsford. After being knocked backwards, the other subject started kicking him in the head. They removed his service weapon and killed him. As a defense, several responses could be a elbow thrust straight down into their back or leaning forward with your feet straight back to come down on top of the attacker. Once there, repeated blows to the kidneys will stop their advances. Then follow the first rule and get back to your feet. A technique to force someone off who is holding you down is to reach and grab their side skin in the area commonly referred to as the "love handles." Grip-squeeze the skin tightly. They will release long enough to allow you to strike at soft tissue. As they retreat from the pain, strike or jab them in the throat, eyes, kick them in their knee or crotch, or any other technique you can imagine.

These examples are very simplistic. In the real world, the only techniques, which will work, are simplicity. (I use simplicity as a catchword at the beginning of several chapters to demonstrate its importance.) I want to stress that these are options only in the event your life is at risk. These strikes must be repeated as many times as necessary to keep the suspect away. One sweep or jab may not work by itself; therefore, you must maintain a barrage of attacks to the soft tissue areas to create separation. You have to overwhelm them with jabs, gouges, kicks, and stomps.

Someone who grabs you straight on can be immediately reversed with a jab to the throat or eyes. Practice these simplistic moves as part of your situational awareness training. Shadow boxing or practicing on a punching bag will make you more efficient. When someone is trying to hurt you, do not try to restrain them. You will always be attempting to restrain someone if all of your training involves restraints and submissions. Train to strike, jab, and knee as hard and as often as you can to create distance. Remember to keep everything fluid. If one thing fails, keep trying various techniques to create separation.

Anyone who will intentionally assault a police officer is a dangerous person. It could be a gang initiation, mental illness, drug or alcohol abuse, or an ex con who has decided not to go back to jail. This person has already committed a felony. You have to assume they will cause serious bodily harm or worse if given the chance. How many videos have we watched where an officer is literally pummeled to the point of near death, brain damage, broken bones, teeth lost, and worse? Do not stand there and take it. Planning has to be fast and efficient. Perform any of these actions with even partial success and you will create the necessary distance needed to deploy a secondary or primary weapon.

Some rules can be definite, like stay off the ground. To get off the ground; punch, gouge, bite, jab, knee, rip, tear, break fingers, or anything else you can think of. Be flexible with every situation. You are in a fight for your life. Stay flexible because no single technique will always work. Any training in self-defense will better your odds on the street.

Steven Varnell

Summary of Hands On:

- MMA is one of the best fighting programs to simulate real life. However, there are many rules which govern the sport that makes it unrealistic.
- Real fights never occur as you were taught in your martial arts classes.
- When fighting for your life, grappling is the last thing you will want to waste your energies on. 25% of officers who go to the ground are injured.
- We are taught defensive tactics. To restrain a suspect requires offensive tactics. They will either try to get away (passive resistance) or try to cause you death or great bodily injury (aggressive or aggravated resistance).
- Your training has to be fast, easy, and vicious.
- Strikes, blows, and kicks are easier to teach and are more effective to practice than take downs, wrestling, and grappling.
- Always keep everyone at least at arm's length.
- If you go to the ground, your priority is to get back to your feet.
- Try to roll out if you are on the ground. If you are unable, use your hips and shoulders to pivot. Keep moving and the first person who resorts to blows, bites, and gouges will come out on top.
- Remember the Fatigue Threshold Study; Upper body strength begins to fade within 30 seconds. Total fatigue in about 2 minutes.
- Palm strike using open hands to avoid hand injuries. Target soft areas with maximum pain infliction. (Eyes, throat, solar plexus, temple, crotch, kidneys, etc.)
- Kick using your entire foot instead of just the toe.
- Knee spikes – point your toe back so the spike moves forward, not up.
- Initial assault, target the eyes because they will cause an immediate defensive reaction.
- CQB targets the eyes, elbows to the side of the head, and knee strikes. The effectiveness is in the number of combination of fluid strikes and kicks.

- All of these strikes or blows have to be maintained repeatedly until separation is created. They have to be overwhelmed with the violence.
- Once separated, retreat and arm yourself with a weapon appropriate for the encounter.
- **Study Train Survive**

KNIFE DEFENSE - 20

The best protection is self-protection.

The best protection against a suspect with a knife is knowing they have it. Only then can you properly respond. If you know they have a knife, there are only two types of defense. One is to pull your firearm at the first sign of a weapon. The second is to try to escape to avoid the confrontation. There were two police officers killed in the line of duty in 2011 by knife attacks. This is a yearly trend and when I see several officers killed every year by a specific method, a chapter has to be dedicated.

If you are carrying a firearm, on or off duty, remember the importance of maintaining distance from an armed subject. A person can cover 30 feet in the average amount of time it could take you to draw and shoot your weapon. The FBI has shown that even with a well-placed bullet in center mass; a person can still run up to 70 yards before the heart stops. A shot into the brain is the only one guaranteed to stop someone. In the chapter on firearms, we will discuss the need for instinctive or point shooting. Practicing these shots will assist in making a fast and accurate first volley; an absolute necessity to defend against this type of attack.

Most subjects will not approach with a knife if you draw a gun. Some will for various reasons from mental illness, drug or alcohol abuse, or suicide by cop. The foundation of this section is about reacting to an unexpected attack from a non-gun armed subject. They may have a knife or blunt instrument, yet the defense will be the same. Create distance by whatever means possible. If the subject is too close, natural reaction will cause you to lean into the attacker to try and control them. However, to lean into a subject with a knife could result in an upper body strike and lead to your incapacitation. Practicing distance creation when confronted by a subject armed with a knife allows you the required time to draw and shoot. If they continue their advancement, I can only say that life is about the choices we make while living it.

What if you are off duty or not in uniform? This means that you are not carrying many of the secondary weapons from a utility belt. The rule remains the same, create distance, and protect yourself. If you have a gun, do not delay its use. Your life is in imminent danger. If you do not have a firearm, utilize whatever is available. A chair with all four legs pointing towards the subject is a good weapon. The assailant is not able to concentrate on defending against them all and you can use it in a thrusting manner. Strike with anything that can keep them away until there is an opportunity to escape. Never use your secondary weapons against an armed attacker if possible. This places you on unequal ground because unlike their knife or blunt instrument, your secondary weapons are not intended for serious bodily injury or death.

Some of the subjects encountered could be former military personnel. Additional care should be taken because they are taught tactics in knife fighting. Take the following various information which is directly from the U.S. Marine Corp Close Combat Manuel, Chapter 3.

"Marines experienced in offensive knife techniques can cause enough damage and massive trauma to stop an opponent."

"The goal in a knife fight is to attack the body's soft, vital target areas that are readily accessible (e.g., the face, the sides, and front of the neck, the lower abdomen {or groin}).

Secondary targets are the inside of the thighs (femoral artery), inside of the upper arms (brachial artery), and the radial/ulnar nerves in the arms.

"Principles of Knife Fighting:

- Execute movements with the knife blade within a box, shoulder width across from the neck down to the waistline. The opponent has a greater chance of blocking an attack if the blade is brought in a wide, sweeping movement to the opponent.
- Close with the opponent, coming straight to the target.
- Move the knife in straight lines.

- Point the knife's blade tip forward and toward the opponent.
- Apply full body weight and power in each of the knife techniques. Full body weight should be put into the attack in the direction of the blades movement (slash or thrust).
- Apply constant forward pressure with the body and blade to keep the opponent off balance."

Thrusting of a knife means penetration. It is the most effective knife tactic because it can cause greater injury by damaging internal organs. Blocking with your arms means standing toe to toe with the subject and should only be attempted as a last resort. If your assailant is skilled with a knife, any attempt to block a thrust with your hand or arms, will result in damaging wounds. The psychological effects of blood loss could prevent you from maintaining a clear mind to determine your next move. Kick, kick, and kick some more, creating space until you can escape.

Although not as deadly as thrusting, slashing injuries are the most common and can have a devastating effect. If you are trying to defend yourself against a knife attack with your arms, a skilled person can easily slice you across the inside of your wrist, damaging the tendons and leaving that hand useless in your defense. In addition, a deep slash across the bicep muscle can disable the arm. If you are not carrying a firearm, escape at all cost.

There are a number of blocks, grabs, and parries (redirection of the incoming knife arm away from your body) shown in self-defense practices as an option against a person armed with a knife. The self-defense manuals I examined showed various arm blocking techniques. We have seen the demonstrations during martial arts exhibitions. The student approaches the sensei with a rubber knife and told to do a slow, overhead attack. The student approaches and follows the instructions. The sensei raises his arms at half speed to demonstrate the effectiveness of his skills. He blocks the knife arm of the student who suddenly stops the attack and cooperates with some type of arm lock, throw, or disarming technique. People are amazed at the skills of the sensei and cannot wait to be taught the same defense. Even if you have an initial block of the knife thrust, a real attack is vicious. They will not stop with a single thrust. Martial arts are most effective when the opponent is following the rules of the "art." Your best plan is to run. Never take on an armed subject unarmed.

The reason anyone ever uses a weapon is to gain the advantage over the other person. We have this mentality based upon our upbringing that fighting should be fair. We are taught the rules of a fight. We learn the rules that govern boxing, wrestling, martial arts, and

MMA. Even from an early age we would agree to meet in the back alley for a fight that was conducted within a learned set of rules. The truth is there are no rules in a real fight. This is the idea we have to wrap our minds around. All is fair when it is a fight for your life.

In the last chapter, we showed the need to use every possible method to inflict pain and injury to an attacker. When a weapon is pulled, the attacker instantly becomes the greatest fighter of all times. Never take on an armed suspect unless you have a clear shot. In a real fact based scenario, the knife-wielding attacker is not going to wait and move in circles with you while waiting for the best opportunity to slip through your defenses. They are going to rush you. When this occurs, none of the martial arts training in the world are going to keep you from getting hurt. Their intentions are to kill you. As you read at the end of almost every paragraph, your best chance of surviving this encounter is escape. No amount of martial arts rehearsing will ever place you on equal grounds with this person.

Always make sure you can see the palms of their hands. An effective method by a trained person with a knife is to hold the knife in the ice pick grip. They will have the knife blade pointing up the back side of the forearm with the cutting surface pointing out to their rear. When close enough, they will punch with a hook technique allowing the cutting edge of the blade to pass forward and across your face or neck. They will stop immediately and reverse with a thrust to the neck or chest. Always know where their hands are and what is in them.

Colonel Rex Applegate said, "Either type of knife defense, parry or block, involves a certain amount of risk." He also taught classes in knife fighting tactics. He developed his own design that was about 10 inches long, shaped like a dagger. The Applegate knife has a round handle, swollen in the middle for the placement of your middle finger and a double-edged blade. This type of blade prevents anyone from grabbing the knife. Both American and British agents carried this knife. Techniques were developed in assassinations of enemies of the state during the war. In his book, *Kill or Get Killed*, Col Applegate demonstrates numerous ways of killing with a knife from sentry guards to crowded street killings.

According to Col. Applegate, the signs of someone skilled with a knife are, they carry the knife with the handle in their palm, blade protruding forward with the edges parallel to the ground in front of their thumb and forefinger. This allows the attacker to sweep the blade left or right to slash the opponent's arms in any attempt to defend themselves. The knife is kept close to the body and their weak hand forward. This arm is used to create the needed opening to thrust the knife. Knife selection is also a consideration. Most inexperienced persons will grip the knife like they are holding an ice pick or hammer. The hammer grip is only good for an upward thrust and the ice pick for a downward thrust. Knife defense techniques were developed for these standard grips. They are the commonly seen methods on movies and demonstrations because they appear dramatic. However, they are ineffective.

Col. Rex Applegate demonstrating proper knife grip and stance.

There is a timetable for death as demonstrated by W.E. Fairbairn for the survivability of a cut artery. W.E. Fairbairn trained the Shanghai Police in the 1920's up until WWII. He was brought back to England to teach Special Forces Units techniques in hand-to-hand combat. Colonel Rex Applegate was one of his students for a train the trainer course. Fairbairn was an expert in knife fighting. It is said he was covered with scares from being engaged in so many knife fights. Though the information in the chart may not to be exactly correct, it does give you an idea of the dangers of a cut artery.

EXPLANATION OF FIG. 112

No.	Name of Artery	Size	Depth below Surface in inches	Loss of Consciousness in seconds	Death
1....	Brachial	Medium	½	14	1½ Min.
2....	Radial	Small	¼	30	2 "
3....	Carotid	Large	1½	5	12 Sec.
4....	Subclavian	Large	2½	2	3½ "
5....	(Heart)	—	3½	Instantaneous	3 "
6....	(Stomach)	—	5	Depending on depth of cut	

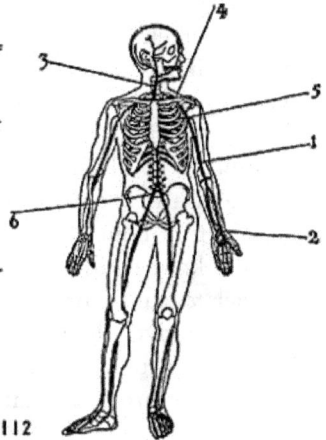

Fig. 112

(This chart is courtesy of *Get Tough* by W.E. Fairbairn)

I have always stressed the importance of determining if a subject has a criminal record because they are inherently more dangerous. Most stabbing methods are developed and perfected in correctional institutions. Watch prison videos and see how fast these attacks occur. They come straight in, fast, and stab repeatedly. Also, watch how their intent to attack is always shown in advance through their body language. Everyone demonstrates behaviors of their intentions. Knowledge of a criminal record should always cause a heightened sense of awareness. We learned earlier that 73% of the subjects who ran from the police had a prior record. Never underestimate the dangers involved to police from a multiple offender facing enhanced prison time.

Remember that there are only two actual defenses against a knife attack. Use your firearm or create distance by running. If you are unable to do either, kick hard and at good targets to maintain the needed distance in order to prevent the knife from causing damage in your torso, neck, or head; and then run.

The charted times above are for when no medical assistance is immediately available. Some injured areas are impossible to stop bleeding. Proper first aid kits and survival information is available to all in law enforcement today. How many officers carry a tourniquet to stop bleeding? It could be an injury to you or a fellow officer. Have you ever thought about what to use like a belt or a shoelace? These will work if you think about and take the time to retrieve them. My suggestion is to always wear a para-cord survival bracelet. If you or someone else is seriously injured, the bracelet can come apart and be used as a tourniquet. You can use them with or without a buckle. I prefer the knot to the buckle bracelet because it is the original design and easier to cut or break apart if needed. Some of these bracelets are more decorative than designated for survival skills. I prefer the bracelets constructed of a single cord rather than the designer multiple lengths. They are more difficult to find, however, any of them will work. Cut off the knot and the bracelet is easy to unravel. Later in Chapter 28, we will discuss better techniques of Tactical Combat Critical Care.

Summary of Knife Defense:

- There are only two types of knife defense, a clear and effective shot or escape.
- If you are unable to do either, keep the assailant away from your vital areas with the use of kicks.
- A knife instantly makes an opponent the most dangerous person in the world.
- Always be sure you can see their hands and what's in them.
- A person can cover 30 feet in 2 seconds. Remember your reaction time to shoot.
- Even after shot in an area of great blood loss, a person can still run up to 70 yards.
- A brain shot is the only shot from a handgun which has stopping power.
- Maintaining distance by whatever means or the use of anything as a weapon is your best opportunity to survive if you are unable to run.
- Understand the dangers of a military trained subject because they have basic knife fighting skills.
- A skilled person with a knife is demonstrated by the way they carry it in their hand. The classic hammer or icepick carries are learned from too much television. A blade protruding forward with the blade sideways, weak hand up, and the knife held close is the proper stance. This person is dangerous.
- You must avoid your normal self defense tactics and understand that you are instantly in a life or death struggle the very moment a knife is brought out. Take the necessary action needed to save yourself.
- Plan ahead with first aid ideas for yourself and others as well. In a knife assault, slashing injuries are most common. A tourniquet may be needed and can be readily available with a para-cord bracelet.
- **Study Train Survive**

FIREARMS TRAINING - 21

The decisions you make when faced with destiny will determine whether you live or die. It simply comes down to taking the correct action in a swift manner.

Shooting practice should never be considered target or defensive shooting. For law enforcement and the safety aspects of this book, it is about shooting effectively against an armed assailant. You have to be able to use your firearm instantly and accurately. Our goal is offensive style training in instinctive, point, or combat shooting. This technique stresses the fast use of the handgun without the sights.

Law enforcement personnel are losing nearly 70% of their gun battles. In *Criminal Interdiction*, I described it like this; "Most police involved shootings occur no further than 21 feet (81%). 58.8% of all police shooting occurred from 0 to 5 feet. In fact, the FBI's "Law Enforcement Officers Feloniously Killed in the Line of Duty" research from 1994 to 2006 showed that law enforcement officers failed to hit their assailants 69.4% of the time."

Police officers are trained in the basics of pistol craft and targeting skills. They learn to take a moment for sight picture, sight alignment, breathe, and trigger squeeze. This traditional style of shooting in order to meet your department's range qualifications alone, fails on the qualifications course of the street. As with many training courses, additional aggressive styles of combat shooting have to be practiced. Force Science Research has shown in their gaze assessment studies that only learning the basic shooting techniques are getting police officers killed. The reasons why the assholes win more often

148

varies. First, they are not on a restrictive course requiring them to shoot regularly in only basic pistol shooting styles. We will perform as our training dictates. Police officers are trying to engage in fast shootouts by doing exactly as they are trained; sight picture, sight alignment, breathe, and trigger squeeze. By the time they reach the sight alignment phase, the assailant has fired. Now the entire process is interrupted and panic sets in as our shots become uncontrolled. If your assailant has military training, they have already been taught to fire fast and keep their eyes on the target. I have the same complaint today that Col. Rex Applegate had about the training received by law enforcement since the 1940's. Basic pistol craft and some stress course shooting is all that is performed. There is no combat style fast shooting. We are teaching our officers defensive training, bulls-eye paper target practices for competition and setting them up for failure. The proof is in the statistics.

Point or instinctive shooting was developed as a natural response to an armed encounter. In a close shooting scenario, you have to fire fast and accurate. There will be no time for the standard sight alignment rules. At close range, you will be shot if you delay or miss. Instinctive shooting relies on all of your natural responses to these dangers with more control.

If you train to shoot where you look without the gun sights, your chances of surviving will increase dramatically. Think how many police shooting videos you have watched where the officer starts shooting until the magazine is empty and still they miss the bad guy. After the proverbial smoke has cleared, there are scattered casings from both sides on the ground. If anyone is shot at all, statistically, it will be the officer. Force Science Research has shown that if you take your eyes off the target to focus on the sights, the chances increase to miss and get shot first.

Actual photo courtesy of www.bobtuley.com

Photo is a freeze frame from the famous Kehoe Brothers traffic stop in Ohio. Armed militiamen versus Ohio State Trooper and deputy in an all out gun battle. The deputy and subject on the right of the photo emptied their guns at one another. Shooting as trained, no one was hit, even at this close range.

Police officers begin their training in the academy. They are taught the basics of pistol craft to pass the qualification course. This is a necessary continuum in the progression of firearms training. You have to be familiar with all of the functions and maintenance of your handgun, train under various conditions of stress to learn how to fire on target, and how to steady the gun on various support items to assist you in making an effective shot.

Under stress, your heart will be pounding, adrenaline flowing, and hands trembling. The shot needs to be steadied to be on target. You can become proficient with fairly long shots with your handgun when you learn to use the sights correctly. This standardized training and other point style shooting techniques requires more time on a range than will be provided to you by your department. Training is one of the first areas cut when budgets are reduced. As I said in *Criminal Interdiction*, "the cost and time necessary to develop these skills rest on you."

I have heard this repeatedly: "If the agency is not going to buy it for me, then I must not need it." This is the common call of the complainers. It is up to YOU to take the additional steps needed to complete the number one rule in law enforcement; Go home safe at the end of the day. You are going to have to spend the money and time to go to the range. This idea of shooting your gun during your annual or bi-annual firearms qualifications course and not pulling it out of the holster again until the next course IS COSTING LIVES! If the reason is being too cheap, then keep all of the receipts for expenses and you may be able to use them as a tax deduction.

I really want to stress to everyone the need for a full and balanced training regimen in the use of firearms. I am also quite aware that most officers will never try to accomplish more with their firearms training than what is afforded by their department. These same officers will be your backup. I have my own opinions on how to train those who want to improve their firearms skills. I am a certified firearms instructor and have taught pistol craft for my agency for a very long time. I can teach you how to shoot with a proficiency to qualify. Teaching you how to win in a gunfight is a very separate endeavor.

As we mentioned in the beginning, this is combat, instinctive, or point shooting. Nearly 60% of gunfights are going to occur within five feet. The person who can fire first and with accuracy is the one who will walk away. We can be on the defensive, but not shoot with a defensive attitude. Do not wait until a subject has fired before taking the initiative to fire back.

In the Force Science Gaze Assessment Study, the rookie cops delayed in drawing their weapon until nearly a second after the suspect turned on them. The elite trained officers had drawn well before the suspects pivoted against them and fired their weapons first in 92.5% of the cases. The rookie officers fired first only 42% of the time. In addition, the rookies took their eyes off the assailants in 82% of the scenarios in order to try to achieve a sight picture. This action essentially removed them from the gunfight causing them to miss most of their shots. They were responding exactly as trained with defensive target practice style, qualification-shooting techniques. They knew as they entered the scenario that something was going to happen and still failed.

Even though this study utilized rookie officers, I am sure that most veteran officers would have the same results. Most of us were never trained for this type of action. It is dumbfounding that agency heads and training personnel do not recognize the need for this realistic style shooting. We need to be proficient in both areas of practice. After a qualification course is completed, stress courses conducted with instinctive shooting and fast draw practices. Fast draw practices can be conducted with dry firing for safety purposes. How often do you see officers on the firing range hang up in their holsters while trying to draw their weapon? How can you expect to quick draw in a real gunfight if you do not practice fast draws? Create a little more distance and then bring the gun up to eye level. Fast draw to a hip shooting position is a common range practice, yet the accuracy of this method is poor beyond point blank range. Speed and accuracy will help you win in a shootout along with the following techniques.

The first concept of instinctive shooting is that you do not utilize the sights. Imagine being in a low light or no light situation or someone pull's a weapon on you during an encounter. It is often called instinctive shooting because the process involved is instinctive. Imagine the handgun as an extension of your hand. Right now, as you read this, quick draw your finger. That's right, pretend your hand is the gun and look around you. Fixate on any object be it a clock, television, or painting. Now draw your hand as the gun and your forefinger as the barrel and point your imaginary gun quickly at the fixated object. Keep your eyes on the item. Look down to see how well you are sighted in. You will be surprised at how simple this is to learn. The same process is followed with the handgun except now your hand and finger are replaced with the grips and barrel. Practice this procedure with a safe gun (always double check that the gun is empty and the chamber is clear). Repeat the process numerous times until the action becomes second nature. Now you are ready for the range.

Start at the 3-yard line and follow the natural process from the draw to the shot. Practice this method repeatedly until you become comfortable and never look at the gun sights. Pay attention to the placement of the rounds and forget about the perfect quarter size grouping. You are trying to hit the target. Never over-think the process and just let your muscle motor skills do this naturally.

Square up on the target with your weak side foot slightly ahead. Face forward in a crouched position. This allows several things to occur. First, your body armor is directed to the front to protect you from a hit in center mass. In the Weaver position, which stresses a sideways stance, exposes the side gap in the body armor and your armpit to the shooter. A round taken into these areas can have fatal consequences.

The second advantage squaring off with the target is your ability to move. You can walk or step in any direction with an almost natural gait. When walking with your gun on target, adjust your gait. A natural walking pattern involves too much body movement. To smooth this out, think about your heel placements and the distance of each step. When you are walking with the gun at eye level, each step will intentionally be a soft heel to toe roll of the foot. This allows for forward body movement without the up and down causation's of a natural gait. In other words, you will be able to maintain a steady eye picture (not sight picture) on the target.

You should practice with a very tight grip on your handgun, even if it is different from what you are normally accustomed. The reason is when faced with the type of pressures involved in a shooting; your muscles will naturally tense with the stress of the events. This grip can affect your accuracy; therefore, practicing a tight grip now will pay dividends later if you are involved in a shooting.

It is always better to move the gun position up from a low ready than a high pointing location (the Hollywood version of holding the gun next to your head with the muzzle pointing up). From the high position or close to the chest, the gun is thrust forward and there is a tendency to shoot low. The natural angle of the wrist along with the frame design of some pistols (revolvers do not have this same frame issue) causes the barrel to point downward at the end of the thrust. From the low ready position, an almost locked elbow prevents thrusting the gun out when brought up to shooting level.

When the gun reaches eye level it should be on target and level. Pull the trigger without hesitation. Keeping the gun in the center of your body and shooting from eye level, you will shoot where you look. If your subject is at an angle, pivot your body towards them, not your arms. By turning your body towards the target, you maintain the gun in center mass. Maintaining eye contact with the mark assures you will be on the objective instantly as the gun rises. Swinging your arms around instead of turning your body can cause the shot to go wide.

Another interesting topic is in the number of shots fired. In most standardized firearms courses, we are given a set of instructions and a time frame like, "For the next course of fire, when the targets turn, shooters will draw to a two handed high point shooting position. Shooters will fire two rounds in four seconds. Shooters will then maintain cover until told to re-holster." At a different area of the course you will be allowed to shoot 12 rounds in 45 seconds. This is fine for the firearms qualifications course. It does not prepare you for the realities of a gunfight.

According to the FBI's firearms training unit, most gunfights will last anywhere from 2.5 to 3.5 seconds. During this time, it will require at least 3.5 shots to the body to stop an assailant. We also learned earlier that a suspect could run up to 70 yards after receiving a shot which severs a major artery. The answer to this puzzle is in your training. You have to learn to draw and fire fast and accurately. You want four or more shots to their body in three seconds. A well-placed head shot is the only one that will take anyone down immediately.

I hope you are beginning to understand the importance of instinctive shooting. When most people are delaying their first shot to aim, you have already fired with a reasonable chance of striking the target. When they are trying to align their sights, they have taken their eyes off you. You have fired and are firing again causing them to react defensively and panic causes their shots to miss. Keep your arm extended, elbows locked, and fire as fast and accurately as possible while seeking cover. With a minimum of practice, this method can be counted upon to save your life. It does not take an excessive amount of time or ammunition to become proficient. Simply practicing with your hand and finger allows the exact pointing position to become second nature.

The accuracy of this method begins to drop at distances greater than 15 yards. Therefore, practice instinctive styles at varying yardages inside this range. In addition, most range courses are drawn out from the 3, 7, 15, and 25-yard line. To help with your proficiencies, also choose yardages that are between these marks because not every shooting will take place at these exact yard markers. 81% of all police shootings have occurred within 21 feet; the same distances you are practicing.

Another area of concern is the use of our shotguns or rifles. Once or twice a year, while at the range for qualifications, we will participate in a shotgun familiarization course. Fire a couple of rounds at a target after trying to load or combat load a certain number of rounds. Occasionally, you may have a course which will cause you to transition between the shotgun and handgun. In other words, few law enforcement personnel spend much time training with their long guns. Stress the importance of basic loading, unloading, stance, shoulder placement, safety, grip, and target acquisition. Low recoil shells can resolve the high recoil complaints against using the shotgun. Additionally, demonstrate proper grip with the push pull technique. As you prepare to shoot, push forward with your weak hand harder than you pull with your strong arm and this will reduce much of the recoil. This also helps you to stay on target rather than trying to realign after bringing the shotgun down from its high recoil position.

Show some advanced techniques after everyone successfully completes the basics. Areas like selective ammunition loading, weapon retention tactics, and transitioning to your handgun. This is another strange truth that has always amazed me. We practice the least with the shotgun, yet it is the most efficient weapons we carry. Additional use in various situations can change the stigma that many people have with shooting a shotgun.

Apply this same philosophy for the use of a rifle. Many officers today are carrying an AR15 rifle that they have taken a dedicated course before allowed to carry it on duty. The problem then becomes the same as the shotgun. Once or twice a year you are required to fire a couple of rounds at a target to qualify. The gun is cleaned, encased, and placed back into the car. Additional training is necessary for the safe operation of the gun. Without regular use, the operations of the weapon like the safety/fire selector switch, clearing jams, and magazine reloads are not automatic. Hesitations will always put you on the receiving, rather than the giving end.

The .223 Cal bullets is a very good round to use inside of a home or building. This will be explained as many of you are squirming over the belief that it is too powerful to use inside because of collateral damage to innocent bystanders. In the next chapter, I will show the importance of correct weapons selection. Tactics for the use of the gun in these confined areas need to be rehearsed. We have learned in Iraq and Afghanistan that our troops are constantly climbing in and out of vehicles. They are also conducting building sweeps and raids on compounds. The same actions transfer cleanly to the warfare at home through law enforcement operations and presented several safety issues which were addressed by various techniques.

The Army has specific training for this style of operations because it is the standard current warfare model. They call it MOUT or Military Operations on Urban Terrain. This came about as warfare shifted from rural to urban operations. First is the length of the weapon inside smaller rooms and vehicle interiors. The second is the extra care needed to prevent soldiers from sweeping others with their gun muzzles. By short stocking, the adjusting stocks assist in both of these issues. By keeping the stock shortened, it reduces the length of the gun. From inside the vehicle, this allows easier access in and out and when the use of the gun is needed from within to fire out.

When you are moving through a building, if you shorten the stock, the gun is usable in the tight confines of a room. Other than some practice with a reduced stock, there is no difference in shooting techniques. The gun can remain on your shoulder for natural and accurate target acquisition. Eyes on target and point shooting techniques are of the utmost importance, not sight alignment. There are other methods of short stocking that take the butt of the riffle off the shoulder. To stay within the model of simplicity, I feel nothing beats a normal shooting style. Different carry and shooting positions can cause hesitations. Every shooting technique I have described is from a normal and natural shooting position. Therefore, they can all be taught easily with effective outcomes. Besides rapid target acquisition, accuracy is imperative and the most accurate technique to fire a rifle is with the stock against the shoulder.

Summary of Firearms Training:

- When practicing with your firearm, stress both the targeting of your shots and combat shooting techniques.
- Almost 60% of police shootings occur within 5 feet of their assailant. Law enforcement fails in nearly 70% of their shooting encounters.
- You are personally responsible for your own safety. Your agency will teach the basics, you have to get to the range and practice yourself.
- When training yourself, emphasis must be on instinctive combat shooting.
- Keep your eyes on the target, not your sights.
- Practice quick draws with a safe weapon. Practice these same quick draws and fire at the range.
- The technique involves a fast draw from a low ready or holstered position. The gun is brought up to eye level and fired.
- Walk deliberately with a rolling heel to toe gait.
- Keep the gun square with your body and on the target. Therefore, the gun will be on the target when it is brought up to eye level.
- Pivot the body and not your arms when the target appears at an angle to you.
- Be very proficient with the operations of your long guns. If you have an AR15, practice firing the weapon with the stock in it's shortest position. This will assist when in a vehicle or building. Shooting from the shoulder is still the most accurate firing position.
- **Study Train Survive**

Steven Varnell

GUN AND AMMUNITION CHOICES - 22

Giving up is the ultimate tragedy.

Robert J. Donovan

There are some agencies wanting to replace the shotgun for many of the popular patrol rifles. Though they are very similar in function there is a place for both of these weapons in your arsenal. I would like to demonstrate when and why you would prefer one over the other.

You often see a police officer with an AR15 over their shoulder on the news. The environment where they are utilizing these weapons should be the determining factor. Would they be better off with a handgun, shotgun, or rifle? For handguns, there are several schools of thought. There are the small and fast groups vs. the large and slow. They both carry facts behind them, however, after reviewing numerous ballistics data comparisons from private testing to the FBI, several things remain in the forefront. You have to hit the suspect in center mass. The bullet has to penetrate deep in order to hit anything vital or there has to be vast tissue damage. There are many misconceptions about handgun cartridges. An important truth about the handgun ammunition is there is no such thing as knockdown power. Critical to this information is the fact that there is enough oxygen in the brain to conduct further actions against you for about 10-15 seconds after the heart stops.

Surrounding tissue damage occurs from the kinetic shock and fragmentation of the bullet. Tissue damage can also occur from the expansion of the bullet itself. The problem is that fragmentation will only occur if the bullet is in excess of 2000 fps at impact. All of the handgun ammunition's are below this velocity requirement. These velocities occur with rifles. Therefore, fragmentation combined with the greater kinetic energy tissue expansion occurs when hit with rifle bullets.

With handgun ammunition, a permanent cavity (the cavity created by the bullet itself) is formed and the kinetic energy makes a temporary cavity. Human tissues and organs have great resiliency to shock waves, which is why handgun ammunition leaves only a temporary cavity. The temporary cavity is momentarily expanded around the permanent cavity, yet returns to its original shape. The damage is caused by the permanent cavity that may be increased by bullet expansion. The size of the permanent cavity conversely corresponds to the size of the bullet. A .38 Cal +P hollow point bullet can leave a permanent cavity with the narrow entry neck and an expansion end to approximately .59 inches, as long as the bullet actually expands. A .38 Cal bullet is actually closer to a .36 Cal and was so named for the size of the chamber that was needed. The .357 mag is closer to the actual size of a .38, which is why it can be fired in the magnum. This is about a 63% bullet enlargement from impact to the point of rest. Compare this to a shotgun slug or a Foster slug from most police smooth bore shotguns. If the slug does not expand, there is a 1-inch permanent cavity created by the bullet. This is a lot of damage depending on how deep it penetrates. With all of this in mind, do not jump on the hollow points and expansion train just yet. The idea is sound, but is the reality of bullet expansion all that important?

A .223 Cal bullet at around 3000fps creates a tremendous release of energy and fragments on impact. The combination of the two forces stretches the permanent cavity so far and fast that tearing and rupturing of the wound channel, which was weakened by fragmentation, causes a significant increase in damage. This is typical of a rifle wound.

We spoke about the .38 Cal bullet expansion. It is essential in understanding wound mechanics that handgun bullets are not dependable in their expansion abilities. There are two key components to having an effective handgun cartridge. The bullet has to penetrate enough to strike vital organs for blood loss and it has to be big enough to leave a large permanent cavity. Remember, handgun ammunition is not fast enough to allow for effective fragmentation. Expansion and penetration also varies from different makes of the same caliber. Not every manufacture creates an equal bullet.

In an attempt to try to resolve this problem, the Glaser Safety Slug was developed. It was touted as the great man stopper and safe to use in your home. The bullet was designed to be frangible so as not to penetrate walls. The selling point was that on impact, the bullet disintegrates and there is a transfer of shot to the body causing devastating damage. The problem was significant superficial damage, but shallow penetration; which violates the first effective requirement of a handgun cartridge. Forensic scientist stated that after being shot with a Glaser Safety Slug, it would take about three days to die and the cause would be by infection. Thus, the cartridge eventually lost its popularity.

Forensic scientists have determined that there is very little difference in the permanent cavity when comparing hollow point to solid ammunition. In fact, hollow point handgun ammunition has been shown to only expand in the body 60-70% of the time. If the bullet impacts anything before striking tissue, it can fill the hollow point and prevent expansion. This includes striking clothing as the material can wrap around the bullet. You will see in some of the following test how this can cause a deeper penetration.

The actual destruction caused by any small arms projectile without high velocity, is too small in magnitude relative to the mass and complexity of the target. An effective bullet will destroy only about 2 ounces of tissue in its passage through the body. This represents only 0.07 of one percent of the mass of a 180-pound man unless it strikes part of the CNS. Sufficient blood loss occurs with hits to the heart, aorta, the vena cava, or liver.

The length of the gun barrel as well as the brand and type of ammunition's used can have significant changes to the bullet velocity. Kinetic energy is energy possessed by an object in motion. Energy is a function of mass and the velocity squared or $E=MC^2$. For our purposes, our energy is possessed by a projectile or bullet in motion. The longer or further this bullet is in motion, the less energy it possesses. The bullet can also sustain a loss of momentum upon impact along its trajectory. The important factor of this energy is that enough of it has to exist to deliver an adequate amount to the target. Too little energy and the bullet does not have enough to transfer to the target. Too much and the bullet passes through the target with limited transfer. The goal is have enough to penetrate and stay in the body so that there is complete energy transference. This is why a .223cal bullet is so effective. It is traveling with a great deal of velocity that correlates to energy. Upon impact, the speed causes a fragmentation and total energy transfer. The combination of the two equates to a lot of damage.

Longer barrels give the propellant more force and time to work on propelling the bullet. At some point, if the barrel is too long, friction begins to play against the bullet. The key is to find an appropriate length. With rifles, a 20-22 inch barrel is sufficient. If they are magnum or heavier loads, a 24-26 inch barrel increase the force-related energy and allows the bullet to achieve its needed velocity. For handguns, revolvers commonly have large barrel variances. Although impractical, the ideal length for maximum energy in a revolver is a 16-inch barrel. Having a four to five inch barrel with a revolver is the ideal length in both power and practicality of use. There can be as much as 150 fps (feet per second) loss in bullet velocity per inch of barrel. A 2-inch snub-nosed .38 will have about 300 fps less bullet velocity than a 4-inch barrel. The same is true for the .357 magnum comparing a 3-inch to a 5-inch barrel. The standard pistol barrel of between four and five inches seems ideal for most of the ammunition used. For more information on barrel lengths, read the "Ballistics by the Inch" web site. They do very detailed studies on these and varying ammunition types.

According to FBI forensic scientist, the critical components of effective ammunition are penetration and permanent cavity, in that order. A bullet must be able to penetrate the human body at least 12 inches, though 18 inches is the preferred depth. These penetrations are needed to reach the vital blood bearing organs. Increased bullet mass can increase penetration and in a gunfight, you will want every available advantage. Big caliber cartridges fire the largest bullets that will cause the most damages; as long as there is a minimum of 12 inches of penetration.

The size of the gun caliber has to be considered for the second component of effective ammunition: permanent cavity. Never buy handgun ammunition based upon its ability to expand because this factor is not dependable. Additionally, the permanent cavity shows no difference between a hollow point and solid ammunition's. Again, as with penetration, the greater the mass of the bullet corresponds to the size of the permanent cavity. However, if the bullet does expand with enough penetration, there are added probabilities of the projectile touching an artery or vital organ. They are all statistical possibilities, but again you should take every advantage allowed.

Both Winchester and Speer conducted ammunition testing at the Burbank Police Departments Firearms Training Center. They fired standard ammunition from a handgun, rifle, and shotgun slugs into bare gelatin to simulate human tissue and then through interior wall material before bare gelatin. The results were as follows:

Average Penetration in Bare Gelatin

.40 S&W 180-grain Hollow Point	16.0 inches
5.56mm 55-grain FMJ	11.0 inches
12-gauge, one-ounce slug	21.0 inches

Average Penetration through Interior Wall into Bare Gelatin

.40 S&W 180-grain Hollow Point	25.0 inches
5.56mm 55-grain FMJ	06.0 inches
12-gauge, one-ounce slug	21.0 inches

If you examine the first chart of bare gelatin, the greater penetrations are from the slower handgun bullet and shotgun slug. Remember, increased bullet mass can increase penetration. The 5.56mm or .223 begins to fragmentize on impact and spreads damage by velocity energy transference exasperated by fragmentation. Because of the additional fragmentation and expansion of damage from a .223, we are not concerned with the reduced penetration. Deep penetration is only essential in handgun ammunition or sub 2000 fps rifle ammunition.

Examine the second chart where each round was first fired through an interior wall before striking the bare gelatin. The shotgun slug has the same penetration. The 5.56mm began to fragment as it hit the wall and penetrated less into the gelatin. The .40 Cal hollow point actually had a greater penetration than the first test without the wall! The hollow point filled with wall material and failed to expand, thus penetrated deeper.

Olympic arms in Washington State conducted another test. Their test mirrored that of the Burbank test results.

Caliber	Testing median	Penetration	Condition of bullet
.223	gelatin only	9.5"	two pieces
.223	wall & gelatin	5.5"	fragmented
.40 S&W	gelatin only	13.5"	mushroomed
.40S&W	wall & gelatin	22"	no deformation
12 gauge slug	wall & gelatin	27.5"	mushroomed

When inside of a house, very little is going to slow or stop that 1-ounce shotgun slug from hitting someone (The same goes with handgun ammunition). Despite what many think about the over penetrating power of a .223 caliber cartridge, the truth is actually the opposite. If you take these ballistics tests and apply them to the real world, the .223 caliber bullets are safer for use inside of a home. They also provide precision and quantity of rounds going downrange at the target. The same could be applied to "00" buckshot. The nine pellets from "00" buckshot provides an effective pattern for the short standard shot distances faced within a house.

Some agencies are discussing whether to stop issuing buckshot. Because of its standard shot spread of about 1 inch per yard, buckshot only has an effective range of between 25 and 30 yards. Some say it is much farther, yet through a smooth bore police shotgun; effective shot placement is questionable beyond this range. A shotgun slug can have an effective distance of about 100 yards. It will have an average gravitational drop of almost 5 inches at this distance. It will hold almost true at 50 yards. Therefore, for those who really want a rifle, you can have an excellent medium range rifle with your shotgun.

In a standard law enforcement patrol environment, if you are issued a 12-gauge shotgun, it should be fully loaded with slugs. However, I do believe that every officer should have "00" buckshot available. These extra shells can be carried in an elastic shell pouch on the shotgun stock or placed in a cartridge belt to throw over a shoulder. If you have to enter a home, transitioning to buckshot is better ammunition to cover the close quarter battle or CQB environment that this scenario presents. In addition to the shotgun, if your agency allows officers to carry rifles, the AR15 is very effective.

As we have seen, the .223 Cal rounds are safe inside a building or home and would assist in reducing the risk of an accidental "friendly fire" incident. For rural patrol officers, it will also give you the ability to reach out to a suspect in open country. In testing, the .223 will penetrate a windshield or door of a car. However, as we have come to expect, the bullet will begin fragmentation and energy loss on first impact. The difference is the rapid multiple round capability and range of the gun.

I said at the beginning of this chapter that there was no such thing as a measurement of knockdown power with handgun ammunition. There are some newer hunting caliber handguns like the .50 Cal and even larger designs in production. These guns fire a tremendously large bullet, which could cause greater damages than our standard weapons. However, most test only include the ammunition's which are feasible. The .45 ACP is the largest used in regular testing. The larger magnums like the .44 and above are too difficult to control to be an effective fighting weapon. Handgun ammunition does not actually have the ability to stop you in your tracks and drop you unless you are hit in the head, shutting down the central nervous system. We have been mentally trained to drop to the ground when shot because this is what is seen on television. We have mentally crippled ourselves into believing that every gunshot wound is fatal. This is far from the reality of an actual gunshot wound. According to the U.S. Centers for Disease Control and Prevention, between 1993 and 1998, there was 114,600 incidents of gunshot injuries. Of this total, less than 31% were fatal.

The FBI's Firearms Division actually tested the impact of a 9mm and a .45 ACP. They measured the muzzle velocity of each and compared the energy to a one-pound weight and then a ten-pound weight. The results showed that a one-pound weight dropped from a height of under six feet would equate to being shot by a 9mm. The ten-pound weight would have to be dropped from a distance of .72 inches. For the .45ACP, the one-pound weight dropped from a height of just over 11 feet and the ten-pound weight from 1.37 inches for equivalency. As you can see, neither of these have the actual ability to knock you down. The knock down comes from our own mental disadvantages.

We must remember that there is no physiological reason for a person to be incapacitated even by a fatal wound except central nervous system injuries. Psychological wounding incapacitates due awareness of being shot and the mental thoughts attached to it such as death, bleeding, pain etc. This is known as neurogenic shock. The mind tells the body it is dying when it is not even hurt. This is also known as emotional fainting. The will to survive often separates those who die and live. The impact of the bullet is no more than the recoil on the hand of the shooter. The ratio of bullet mass to target is too extreme.

Knock down power is the transfer of momentum to cause the target to move in response to the blow received. It does not exist.

Incapacitation is a requirement of deadly force confrontations. All advantages should go to the officer to win this fight. One of these is minor but an advantage just the same. If one caliber is large enough to destroy 0.04% of mass vs 0.07%, the later still is an advantage to hit something critical.

This demonstrates the importance of a positive winning mental edge so you can fight through the injury and survive. Understand that if you are shot, the odds are in your favor for surviving the incident. For others who fall into that defeated status, "I have been shot, I am going to die" attitude may simply will themselves to the "light." I have always said that success in this job is as much mental as it is physical.

As for off duty carry, studies show it is best to carry the same or similar gun as your on duty. This is the weapon that you are familiar with and utilize the most. You have had the opportunities to clear jams, reload, and draw. Many officers carry a completely different type of firearm when off duty. I agree with this only if you are very proficient with many hours on the range with the gun or an equally designed model. An example of this is if the Glock model 26 is your on duty weapon and the model 27 as off duty. They are both functionally identical.

If you do carry an off duty gun, it is imperative that you also carry extra magazines or speed loaders. We have already seen how often we miss in the violent explosion of an armed encounter. The ability to reload is as important as carrying the gun itself. One without the other is a definite risk to your life.

As far as our on duty weapon, most everyone is restricted to carry their department's gun. For those who still tout the effectiveness of smaller cartridges, I can only go back to the testing. You may be able to carry more rounds per magazine, but the essential elements lay with the damage done when you actually strike the target. Yes, there have been more people killed by .22 Cal LR ammunition than any other in America. However, that has to do with the cost and availability of the cartridge, rather than the power. The issue is placing a firearm in your hands that provides the greatest opportunity to stop an aggression, not if it can kill. Larger is always better. The single most important factor in handgun ammunition is penetration. Having a gun without proper penetration capabilities has caused the lives of officers. I again stress that you should never buy ammunition for its ability to expand. The greater mass of the bullet will increase the penetration as will the design. Hollow points may or may not be the best option. Explore the various manufactures of ammunition because they are not all the same.

My advice is that we will get back from something what we put into it and this includes the cost of ammunition. Based on penetration and permanent cavity as the known factors of effective handgun ammunition, bigger is better, and wins the argument.

Summary of Gun and Ammunition Choices

- Educate yourself with the science behind ballistics.
- If you are able to, carry a large caliber handgun.
- Never buy ammunition for its ability to expand.
- The two determining factors of effective handgun ammunition is penetration and permanent cavity, in that order.
- Any caliber cartridge can kill; you need effective penetration from a heavy bullet and multiple hits to vital areas to ensure that the assailant is stopped.
- Most shootings have shown that it takes at least 3.5 hits to stop someone. Practice firing in groups of four or two sets of double taps.
- .223 caliber rifle ammunition is a good choice for rural patrol and building entries. With the stock shortened, the length of the weapon will be no more than your extended hand with a handgun.
- Shotgun slugs are excellent for medium ranges up to 100 yards. They have tremendous penetrating abilities and should not be considered for building entries. A 5.56mm or "00" buckshot are better alternatives.
- Hollow point handgun ammunition will fill or wrap itself in any material before striking tissue. Even without this expansion prevention, hollow points fail to expand in 30 to 40% of the cases.
- A positive mental attitude will assist you in continuing the fight.
- When off duty, carry the same or very similar weapon as when you are on duty.
- Always carry extra magazines and/or speed loaders.
- **Study Train Survive**

Steven Varnell

OFF DUTY/PLAIN CLOTHES - 23

The mystic bond of brotherhood makes all men one.

Thomas Carlyle

I write about this topic for a very simple reason. In 2011, there were four police officers killed by gunfire while off duty. Included was three officers (one of them from the off duty status and two plainclothes officers) who were shot and killed by other police officers! This is actually a yearly average not a sad single event. What the hell is happening here? One problem is the mentality of off duty officers feeling a need to intervene in crimes in progress. The other problem is in the poor procedures of identifying yourself as a police officer.

Whenever you are off duty, evaluate any situation you encounter as to the importance of your involvement. Consider the many factors involved. Many of us have never discussed, much less mentally prepared for these situations. Therefore, when they do occur, reaction to them is the same as if you are on duty. However, you are not on duty and not easily recognized as a police officer.

According to the FBI's Law Enforcement Officers Killed and Assaulted or LEOKA reports, from 1975 to 1985, 130 off duty police officers were feloniously killed. In the three years of 1991 to 1993, 35 officers were feloniously killed while off duty. Almost half of these occurred when the officers tried to intercede in robberies. Often times, off duty officers tried to intervene in a robbery when they themselves were unarmed. Other times they tried to intervene when there were multiple suspects. In each of these situations, the odds are stacked against us.

When an officer is off duty, they are not properly equipped to handle criminal situations. They may carry a handgun, but how many carry extra magazines, handcuffs, radio, secondary weapons, body armor, or a radio. In addition, there can be confusion in the minds of other officers arriving at the scene as to your identity. Great care needs to be taken in the decision-making of the off duty officer who witnesses a crime. Are you with your family at the time? If so, could your actions place your family members in harm? What are the policies of your own agency? Even the simple act of stopping to assist disabled motorists has had its tragedies. Recently, an off duty officer was struck and killed and another was stabbed to death while trying to change a tire for someone else. In addition, you do not have emergency lighting to warn approaching traffic to slow down. Sometimes it is best if you pick up a phone and call it in to the proper authorities. There was a time when it was all right to pick up hitchhikers and stop to help strangers on the road. Today is not that time as morals, values, and respect is a thing of the past. Be smart for yourself and love ones.

Put yourself in the shoes of a responding on duty officer who arrives at the scene of a violent crime in progress and they see you holding a gun. At that very moment, what separates you from the criminal in the eyes of the officer? Several off duty officers have been shot and killed by responding officers when the bad guy dropped their weapon and the officer stood there with their gun. We are trained to never surrender our weapon. In our mind, we know we are the police and did not think to drop the gun. In the mind of the responding officer, they only see someone holding a gun which makes you an immediate threat to themselves and others!

I am not saying that you should never take police actions while in an off duty capacity. I am saying to place more thought into these actions than if you were on duty. The difference is in whether or not your inactions could be as effective as your actions. Many times while off duty, your best option will be a good witness. Unless you or another person's life is in immediate danger and you are in an armed position to take action, being a good witness is the best offensive. Think about what to do in this type of event before it happens. Are you armed? Do you have additional ammunition, your credentials, badge, and identification card? Is the act you are witnessing an immediate life-threatening event? If you observe a property crime like theft, burglary, or even a robbery, try to be a great witness. These events can easily escalate into violence. Even if the asshole is unarmed, without your secondary weapons, you are on equal ground should they resist, a position I have preached about avoiding.

If 911 is contacted, be sure to notify the operator that you are an off duty officer with a description of your clothing. Tell them everything about the events, suspects, victims, and yourself to inform the arriving officers with as much information as possible. This may sound ridiculous, but uniformed officers have killed several off duty officers over this lack of communications. If the responding uniform officers tell you to drop your weapon, immediately follow their orders. Advise them you are a police officer and the location of your credentials, but do not reach into your pockets or take any action that could cause them to take further actions.

When you are on duty and working in a plainclothes assignment, be aware of your appearance when responding to events. Just as in the off duty capacity, many on duty plainclothes officers do not have all of the necessary equipment. They should have some type of outerwear identification like raid style jackets or vest. Take for instance a recent event of a armed man call in an apartment building. The first officers on the scene encountered a man with a knife who attacked them and they shot and killed the suspect. You can only imagine the adrenaline rush of the officers on scene and the responding officers tensions as they listen to the events unfold over the radio. Responding officers want to get there as fast as possible. Immediately after the gunfire and the suspect goes down, a uniform officer sees a man running with a rifle towards the front door. He immediately thinks it is another suspect and opens fire. The man is shot in the chest and dies at the scene. He is a plainclothes detective running to help his fellow officers. He has no vest or other markings to identify himself as an officer and failed to realize how his personal appearance would affect the others on the scene.

The solutions to these events are simple. We have to think about the consequences of our actions in advance. We have to remain calm and remember when we should and should not be involved. Follow the procedures laid out by your own agencies. Failure to do so could lead to personal civil liabilities. We sometimes have to learn to be a great witness to create a safer environment for all. Control your actions and concentrate on the suspect(s) to assist the responding officers. This is the same scenario seen in the Foot Pursuit Chapter. Excitement and over reaction can lead to a poor physical identification. The on duty officers will have to face additional dangers of not knowing the correct description of the suspect. The last thing we need is unknowingly facing off with another officer. One can only imagine the strain of having to live with the actions that led to the injury or death of another officer.

Summary of Off Duty/Plainclothes

- Be very up to date on your own departments' policies about your responsibilities when off duty.
- Understand that when off duty, you are not properly equipped to handle most scenarios.
- Try some mental preparations for off duty situations to assist with a controlled response. These preparations should include understanding the off duty requirements of your agency, the type of crime, are you equipped for the event (extra magazine, clear and proper identification), and is it a life threatening crime. Property crimes should never be intervened.
- Try to resist that police officers urge to instantly jump into an event.
- You should in most cases, unless it is an imminent life or death situation, try to be a good witness for the on duty officers. Nearly half of the off duty officers killed occurred while trying to stop a robbery.
- When you pull your weapon without a uniform on or without proper identification, think how another officer would respond seeing a civilian with a gun.
- Remember you are not on duty. Follow all instructions given to you by the officers on scene.
- Several off duty or plain clothes officers are killed each year by on duty officers.
- **Study Train Survive**

BUILDING ENTRIES - 24

The absolute pacifist is a bad citizen; times come when force must be used to uphold right, justice, and ideals.

Alfred North Whitehead

Patrol officers are frequently called upon to enter homes, offices, and buildings. There is nothing routine about a building search. Tactical teams have the advantage of practicing these entries during their regular training sessions. I was assigned to our SRT (Special Response Team) for over a decade and received good training from various sources. The advantage of being assigned to these specialty units are they routinely train with other agencies. It is here officers can see advancements in equipment and tactics used by others. I am writing this section for the patrol officer, but not to exclude officers with tactical training.

As with many of the things we do in law enforcement, never enter a building alone. There are too many areas of concern and points of ambush to consider. In certain areas of the country, some agencies are so small that many of the officers are lucky to have backup. However, first decide the reason for the entry. Call in a tactical team if you know there is a person inside with a gun. They are better equipped for these types of operations. Different approaches are possible depending on the type of call you are on. You and your backup can complete calls of nonviolent crimes that require clearing the home.

The initial decisions are what type of entry is being made, what are your objectives, and compare the objectives to the risk. Once this is determined and the decision is made for the entry, be sure to have an advance meeting. I do not care how many times everyone has worked together, meet in a neutral location, and discuss the plan of action. This can be as simple as a brief talk to a detailed operational plan.

The majority of actions I was involved with were drug warrants. Others included arrest warrants, knock and talks, and several hostage situations. For the street officers, you will be involved in investigating calls for service. An alarm has sounded and you need to clear the structure or the scene of a 911 call and be advised that the suspect is still inside the house. The first course of action is to determine the type of crime involved, whether a weapon was involved, where that weapon is now, are there any other available weapons including firearms in the home and how many suspects are inside.

Next, try to gather as much information as possible regarding the layout of the house, any other suspects or victims inside, and the last known location of the suspect. Be sure to have enough officers to secure the scene and enter the home. Notify a supervisor of your plans and follow all of your departments' rules in these actions.

If needed, two officers can cover the home's exterior. Positioned at a corner of the home opposite of one another, two sides can be watched at the same time. Be sure you watch your zone from a position of cover or concealment. Once the home is secured on the outside, how to enter can be decided. Entry into the home should be through only one location to prevent any cross firing.

The house will normally be entered through an open door, however, try to use every possible access point to your advantage because the suspect will also concentrate on the doors. Try to gather some intel through quick glimpses in a window that exposes the room you are going to enter. A good extension mirror, used to search vehicles, can also be utilized. Avoid the windows if the house is dark as street lighting or simple moonlight can easily silhouette you. Again, if you believe there is an armed subject inside, avoid all windows and call for a tactical team.

The first aspect of the entry is a quick ingress and seizure of the property. Determine the size of the room to decide on the number of officers needed. For a standard home, a clear and search team of two officers per room should suffice. Placing more officers in these small areas can cause them to bunch together while trying to maneuver around the common furniture. At least one or two officers should follow the initial team. This first phase is the control phase. The officers need to make entry and rapidly secure any visible suspects. The military model of entry is acceptable. This is where the first two officers enter through the fatal funnel (so named for the area where the officer is silhouetted in the entry point as seen by anyone in the room) and turn left or right to cover the sides. The third and fourth officer can move forward, yet out of the funnel. These forward moving officers should not over step their side covering distances being provided by the first and second officers.

The first officer will move in and away from the opposite side of the door, which is hinged, or the side with the door handle. The second officer can then move in the opposite direction of the first. The initial officer, if they move in and to the right, should cover everything in the right quadrant of the room. The second officer who is moving into the opposite side of the room covers the other quadrant. The side officers need to maintain their attention to the sides to protect everyone else entering the structure from side fire. Many times a suspect will move to the sides of the entryway. If all of the officers move rapidly forward, they will pass this suspect who will then be in a dominating position behind the officers. Once inside, if there is no area to the side to cover, like a wall, move forward at the pace of the team to cover any approaching areas to your side of the room.

With the main area cleared, the teams can move toward the other rooms. The lead officer can "cut the pie" to each room before entry. By watching "slices" of the target room and sweeping past to see all angles, assures there is not a suspect in a position of ambush. Once completed, the two entry officers can enter the room. The one or two other officers can cover the unsecured areas until the entry team retreats from the room. The two officers, who enter the room, should immediately enter left and right out of the fatal funnel again. Once the main areas are cleared, they can initiate covering techniques for a more definitive search of the room.

Care should be taken when opening closet doors and cabinets because they are also fatal funnel areas. Your baton or other device can be used to open these from the side while the other officer is covering from the opposite end of the room. Do not bunch together and keep talking to a minimum. Noise control is important for making it difficult for the suspect to know exactly where you are in the house. Always enter a structure with a flashlight, even in the day light hours because the areas searched are usually dark. Once the room has been secured, the search team can reenter the hallway with the cover officer(s) and repeat the process again until the structure has been secured.

This has been a quick overview of the basic processes involved in this type of action. It is imperative to discuss and try to obtain at least annual practice on the current techniques of structure clearing.

Definitive instructions need to be in place for officers as to when to call in a tactical team and/or supervisor. If any of these instructions are contrary to your agencies directives, always follow the departments' policies. However, if anyone feels a specific policy should be readdressed, they should take action through the appropriate chain of command. It is not about right or wrong, it is about safety.

Summary of Building Searches

- Determine the nature of the entry and whether it should be conducted by a tactical team.
- Determine the size of the structure to be searched to ascertain the number of officers needed.
- Have an advanced plan so everyone understands their specific role.
- The exterior can be covered with a minimum of two officers on opposite corners.
- Simple entries should be made by three to four officers. The military option is acceptable with the first officer in moving opposite the hinged or the door handled side. The second to the opposite direction of the first. The third and fourth moves in and forward, yet out of the fatal funnel of the doorway. These officers have to be careful not to over advance their side cover. The side officers are to cover the sides until clear to advance.
- Rapidly clear the areas for any suspects in plain sight to secure the premises.
- Have the lead officer "cut the pie" at all doorways to assess the open areas of the rooms.
- No more than two officers to enter each room. One to search and the other to cover. Additional officers maintain cover of the unsecured rooms.
- Stay out of fatal funnels which include all cabinets and closets.
- **Study Train Survive**

Steven Varnell

S.T.E.P's

Stress, Training, Empirical Perspective's

Introduction

I have spent most of my life in the pursuit of discovering and presenting police officers around the country training, tactics, techniques, and explanations of various approaches to situations involved in the profession of law enforcement. Law enforcement is a profession like no other. With service provided to every square inch of our country 24 hours a day and 365 days a year, no other profession can compare. It is part of the excitement of the job as each day starts with a mystery of the events to come and how each will end.

Societal events take place which requires the police officer to re-evaluate what they know. Then a determination is required as to the best way to use this information. It is a learning curve with no end. I have always said that the day we quit learning it is the day to stop to prevent hurting yourself or someone else. Outrageous events take place around the world that requires continual fine-tuning.

Agencies are always looking for practices to use to protect themselves in these litigious times and not always in the best interest of the officers. Police officers must understand and accept this simple fact. They must self-prepare to face the dangers of the street because most agencies do not have the resources to do everything necessary. As with any other profession, police officers must step outside the box of departmental education and strengthen their areas of weakness. Many organizations around the world are always testing and evaluating law enforcement tactics. They use studies based on real life events to determine if alternatives existed, that could have prevented officers from becoming victims.

It is along this informational path that created this collection of my books with expanded chapters. I have produced four books, *Criminal Interdiction, Tactical Survival, Behavior Analysis and Interviewing Techniques, and Statement Analysis*. I have taught these topics extensively throughout the United States.

Our lives are defined by millions of tiny decisions and only a few big ones. We tend to focus on the big ones, but it is the tiny decisions that stack up over time and define who we are.

From Sealfit by Mark Divine

Stress - 25

Stress is a reaction to a stimulus that disturbs our physical or mental equilibrium. Even though stress lets us know we are alive, it can have both positive and negative effects on our everyday lives. Our responses are controlled as stress amps up our survival and performance levels. Allowed to over exert, and stress becomes our first enemy in a dangerous life-threatening event. Once we know how stress affects the system, we can counter any negative effects.

How the brain works in relation to perception, based on memory exemplifies object/action recognition. Our brain must analyze the observation and compare the results based on the information stored in the brain. Three components make up memory functions; the Short Term Sensory Store (STSS), the Short Term Memory (STM), and the Long Term Memory (LTM).

The brain receives the relevant data via the sensory nervous system (i.e. sight, sound etc.). This information goes into the Short Term Sensory Store, which holds a picture for 5 to 15 seconds depending on the intensity of the stimulus. The Short Term Memory (STM) then processes the information. The Short Term Memory analyzes the stimulus (information) and evaluates it to the relevance to the moment. Based on the results of this evaluation the STM will develop a motor response best suited to the moment based on its experience. In the event that the STM does not have any readily available data to cross-reference to, it will begin to search the Long Term Memory (LTM) for a similar situation to develop a suitable response. This all takes time.

The amygdala is that portion of our brain that stores information related to fear and emotional responses. If your amygdala recognizes a threat, it will bypass the cortex or our normal processing regions and initiate the Sympathetic Nervous System (SNS). The SNS is part of our Autonomic Nervous System that is divided between the Parasympathetic Nervous System (PNS) and the Sympathetic Nervous System. We can view them as the ying and the yang of our emotions. The SNS fires off our excitement emotions and the PNS relaxes us.

After passing through the amygdala, which initiates protective reflex, sensory information goes to the cortex to determine if a real threat exists. It is our brains back up plan. Is this a real or false alarm? Based upon this information return after a quick check, the amygdala is signaled to either continue the physical response and deal with the threat or abort action. Note it is a physical response.

As discussed with the OODA Loop Concept, Hicks Law, one of two psychomotor skills of the autonomic nervous system, determines the speed of your response based on the number of reactionary options, which exist in your memory. Fewer reactionary options equates to a faster response. Since action is always faster than reaction, any timesaving's is a benefit.

Because the amygdala is aroused before the cortex can accurately assess the situation, an individual will experience the physical effects of fear even in the case of a false alarm. These self-preservation actions, the acute stress response system, activate. The hypothalamus (midbrain) controls stress and is triggered upon danger recognition by the amygdala activating the pituitary gland next to it.

The pituitary gland does two things: It sends a message to the adrenal medulla (adrenal gland) and gets the body ready for the fight or flight syndrome and then sends a chemical, ACTH to the adrenal cortex, another region of the adrenal gland. The adrenal cortex releases corticosteroids into the bloodstream that causes the liver to release glucose, inhibits immune response for inflammation and white blood cell production, and converts fats/protein into glucose.

The adrenal medulla triggers the sympathetic nervous system that releases adrenaline. This adrenaline release causes increases in heart rate and breathing, slows digestion, dilates the pupils, releases glucose into the blood stream, and causes the fluid production systems to slow. These fluid reductions affect teardrops and saliva production. This is why someone who is observed rapidly blinking their eyes or constantly licking their lips is indicative of high stress.

Our heart rate is the determining factor of stress and its effect on our systems. To overcome the effects of high stress involves controlling our heart rate. When your heart rate accelerates from a standard of 60-80 beats per minute (bpm) up to 115-145 bpm, this is known as the optimal survival and performance level for complex motor skills, visual, and cognitive reaction time. This is when we perform at our peak. However, with this increased heart rate you have lost your fine motor skills. A fine motor skill would include any action that requires precision hand eye coordination, such as precision shooting with a firearm.

Our heart rate accelerates as the threat and stress of a situation increases. Above 145 bpm, complex motor skills, which include a combination of complex muscle groups and include shooting stances or takedowns that have multiple components, begin to diminish.

At a heart rate of 175 bpm or above, only our gross muscle skills – simple strength skills, push, pull, and run operate. These are the large muscle groups only.

Over 145 – 175 bpm, peripheral vision which detects motion, provides night vision and depth perception begins to lessen as focus is directed to sharpen your center gaze focus via pupil dilation and lens flattening. The auditory systems begin to fade as focus accentuates upon our primary sensory option, sight. A loss of so many mental and physical skills can mean the loss of ability to talk on the radio, reload a magazine, provide medical care, etc.

There are four heart rate categories

- Resting 60-80 beats per minute (bpm)
- 115-145 bpm – optimal combat losing fine motor skills
- 145-175 bpm – losing complex motor skills
- 175+ bpm – only gross motor skills are functioning yet functioning better than ever

The increase in heart rate and breathing initiates vasoconstriction. As the arteries opens, the heart pumps more arterial blood to the heart to transport the extra glucose required by our muscles. The digestive system starts to shut down along with other fluid producing systems to protect the core. Cognitive thought fades as we move into auto functioning. Our forebrain, which controls our voluntary movements, speech, pleasure, pain, blood pressure, thirst, and visceral functions, turn off as we begin to function within our midbrain.

Above 175 bpm, begins irrational freeze, fright, flight, or fight reactions and voiding of the bladder and bowels. It is normal to urinate or defecate on oneself when highly stressed. This is full sympathetic nervous system activation. Most people are familiar with the flight or fight syndrome, but most are unaware that it is actually the freeze, fright, flight, and fight syndrome. Once the intense startle occurs, there is initially a freeze as the brain processes what is happening. As this processes, the heart rate in response to the SNS activation accelerates to the level of the threat and creates the fright response. As with all creatures, if given a chance to flee or flight, we will. Only a police officer loses this option. It is not our job to flee. We can make a tactical retreat but only to try to regain the advantage. Then comes the fight and pain becomes a factor only after a stressful event concludes.

Your training develops around reflex and gross motor skills once we understand they are the only skills that function correctly. With the loss of fine motor skills, combat shooting skills are required. With the loss on complex motor skills, strikes and kicks become our defensive tactics. This includes weapon retention drills.

Knowing that your heart rate is responsible for these losses, there are ways to control it. It is important not to allow your heart rate to climb too much higher than 145 bpm. To combat the negative effects of stress is through tactical breathing or autogenic breathing.

It is believed that when we are rapid breathing, we are trying to take in more oxygen. This is a semi truth. We are always trying to take in more oxygen but, when we are breathing rapidly; our breaths are too short. Rapid breathing causes you not to take in as much oxygen as is needed. In stress, your body uses up the oxygen causing cells to produce lactic acid. This lactic acid converts to carbon dioxide and releases through your lungs. Rapid breathing is actually your system trying to remove the excessive carbon dioxide more so than take in extra oxygen.

Autogenic breathing is the most effective measure to reverse some of these symptoms. How does autogenic breathing work? It is a form of the Valsalva maneuver which if you have ever flown may have utilized. When your ears clog up, the most effective way to clear them is by holding your nose and blowing. This equalizes the pressure between your ears and sinuses

Another way to use this to slow down our heart rate is by increasing pressure in the chest cavity, which increases pressure on the vagus nerve, which supplies nerve fibers to the heart. Pressure on the nerve signals the heart to slow down. According to Dr. Andrew Dennis, who is a trauma surgeon, police officer, SWAT team member, and author of *"Officer Down! A Practical Tactical Guide to Surviving Injury in the Street,"* there is a specific technique to use. Hold your tongue against the roof of your mouth and inhale through your nose. As you inhale, hold your breath, bear down through your chest, and extend your abdomen as if taking a bowel movement. The diaphragm muscle, which is between the chest and abdomen, is forced down, and extended, allowing maximum oxygenation into the chest and held when inhaling.

Exhale forcefully through pursed lips. Exhaling pushes the diaphragm muscle back up expelling the used air.

Studies have found that a 3-cycle count of autogenic breathing decreases one's heart rate up to 30% for up to 40 seconds. At 175-220 bpm, autogenic breathing would help bring them back down into that target range of 115-145 bpm. This is also why unhealthy people with heart disease die on the toilet when pushing a bowel movement. The weakened heart is slowed and stopped.

Other ways are:

- Skill Confidence: This takes place through both mental and physical training
- Dynamic Simulation Training: Increases and builds confidence - reduces "newness" of stimulus
- "Realistic" stimulus/response training with doses of stress to help inoculate against it.
- Visualization (mental imagery)

Peripheral vision is a part of the vision that occurs outside the very center of gaze. It is for detecting motion, our night vision, and depth perception. Our peripheral vision sees motion around us and the brain will provide attention to a motion on our perimeter. Tunnel vision is the loss of peripheral vision while maintaining center of gaze.

Stress causes the brain to focus attention to the center of gaze essentially turning off our peripheral vision. Once this occurs, you can no longer recognize a threat flanking your position. It is also the primary reason not to deal directly with more than one person and to maintain distance. Once your focus is distracted to the actions of one person and the other tries to assault, you will not see the actions of the other suspect in time.

The visual system is the primary sensory organ of the body because the visual system sends needed information to the brain during combat for self-protection. At approximately 175 bpm, a person will experience an eyelid lift; pupils will dilate and flatten causing a loss in depth perception and experience visual narrowing (commonly known as tunnel vision). It is also now, that a person becomes "binocular" rather than "monocular." This can improve one's depth perception by 20-30%. Because of this fact, while combat shooting, we must teach only two eye "binocular" shooting rather than one eye aimed shooting.

At approximately 175 bpm, it is normal for a person to have difficulty remembering what took place or what they did during a confrontation. "Critical Stress Amnesia" is a common recall problem. After a critical incident, it is common for a person to only recall approximately 30% of what happened in the first 24 hours; 50% in 48 hours; and 75-95 % in 72-100 hours. Firing more shots than someone remembers is a common occurrence. Firing additional rounds as the subject tries to flee or falls is common. This change in violence, which precipitated the shots, requires the brain processing and reaction to stop. During controlled testing with electronic timers, 20 LEO's were told to shoot as many shots as possible between two audible signals. 17 or 85% of the 20 fired one or two shots after given the signal to stop.

The worst factor experienced in high stress scenarios is memory. It is difficult even in the most nonthreatening situation. It becomes worse as the incident becomes volatile. *"In Defense of Self and Others,"* by Urey W. Patrick and John C. Hall, states that, "Startling in onset, brief in duration, and sudden in termination," is a deadly force encounter.

They described memory as, "Memory is constructed from stored bits of information we unconsciously fill in with inferences. When all of the parts are filled in that make sense to us, we call this memory. Memory relates to visions. Due to center gaze focus after a horrific event, memory is incomplete and gap filled. The memory will try to repair these. All memory involves reconstruction. We connect pieces not well connected and then make judgments as to whether or not they fit. We are not aware when this happens but is normal. Our memory is constantly updating itself, pushing pieces of events around, filing them in incorrect orders and emptying parts not used."

Tachypsychia is a neurological condition that alters the perception of time, usually induced by physical exertion, drug use, or a traumatic event and results in unreliable mental track. This includes Time Space distortion/ Memory loss - slow motion – what did I do? When our SNS activates fine motor skills and dexterity diminish in favor of major muscle groups. Stress alters perceptions of events. People who witness an event may see more and not understand how an officer thought this and that. Various officers may call out commands from which lawsuits will claim training issues and incompetence exist. Our conscious mind is a hindrance in a stressful scenario and our subconscious takes over in a threat event. Habits and reactions created through training and experience takes over.

Our memories are not comprehensive and are vulnerable to post event information and suggestions. It is not always exactly repeatable. It only provides the outline and the mind fills in the rest. Change is probable and indicative of the truth. Consistent, unfailing recollections are more indicative of a lie script.

Training - 26

As a Greek philosopher once said;

"We do not rise to the level of our expectations; we fall to the level of our training."

Contrary to public belief, training for law enforcement is almost nonexistent. Agencies are unable to provide all of the necessary training that any officer requires to help them do their job safely. Because this is a 24/7/365 job, few agencies can afford to have their officers "down" for training. Annually and sometimes bi-annually, agencies require their officers to complete the minimally necessary training courses required by their State. This is like making a minimum payment.

About 150 police officers are killed yearly and 60,000 assaulted resulting in over 16,000 injuries. The need for practical and reasonable training has to become mandatory. If not by the agencies, then the officers themselves must self-prepare. It is not a morbid fascination in death, but knowing how cops die lays the groundwork for how to train them to survive.

We have to recognize where those needs are and address them. To find them we can start at two places. One is the areas that I teach to address in recognizing danger signs. These areas are what I call Critical Observations. Since 50% on average of all police deaths have a traffic component, we have to watch for brake lights and turn signals. These cues are indicative of their mindset. They are overly concerned with your presence and not on paying attention to their actions.

Next, we can look at a related issue I call command repetition. Once we have made contact with a subject, if they are paying attention to us they will respond to any directions you provide. Once you have to start repeating your request, they have begun to internalize and are not following your request. If this occurs repeatedly, this is a strong danger signal. It indicates that they are operating primarily in the internal dialogue, which is the weakest of the Representational Channels.

The last two areas involve asking questions. They are directed closed in questions that require a simple yes or no answer. "Have you ever been arrested?" If they answer yes, ask them to tell you about all of their arrest. Only 3% of cop killers have no criminal history.

The next question is, "Do have a weapon on you now?" Their subconscious will often give you a signal that they have a weapon and where it is located. Their hand or arm will lightly tap it or they may look down at it.

According to Urey W. Patrick and John C. Hall, noncompliance is the first and most common danger sign after the encounter has initiated. The context of the event is essential. Is there prior knowledge of the subjects' actions, the offense under investigation, and any preceding events that have occurred? They like to ratchet up our concerns based on the number of issues present. Two or more danger signs such as noncompliance and failure to show hands are signs of immediate danger. Any additional signals are indicative of imminent danger such as aggressive movements, surprise actions, or the presence of other individuals. A similar strategy is also used in combat hunter techniques, which are covered in this chapter.

Police officers are not responsible for the actions of subjects they confront, regardless the subjects intentions. They are only accountable for a reasonable response to what that subject chose to do. Everything that any of us do daily is based on the choices we made. Bad guys like to blame this cause or that catalyst, but it is only about that specific choice they choose to make at that moment. If the result is not what someone thought it should be, regardless of the twisted reviews of the media and others, all rest solely on the shoulders of the individual who created the events that led to the results. Do to pressures of past events and the inability to depend on the support of our administrations, officers will accept a level of risk to their own safety that is unnecessary while failing to deploy the required force.

A 15-year study by the FBI found that the bad guys:

- Will often show signs of being armed that we miss.

- Have more experience in deadly force use.
- Will not hesitate to use a weapon.
- Primarily handguns were preferred.
- No gun law had ever deterred any of the offenders.
- Practice more often with their firearms - Most offenders averaged 23 handgun practices each year.
- LEO's averaged 2.5 per YEAR.
- 50% prior gun battle; 7% LEO.
- They preferred to carry their gun without the hindrance of a holster in their waistband. 93% of cop killers carried their gun in the front waistband, 3% in the small of their back.
- Practice fast draws and 60% shoot instinctive styles to draw first, fast, and start putting lead downrange.
- We lose 70% of our gun battles.
- 50% of bad guys carry a backup weapon .
- 12% for the victim officers.
- Criminals show no remorse to the use of a firearm. We are given 3 days leave.
- Over 70% of officers have been involved in a situation where deadly force was justified, but they failed to react. This causes additional complacencies which could affect their future decisions towards their own demise. "I did not have to shoot last time and I did alright."

In cases of specialized training requirements like deadly force encounters, a combat mindset and shooting style is required. We must distinguish between qualification shooting and training. Annually or bi-annually, we go to the range and shoot a standardized target course to demonstrate our ability to carry a gun on duty. It does not prepare us to use a gun in a gunfight. This requires training, which is when those who are qualified can take those skills and learn new ones in realistic and job specific lessons.

Training must focus on speed first and accuracy second because law enforcement loses nearly 70% of shootouts. Qualifications have its focus on accuracy. When 81% of all shootings occur in less than 21 feet, the first person to fire and hit their opponent will probably win. Almost 70% occur in less than 10 feet and 60% occur in 5 feet or less. The person who shoots first has the advantage. We have a hit ratio of less than 20%, which means a miss ratio of greater than 80% with an average of 10 rounds fired per event! Little has changed in the centuries of this country when we see that in the old west most gunfights occurred in between 10-20 ft.

Practice is mandatory with our level 3 high security holsters. This was the simplistic logic of our agencies to deal with having about 10% of officers killed with their own gun. Instead of training them offensive aggressive techniques in the hand-to-hand combatives to prevent having the gun taken, they choose to make the gun difficult to draw from the holster. Considering speed is the essential element of gun fighting, this appears and is wrong. However, since most agencies now require this style holster, they must be required to draw it regularly to develop the correct muscle memory to respond in a high stress event. Of course, this is not the case. Few ever draw their weapon except during their required once or twice a year qualifications. This is also the fact that is driving the research today to move the security of the holster to a level 2. With a lot of practice, we can speed up our draw from the level 3 holster, but we all know how often we will all practice. This makes the level 2 more practical.

The FBI determined that qualifications are require at least 4 times per year to maintain basic skills. Additional training is required to make these officers efficient in their skills. A sufficient multifaceted training program has to encompass tactical issues, judgmental, survival, and high stress realizations. Only the training staff will like it when a training curriculum is its qualifications course. Everyone qualifies and it makes them look good but, it does a disservice to the officers as they only complete routine goals.

Proper training is a well-rounded course designed like this: Qualify first. Get this mandatory skill set determination out of the way so training can begin. Perform stress courses that vary on training days. When possible, train with dynamic force on force scenarios. Practice fast draws (How many hang up in their security holsters). Train with the Instinctive shooting concept - target focus, draw and point at the target to initiate the muscle memory skills. Start with an empty gun and sight on the target, not the sights. Practice live fire from a low ready position, not pushed out from the body. Pushing the gun away from the body can cause the shot to go low. Fire single rounds from the 3-yard line into the target, without looking at the sights and watch where they hit and make fine adjustments to improve each shot. Fire instantly as your hands comes into view while the gun comes to target. Move to double taps, triple taps, and then two double taps.

As you improve, move back, not to the 7-yard line, but one-step back. Get used to shooting at various distances other than the standard yardages. Practice this repeatedly until the majority of your shots are effective. You can continue to move back to the maximum distance of the 7-yard line, which is 21 feet away. Combat shooting begins to lose effectiveness beyond the 15-yard line. This is the perfect place to stop considering over 81% of our shootouts occur within this range.

Teach each component of a specific tactic separately in the static mode. Then we pick up the pace and practice the movements repetitiously and half speed. We are developing the stimulus-response training principle, which means many repetitions (muscle memory) in response to a given stimulus.

Dynamic training is the final stage of training that is full speed role-playing and tests the student's ability to respond to a particular type of resistance. These scenarios can change regularly so the trainees never get used to a routine.

Have participants go through a scenario as many times as necessary in order to succeed. Scenarios designed to make the trainee look foolish or fail prove that the training designers are in the wrong profession. Never trash talk students. Never talk about mistakes made by other students. Criticize in private, praise in public. Encourage participants not to worry over a 'bad' day of training. Fix the problem, correct the deficiency, strive to improve and move on. Encourage everyone to habituate this practice on their own.

Most importantly, the number of rounds fired or time spent on the range should not judge training. Effective training is frequent sessions of specific actions. As a state trooper, much of my exposure was in and around motor vehicles. With this, much of my firearms training needed to be around cars. Yet, in over 29 years, we rarely trained around cars. We are all in a vehicle at some point, so I have to ask how much training has any of you attempted from inside your car. Have you tried to draw your weapon from within a car with the seatbelt on? You will discover how difficult and if the first time you try or attempt having not tried this in a long time, your response will be poor. First, as you reach for the weapon grip, use your left hand to release the seatbelt and twist to the left. This will bring your weapon out and away from the seatbelt receiver, center console or other items in the way. Now you can draw the weapon with options to use when faced with various threats. Practice what you would do if someone was beside you, approaching your window both driver and passengers side, at an angle to the front or trying to come through the window after you. Practice various techniques until you are satisfied which works best for you. We all carry our weapon differently with different holster security measures and holster placement. As a K9 handler, I carried my weapon in a thigh holster, which made it easier to remove from the seated position of the vehicle. In addition to our holsters, our agencies equip our vehicles differently. Train in the best measures for your fastest response.

Training for the high liability issues is paramount. We have discussed the needs of close quarter hand on combatives and the requirement to stay on your feet and never go to the ground in an aggressive fight. (Refer to the "Hands On" Chapter previously covered) I believe that we should all take self-defense courses because it places additional tools in our tool belts. Understanding our limitations due to stress is critical to the training standards. All deadly force incidents are fluid, unpredictable and entail unanticipated random developments that require LEO's to adapt and resolve.

In high stress, our eyes, which are normally convex, begin to flatten for center gaze focus, known as tunnel vision. This causes us to lose our peripheral vision. With the loss of peripherals, you lose night vision and near sightedness. Binocular shooting assist with the night vision and is necessary in shooting less than 25 feet. Once tunnel vision occurs, you have to shoot from instinct due to a loss of complex motor skills. Sight focus and alignment will not work. You must respond with motor programming developed only with training.

Fitt's Law is a model of human psychomotor behavior based on time and distance. It enables the prediction of human movement and human motion based on rapid, aimed movement. Fitt's Law states that where time is critical, speed increases and sacrifices accuracy. This is particularly pertinent to technique selection in a survival stress situation. The larger or closer the target is to you, the faster your response. Smaller or farther requires slower more careful aiming. This is the rule that necessitates the combat instinctive shooting technique. Fitt's Law provides us a rapid and accurate survival response to a close up threat. The closer and more imminent the threat, the more immediate your need to fire is.

Sight shooting is only effective in the following areas:

- Time to shoot
- The distance of the shot
- Cover available and used
- A stationary target

Shoot only as fast as you can achieve good shots. Habituated training improves the speed.

A Force on Force study for Urban Combat, completed in 2013 by the Royal Military Academy, found that soldiers ready to ship out, had specific training. They conducted solo building clearing first on paper targets and second with live subjects with Simunitions. Soldiers knew exactly what they were to face inside prior to entry. It discovered that they were 30% less accurate in the second phase. Their stress levels and heart rates were significantly higher when they knew they would face an individual and not a paper target. These test proved the need of stress habituation.

When faced with a deadly force situation, survival depends on the officer to continue shooting until the threat is stopped. All officers hear this training axiom throughout their career at the qualification and training ranges. However, our qualifications are designed around specific number of rounds fired throughout. Then we will move into a training session with limited ammunition and told to fire specific numbers of bullets at a target. This completely misses training our officers who need to fire more than one or two rounds at a target. It can be used with multiple threats when an officer is required to fire at them one at a time. Determine the immediate threat, fire a minimum of two rounds, and move to the next returning to the original once the second threat is stopped. Even if not stopped, this may pause the attacker and allow the officer to transition to others.

Training only with full frontal unobstructed targets as is the range practice, can result in uncertainty, hesitations, and a failure to respond properly to a threat. This is the disadvantage of center mass shooting practices. It is better to focus on the center of whatever a target presents. Target whatever is presented as a target and shoot for multiple hits. When required to shoot at targets as various angles where only certain parts are visible and then after some physical stress is added by physical activity, we will see who is best prepared to face this common real-life challenge.

Only a minimal of qualification and almost no training is conducted with our shoulder weapons. In a high stress situation, though it is our best weapon to deploy. Demonstrate their accuracy differences by requiring officers to run the same course with a handgun and then a shoulder gun. Transitioning between them can also be effective.

Since speed of response is critical to our survival, we can explore reactions. Our reaction to an action taken against us is comprised of three areas, decision time, response time, and mechanical time.

Decision Time is the accumulation of that time necessary to perceive a stimulus. The visual start point was the starting point and the muzzle flash was the end. .576 seconds was the average for easy threat recognition. By deducting .365 seconds (response/mechanical time), we are left with .211 seconds as the decision time.

Response Time is the time required for the brain to send the required nerve signals to the necessary muscle group to respond.

Mechanical Time is the time necessary for the bodily movement's response to occur.

Decision and Response times occur only once in a reaction time sequence while Mechanicals can accumulate with repetitive responses. Reaction time is the time necessary to recognize a stimulus, decide upon an action, then initiate, and complete the response. OODA is reaction time. (See the OODA Loop Chapter starting on page 279). Most deadly force confrontations start and end within three seconds. In testing of Reaction time with their gun on target and finger on the trigger, with an anticipated response using firearms testing, the best-estimated response time was 0.7 seconds. Decision time was about 0.3 seconds and 0.4 seconds is the response/mechanical time. This is the time between the signal to shoot and the muzzle blast of the weapon. The officers knew what was going to take place and had their weapon drawn with their finger on the trigger. This eliminates their reaction and decision times because they were pre-determined.

Decision/response/mechanical reaction times all require time. The mechanical average is .3-.4 seconds. Reaction time is based upon what is and is not expected from an event. A best-case total expectation has a total time of 0.7 a second. Of this, 0.5 second is decision time while 0.2 seconds is response. A surprised event is 1.25 − 1.5 seconds. 1 second is decision time.

Forty six officers had their weapons drawn and on the target ready to fire. Using electronic timers, an audible signal sounded and stopped at the sound of the muzzle blast. Each fired three rounds with their fingers on the triggers and three off trigger. Recognition and decision was removed from the formula this way. There was a reactionary gap of .365 seconds (response time) on trigger and .677 seconds off trigger. These are the response/mechanical times to fire a shot. In video testing of shooting incidents, this response/mechanical time is consistently 0.3-0.4 seconds.

Stress alone and choice options increase reaction by 50-100% training and experience can help reduce these hesitations experienced by officers. Drawing your weapon from holster can add another 0.5 - 1.5 seconds for a total time of up to 3 seconds.

In 0.7 − 1 seconds is the accepted standard for an officer to first recognize another's actions and in that time an unseen weapon can be raised and fired several times. We must recognize the threat has stopped and decide to stop shooting (decision time). The nerve impulses must send a signal from the brain to the gun hand (response time) to stop pulling the trigger. Then the gun hand has to stop pulling the trigger. Typically, this requires 0.5-1.0 seconds. This explains why officers continue to fire several rounds even after the threat has stopped.

Officers can only react to the actions of a subject, not read what their intentions are. 64% of officers who were the victim of violent and potentially deadly attacks were not aware of the attack. Of the 36% who were aware of the pending attack stated that they had no time to prepare. Law enforcement officers are always in the position of reacting to what their adversary does.

In a surprised event, reaction time was 1.25 seconds due to an increased decision time of .85 seconds as the mechanical/response time remains constant at 0.4 seconds. Decision time alone was longer than total response of an expected event. The secret to time compression is Hicks Law – the time it takes a person to make a decision because of the choices available. In Reaction Time, the best response occurs when the choices are minimalized. The fastest response occurs with one choice. Each additional choice adds 58% more time. We have to train in specifics to avoid this lag time. As we will learn, the OODA Loop principle reinforces us to train in the most effective measures based on proven facts. It initiates us mentally to be more efficient in behavior recognition and the appropriate response to those actions.

Dr. Gary Klein developed Recognition-Primed Decision Making or RDMP. It focuses on the importance of experience to our decision making. He found that two processes: the way decision makers' size up the situation to recognize which course of action makes sense, and the way they evaluate the course of action by imagining it affects their decisions.

Decisions evolve with circumstances. Some decisions are made simply, with more time to decide, other decisions require quick if-then thinking in order to achieve results. Rapidly changing circumstances that allow little time for making a decision is the norm for law enforcement. If not prepared through training, education, and experience, time sensitive decisions are not made properly and effectively, and the advantage then goes to the adversary.

Training must be simulated situational stress and threat recognition based. We are seeking responses that require a rapid sequence of recognition, decision, and action performances that involve reaction skills. An expert based on experience and training may not make a better decision but they will make a faster decision.

Speed is our training focus. Even if you are a better shot and/or gun handler, allowing the bad guy to advance too far without taking action places you at a distinct disadvantage that you may not recover from.

Think about specific training topics and how it is taught to occur after you are in trouble. Weapon retention begins after they grab your gun. Defensive tactics after they grab you or shooting after they have the advantage. Training in preparation of these events decreases critical time to your success.

Behavior understanding and recognition are so important that the military created their combat profiling or hunter program. The military developed the program as a response to defend troops from IED's and other threats. Prior to its creation, the military answer to IED's and other attacks was heavier armor, which is treating the symptoms not the cause. Our holster design is a symptomatic answer to the 10% plus number of officers killed with their own weapon.

According to retired Marine Officers Patrick Van Horne and Jason Riley in their book, "Left of Bang," combat profiling is analyzing a person's behavior to determine their emotions and intentions. They explain that there are two requirements – mindset to actively search your area for people that don't fit in and knowledge to know what causes someone to stand out from the crowd. Intuition is a person's sense of a situation based on training and experience, which has been proven repeatedly with the RDMP as effective. It allows no deliberations, just actions.

There are six domains of the process. These domains are

- Kinesics or the observation of people's behavior. Baseline establishments determine the characteristics used to classify a person. A Kinesic anomaly is a person's behavior that does not fit their baseline – too dominate or submissive or very uncomfortable. Kinesic slips are when someone's behavior betrays their words. Watch how we get up and check to make sure we have our keys, wallets, phones etc. Bad guys do the same with their weapons and contraband

- Biometric cues or the characteristics that exist because of stress, such as heartrate, perspiration, etc. They are the SNS reactions to stress. The eyes are one of the cues and have three biometric measures, pupil dilation/constriction, blinking, and tunnel vision. A person's normal blink rate is 6-10 times per minute. Shivering, arm, chest rubbing, and arms across the chest are all symptomatic of the SNS sending blood to the major muscles and organs. This causes the person to feel cold.

- Proxemics involve two elements – distance based on relationships or attitudes and movement to, from, or idle. Movements to, is a proxemics pull and away is a proxemics push. When someone is trying to get close it is a proxemics pull or to get away from something a push. Allowing them too close means a limited reaction time, increasing the subject's options to assault and they require less skill. A businessman who is scolded by a superior may move his chair back or sit back and pull their feet under the chair. Proxemics push baselines are determined by watching how people interact with one another. As you pull into an area, we may see people suddenly begin to move which is a push and ask why

- Geographic's are an area that someone is familiar with and will move through with confidence and fluidity. Uncomfortable is someone not familiar with the area. You must see how people move through an area to obtain a baseline. In Geographic's, we are watching for Natural Lines of Drift (NLD's). These are the areas people are familiar and will commonly travel. Bad guys have an advantage of knowing the lay of the land. We have to watch for their common paths of travel. People will travel a path that is safest, simple, and obstacle free. These paths are not always the shortest. The neighborhood knows the avoidance areas. People do not move randomly through areas. Criminals have habitual areas that they can move to and commit their acts like malls and anchor points where they go for safety like home or a clubhouse. Humans are territorial and always claim turf. People are more vulnerable when they are on the move. The identification and elimination of anchor points is critical to keeping them on the move. Using geographic profiling, we can see where people are committing the most crimes (habitual locals) and discover their NLD's back to their anchor points. As creatures of habit, they will continue to commit crimes the same way and travel the same NLD's.

- Iconography is visual language with symbols placed on people and in environment. The three main types are Tattoos, t-shirts, and graffiti. Timothy McVeigh wore a t-shirt the day he was arrested that said on front, "sic semper tyrannis" (Thus always to tyrants) which is what John Wilkes Booth yelled after killing Lincoln. On the back was a Thomas Jefferson quote – "The tree of liberty must be refreshed from time to time with the blood of patriots and tyrants."

- Atmospherics are the moods and emotions of the people in the area. Are they nervous or relaxed? When they are anxious and afraid something has occurred or is about to occur. Emotions and moods are driven by the autonomic and subconscious. The amygdala is the part of the brain that recognizes mood and emotion and since it occurs in our sub conscious, we will feel the change before we realize it. That funny feeling you get.

- Order and disorder affects the way an area looks. "The Broken Window Theory" says that even one element of disorder, graffiti, and old bike chained to a fence, of garbage on the street creates other disorder and attracts criminal elements.

Each of these domains is examined once there is an establishment of baselines. Baselines and anomalies exist because we are creatures of habit and baselines are those normal patterns. Anomalies are changes in normal.

The key to responding well to a situation is knowing when to make a decision, knowing what decisions to make, and rehearsing those decisions so that when it comes to act, your actions are immediate and spontaneous. This all falls back to our own situational awareness. Situational awareness is understanding both the physical and environmental around you. We must have mental preparedness to take action, even deadly action.

Heuristics experience-based techniques are for rapid problem solving, learning, and discovery that find a solution, which is just good enough for survival. Heuristic methods are used to speed up the process of finding a satisfactory solution through cognitive shortcuts. Examples of this method include using a rule of thumb, an educated guess, common sense, or specific training techniques. We will learn that heuristics plays a part in our interviewing techniques. Since it is based on general acceptance rules, it can cause us to see everyone as guilty before proven innocent.

Heuristic decision-making will help in determining thresholds of decision. These are necessary once enough characteristics are recognized. In combat, like interviewing, it is the rule of three. When at least three anomalies are observed, you must take action. Dominant /submissive, uncomfortable/comfortable, interested/uninterested (where their interest lies compared to what it should be, pretending to do something.) are some of these anomalies. Dominants make you look larger, feet spread, legs out seated, hands behind head, on hip, stretching to be taller, finger pointing, eye gaze, proxemics, and touch. Uncomfortable – legs crossed to block, leaning towards the door, eye glancing, feet bouncing, increased pacifiers. Any three clusters of indicators have to be investigated. However, just like in a field interviews, if the threat is there, action can proceed after one characteristic if it is a threat to you or another.

The military follows a decision pattern of kill, capture, or contact. They have to be ready to kill, and if not needed, determine if they are a threat or of intelligence value and if not, simply make contact with them. For police it is shoot, arrest, or question. This is the opposite of our former threat continuum. In a dangerous situation is easier to back down from a decision to kill than it is to ramp up to the decision. Force science study of experienced vs rookie officers demonstrated this. What this rule tells us is we must be mentally prepared to take deadly force at any situation. If it is determined not necessary, then we can use safe arrest techniques to take the person into custody. However, if this is not required, we can approach and question them about the events that caused us to take the initial actions. At any time, we must be prepared to return to our other options.

Our safety and well-being must have strong situational awareness skills backed by training and experience and apply them whenever possible to stay ahead of the problem. We are always looking for the opposite behavior of expectation. If there are negative atmospherics, is there someone behaving calmly? Once we see three behaviors, we will need to do something. It may be as simple as approach and question to let them know you are here but you cannot wait to allow too many indicators to build.

Empirical Perspectives - 27

The word empirical is when something is verifiable by experience or experiment. Law enforcement, like the military, has to determine the best practice applications for real world scenarios. I call this section *Empirical Perspectives* because we will explore law enforcement situational testing and deadly force information conducted around the world. Much of this testing information is the backbone of this material.

Between 1999-2008, 486 officers were killed with firearms. 44 of these with their own weapon. In 2008, 35 officers were killed by firearms, 4 of these their own firearm. One counter to these statistics has been for agencies to require the use of security holsters. This sounds good in theory but is very risky.

Speed is the quintessential factor of action vs reaction and these holsters slow our ability to engage. The requirement of security holsters is fixing a problem in the wrong direction. Enhancements of officer's awareness and effective combative countermeasures are a better practice. To say an unarmed assailant is less dangerous than an armed one leads to many of these officer deaths. In fact, unarmed subjects kill about two officers a year on average. Officers will treat an unarmed subject differently even when they are aggressively assaulting an officer. They can easily become armed if they take the officers weapon away. We train to fight fair instead of for our lives. If an officer becomes involved in a physical struggle with a subject and is overwhelmed, that officer's life is at the hands of the offender. We must always remember that a physical confrontation with an unarmed person has the same potential as that of an armed subject.

Contrary to public beliefs, officers are not expected to take a beating or be harmed. Yet to remain engaged with a subject who gets lucky and renders the officer unconscious, they are a deadly threat.

If a weapon is not visible, we must evaluate them for the probability of possessing a weapon. There are two different categories to indicate a gun: Behavioral Traits and Concealment Characteristics.

Behavioral Traits include:

- Adjusting the clothing after changing position, touching
- The weapon ensures concealment and security
- A change in gait
- Standing with the body bladed from the officer while talking to keep the weapon away
- Arms not swinging evenly while the suspect is walking (Less movement on strong side)
- Running while holding one arm or elbow tight against the body
- They will not bend over, yet squats down to pick something up
- Direction avoidance when exiting a vehicle.
- Pay attention to your own actions when in plain clothes. Your behaviors will be similar to theirs.

Concealment Characteristics are:

- Clothing, especially shirts and jackets, wrinkled on one side, smooth on the other.
- Bulges
- Weighted pockets
- Shirt tail out
- Clothing vs. environment -
- Hot wearing a jacket
- Cold and the jacket is open

Survival relies on winning the first few seconds. To help, understanding behaviors are mandatory. When you are standing with anyone, keep your eye focuses moving between their eyes and the movement triangle. The triangle is the area between the chin out to both shoulders and across. Should anyone try to initiate any type of movement or attack, whether it be from the arms or legs, it will register in the triangle.

Secondary weapons are an option for each officer who has trained in the weapons use. Chemical agents are effective in certain situations but not in close quarter battle. Every officer will tell you that chemical agents have worked every time in harming them and questionable against the assailant who is often high on drugs or alcohol. Besides, we can never forget their use. They are irritants, not incapacitants.

Often, because of the retribution concerns from both the public and their administrations, many in law enforcement will not draw their weapon except as a last resort. It is easier to re-holster a weapon when not needed than to draw it when necessary. If you have cause of concern, draw the weapon.

Physical fitness is a necessity of the job yet not a reality in life. It is estimated based on surveys that of 226 US officers with time on the job, only a minority felt they could 'very well' perform such relatively simple tasks as completing 21 push-ups, negotiating an agility obstacle course, performing 36 sit-ups, sitting and reaching 16-inches, and bench pressing their own body weight. I bring this up because there was a recent study conducted in Norway and Reported by Force Science Research News, episode 262. Not surprising was that a person's physical conditioning played a critical place in overcoming an aggressive subject. They utilized officers who were able to bench press--235 pounds; chin-ups--15; long jump--8 feet 4 inches; time for the roughly two-mile run--11 minutes 53 seconds. The average participating officer weighed 181 pounds and stood just less than 6 feet. Seeing these test participants abilities, Dr. Bill Lewinski of Force Science stated, "In all likelihood, fewer than 10 per cent of officers upon graduating from any academy in North America would be able to match these performance standards. And from a fitness standpoint, that is when officers tend to be at their absolute peak."

The study found that as officers became older, their physical abilities declined, and that some minimal physical requirements should be mandatory to stay on the job. This same topic has been brought up many times over my career. Because of our inclination for litigation over every issue and the involvement of unions in the name of the officer's best interest, implementation except in specialty programs has failed. The best interest of the officers is unquestionably in an exercise program.

"In the study of physical exhaustion conducted by the Force Science Institute a few years ago, they found that the average officer's pulse rate hit 180 beats per minute within 20 seconds of all-out exertion, such as would be experienced in a struggle with a resistant suspect. That represents a dramatic stressing of an officer's physical system and capabilities." At least, let this remind you to get into physical fitness training for the defense of yourself and others.

Another aspect of stress and motor skill performance is a neurological response called "Interlimb Interaction." It is defined as "any action of one limb, real or imagined, having a similar effect of a lesser degree upon another." Interlimb interaction is most commonly associated with accidental discharges during high stress instances. Any action that causes the weak hand to flex can cause an overflow to the opposite hand. This action will involuntarily initiate a contraction in the opposite hand resulting in an accidental discharge.

One example is when making a high stress felony arrest and you are holding your gun. Should the subject do something to cause you to push them away with the weak hand, this can cause an equal force to the strong hand, discharging the weapon. Another is a loss of balance or when the body attempts to right itself. This will cause one hand to reach out and grab an object to stop the fall. A force will apply to the strong hand and cause the finger to squeeze and discharge the weapon. The final cause of Interlimb interaction is the startle response. When we are suddenly startled, fist gripping can initiate the discharge.

Unless it is an immediate threat issue fingers can be off the trigger. Just remember that we can shoot .312 seconds faster with our finger on the trigger. Determination can be made as to the situation you are entering and if fellow officers are in your line of fire.

Being startled will result in four involuntary actions occurring within 150 milliseconds. First, the eyes blink; second, the head, and upper torso move forward; third, the arms bend at the elbow; and lastly, the hands begin to tighten into fists.

In a high stress situation, we will do the following:

- Crouch
- Square off to the target
- Focus vision to the target
- Have convulsive muscle contractions
- Use binocular vision

Freeze, Fright, Flight, Fight are the order of our fear response. 10% of officers killed by gunfire never drew their weapon even though recognition of the situation is made.

In a recent Force Science review, using 93 officers in a reactionary response study where the officers were fired on by the driver of a car, which was not anticipated, 10% of the officers never pulled their weapon. Training needs to be lifelike and as stressful as possible. Many have said that doing something is better than doing nothing. This may be true for non-life threatening events, not for tactical application. Poor tactics can, has, and will get you and others killed or injured.

Fear is a neural circuit designed to keep an organism alive in dangerous situations. There is a difference between physical and emotional exertion because physical exertion cannot replicate the emotional responses to fear. Emotions are distinct patterns of behaviors of neurons and the emotion of fear is an unconscious process blueprinted at the neurological level, and when triggered, has physiological reactions that we may have little, if any, control over, but which can be molded. All of this compounds the difficulty in dealing with a potentially lethal situation and increases the need for reality-based training.

Once an emotion turns on, it is difficult to exert conscious control over it at will. This means that in an unexpected spontaneous attack, if you are training motor skills that are not consistent with what the amygdala will cause the body to do as a protective reflex, no matter how well trained the response it may be overridden.

A trained response may become the dominant response through repetition and training using stimulus/response training methods given some stress issues and Hick's law, but the answer will only be "yes" as long as the motor skill taught is consistent with the automatic protective reflex the amygdala will cause the body to take. Effective reflex training for all areas of self-defense should be simplistic. For hand-to-hand combatives, reflex strike training and instinctive or combat shooting for shooting,.

The first few seconds on an attack are the most critical. Your response has to be a natural reflex with gross motor skills. The bulk of our survival strategy has to adopt the gross motor skills and we should work at honing those skills through training.

Repetition is the mother of all skills and develops competence. Competence breeds confidence, and the more confident in your skills you have, the less you will be affected by stress. Finally, we should engage in dynamic training scenarios.

Action is always faster than reaction. An officer cannot tell what is in the mind of the offender and needs to act on perceived threat cues before the suspect acts, which places the officer in the advantage. Reality training is necessity. "The battle is not won with the first shot. It is won with the first accurate shot."

Psychological resilience is an individual's tendency to cope with stress and adversity. Good outcomes, constant competence under stress, using challenges for growth that makes future hardships tolerable, and better recovery from trauma all enhances resilience despite a high-risk status. Resilience is a learned process and not a trait of an individual. We have to train in the most realistic fashions to prepare our mind and body for the possibilities that exist. Going to the firing range twice a year is not preparing you for events that we face on the street.

Simplicity is a powerful principle that allows us to channel our energy like a laser beam and avoid the rut of rigid thinking and acting. For some reason, we have found that it is easier to create complexity training rather than simplicity.

Targets are static and non-reactive to human interaction. A target poses "no real threat, no stress, and no penalty for failure. Outdated firearms' training does nothing to teach us the judicious use of deadly force if every time a target turns you fire upon it.

When we think of force continuum, it must be based upon any type of means to negate or stop the threat and not along some imaginary and impractical checklist; which begins with the least injurious and ending in deadly force. Whether the suspect holds a gun, knife, club, or is unarmed and threatening to harm an officer, the threat is the same. Any weapon display requires the officer to immediately escalate to their top tier weapon.

Human Movement Sciences at VU University in Amsterdam, in real-life deadly force encounters, LEOs typically hit what they are shooting at only 15-50% of the time. Annual shooting tests "almost all officers are able to hit well over 90% of the targets."

The culprit, "anxiety" stems from the possibility of being shot in real gunfights, which causes officers to "reduce goal-directed attention, speed up their shot execution, and shoot with less accuracy."

Mental imagery is effectively used in high-stress sports to improve motor performance. If the imagery accurately reflects real-world conditions, it activates "the same neural networks that are involved" in the actual movements imagined and "strengthens the neural pathways needed to perform the intended action in real life."

After an initial shooting exercise to establish a baseline, some officers were exposed to a seven-minute session during which they imagined themselves shooting with consistent accuracy even when under the stress of an attack, while a control group merely listened to unrelated audio input. When exposed to a simulated gun battle, the mental imagers consistently out-performed the others, whose targeting skills under fire tended to erode from their "normal" level of accuracy.

Most deadly force encounters begin and end within 3 seconds. Force Science Research Study in 2013 used 93 officers, studied the safest position in a traffic stop. There is a safe zone considered the back half of the suspects' car. Twelve officers, all on the driver's side tried to neutralize the shooter (grabbing for the gun), three succeeded. If attempting to use neutralization techniques after a driver's side approach, training and practice is required. (Motor programs have to be developed). The most common startled first response by the officers was to raise their hands as if a shield, an indication of SNS activation. Once a threat was recognized, 1 in 5 officers failed to move directly to the safe zone. Some moved at angles while the other backpedaled. From the passenger's side of the suspect's car, officers made it to the safe zone on average of a half second faster than the driver's side approach. Understanding Hick's Law of psychomotor behavior and the rule of choice, officers who moved first and then drew to fire once in the safe zone did so faster. When trying to move and draw simultaneously, our time for each action was slowed by as much as 50%. This teaches us to mentally prepare to move first before drawing to shoot. It removes you from their field of fire faster and allow you an advantaged position from which to return fire.

Force Science Research released its findings on determining how safe it was to have someone sit on a curb and is one position better than another is. They tested subjects sitting on a curb with their;

- Legs straight out
- Crossed ankles
- Crossed legs

A buzzer was on a table five feet away. Each suspect had to hit the buzzer as fast as possible from the various positions. The average total time was 1.3 seconds to come up and hit a buzzer that includes .2 seconds to listen for the buzzer and react. Surprisingly, they found that no position was any slower than another was.

In light of the test, officers should stand about five feet from the subject's feet and at an angle. The common pre-attack clue came from their hands because all 42-test subjects used their hands to lift up and propel forward, not stand up. They moved to the area equivalent of between the waist and knees. Most officers would stand about five feet from the subject's body. By standing five feet from their feet, you have a measurable distance to apply in each situation. By standing at an angle to them, it was more difficult for the subjects to propel themselves at an angle compared to straight on.

In a Force Science Fatigue Threshold Study, they were able to provide imperative information to your survival when determining one's ability to stay in the fight. Using younger and fit officers, this study showed that:

- The body begins to fatigue within 30 seconds of a fight.
- More energy is used while restraining than resisting.
- Upper body loses total strength within 2 minutes.
- To fight at 100% of ability, the fight can be sustained for only 10-15 seconds.
- If unsuccessful and the fight continues, the body begins to use lactic acid which will give you about 45 seconds, but at 55% of previous levels.
- If it continues, our aerobic system will burn longer but provide only 31% of max output.

The Threshold Study tells us that in an all-out fight, you must win in the first few seconds. If the fight exceeds 30 seconds, you could be hurt or killed. This is the foundation of strikes and kicks and no grappling. It has been shown that in a high activity training fight, your heartrate can easily reach 180 beats per minute. The SNS will start taking away many of your fine and complex abilities and mental thoughts.

In another Force Science Study, released March 2014, which examined batteries against police officers utilizing statistics from the Orlando Police Department, this test found that:

- Females are more likely than males to batter
- Odds of a battery at 40% when alcohol involved
- 90% higher battery probability when multiple officers are on scene vs single officer because:
  - When there is an event with multiple officers present, the subject is more likely to be violent
  - Other officers are more likely to become over-involved and can exasperate situation
  - Officers get more complacent around other officers

With these results some recommendations are:

- Regardless of intoxication level, be cautious
- No complacency with females
- Explore team tactics when arresting violent persons with multiple officers because each officer has a tendency to deploy their individual arrest tactics, which often times disrupt the other officers and cause injuries.

An example of team tactics is predetermining the order that each officer directs attention. The first can gain head control, the second grabs an arm, a third grabs the other or free arm, and the forth controls the legs, etc. Now with a coordinated group effort, the likelihood of officer injuries is reduced.

In a study to determine how fast a subject can run towards an officer to assist in response determinations and distance controls, the following charging information was released.

Charging forward information (Suspects):

- 1st stride >3 feet
- 3rd stride >4 feet
- 6th stride > 5 feet
- 6 strides in 1.5 seconds (ALREADY ABOUT 24 FEET)
- 13 mph by the 5th stride
- From 9 feet, reach out and cut >½ second
- From 5 feet, reach out and cut <1/3 second

An officer's initial response was to start backing up so these strides and distances were measured.

Back peddling (Police Officers):

- 1st stride 2 feet
- 2nd stride 3 feet

They will overtake you rapidly. Your decisions have to be predetermined and reactionary based on training for fastest and best response.

The Center for Injury Research and Policy – John Hopkins School of Public Health in Baltimore conducted a study in 2013 on occupational homicides of nearly 800 officers from 1996-2010. They discounted the 72 officers killed on 9/11. The three most occurring instances were disturbance calls (23%), vehicle stops (17%), and investigations (17%) all total 57%. One in ten homicides was a result of using the officer's own gun. Most officers underestimate takeaways.

Over 90 percent of these homicides of officers were committed using firearms, with short-barreled weapons being used 72 percent of the time. The most common encounter that resulted in homicide of an officer was response to a "disturbance call." In 29 percent of these cases, the assailant was waiting to ambush the officer. Eighteen percent of all response calls resulted in a "secondary ambush" of the officer after the initial encounter had begun. More than half

(52%), of these "secondary ambush" encounters involved high-powered, long-barrel weapons.

- Most fatal wounds are to the head and neck – 55%
- 58% they were wearing body armor
- The officer was working alone when killed in 43 percent of incidents.
- More than one officer was killed in 30% of instances and more than one assailant in 17%
- Officers are up to 5 times more likely to be murdered than anything else in the private sector

An interesting development of this study was the number of officers shot in the head and neck and killed. This is not the first study to point out this dilemma.

A two-year hit probability study with 103 volunteers most with little to no gun experience was conducted. To simulate results presented by the 15-year FBI study, shooters started from four locations without holsters.

- Hand on gun in rear waistband
- Gun in front waistband, garment covered
- In hand behind leg
- Gun held to a baseball cap as if hostage taken

The results of this test helped explain what has been occurring. Inside seven yards, each participant used one hand. They changed to two hands beyond seven yards. All of them shot instinctive style and fully extended their arm. Inside three yards, more than half shot at the head with at least one hit every time. From five to seven yards, most shot at the chest, but due to poor gun control they shot high into the neck and head.

This explained that we tend to shoot where we are looking and at close range, it is eye contact. The chest was the second target area. Most fired three rounds in 1.5 seconds. The researchers were surprised how fast these untrained volunteers were able to draw and fire.

From inside three yards, most assailants will fire fast and aim for the head – distance control. Collateral damage existed as far out as four feet and again poor recoil control was the culprit. This calls for officers to stay spread out when facing a dangerous armed subject. I have taught that the five-foot rule is necessary roadside in an encounter. We can apply this to the spread of the officers in the encounter. The investigating officer stays in front and five feet back while cover officers maintain a five-foot outer spread rule. In addition to the other factors, inside three yards, officers may experience muzzle flash blindness even from near misses.

In reviewing the FBI-LEOKA results of 2009-2013, there were 251 felonious law enforcement officers murdered. 175 of these were patrol officers, 168 were wearing body armor, 91 shot in the head, 20 in the neck, 16 in the upper chest, 7 in the upper back, 5 in the lower back.

- 13 of the officers were killed with their own weapon
- 10 had their weapons stolen
- 58 officers fired their weapon
- 31 tried to fire their weapon
- 94 of the killings occurred in 0-5 feet

The top events involved were making an arrest, ambushes, dealing with suspicious persons, and traffic stops.

The body armor statistics of these were:

- 2008-41 killed, 32 (78%) were wearing body armor and 29 of these by firearms.
- 1999-2008 – 486 killed with firearms 309 of these with body armor (62.6%)
- Of the 309, 207 were hit in the head, 79 in the torso covered by body armor and 23 below the waist.

Body armor is nothing more than a partial protective shield and police officers should not take any additional risk while wearing it vs not wearing it.

In a unique study conducted by the FBI, they reported that 28% of cop killers were in the company of others 14/51. 11 of those (79%) were not the focus of the officer's attention. 22% were killed by someone else other than the focus of their attention.

All reviews of deadly force encounters have to be examined from the point of the officer involved and under the threat of danger. We have difficulties deploying deadly force against someone attacking another. In fact, in incidents when the victim officer had a partner or back up arrived during the attack, 92% of the time, deadly force was not used. Failure to shoot in the defense of others is common and due to several factors. When an unexpected event occurs, there is a reluctance to act immediately due to a sense of disbelief. There is a reluctance to shoot in the defense of others. A reluctance to use deadly force against someone who is clearly dangerous, but not acting is still dangerous. This delay in action causes an officer to act in reaction. Officers will commonly accept a level of risk to their own safety that is unnecessary and unreasonable while foolishly failing to deploy deadly force.

Statistics demonstrate that officers are quick to put themselves in harm's way and reluctant to use significant force. We are authorized to use deadly force to protect others and ourselves and do not have to wait until a subject commits the first act. The National Institute of Justice found in 2011 that there were about 40 million contacts with the public by police. The percentage of these encounters that involved shootings was 0.00002865%.

Almost 60,000 officers are assaulted resulting in over 16,000 injuries. Of these over 11,000, involve a deadly weapon. You have to do something fast and unpredictable to keep them off guard. Remember Hicks law and rule of choices. Just adding one additional choice causes a 58% slower response as your mind has to make the determination. We must train extensively in all areas that effect your safety.

Tactical Combat Critical Care - 28

In no way can anyone take the information I provide in this chapter and consider it appropriate lifesaving training. It is here as informational only and I advise everyone to seek out additional medical training from trained medical professionals. I report this information in an effort to encourage everyone to always expand their medical training because the proof is in the statistics. With the right training and equipment, many officers can be saved, our ultimate goal.

In 1993, the Naval Special Warfare Command researched combat associated deaths due to penetrating injuries after the Battle of Mogadishu. The result was TCCC for medical care and tactics and has now been adapted throughout the military community. The military community is now initiating training throughout the United States for law enforcement. Dr. Matthew Szainkrycer emergency medicine consultant at the Mayo Clinic as well as the tactical medical director for the Rochester PD began comparing military combat and law enforcement injuries and whether or not any of the victim officers could have survived. 533 victim officers were examined over a 10-year period. After eliminating cases resulting from traffic accidents, the number reduced to 341. The data showed:

- Ballistic vests were worn by 218
- Based upon the nature and location of the fatal injury, 123 victim officers (36%) had potentially preventable deaths.

- 196 victim officers died in the presence of another officer.
- 29 incidents resulted in the death of two or more officers.
- 79 officers with potentially preventable deaths died in the presence of other officers, who might have been able to render aid with an advanced medical skill set.
- The most common cause of death was head trauma (198), followed by chest trauma (90). Two officers died from isolated extremity hemorrhage.
- Most of the preventable injuries were to the chest

This study shows us the need to think and prepare for a future possible event. Where are your first aid bags and the type of equipment in them and how accessible are they. Simple equipment carried on the officer is available. When a situation goes bad and you are hurt in a hot zone, EMS is not coming in until the situation is contained. Medical professionals have determined that you must be able to care for yourself for a minimum of 15 minutes.

What is shock? Shock is the body's inability to deliver oxygen to its tissues. Shock is a life-threatening condition that occurs when the body is not getting enough blood flow. Lack of blood flow means the cells and organs do not get enough oxygen and nutrients to function properly. Multiple organs can suffer damage as a result. Shock requires immediate medical treatment and can get worse very rapidly. According to the National Institute of Health, as many as 1 in 5 people who suffer shock will die from it.

Even though there are various types of shock resulting from different origins, for our purposes the focus is blood loss from injury. Blood loss prevents cells from receiving oxygen. Therefore, we must always treat any injured person for shock. Ask them their name, where they are, and what happened. This shows they are breathing and coherent. Confusion is a sign of shock onset. Elevate their legs to get the blood flow back to the heart and brain and wrap them to keep them warm. Why? Warmth helps to maintain the body's ability to clot, improving outcomes for victims of blood loss. Cells need oxygen and a reduction of oxygen causes the cells to produce lactic acid lowering the body's PH level and becoming acidic. The more a victim bleeds, the more acidic their blood becomes. The more acidic the colder they get. The colder they get the more they bleed due to their inability to clot. Blood will not clot below 93 degrees so keep them warm!

The very best medical intervention is often the best tactical option. We must be practical and smart in a real life deadly force situation Threat elimination is overriding to rushing a victim to medical care if the latter requires you take unnecessary risk in the face of the threat that has already used deadly force against one of your own. The only thing worse than an officer down, is to have two officers down. Be medically self-sufficient and understand that if you are not dead you are still in the fight. Even though 90% of survival is how fast you are transported, preparations and actions through self-dependence can sometimes delay this time threat.

Some considerations are:

- Israeli Bandage Battle Dressing, First Aid Compression Bandage
- C-A-T Combat Application Tourniquet or Special Operations Forces Tourniquet Combat Application Tourniquet Wide (SOFTC-A-T –W)
- HALO Chest Seal – Remember to seal only three sides!

Once again I want to stress that everyone should seek out and take certified courses in Tactical Combat Critical Care. This section is only a reminder to find these life-saving training opportunities for officers.

Mental Armor - 29

There are but two powers in the world, the sword, and the mind. In the long run, the sword is always beaten by the mind.

Napoleon Bonaparte

There is a three step formula For Physical and Psychological Survival:

- A vision that moves you - Motivation
- Constant innovation – Accepting new ideas
- Daily action - Training

Training academies emphasize physical training. Yet, the Psychological factors can be 3-times more important than the physical. Napoleon said, "In war the moral is to the material as three is to one." In every theater of combat, the highest number of casualties is the psychological injuries.

Post-Traumatic Stress Disorder or PTSD is what we used to call Psychological collapse. PTSD is a psychiatric disorder that can exist when both of the following have occurred:

- Following the experience or witnessing of a life-threatening events such as military combat, natural disasters, terrorist incidents, serious accidents, or physical or sexual assault in adult or childhood.

- Response involved intense fear, helplessness or horror

Most survivors of trauma return to normal given time. However, some people will have stress reactions that do not go away or may even get worse over time. PTSD is a re-experiencing of the trauma in

- Thoughts
- Feelings
- Dream content
- Together, these cause emotional numbing which explains why the first symptoms may not be recognized until later
- PTSD is often characterized by
- Depression
- Loss of interest in work or activities
- Psychic and emotional numbing
- Anger, anxiety, cynicism and distrust
- Memory loss and alienation

Emotional stress can build very fast and if there is no permissible emotional outlet, we will "convert" symptoms into physiological conditions. PTSD in law enforcement exists at a greater rate than most realize. Out of every 100 officers, up to 18 are working and suffering from posttraumatic stress disorder without knowing.

The most important survival resource is mental clarity. We will see throughout this book that the strongest connection between safety and the profession of law enforcement is mental. With only seconds to react, this loss of emotional edge means the difference between winning and losing. A preoccupied officer in an emergency is easy prey in those first seconds, walking up on a car with a mind distracted by anxiety, job dissatisfaction, and concerns over a divorce and financial worries.

We are always training for the physical factors of the job, which are important, but we must prepare for the mental issues as well. We need to recognize the important role of cumulative stress in police work—the daily wounding of the soul over years and decades. Many experts say, "In some ways, a cop's work may be even more traumatic than that of a soldier sent into a war zone. The police officer's job, over many years, exposes and re-exposes them to traumatic events that would make anybody recoil in horror."

Observations where police officers and other emergency workers, such as firefighters, experience the same traumatic event, it is more likely that the police officer will have difficulty dealing with the long term emotional effects of the traumatic event. The academic literature suggests that the causes of occupational stress are more complex for police officers because they encounter stressors in call after call, which sap emotional strength. Debilitation from this daily stress accumulates making officers more vulnerable to traumatic incidents and normal pressures of life.

The weakening process is often too slow to see; neither a person nor his friends are aware of the damage done. First, prolonged stress causes people to regress. Their psychological growth reverses. Second, chronic stress numbs people's sensitivity. They can't stand to continually see human misery. They must stop feeling or they won't survive.

The mind has a defense mechanism so people can continue working in horrible situations. If they kept their normal sensitivity, they would fall apart. As they become insensitive to their own suffering, they become insensitive to the suffering of others. (An abnormal response to an abnormal situation is normal behavior)

The daily work of a police officer involves certain paradoxes and conflicts that may be difficult to deal with, such as:

- Being on guard for an attack makes the police officer appear cynical, brutal, and detached.
- A police department is both a professional and military organization, and these two aspects oppose each other.
- The community and department expect officers to use judgment, but when they do, there is a danger of being disciplined or complained on; another unnatural no-win situation engendering chronic stress.

Most occupations involve a combination of good and bad results. In police work, almost everything is bad, and everybody you deal with is perceived either bad or foolish.

Another is that police officers develop a 'street wisdom' and possess a degree of authority that tends to make them perceive themselves as being morally superior to the rest of society. The public perceives it and tend to reinforce the divide.

Other sources of stress are:

- The fear of killing someone in the line of duty.
- Feeling responsible for a line of duty.
- Lack of support by the department or superiors.
- The disruption of family time or events due to work demands and scheduling.

- Shift work disorder – improper sleep habits and insomnia.
- Exposure to neglected, battered, or dead children and other traumatic experiences of human suffering
- Organizational culture and workload

Police Officers:

- See the dark side of humanity and are exposed to extraordinary brutality and horrific imagery.
- Tend to become socially isolated.
- Are required to remain in a constant state of hyper-vigilance which is an enhanced state of sensory sensitivity accompanied by an exaggerated intensity of behaviors whose purpose is to detect threats and is accompanied by a state of increased anxiety which can cause exhaustion

The youth of today is and will continue to be our greatest threat. Societal and parenting parameters are changing to allow for more behaviors without consequence. There is no compliance without consequence. The desensitizing of our youth towards discipline and respect is producing an undisciplined youth with no regard to authority. Confrontation or interpersonal human aggression is one of the leading causes behind stress for everyone.

Police Suicides Studies show there are 125 to 150 police suicides per year, at a rate of 17/100,000 (the public is 11/100,000 and the military in 2010 was 20/100,000). More cops commit suicide than are killed by felons. In 2011, there were 147 police suicides and 164 line of duty deaths, of which 65 were by gunfire.

The Department of Commerce says 56% of officers retire on disabilities. Approximately 18 percent of working police officers in the US are having undiagnosed symptoms of PTSD. By the most conservative studies, there are 216,000 officers either suffering from PTSD or some other form of emotional stress that is significant enough to alter and disrupt their lives.

Lt. Col. Dave Grossman says this; "Denial kills you twice. It kills you once, at your decisive moment when you are not physically prepared: You didn't bring your gun; you didn't train. Denial kills you a second time because even if you do physically survive, you are psychologically shattered by fear, helplessness, horror and shame at your moment of truth."

Sleep - 30

A two-year sleep study of 5000 officers showed that:

- 46% had nodded off while driving, 40% had sleep disorders, 53.9% of night shift had shift work disorder – improper sleep habits and insomnia.
- Significantly higher administrative errors, falling asleep while driving, fatigue related safety errors, uncontrolled anger, citizen complaints, frequent absenteeism, mental and health problems including depression, burnout, exhaustion, increased heart disease, anxiety, and diabetes.
- Officers with sleep disorders are twice as likely to experience events with negative consequences.

Sleep or the lack of proper sleep has a profound effect on our mental and physical abilities and is a key factor in stress casualties and PTSD and illness. Sleep loss destroys the immune system.

- 24 hours of no sleep equals .10 BAC
- 30 minutes is the minimum time for an effective nap
- 4 hours sleep daily equals 15% peak efficiency
- 5 hours sleep daily equals 28% peak efficiency
- 6 hours sleep daily equals 50% peak efficiency
- 7 hours sleep daily equals 87% peak efficiency

The Circadian rhythm is our 24-hour internal clock or our sleep–wake rhythm. Our eyes have ganglion cells, which are photosensitive. They receive light signals and pass the information to the brain, which measures the length of day and night. This measurement is utilized in the secretion of melatonin to allow for sleep. To have deep sleep, it needs to be in the dark. Remember that one of the major causes of stress in the profession is the rotating shift, which produces poor sleep habits. These sleep habits reversed from what our brain says is necessary. We were created mentally with an internal clock that goes dark when the sun goes down and on when it rises. Most still follow this pattern of nighttime sleep and daytime work, except law enforcement. Therefore, we must imitate nighttime conditions as strictly as possible to allow the rhythm to adjust.

HAVING THE EDGE - Emotionally, law enforcement is the most toxic career field in the world. Buying bigger guns, putting in more intensive combat ranges and purchasing a tank for your department are all fine ideas, but they aren't nearly as important as sending your officers out into the field in prime condition, psychologically. An emotionally healthy cop, at home and on the job, is an alive cop. We can make sure of that by providing good mental health programs that will keep them alert and on the defense more than ever before. It's called "giving them the edge."

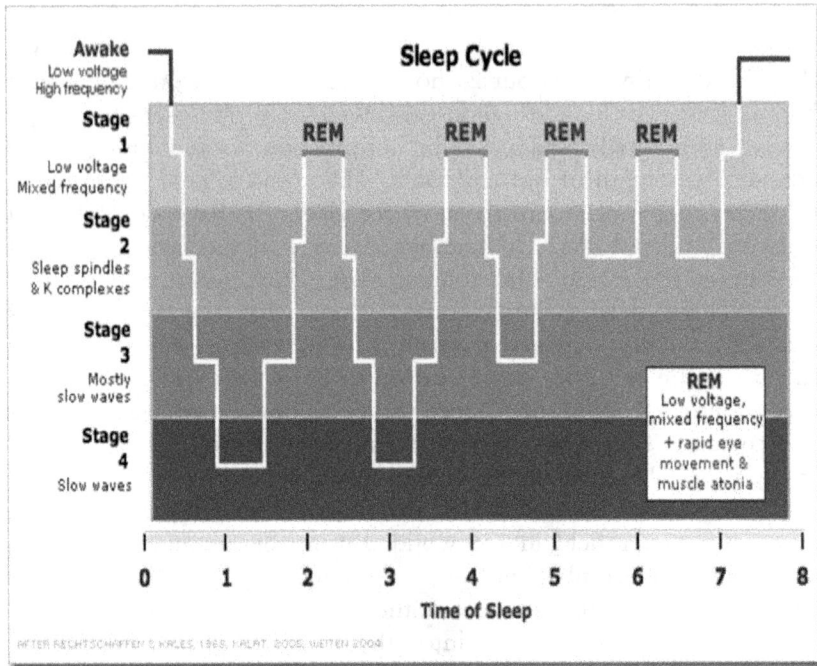

Sleep Cycle

Awake Low voltage High frequency				
Stage 1 Low voltage Mixed frequency	REM	REM	REM	REM
Stage 2 Sleep spindles & K complexes				
Stage 3 Mostly slow waves				
Stage 4 Slow waves		REM Low voltage, mixed frequency + rapid eye movement & muscle atonia		

0   1   2   3   4   5   6   7   8

Time of Sleep

AFTER RECHTSCHAFFEN & KALES, 1968, KALAT, 2005, WETTEN 2004)

Steven Varnell

Behavior Analysis and Interviewing Techniques B.A.I.T

Surprise? It's only in the mind of the victim. Surprise is simply the perception that something (an event and/or the process by which it changes) is happening contrary to expectations.

-------------Barton S Whaley

INTRODUCTION

Since the release of *Criminal Interdiction* and *Tactical Survival*, I have wanted to write a book about human behaviors and interviewing. My goal has been to discover how I could write a book on interviewing and still give the topic an original foundation. After all, few topics are covered more than these. Another requirement is the new book has to be in an area of officer survival and safety.

I have initiated a series of lecture-based training courses derived from the books and present them nationwide. Together with former partners, I have started our new instructional group called Interdiction and Survival Strategies (ISS). Instructing your peers is hard enough, teaching new concepts to law enforcement officers is another category by itself. The research for this book requires a vast amount of time to make it a topic that anyone will look forward to receiving.

Behavior Analysis and Interviewing Techniques (BAIT) takes us deep into the minds of suspects while seeking solutions to many of the problems experienced by police officers for effective evaluation and interviewing. I sought out research from around the globe and applied it to my own experiences.

In my 29 plus years in law enforcement, I have completed many Interviews and Interrogation classes, including specialized courses for instructors, and conducted thousands of interviews. Any concepts that deal with the human psyche have always been a favored topic of mine and the foundation of my training courses. The knowledge learned can save your life. Safety and survival is the preeminent result of our job and my writings.

I will introduce you to an actual event that led to the officer's death. Never will or shall any of these accounts be considered a criticism of any officer. Never should anyone read this book and say, "I would never do that!" You need to say to yourself, "I have to do my best to never repeat that situation."

Criminal Interdiction literally was written "off the top of my head." The ideas and chapters are from my own experiences. Except for statistical data, little research was required. *Criminal Interdiction* was what I did each day of my career for over 29 years. Officially, I retired from law enforcement on June 30th, 2011, but I never retired mentally;

does anyone? The information I retained to recognize and arrest the bad guys continues to this day. Imbedded this deep, no switch can turn off the mental processes. I am not on patrol, but I will always be on the streets. My eyes will always be watching and my mind will always be trying to discover new ways to safely complete various police task. The difference is that now I have the time to conduct research. I read books, research papers, conducted countless interviews, and searched the World Wide Web to make the information "cutting edge."

In *Tactical Survival,* we discussed areas of self-defense in ways that are no longer considered yet have a proven record of accomplishment in combat. As I travel around the country teaching, I learn new ideas. Due to the controversial ideas, questions and challenges to my concepts exist. I welcome all ideas, considerations, consultations, and complaints. To me, this is how to obtain the best approach to a situation. It indicates that they listened and are applying the ideas into their own. Some are convinced and others not sure, yet not one has ever said these ideas will not work and here is why. Many officers have contacted me after reading the books or attending a class. By applying what I teach, they explain how particular events were overcome. Now that is excitement of the ultimate degree in my soul.

For me, the learning continues. Incessantly, I conduct research and make minor adjustments to my presentations. I demand the information is current and cutting edge when lecturing to law enforcement because they deserve nothing less. As more information comes out, I will create expanded chapters in the current books and expound on the information to the courses.

Agree or disagree, pick at the small insignificant issues, complain about layout or a lack of photos, editing errors and what not. This is a book of ideas and learned practices to help you survive and become a better truth seeker. No photo will increase your knowledge like expressive words. As is said so often, a picture is worth a thousand words, but here we let the words become our mental pictures. Stay focused on what is important; the events in front of you during your shift. In the end, be open- minded and at least try the ideas I expose to you. As you read, think how often the small things could have changed the outcome of so many events.

Behavior Analysis and Interviewing Techniques, (BAIT) is a new approach to the topic and I hope it finds its way into the minds of officers everywhere. Use the BAIT acronym to help you remember that we first observe their behaviors, and then we recognize their deceptions through effective interviewing. BAIT is a process of effective criminal recognition and investigation. I know the techniques work and I am certain the foundations are sound because I tested them for decades.

Experiment with them with an open mind. See how they stand up to your own ideas. If you are not pleased with one, change it to meet your needs. The result is still a success. What I ask is to be flexible and understand that not one of us has all of the answers, but we can always improve. Incorporate them into your own techniques and have fun taking out the bad guys.

In 2011, the United States Department of Justice, COPS Program, released their "Officer Safety and Wellness" Report by Mora L. Fielder. It describes many things about our changing society and the propensity of criminals to use a firearm leading to a potentially more dangerous work environment for law enforcement. The issue of training in the report caught my eye and I agree with wholeheartedly. This is the quote from the report in regards to training:

"Training is another fundamental factor for officer safety, health, and wellness and thus is not the area to cut corners or cost. It should be the primary investment made by an organization. Yet, when economic times tighten budgets, the elimination of training is usually the first. Most agencies have annual hours dedicated for in-service training, but often the additional or advanced training opportunities are what enhance officer knowledge, minimize risks or mistakes, and help hone duty-specific skills, knowledge, and abilities. Tactical training enables officers to keep honing skills such as driving, handling violent encounters, and operating less than lethal or lethal weapons."

"Violent encounters are one of the most hazardous risks for officers. Attacks can be direct, physical, or with weapons. Constant training and practicing techniques that prepare officers for situations such as these are crucial in safeguarding their lives."

We can never train or study to learn new ideas enough. If your agency will not provide everything, it's up to you alone to seek out the best techniques to help complete the job. Many will complain that if the Department will not provide it, I must not need it. I hope those words do not come back to haunt and follow you to the hospital after you responded ineffectively or worse when you or your fellow officer's ass is on the line.

Many books are on the market that explains various ideas of interviewing and interrogations. Many more cover body language when it applies to everyday personal situations. Good books are available by former law enforcement officials that discuss body language in terms that a civilian can understand. For the street officer, uniformed or not, there is a need for understanding verbal and nonverbal communications as it relates to safety. No other person has to conduct more interviews and be as observant to behaviors as a police officer. Throughout the course of their day, they will encounter people through traffic stops, pedestrian encounters, accident scenes, crime scenes, domestic calls, and more. Never has another job needed more guidance than that of the police officer. For many members, they have the advantage of moving the interviews into special interrogation rooms. Barren of anything other than chairs and a desk, with a surreptitious audio video system, designed to create an uncomfortable environment for the person interviewed. Once completed, they have time to review the tapes and have other officers watching the interviews from another room. The collection of the information and are ideas brought about by all of the people involved. This is an important aspect of acquiring a good confession. These same investigators will go to the field and interview people at other locations, involving various cases, but time is on their side.

For a street cop, time is often against them. It does not take long before dispatch calls them on the radio wanting to know how long before they complete their assignment because other calls are holding. Rapid recognition of certain behaviors is necessary. As we have seen, a second can mean the difference between life and death or injury for a street officer. Within this period, we can develop recognition and motor skills to recognize in advance an action for which a proper response will succeed.

For these very reasons, I wrote *Criminal Interdiction*. Because of these exact threats, I wrote *Tactical Survival*. For this very cause, I am presenting *Behavior Analysis and Interviewing Techniques or BAIT*.

Pelham, Alabama - 31

What we have done for ourselves alone dies with us; what we have done for others and the world remains and is immortal.

> Albert Pike, a 19th century attorney, Confederate
> Officer and writer

December 2009 in Pelham, Alabama, people were just getting over the Thanksgiving holidays and preparing for Christmas. The weather is getting colder and everyone can feel the excitement of another year ending. Lights and manger scenes decorate houses around town. Plastic reindeers and Santa Claus' stood on rooftops and in yards. The feeling around town is growing festive. Smoke rises from the chimney tops as the smell of burning wood lingered in the air. The combination of the sights and smells adds to the excitement as everyone's favorite holiday approached.

Pelham is an upscale city south of Birmingham just off Interstate 65. It is a quiet place where little happens when compared to the big city crime 20 miles to the north. Housing cost and income is above the states average and below the poverty levels. Pelham is a good place to live and raise a family. The Pelham Police Department employs less than 100 people and is considered a progressive agency. Statistics show that from 2000-2008; there were only four (4) murders within the city limits. The largest percentages of crimes involve thefts and burglaries.

Pelham Police Officer Philip Davis has been on the force for four and half years. Before joining the Pelham Police Department, he worked with the Calera Police Department and the University of

Alabama Police Department. Officer Davis is part of the Departments training program. Not only is he involved with his own agency, like most officers, he also takes a personal interest in the betterment of the community. Davis teaches women's self-defense classes at Valley Christian Church in Birmingham. He is a Christian man and a proud officer. Again, the city of Pelham has attracted a good officer.

2009 had been a difficult year on law enforcement. On March 24, a lone gunman kills four Oakland, California Police Officers. The next month, on April 4th, three Pittsburgh, Pennsylvania Police Officers are killed in a gunfight. Then just days earlier, 29 November, a psychotic paroled killer guns down four Lakewood Police Officers in Washington State, paroled killer. The death of our countries law enforcement officers is again above the yearly average.

On Thursday, December 3, Davis began his shift earlier in the afternoon. He later drove to Interstate 65, a north/south interstate highway that starts in Mobile, Alabama and ends in Gary, Indiana. At about 11:50pm, he is monitoring traffic on the highway when he clocks a gold colored Acura speeding in a construction zone. Davis proceeded to make a traffic stop. Still fresh in his mind is the deadly events of Lakewood, Washington. That day affected Davis as it had all of us in law enforcement with a touch of shock. Davis writes in Facebook his feelings about the incident. Thoughts of each of these incidents were in my mind. I wondered how so many of us could continue to be killed in these senseless acts of rage.

Davis catches up to the speeding Acura that he had clocked at 76 miles per hour (mph) in a posted 55 mph zone. A traffic stop is conducted between the 242 and 243-mile marker. The 242-mile marker is the exit from Interstate 65 to the city of Pelham. It is also known as Shelby County exit 52, the former exit number. The exit numbers for interstate systems have been changed to the mile marker where they make locating easier in times of an emergency. The driver of the Acura pulls off to the right side of the road onto the emergency shoulder and stops. Davis exits his patrol car and approaches the driver's window of the car. He sees that the driver is the only occupant. Davis is wearing a microphone and has a dash-mounted video camera in his car. The events that follow are strange, unprovoked, unnecessary, and conducted by the one person no one would have ever suspected.

Unexplained Evil - 32

Bart Wayne Johnson is driving on Interstate 65. He is a pharmacist in the town of Jasper, located 40 miles northwest of Birmingham. Johnson lives in Kimberly, a town 38 miles north of Pelham or 34 miles east of Jasper. He is married with two children. His wife Dana is also a pharmacist. His salary alone is over $100,000.00 per year. They live in an upscale neighborhood and their house is decorated with lights and plastic candy canes in anticipation of Christmas. He is a graduate of Samford University, School of Pharmacy in Birmingham. Johnson has a brother in law enforcement. He is a police officer in the city of Trussville, a small town 15 miles northeast of Birmingham off of Interstate 59 in Alabama. You can definitely say that Johnson has spreading roots in the area.

Bart Johnson is considered by his employers as a "go to guy." You can count on him "in a pinch." He understood the day-to-day operations of a pharmacy. Fred's Pharmacy schedules to open a new store in Bayou LaBatre located off Interstate 10, down near the coast of Alabama with the Gulf of Mexico. Because of his understanding of the required work and policies of the company, they ask Bart to travel and help prepare the store for their grand opening. He agrees and schedules to be there for several days. He arrives on November 30th and intends to stay until December 3rd to travel back home. He is "energetic" while working there and as said by another co-worker, "He kept me going." There were no signs of trouble, anxiety, headaches, or other ailments. He worked the same hours as everyone else in their efforts to make the pharmacy grand opening successful.

On his last scheduled day, Bart Johnson had already checked out of his hotel and gone to work. The day is December 3, 2009 and he is ready to go home. It is another long day of work that ends between 8:00 and 8:30pm. He walks to the parking lot with another pharmacist from the new store and they say their goodbyes. Johnson has a few more hours of driving to reach his home north of Birmingham. Before getting in his car, Johnson tells the co-worker, "I don't know if I will make it all the way home tonight." It is not a premonition, but a statement that anyone would make when they are tired and still have a long drive ahead. In this case, though it is the truth and not one that anyone expected.

Bart Johnson travels north from Fred's Pharmacy located on N. Wintzell Ave. onto Highway 188 and then west on Interstate 10. He picks up Interstate 65 northbound for the trip home. This is the start of Interstate 65 and designated as mile marker 0. Pelham is at mile marker 242 or 242 miles north. The speed limit is 65mph but increases to 70 around Saraland. It slows again around Montgomery and varies the remainder of the trip. Near Pelham, there is road construction and the speed limit reduced to 55 mph. He should arrive in the Pelham area around midnight.

A *Routine* Traffic Stop - 33

Pelham Police Officer Philip Davis drives to Interstate 65 to work traffic enforcement. He sets up to run radar and clocks a northbound Acura at 76mph, 21 mph above the speed limit. He accelerates and conducts a traffic stop of this speeding car between the 242 and 243 mm. The car has an Alabama tag number of "JCREW1." The driver of the car activates the turn signal and moves to the outside shoulder of the road. He never takes his foot off the brake. He turns on his vehicles interior lights as Officer Davis approaches on the drivers' side of the car. The Officer explains to the driver that he has stopped him for speeding. He proceeds to ask him if he has his drivers' license and if the car belongs to him. Sarcastically, the driver replies, "no, I just stole it." Officer Davis responds in an equal manner and says, "I'm glad you are in a jovial mood." He proceeds to tell the driver that he asked the question because sometimes when people borrow someone's car, they do not know where the proof of insurance is. He then tells the driver, "I'll be right back."

Officer Davis returns to his police car. He writes out the majority of a traffic ticket for unlawful speed. The driver of the car turns out the vehicle interior lights. In his right hand, he is holding a Glock .40-caliber handgun tucked under the outside edge of his right leg. Officer Davis returns to the drivers' window of the Acura and asked, "Where do you work?" The driver responds, "Why does that matter?" and then tells Officer Davis that his brother is a cop. Davis responds, "Now he wants to start acting reasonable." He then instructs the driver to have his brother call him and he would explain how he had acted towards him, and "we'll see how that works out."

Pelham Police Officer Philip Davis will not speak again. The driver of the car pulls the .40cal Glock from under his right thigh and shoots Officer Davis in the left side of his face. In fact, the bullet enters between his lip and nose, fractures the face bones, teeth, and fragments upon striking Officer Davis' spinal cord. He fell straight back with no attempt to catch himself which caused lacerations to the back of his head. The time is 11:57 pm.

A passerby sees Officer Davis go down to the pavement and calls 911. Responding officers to the scene discover the ticket book lying in between Davis' legs. The name of the driver of the car that shot him is Bart Wayne Johnson. On the traffic citation, his employment is listed as "Unemployed."

The first person on the scene is a truck driver who sees Officer Davis lying in the outside lane. He stops and runs to the officer. He calls 911 and is told to check for a pulse. He says there is a pulse but no movement. There is a gurgling sound coming from Officer Davis' mouth "almost like he was trying to speak." Other Officers begin to arrive at the scene and start CPR. Another Officer states that there's no pulse, his eyes are open and fixed, and blood from his head runs across both northbound lanes of the interstate. In all likelihood, Officer Davis died instantly.

Officer Davis is pronounced dead at the University of Alabama, Birmingham hospital. The clock has passed midnight and the date is now 4 December 2009. Davis becomes the first Pelham Police officer killed in the line of duty in the city's 45-year history.

Another officer, family man, dedicated civil servant has passed at the hands of evil. His death takes a small part from each of us with him. The job entails more than most realize and produces a brotherhood that few understand.

Reviewing the video tape from the dash-mounted camera of Officer Davis' car, investigators are able to see the events unfold. The brake lights went out 2 seconds after the gunshot and the Acura drove away northbound 6 seconds from the shooting. At the time of the first traffic stop, Bart Johnson was on the phone with his brother, the City of Trussville Police Officer. A few moments after murdering Officer Davis, Johnson's brother calls him back and asked if he had gotten a ticket. Bart Johnson responds, "Nope, not this time."

His plan is to travel north and ditch the car before traveling south again. If he can get south of the scene of the crime, most law enforcement efforts will be directed towards the direction he was last seen driving. Additionally, all of the drivers and vehicle owner's information are for locations north of the crime scene. It makes sense to direct assets to the north of the murder. He had to get rid of the car, the gun, and his shirt because they had Officer Davis' blood on them.

After midnight in the early morning hours of December 4th, a woman is making coffee in her home. She lives in the area of Birmingham known as Inglenook, located on the north side of Birmingham near the airport. It is a low income and low cost housing area. The average home sells below $50,000.00; 4 times below the average home cost of Birmingham. She hears a squealing noise outside and walks to the window. She watches as "a white man" stepped out of a car and starts to walk down the sidewalk towards her home. It's too dark to recognize the man, but he steps into her yard and tries to open her daughters' car door which is locked. She opens her front door and questions the man trying to break into the car. He looks up and motions her to go back inside; frightened, she did. At once, she calls the police and tells them about this man who is trying to get into her daughters car. He does not care that he is being watched. She tells the 911 operator that the tag on the car driven by the stranger is "JCREW1." The police tell her that the man outside is a suspect in another incident and instruct her to stay inside behind locked doors.

After locking the door, she looks outside again. She sees the man walk out into the street towards another vehicle that has arrived. She sees the man get into the passenger's side of the vehicle described as a gray colored Toyota Tundra pickup truck and together they speed away. She does give the 911 operator a scene-by-scene description as the events unfold in front of her house, including the full description of the truck. The Acura that the unidentified "white man" had arrived in and the same car stopped by Officer Davis, is left on the side of the street.

A "BOLO" or Be On the Look Out is broadcast to every agency. Cars and motorcycles today are fast, but they can never outrun the radio information broadcast. All known information regarding the car and subsequent events are dispatched across the State of Alabama and the neighboring states.

There is a sick feeling that comes over you when you hear an "officer down" call go out over the radio. At this one moment, all animosities, problems, departmental bickering, dislikes, and inner agency rivalries, dissipate. Officers, Troopers, Deputies, Agents, Detectives, and anyone else, who carries a uniform or a badge, come together. We all know that any homicide is terrible, but the murder of a police officer places it into a different category. Law enforcement officers represent justice, authority, and that barrier between right and wrong. When someone is willing to cause harm to the badge, that person is willing to do anything to anyone. They are at that moment a rabid dog. Every sense of right or wrong has vanished. They have committed an atrocity to the very fiber of our society. Remember that we place ourselves at a much greater risk and are therefore provided greater protections.

There are people who have always taken issue with this topic. It is said that by placing greater penalties against someone who harms a police officer gives the appearance that their life is more valuable. It is a shallow argument that some people will never understand. Remember in *Criminal Interdiction* the story of the sheep and the sheep dog? The sheep always hate the sheep dogs until the wolf shows up. Just as you have seen in every disaster, the public runs from the catastrophe as the police run into them. As I like to say, the job entails more than most realize and produces a brotherhood that few understand.

In the City of Trussville, Alabama, broadcast the BOLO information. A Trussville officer runs the "JCREW1" tag and sees the name and address of the registered owner. He knows the car belongs to Bart Johnson, the brother of fellow Trussville Police Department Officer Johnson. The time is now 12:40 am. A Trussville Police supervisor contacts and instructs Officer Johnson on three separate occasions to go to his brother's house in Kimberly. Officer Johnson never goes there. At 1:06 am, the Trussville Police Supervisor is told that Officer Johnson is traveling south on Interstate 65. At 1:30 am, the Trussville Supervisor states that the Acura from the murder scene of Officer Davis has been located near a home in the Inglenook area of Birmingham. Further information indicates that the man driving that car has now entered a gray Toyota Tundra pickup truck. The supervisor knows that the Toyota description matches the vehicle driven by Trussville Police Officer Johnson. I can only imagine the confusion and shock befalling everyone involved.

The supervisor then calls his officers and advises that there is now a BOLO for the gray Toyota truck belonging to their officer. A few moments later, a gray Toyota Tundra pickup truck approaches and stops at a roadblock on Highway 31 and Interstate 65 manned by members of the Hoover Police Department. The two Johnson brothers occupy the truck. At gunpoint, both men are placed face down onto the ground. The passenger in the truck, Bart Johnson states aloud for the arresting officers to hear, "I'm the one you're looking for." Both men are transported in separate cars to the Hoover jail. In the glove box of the Toyota is found a bloody Glock .40 Cal pistol. Bart Johnsons Acura is located within the City of Birmingham at the location where he tried to steal a car and was picked up by his brother. There is blood on the driver's side door and roof. Later analysis will show it is the blood of Officer Davis.

Bart Johnson is placed into jail on no bond. His neighbors are shocked to hear the news. One states, "They had a nice house, nice cars, a boat, a motorcycle. The only thing missing was the white picket fence. I thought they had it all." We may never know why this happened. "As best I can determine, he didn't like police," says a prosecutor on the case; His brother is an officer. Officer Johnson is not charged with any crimes and released. Though trapped between the natural desires to help a brother, he follows his oath of office. In doing so he stops the madness of the night and saves the life of his brother. He had taken him and turned him over to the authorities.

The actions taken by Johnson clearly show that he knew what he was doing and that it was wrong. All of the evasive actions from calling for help, dumping the car, and trying to steal another dashes the idea of temporary insanity. Of course, when the case first breaks, there are all types of things running through our mind. Was Bart Johnson transporting illegal drugs? Was he bringing home prescription drugs stolen from the pharmacy? Was he stealing other things from the pharmacy? When stopped by Officer Davis, did he panic with the thoughts of something he had in the car or had recently done? Maybe he was high on illegal drugs or prescription drugs. His defense later would argue that he suffered with migraines and had mixed a migraine medication with alcohol.

During the trial, an inventory of the Fred Pharmacy store showed that nothing was missing. His co-workers, who worked with him during the crucial and difficult week of the store grand opening, testified that Bart Johnson showed no signs of suffering from anything. They never saw him take medications and he never complained of headaches. There were no signs of anything illegal in the car. The arresting officers at the roadblock stated that Johnson did not show any signs of impairment nor complained of any. He was coherent and complied with all instructions.

To commit murder, face to face, and on top of that to commit the murder of a uniformed authority figure is evil. Remember, Bart Johnson was talking to his brother, a police officer, at the time he of the stop.

Why did this happen? There are many reasons and none of them makes sense. The facts from his trial are: Bart Wayne Johnson had already received 18 traffic tickets. Even though his own brother is a police officer, he generally dislikes cops. Bart Johnson's traffic citation, which was found between the legs of the lifeless body of Officer Davis, was his 19th and would have suspended his license. The emotions of the moment had overcome the tired Pharmacist to the point he committed murder over a traffic ticket!

Johnson then had to develop a plan of escape. Why? He knew what he had just committed was wrong and he had to devise a reason that cleared him of the capital punishment act. In my opinion, these are not the actions of someone who suffers from mental illness.

A psychiatrist testifying for the defense asked Johnson about the evening when he was pulled over by Officer Davis. Johnson said that he does not remember much about that night but does say, "I guess I shot him." When asked why, he says he has no idea. Johnson said that he stopped at a McDonalds Restaurant for a coke and mixed it with rum and was taking Imitrex for migraines. When driving, he saw blue lights ahead on the interstate and thought the police were conducting a sting operation to get him. He stated that it felt like he was driving into a cemetery and that is when he called his brother.

When there is not another rational reason and there are no reasons for the act of murder, blame it on illness. He thought he was driving into a sting operation, yet he was speeding. Not trying to outrun anyone or drive overly cautious, just speeding. He pulled over and stopped when the blue lights directed to him from Officer Davis' patrol car. He is rude and belligerent towards the officer who is just doing his job. Johnson tries to take another approach by saying his brother is an officer as an attempt to try and get out of the ticket. It is too late. Officer Davis is going to do his job. Nothing else has worked, but Johnson is not taking this ticket. Many things are passing through his mind but only he knows for sure. After killing Officer Davis, Johnson drive's into town to ditch his car. He could later say it was stolen. He could say to investigators, I was not driving the car it was stolen. I am a Pharmacist, my brother is a cop, and I have never done anything wrong except traffic violations. That was until this night when he committed murder.

On May 13, 2011, a jury decided Bart Wayne Johnson was guilty of murder and deserved to die at the hands of the State. Amen.

The cause of this tragedy is the choice made by Bart Johnson. Choices we make in response to an event determines each event in our lives There are no other reasons that this entire incident occurred except for the delusional acts of Bart Johnson. That said, in no way are the following sentences derogatory to anything that Officer Davis did that night. This never should have happened, but it did. In *Criminal Interdiction* and *Tactical Survival*, I speak at length about the tactics of a traffic stop. There were measures that Officer Davis could have taken to reduce the odds against him. Another event unfolded that we will discuss later that neither Davis nor Johnson realized at the time. Non-intentional, top down Attention Manipulation was directed towards Davis. When Johnson spoke about his law enforcement brother, Davis directed his eyes and attention away. He reached for and looked at a note pad to get the brothers information. This split second occurrence opened the door for Johnson to choose his course of action.

Two families destroyed. Officer Davis leaves behind a wife and two children. The Johnson family is also fatherless now. He leaves a wife and two children behind as well. How does anyone ever explain the actions of December 3, 2009 to any of these children?

In the proud tradition of law enforcement, his family and friends remember the memory of Officer Davis by sharing their love of community. Please visit The Philip Mahan Davis Foundation at http://officerphilipdavis.com/. It is "a not-for-profit organization dedicated to honoring the lives of our fallen heroes. The Foundation provides support and assistance to the families of Alabama Police Officers who were killed or catastrophically injured in the line of duty.

Established in 2011, the Foundation strengthens the relationship between the Alabama Police, its business and civic leaders, and its citizenry. It allows us to express our gratitude to the fallen Officers' families for the ultimate sacrifice of their loved one."

Pelham Police Officer Philip M. Davis

OODA Loop - 34

Radical uncertainty is a necessary precondition of physical and mental vitality: all new opportunities and ideas spring from some mismatch between reality and ideas about it.

– Col. John Boyd

Officer safety is paramount in every decision we make. After 29 plus years of working the street, I learned early that understanding the behavioral habits of people could give me the edge needed to overcome the advantages held by the criminals. They know what they are intending to do and have the benefit of surprise, yet still it is up to you to overcome. It is action vs. reaction, in which reaction rarely is victorious. To comprehend our ability to overcome this deficit, we need to understand the groundbreaking research and development of the OODA Loop concept. OODA stands for Observe Orient Decide and Act. USAF Colonel John Boyd first developed the process. He had developed the Energy-Maneuverability theory (a model of aircraft performance, which led to the development of the F15 and 16) based on his observations as a fighter pilot in the Korean War.

Colonel Boyd had an amazing mind in terms of combat strategy. Young pilots always wanted new strategy, which led to his first research project called "Fast Transients." It dealt with ones abilities to adjust faster than your opponent to keep them off guard. Later he will re-name it "Patterns of Change" before settling upon the "OODA Loop." Boyd began researching ground combat and was amazed at how so many battles throughout history has been fought when small armies easily defeated vastly superior ones. An example is how the

Roman legions lost 70,000 soldiers compared to 3,000 soldiers lost from the armies led by Hannibal and the Carthaginians. He discovered the common thread was that none of the leaders threw their armies head to head against an opponent. They avoided attrition and adapted to maneuverability. Success rested upon their ability to transition quickly from one maneuver to another. He explored the German blitzkrieg and the Israelis attack on Entebbe in Uganda as other shining examples.

I will begin with the concepts behind the OODA loop theory as it can have an effect on every other process we encounter. According to Col. Boyd, decision-making occurs in a recurring cycle of observe-orient-decide-act. Observe – seeing what is happening, Orient – interpreting what is happening, Decide – how to respond to the action, Act – your response to the action taken. The officer who can process this cycle quickly, observing and reacting to the unfolding events faster than an opponent, can thereby "get inside" the opponent's decision cycle and gain the advantage. Boyd developed the concept to explain how to direct one's energies to defeat an adversary and survive. Boyd emphasized that "the loop" is actually a set of interacting loops that are to be kept in continuous operation during combat. He also indicated that the phase of the battle has an important bearing on the ideal allocation of one's energies. In other words, at what point do you understand what is occurring and how fast do you react. An example of this is once a subject starts to draw their weapon on you; they are already at step four of the OODA loop. They have already Observed, Oriented, made the Decision and initiated the Act. You are only on step one or the Observation phase, decidedly behind them. Action beats reaction almost every time. You will never want to play catch up in a gun battle. Your actions have to create pause or confusion, which stops their progression to react to yours and will cause them to over or under react to your action. The key to survival is in our ability to adapt to change, not perfect adaptation to existing circumstances. (Doing the same thing repeatedly and expecting different results). You have to constantly think about if they do this; I will do that, an ever evolving and fluid movement. You have to do something fast and unpredictable to keep them off guard

It is also imperative to understand that the Orientation phase is the single most important loop. Up to five influences affect Orientation: Cultural traditions, genetic heritage, previous experiences, ability to analyze and react, and processing new information. Because of these factors, it is the most important part of the loop since it has an effect on the outcome and shapes the way we observe, decide, and act. This is when our training and experience plays the primary role.

Training and experience affects everything we do. It is through training that we learn what the most effective tactics are and experience shows what will work. Only when we can observe the threat, based upon our training and experience, orient to the threat, and decide the most efficient course of action and act will we be successful. This necessitates the need for not only training, but also effective training. We all receive training to meet our standards requirements, but much of the training we receive is not realistic.

An example of this unrealistic training would be in defensive tactics. Once a year we meet for an 8-hour training session. We are introduced to various holds and grabs similar to MMA style fighting. Defensive measures teach if someone mounts us while on our back. The reality of this, as I have shown with an entire chapter dedicated to this topic in *Tactical Survival*, is that this training will actually place you in jeopardy, not benefit your survival. The tactics taught have to be swift and easy and never should any of us go to the ground with an assailant. The skill necessary to properly learn these tactics requires too much time. As Boyd said, the key to victory is maneuverability not attrition. Never stand toe to toe and battle it out with an assailant. The victory can easily go either way.

True success occurs when we develop the proper feel or reactions for the situations. We want to increase the tempo to bypass the orientation and decision phases. This causes observation and action to occur almost simultaneously. We are in essence compressing time while forcing them to extend time all the while placing them further behind us.

An example of this is when we are driving and the driver in front of us brake's their vehicle. We see and instantly respond by breaking ourselves in order to prevent an accident. We observed the action, but we are not required to pass through the orientation and decision phases of the Loop. The action taken is a "known response" to a "known action." It is a process, which takes time and practice. Another example is when firing your service weapon and a shell jams. We instantly respond with the "tap, rack, and shoot" method of clearing the weapon.

To help us reach this time compression state, Hick's Law explains the time it takes a person to make a decision because of the choices available. It only makes sense that the more choices made available to us the longer it takes to decide which to apply. Lag time reduces with choice minimalism. This is the imperative reasoning behind training hard in specific actions towards specific threats to reduce the lag time created. This produces the required compression of time discussed by Boyd. Simplification has always been the most successful people's plan of action. Not only Boyd and Hick's, but also Rex Applegate and his proven philosophies of hand-to-hand combatives, knife fighting and shooting skills. They each rest upon the simplification of response techniques with speed and accuracy.

With visualization techniques, you are initiating motor programs. I have always preached the necessities of mental planning for various situations. Whenever anyone engages us, always preplan the event with the ideas of, "if they do this, I will respond with that." We are creating "known responses" to "known actions" and thus reducing lag time. Our fast response will cause them to pause to observe, orient, decide and then act. Their actions are stretching out time forcing them to fall further behind and thus incapable of overtaking you.

Boyd's diagram shows that the process is ever evolving, a fluid movement forward, and re-initiating again with change. Every observation requires new orientation, decisions, and actions.

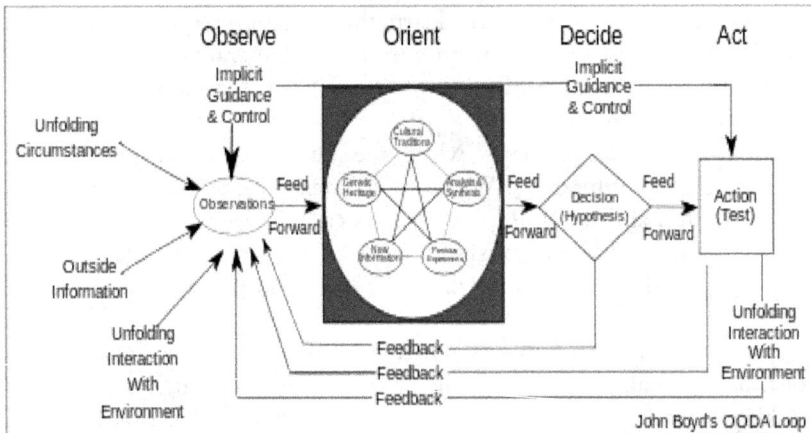

Diagram is from en.wikipedia.org

So how can the OODA loop principle apply to law enforcement? Let's see how it is designed to win and then apply it to ourselves. Boyd said that in order to win, we should operate at a faster tempo than our adversaries should or even better would be to get inside the adversary's OODA loop and disrupt their actions. This action can create confusion for an adversary caus ing them to stop their progression and react to yours.

The key is to obscure your intentions and make them unpredictable to your opponent while you simultaneously clarify his intentions. That is, operate at a faster tempo to generate rapidly changing conditions that inhibit your opponent from adapting or reacting to those changes and thus suppress or destroy their awareness.

Therefore, confusion and disorder will occur and cause them to over- or under-react to your activities. You have to do something fast and unpredictable to keep them off guard and second-guessing your actions.

Originally designed for the fighter pilot, Boyd's idea of the loop in action is explained as a fighter pilot when you know an encounter with an enemy aircraft is imminent. Based on your intelligence you have to make a reasonable assumption of what type of aircraft and how trained is the pilot. As the enemy comes into radar range, you determine speed, numbers, and size. You decide to climb based on their altitude and approach with the sun at your back. This is the first completion of the loop. You observed, oriented, decided, and acted. Now based on their reaction to your actions the loop repeats itself. Your training and experience determines how fast you can flow through the loop. How does one interfere with an opponent's OODA cycle? One of Colonel Boyd's primary insights into fighter combat was that it is vital to change speed and direction faster than the opponent is. This is not necessarily a function of the plane's ability to maneuver, rather the pilot must think and act faster than the opponent can think and act. To get "inside" the cycle—short-circuiting the opponent's thinking processes—produces opportunities for the opponent to react inappropriately.

At another level, an example could be that of a football player. A running back is handed the ball where he approaches a defensive player who is bigger and stronger. He knows he cannot simply run through him with much chance of success. Therefore, he slips aside and uses a series of short and fast body fakes that causes a moment of pause for the defensive player and eliminates his attributes of size and strength. Based on the running backs training and experience he takes advantage of the situation by accelerating past the opponent who over-reacts to his movements and slips by them. By taking advantage of the opponent's over-reaction to his fake, he has now broken the opponents loop and the opponent now has to react again based on the new parameters, but it will be too late as the running back goes past his position.

He has taken control of the situation by creating an advantage rather than reacting to the action. It is not simply a matter of moving through the loop faster, but most important is taking control of the situation. The OODA loop favors agility over raw power in dealing with human opponents in any endeavor. Boyd's practices created the idea of smaller and more agile fighter aircraft still in use today, the F16 and F18.

Now let's apply this theory to law enforcement. Most gun battles (81%) will occur in less than 21 feet. Almost 60% of them will occur at 5 feet or less. The most common method of public encounters is a traffic stop. You know that the preferred weapon of choice is a handgun or knife, especially at the common distances of a couple of feet. The subject is nervous and quickly reaches into his waistband and pulls a gun while stepping back. This is a difficult situation for the officer. If he stands there, he will be shot or taken hostage. You will also be shot if you stand and try to draw your gun. Look at the loop. He has observed you, oriented by knowing his arrest record and will serve life if arrested again. He has decided to kill you rather than run away, and acted by drawing his gun. When you observed the action of him drawing the gun, you are at step one of the loop, observation. You still have to orient and decide on a course of action before acting on the decision. This can occur fast, but every second delayed is a second closer to death.

The only plausible action with any hope of success is to move laterally in the opposite side that the gun has been drawn. If they draw right handed, as 93% of the population will, your best course of action would be to run to your right while drawing your gun to return fire once reaching a reasonable position. Your movement will cause them to re-initiate the loop to respond to your actions. With any luck at all, you can fire rapidly while moving and strike or disrupt their ability to shoot properly. This has to be determined by a case-by-case scenario and using the above-mentioned scene, both you and the bad guy are standing face to face. With the bad guy stepping back while drawing their weapon, you will not get to him in time to stop his action. Statistics show that you would have to be inside of 3 feet from the subject to effectively grab and try to overtake him. In the case of a traffic stop, a passenger's side approach is the safest and your first action upon seeing a weapon is to move to the rear of the car before drawing your weapon. This position provides you with cover and protection.

A better scenario is to keep the driver in their car. If they are outside with you, ask them, "Have you ever been arrested?" This is single question can save your life by heightening your awareness. Only 3% of offenders who assaulted and killed a police officer did not have any prior arrest. With this question, you are already observing and can now move forward to orientation. Your previous experiences have told you that this person can be more dangerous. This causes your natural instincts of awareness to initiate. Now you also see that they are very nervous and starting to look around, all indications of the fight or flight scenario. They are observing and orienting as they try to decide the next best course of action. They are in step three of the loop. Remember, it is always better to get inside and disrupt their loop, thus short-circuiting their thought process. You can initiate hands on or you can say, "Today is your lucky day. I have to let you go." This creates a break in their orienting phase, which disrupts their decision before they act. Then you can seize them with an element of surprise or wait for back up to arrive.

Training and preparations for these situations are vital for their success. Remember Hick's Law and examine various events and situations that you will encounter based on your experiences and explore the best-case scenario. When standing toe to toe interviewing a subject, say to yourself "If he tries to grab or hit me, I will instantly strike him in the throat." You are preparing your motor programs for an instantaneous response to their behavior. Should the subject grab or strike, rather than standing there stunned for a second, you will instantly respond. You are compressing the reactionary steps. With this preplanning and practice of your reactions to various scenarios, you are compressing time. When action is required, it will be instantaneous because you have already developed the mental and motor response of the actions. Otherwise, you will have to receive whatever they give as your mind decides the best course of action.

You approach the passenger's side of a vehicle and suddenly see a gun on the subject. Preplan that the safest response to this action is to run to the rear of the car and draw your weapon. Past demonstrations proves trying to draw and run takes longer (too many options) than to first move to a safer zone and then draw your weapon. You mentally prepare and even practice this move several times. You think about the processes involved during each stop and passengers side approach. In the event that this description does occur, you are again compressing the time with a known response to a known action and dominating the scenario. To preplan will allow you to observe the gun, orient to the fact that there is a gun, decide what your best course of action will be and act. In this time frame, you are delaying or creating a lag in your reactionary time, thus falling victim to their action.

You recognized their behaviors fast enough by paying attention. You interrupted their process thus gaining the advantage. In the first scenario, you were simply responding to their nearly completed action and placing yourself at a disadvantage. In the later examples, you are rapidly responding to a known or anticipated action with a planned reaction, which then places them at the disadvantage. It can almost classify as maneuver warfare by defeating an opponent by incapacitating their decision-making by shock and disruption brought about by movement. It is one of two accepted practices of military theorist, a war of attrition or of movement. Movement is very effective when you are few, quick, and fluid. An agile opponent has defeated much greater armies. The same goes with law enforcement. In our gun scenario, lateral movement is critical. The same applies to an edged weapon. From a distance of 30 feet, an assailant can overtake and stab you by the time you recognize the threat, draw and shoot.. Again, movement opposite their weapon creates or maintains distance and provides you with the time needed to bring your weapon into play. Also, it moves you to a direction away from their weapon. They have the additional movements needed of bringing the knife around to the opposite body side, thus a longer distance to hit.

Preplan and practice a fast movement to your right under these scenarios. We are playing the odds that 93% of the population is right handed. Your movement requires them to turn their entire body to respond to the action.

The last of this process is in understanding that once you begin, you have to continue until the threat is eliminated. As soon as you see them pulling a gun, instantly move and keep moving while drawing and firing continually. In the scenario of the traffic stop, move to the safe area, draw your weapon, and be prepared to eliminate the threat. If they take no action, continue to move to the safety of your vehicle. Access and bring into the fight any long guns that you have available. In the other scenario where the subject physically assaults you, one strike to the throat may not be enough. Be prepared to take any action against them, which will allow you the opportunity to separate. Use this separation to protect yourself with any additional weapons at your disposable. Their actions will dictate your level of force. It is not good enough to initiate a great plan and suddenly stop. Only consider stopping once you are no longer in danger.

Fatal Errors and Flaws - 35

Over here, over there, everywhere,

Today, tomorrow, always:

Bad men there are.

Hate you they do.

Kill you they will.

Watch out you better.

  -   Old Shoshone Refrain

I have always mentioned the Fatal Errors and everyone has seen them many times during training. However, it is apparent that no one has retained the information that these simple commandments, if you will, express. Nearly all of them deal within the realm of mental planning and preparations. Like most actions in life, police work or shall I say effective and safe police work, is mental. When we lose focus and attention, we get hurt and killed. Add to this the fact that police work is the most stressful job in the civilized world, mental planning is everything. Let's look at the ten most common Fatal Errors. I will place "physical" or "mental" at the end of each to denote if this category is a physical or mental task.

1. Attitude – This does not indicate our projected attitude that people see such as, anger, happy, aggressive, etc. This is the title given to attention failure. Attention is one of the most important mental states we possess and is why attention is Chapter 6 by itself. It affects almost everything we do. Understanding how to control your attention is paramount to safety. Because of a lack of proper attitude, we fail ourselves, our families, and the citizens we protect. This is how we mentally prepare ourselves to face the day. Are we going to focus on the task as they occur or fail to keep our head in the game? Are we going to let uncontrollable events affect the way we approach our job? Things like no pay raise again, my supervisor sucks, my kid failed a class, my wife lost her job, or my air conditioning broke. Any and all of these can affect your attitude, creating distractions and blocking your ability to "see" the dangers when they approach. The number one rule of law enforcement has always been and will always be, to come home safe at the end of your shift. **"Mental"**

2. Tombstone Courage – This is known as the "John Wayne" effect. An approach dates back as far as law enforcement. I wear a badge and carry a gun. I possess the authority to enforce the law. I will be respected and obeyed. This may have been true in centuries past, but times, society and parenting have changed. Parents teach their children to resist authority and it shows. The family has broken down and with it the necessary nurturing from two parents to instill moral and family values in their children. Bad guys often receive more respect than law enforcement. No one believes they have ever done anything wrong; the parents support the children over the school and the judicial system. Once tragedy occurs, they will complain that everyone, except for themselves, has let this child down. Respect for your position, as anyone who has worked the streets for any time will attest, fades further each year. Everyone wants to argue, has an excuse, feels profiled, or thinks they are innocent. We understand the dangers involved. I even explained in my previous books how the streets of America can be more dangerous than the battlefields of Iraq and Afghanistan. The days of the "One Riot, One Ranger" philosophy is gone. Wait for back up when taking police actions that could lead to a detention. **"Mental"**

3. Rest – Most research today consider the lack of rest as the most important of the errors. There is no replacement for the necessary hours of sleep on your performance. Force Science Research has shown that police officers who do not get the necessary sleep each night have various medical problems and dangers associated with this simple process. Athletes have been shown the three necessities of a successful career; proper diet, sleep (at least 8 hours each day), and exercise. No single one of these is any more important than the other is. Failure to accomplish one and the entire process fails. After a 2 year sleep study involving 5000 officers, 46% had nodded off while driving, 40% had sleep disorders, and 53.9% of the night shift had improper sleep habits and insomnia. Officers with sleep disorders were twice as likely to experience events in their career with negative consequences. Though 94% considered themselves in good physical shape, 79% were overweight. Lack of sleep had adverse effects on decision-making and performance. You are a warrior. The proof is in the statistics. Warriors fight, get injured, and sometimes killed for the cause they believe in. Few mourn your loss more than your fellow warriors do. It is a simple solution to a simple problem. **"Mental"**

4. Bad Positioning – Good situational awareness techniques will assist you in proper positioning tactics based on the type of action involved. There are many various observations needed in an encounter. Notice any changes in behaviors, consciously exercise your mental planning and tactics, always place yourself in a position of advantage, and have good situational awareness skills. When you make traffic stops, observe their pre and post stop behaviors, watch for the critical issues like brake lights and turn signals. Stop your car at least two car lengths back, keep everyone in their car and approach on the passenger's side if possible. When backing up another officer, determine the situation and position yourself to cover the occupants while not becoming involved with the stop. If you are involved in a foot pursuit, follow the proper tactics to always maintain a position of safety. Everything we do involves positioning and situational awareness of the environment. Be sure to follow these simple rules. **"Mental"**

5. Recognizing Danger – This is the attention and recognition of the critical issues that are presented each time you come across someone. I can assure you that someone on a regular basis has considered harming you during your shift. Take the initiative to follow the maxim I proposed in *Tactical Survival* of Study Train Survive. Study the intricacies of the job and always learn the newest tactics and techniques through training. They have the advantage of surprise in their favor and action usually beats reaction. Utilizing attention with training and experience can give you precious seconds with advance recognition of a behavior. This allows you to move to the all-important phase 2 or time compression of the OODA loop. Your next actions can have lifelong consequences. Understanding these philosophies and the reactions to them can increase your survival odds. **"Mental"**

6. <u>Hands</u> – These are the two primary body parts of the suspects, which will hurt you. Know where they are and what is in them at every second of your encounter. They are the source of all bad events to come and must be controlled. 16,000 officers will be assaulted and injured each year and it is in your best interest to try and not be one of those victim officers. How do you do that? I am trying to answer a multitude of questions in my books. We are studying behaviors and reactions to those behaviors. I will repeat this phrase numerous times, but action always beats reaction. If you know from where the assault will initiate, then you have to make a conscious effort to keep track of their hands. Never let them reach into a pocket, stand with their arms behind them, approach a car without being able to see them or become involved with anyone without their hands in plain sight. The FBI has reported that this single action of keeping their hands in sight can greatly reduce the chances of the officer being killed. There are some of you reading this and saying, "This is common sense." It is common sense, but is also a common error repeated by everyone each day as we allow diversion of our attention. **"Mental"**

7. <u>Relaxing Too Soon</u> – Another word for this is complacency and we have already discussed how it occurs. Never trust the person encountered. Un-events will occur on a regular basis. What I mean is that each and every day many of the things that we do, begin to seem routine. As these un-events fail to unfold anything new, we start to perceive this state as normal. Later in this chapter, I will explain in detail the Normalization of Deviance. We begin taking short cuts. We feel over confident on our experiences and believe we will recognize an event before it can happen. The truth of the matter is that we must maintain a consistency in the way we conduct ourselves with nearly everyone. This helps to prevent the shortcuts. Relaxing too soon is taking a short cut. We know we cannot afford to play catch up as action always beats reaction. Relax after the encounter. You can never let your guard down when dealing with the public. **"Mental"**

8. <u>Handcuffing</u> – This is usually the lack of handcuffing or poor handcuffing tactics. You can always take them off later, but if you are suspicious enough to detain them, handcuff them. It eliminates the threat of number 6, the hands. It is not only important to handcuff the suspect, but you must properly handcuff them. We have all heard about someone escaping an officer's custody by slipping out of the handcuffs. It occurs more often than we like to imagine. Again, what we are talking about is taking a short cut. Secure them with their hands behind the back, palms out, tight enough to prevent them from slipping out, and double lock the cuffs. Many of you will read this and say, "This is the basics we learned on the first day!" True, oh so very true. However, each day we work without an incident the un-events begin to feel normal. Ignore all of the complaining from the suspects about the cuffs. They were never intended to be comfortable. Pay attention to the basics. **"Mental"**

9. Search – When the conditions are correct and safe, conduct a search. If there is a need to search and not just a quick pat down, remember number eight, handcuffing. Everyone will miss something in a search at some point in their career. We have to take our time and be methodical. Start and finish at the same place each time. Make it a habit to be thorough. Many officers have been killed because we failed this simple task. Never assume someone else conducted a thorough search. Search them again if you are transporting for another officer. This is also the place to bring up search locations of persons. The bad guys know that we will not thoroughly search females and usually fail to conduct a great search on men. They will hide weapons and contraband in the one area most frequently overlooked the crotch. In fact, 75% of criminals will hide their articles of contraband in the crotch because they state that they have either never been searched there or not very well searched. In men arrestees, you have to thoroughly grab all of the area to see if there are more objects in place than are supposed to be there. For female arrestees, male officers are getting away from the basics out of fear of complaints. Run the back of your hand around their waist and pockets to ensure that there is nothing immediately available. Have a female officer conduct a thorough search later if they are arrested. Explain to them that they will be strip searched at the jail facility and if they have anything on them, it will result in additional charges. Also, search the rear of your car each and every time anyone is placed there to ensure anything found can be charged to the current suspect. They may be afraid to tell you they have something secreted and remove it in the rear of your car. **"Mental"**

10. Equipment – Be proficient with your equipment and understand the need for back up gear for your primary tools. Keep a basic survival rule of our Special Operations Forces; 2 is 1, 1 is none. If your primary equipment fails and you do not have a backup, it is the same as not having anything at all. A gun that fails when it's needed or a flashlight dies when lighting is critical jeopardizes your survival. Carry a backup weapon, two flashlights, two knives, multiple handcuff keys, and a go-bag in the trunk of your car. In the bag, you can carry a change of clothing including boots, snacks, and a camelback or bottled water.

Never allow this simple action to endanger you or prevent you from continuing your work when needed. **"Mental"**

In addition to the "Fatal Errors" committed by law enforcement, another area of review conducted by the FBI was the "Fatal Flaws." These are the areas determined by the researchers to be the primary mistakes committed by the officers, which led to their deaths. After the completion of each three-part study, the FBI maintained a Fatal Flaws list. After 15 years and the completion of the study, the list remained the same. The reason is we rarely change our training modules and believe we would never commit them. Each and every one of these mistakes is directly contributable to failed mental planning. In both of my previous books, *Criminal Interdiction* and *Tactical Survival,* I have discussed these issues. Understanding how vital they are is essential.

1. **Failure to wait for back up.** This is the number one reason, in my opinion, why we are continually killed and injured on the job. There is this false impression that everyone will respond to your lawful commands and authority. The truth is nowhere near this belief. At the time of arrest, they are on equal ground with you. This is the time to expect things to go wrong. I know we have all arrested people without incident while alone or had them flee after passive resistance. Eventually, you will find the one person, who knows they have multiple previous arrests, and are facing enhanced prison time and will aggressively assault you in an effort to escape the situation. Wait for backup whenever it is at all possible.

2. **The failure to draw your weapon when the situation called for it.** Too many of us have had the "best interest of the department" pounded into our psyche, especially from inside the training academies. Many agencies have gone too far to the left with their political correctness and called the display of your firearm in the performance of duties a "use of force." This is in my opinion a "show of force." The more it is pounded into your mind that every time you draw your weapon it equates to a negative act, your life is being placed in greater jeopardy. It becomes a Normalization of Deviance and creating a negative impression in your mind. This short-circuiting of an essential action creates a lag in your response time and ultimately endangers your life. If the situation calls for it, draw your weapon. This simple action is moving you forward into the OODA loop and better preparing you to meet the possible threat.

3. <u>Tunnel vision when dealing with more than one suspect.</u> This is another common mistake by law enforcement. It deals with the concept of attention redirection. If it is at all possible, we should always try to avoid dealing with multiple persons without backup. It is simply impossible to properly cover more than one person if you are alone. Remember, if you are a cover officer, it is your job to only be a cover officer. It is required that you stay back to oversee the entire scene and not become involved at all with any facet of the investigation unless it is required. The tactical discussion of the cover officer is in the next chapter. For this topic, let's explain peripheral vision. Peripheral vision is a part of vision that occurs outside the very center of gaze. It detects motion. The loss of peripheral vision, while retaining central vision is tunnel vision. In other words, the purpose of peripheral vision is to recognize motion that occurs around us. In a stressful event, all focus is on the center of gaze, thus giving us tunnel vision. This bodily response to stress also places us in grave danger when dealing with more than one person. We will never see the others begin to move toward us from a flanking position.

4. <u>Failure to keep people in their cars.</u> This is again an issue of the previous scenarios. Once a person exit's their car, they are on equal footing with you. Equality is not a logical feature of this scenario. The advantage must always be with the officer. If more than one person exits a car, there are the dangers of tunnel vision. Without a cover officer, you are at a disadvantage.

5. <u>Proper vehicle placement after a traffic stop.</u> Proper vehicle placement after a traffic stop carries with it a double front line of protection. First, most officers will correlate the positioning from the threat that could exist from within the car. The second threat is from the approaching traffic from behind. This is a very critical consideration because statistics show that more than 50% of all police officer deaths have a traffic component. First, when conducting a traffic stop, you should stop at least two car lengths back if possible, from the target vehicle. In addition, you should pull as far off the road as is reasonable. This helps you against both threats. If the subject was to exit the car with a firearm, you have allowed yourself some distance to provide a reaction. Second, if your car is struck from behind, this distance allows absorption of energy. It will also reduce the impact to the violator's vehicle, which provides you additional protection from the energy of the striking car.

6. <u>Failure to immediately control a known suspect.</u> This is directly attached to number 8 in the Fatal Errors category of "Handcuffing". If you have a known or even a suspect of a crime, it is essential to your safety to control the two body parts that can cause harm; the hands. As I said before, if you can legally detain them, handcuff their hands behind their back, palms out.

7. <u>Mental planning of different scenarios.</u> I have talked about the importance of this this topic in terms of the OODA Loop, Hick's Law, and Rex Applegate's training. There are those in the field today who will say that visualization techniques do nothing. Yet, everyone in the business of self-defense, law enforcement, athletics, and combatives can all explain how effective mental planning is to any scenario.

Again, I believe that it all falls back to "The Normalization of Deviance." This is a term developed by NASA and former shuttle commander Dr. Story Musgrove after investigating what happened to the Challenger and Columbia Space Shuttles. NASA had identified both of these failures on previous missions. Noted on the prior missions of the Challenger shuttle was the degradation of the O-rings. The manufacturer notified NASA that they could get worse in cold weather.

Minor tile damage had become common and expected after shuttle take offs. In both cases, NASA had determined the damage as "acceptable." With each successful mission, the acceptability of problems (quality control) worsened because nothing negative had ever happened. Sadly, as with most things in our lives, there are no compliance without consequence.

The Normalization of Deviance is the downward change in standards each time a successful mission is completed, even with the forewarned knowledge of trouble. This is a condition, which applies to all areas of human existence including law enforcement. Each time we rush through or take short cuts in the processes, we mentally cause deviations in our thinking. "I am able to do this without ever doing that and nothing ever happens to me." It creates "acceptable" dangers in a profession where there can be none. It is a simple process of mental concentrations to the processes taught which we know will work. Eventually, the short cuts will lead you down a very slippery trail; One that can cost you your life.

Another important cluster of facts can also play out in regards to all of this information. During the FBI's 15-year study, they also looked at the officers and their personality/ behavior traits. Each of the 54 murdered officers in the study carried at least two (2) or more of the descriptive traits as described by not only the officers who knew them, but from the assailant who murdered them. Here is the list:

- Friendly to everyone
- Well-liked by community and department
- Tends to use less force than other officers felt they would in similar situations
- Hard working
- Tends to perceive self as more public relations than law enforcement or very service oriented
- Use force only as a last resort – peers claim they would use force at an earlier point in similar circumstances
- Doesn't follow all of the rules, especially in regard to:
  Arrest
  Confrontation with prisoners
  Traffic stops
  Does not wait for backup
- Feels they can "read" others/situations and will drop guard as a result
- Tends to look for "good" in others
- "Laid back" and "easy going"

What we see is a combination of many of the areas of concern I have wrote about previously like, not waiting for back up, being too friendly, not recognizing or reacting to dangers, and taking short cuts. Often time's police are seen as rude, rough, and mean. There are times for "Officer Friendly." You cannot be hard in every occurrence. Common sense, an attribute that is so often lacking, has to come into each scenario. Each time you encounter someone in a traffic stop for instance, you do not have to be a machine. You can be firm when needed yet remember this is not a social call it is a traffic stop. You should have a stern and serious attitude by appearance or presence only. If you stop a mother with her children or an elderly couple, you can still be polite and firm.

Unfortunately, many agencies and supervisors do not understand that this is a job of confrontation. Everyone receives complaints at some point. It is the job of the supervisor to handle these issues, but many see it as just more paperwork and chastise the officer. Many of the "mottos" can themselves lead to unrealistic expectations from people who have not worked the street for years and civilians alike. "Courtesy, Service, and Protection" are mixed with departmental attitudes of "Officer Friendly." This consistent laid-back attitude of many officers raises the odds against you. Society changes on a regular basis and continually becomes more violent. Do the job with your safety as the principal issue each day. Follow the rules as taught and continue to learn. Together you will raise the odds in your favor should one day evil approaches with a smile on their face.

Attention - 36

-moral ambiguity is what the threat counts on during the initial phase of his assault, to delay your appropriate response just long enough to kill you.

- Mike Straw

If you read this chapter and parts of it appears familiar, that is because it is from my book, *Tactical Survival*. I spoke at length about the importance of attention to the safety of a police officer. I have included it again as a refresher with additional information on the Colavita Dominance effect. This is an important scientifically proven event that occurs in all of us. Recently, the Colavita Dominance theory was brought into a trial in California as a cause and affect involving a police-shooting event. Attention plays a vital role in maintaining the correct mental focus to avoid all of the negatives from the last chapter.

I included these topics together because you cannot read one without being aware of the others. We know about learning to read body languages, voice commands, and responses (all of which I will discuss), but attention? Attention or our attention to detail is an important aspect of officer safety. Attention is how the brain operates when receiving the information from our surrounding environment through all of the various sensory receptions. Think about the various mental distractions that we have to work with each day. However, our brains can only focus its attention on one thing at a time. It will remove all other issues from your attention span to focus on that issue.

Despite how good we think we are at multitasking, we are really only good at one thing at a time. When we think we are multitasking, our minds are actually switching from one activity to the other. There are many who believe they are excellent at multitasking. You can drive, watch the calls on the computer screen, listen to the patrol radio, and talk on the cell phone. In reality, your brain is only programmed to handle one of these situations at a time. When you are involved in one, the others are not getting any attention. You say to yourself, "but I am on the phone all of the time and driving while watching the calls on the computer." Yes you are, just not at the same time. Think back to when you were trying to read the notes on the computer and talking to someone on the cell phone. One or the other actually gets cut off for that moment as you switch your attention between the two. Then suddenly, because you are not paying attention you brake hard to avoid a collision. When we have been driving for many years, the actions we take are more reactionary. You do not have to think about when to brake, accelerate, or turn the steering wheel. They are simply trained motor skills. Accidents occur when you do not notice to take the action in time.

The brain is unable to focus on everything so it tries to prioritize the most important. What it considers important at that moment may not be the most significant thing to you. Additionally, thinking about other issues in your life will lead to an inability to focus. Attention is like a spotlight and you will only notice the objects in the light. If you spotlight on one person, you will not notice anyone else. This is the inherent danger of dealing with multiple suspects. When they are out of the car or as pedestrians, you cannot deal with them all.

As we enter the topic of attention focus, let me explain how the eyes work in conjunction with the brain. The entire eye is designed to track motion. We have two types of eyesight, central and peripheral. The central is the eyesight that is directly in front of us. The peripheral is the sight zone to the sides of the center. The central sight zone observes more than the peripherals. The peripheral sights are not as strong and capable of recognizing only one movement at a time. This movement recognition is for faster motion. In other words, if two movements of various speeds occur in your peripheral zone, the faster moving object is observed while other movements can be missed. Keep this concept in mind as we explore the upcoming topics of attention and redirection. Understanding why a process works will explain the outcome of the event.

Keep everyone in their cars until a situation arises that requires them to be out. Try not to deal with multiple suspects until you have backup. Without standing back to take in the entire event, you cannot handle them safely. If you must take action, separate one and make the others stay away. As additional officers arrive on the scene, direct them to focus on the others. Recently, in central Florida, an officer patting down three suspicious subjects, was shot in the head and killed. He knew back up was on the way and failed to wait. We have all done this same thing many times before in our careers. This is NOT criticism of this fallen officer. It is a harsh lessens for the rest of us. When trying to do multiple things when dealing with a suspect, you will only do one thing right. This one thing will then be something else, then something else, and so on. If you will remember this simple fact of attention, it may one day pay off in saving your life. Remember the FBI statistics that 38% of officers were killed during a crime in progress. 60% of those officers were killed while trying to make an arrest of the suspect before backup had arrived.

Attention can be controlled by distraction or misdirection. One person could start going through their wallet, which will focus your attention. The other suspect recognizes that you are concentrating on the item and pulls a weapon or discards contraband. If focused on a specific item or subject, you may not recognize the developing dangers.

In order to prevent this, stand back and control the encounter. Do not move close and wait for back up. By standing back and not focusing attention to a single person or object, you are keeping your attention on the entire chain of events. The moment you start reading driver's licenses or writing notes, your attention is misdirected from the overall situation. Make sure they keep their hands out of pockets and in sight.

This brings up a fascinating reality called inattentional blindness. The brain is simply too overwhelmed with everything in our environment. Therefore, we developed attention to keep us focused on specific items of interest. Remember that we can only focus on a single event. To allow this to happen, our brain ignores everything else. Because of this normal psychological event, large things can occur around us and we never see it happen. Think of magicians when they have you concentrating on one thing while changes occur in the background. They are not expected and your focus is directed; therefore, you will not notice it. You may not always recognize change where it is not expected. This is a common cause of motorcycle accidents. We look down the road before pulling out from a side street. We take a quick glance. Our mind focuses on cars, vans, trucks, etc. you do not see a motorcycle, bicyclist, or pedestrian approaching. An accident occurs and we are left telling everyone, "I looked and never saw anything. I have no idea where they came from."

The same psychology applies to law enforcement. Knowing how this "change blindness" occurs, train yourself to focus on a series of events. For instance, you are about to stop a car. Training teaches us to watch the people inside the car and their behaviors such as, how the driver operates the car, where the driver is looking, the brake lights, and turn signals, how they pull off the road and stop their vehicle. Can you pay attention to all of these things at once? From a distance, your center of attention is the car. As you focus on more specifics, create a checklist of things before, during, and after the stop. If you follow this checklist of indicators, then one by one, eliminate them from the list. You catch up to the car and do not immediately activate your emergency equipment. You observe the driver and passengers. How are they behaving? Is the driver watching you in the side and rear view mirrors? What about the car, is the license plate proper? Now is the time to run the tag, not after the stop. Are there air fresheners, bumper stickers, rental car signs, or other things that could heighten the event?

In your mind you have check listed the occupants and the car itself. Initiate the emergency equipment and proceed with the traffic stop. Does the car stop in a reasonable manner or travel some distance before stopping? What are the occupants doing? Did the car stop a safe distance from the road? Are you stopping about two car lengths back from them? Are the brake lights and/or turn signals still activated?

You can see how placing the item into a mental checklist allows you to safely conduct the stop. Most officers will observe the car and make the stop. They may notice a couple of the items, yet miss many more. There are just too many things to pay attention too at the same time. The ones missed could be the signal needed to save your life.

Attention redirection is an action we use more often without realizing. A pickpocket artist will be good at redirecting your attention. They get you to look at one thing while they concentrate on taking something else. Magicians and illusionist do the same thing. "Watch the cards," they will say which focuses your attention. Once that has happened, they can do most anything else they want. Keep in mind that attention is single topic focused. If your focus is where someone does not want it to be, they will cause a distraction to redirect your attention. Remember the Lunsford tape out of Texas? He has two subjects out of the car while searching the trunk. There is no way to see everything they are doing. They distracted and then rushed him. In the first chapter of this book, we see another example of attention redirection. Bart Johnson tells Officer Davis about his brother the police officer. Officer Davis reaches for a notepad from his pocket, which opened the door of opportunity for Johnson to shoot him. An attention redirection was added which caused the officer to be distracted

Suspect behaviors tell all if you can maintain your attention to the details like developing a baseline. You've experienced hundreds of different people during the course of your job and developed a baseline for normal behaviors. When you come across someone behaving completely different, focus on them and investigate the reasons for the mannerisms. It is comparable to animal behaviors. Domesticated animals like to interact with people. They are curious and trusting. Wild animals never want to get close to humans. They are not curious and live in a constant state of fright, flight, or fight. Given the chance, they will leave. Left with no options, they will fight. This is the same with criminals and the average person. Normal people have no problem being around you while the crook wants to stay away.

The limbic system is a set of brain structures, which support a variety of functions including emotion, behavior, motivation, long-term memory, and olfaction. When you are observing people, constantly search for overt behavior displayed due to nervous emotions and feelings. When someone is nervous, the limbic system in the brain will recognize that stressor and begin to generate energy for the fright, flight or fight response that follows.

I've talked about this topic in every class and book. Body language or Kinesics is the study of nonlinguistic body movements. We all have behaviors that will exaggerate under pressure. Just as a polygraph machine measures changes in blood pressure and heart rate, so can you. These changes cause a person to sweat and adjust behaviors. Start watching everyone's behaviors when you have them stopped. Pay attention to their breathing, their pulse rate in the suprasternal notch of their throat, and their hands. The standard for a resting heart rate is 60 – 100 beats per minute. If you are out with someone and you have back up present, ask them if you can check their heart rate. Check the brachial pulse in their arm, or if they say no, simply watch the pulse rate in their neck. Count the number of beats in 10 seconds and multiply that by 6. This will give you an approximate heart rate which will help you to determine how stressed they are.

Do their hands shake, but relax as the encounter progresses? This shows how they are calming down in your presence and therefore not feeling guilty. Pay attention as they fumble through their wallets and purses. Do they tremble, try to hide the contents, or start to look and then stop to say they cannot find what you have asked them for? Pay attention to their eye movements and the direction they are looking. They will often seek a way out or towards your weapons, their car, their accomplices, etc. Observe their inability to stand still while asking them questions. Make a mental note of the items in plain view around them. They can tell a lot about the habits of the person. Is there Visine or lighters in the console or seat next to them? Ask them if they smoke. People keep close the things they use regularly. Why have a lighter immediately available if you do not smoke? Chapter 9 of *Criminal Interdiction* is dedicated to this topic.

There is one behavior which I believe is the single most important an officer can pay attention to; audio occlusion. When you repeat your commands, be prepared. Command repetition occurs when the person is beginning to shut you out because their mind is occupied. This is an ideal time to discuss the Colavita Visual Dominance effect. This phenomenon is whenever you have two separate stimuli of a visual and auditory nature, the brain automatically overrides towards the visual. In other words, a suspect you stop is stressed. You are giving him verbal commands. His visual channels will override the auditory and he will fail to hear you. A visual can be internalization as well when they are trying to decide their next course of action. They will never hear your complete sentences and fail to obey your commands. They are redirecting their focus internally and we can only direct our attention on one thing at a time. The internal thought processes are unlikely for anyone confronted by the police. They are entering their fight or flight, over stressed, adrenaline pump. They are very scared and are mentally deciding their best course of action. In almost every video of an officer who is assaulted or killed, you will hear the officer repeat themselves to the suspects at some point before the attack. It may occur only once, but you will clearly see the behavioral change of the suspect. Just as you, pay attention to the video, pay attention to your suspects. Avoid distractions because this is when they will initiate their actions.

Situational awareness is a topic we need reminding of to keep it in the forefront of our minds. You are taking stock in your surrounding environment. You have to be aware of the areas and the people in them. When we stop and write reports, be cognizant of the area you park, the accesses and blind spots, as well as looking around frequently for anyone approaching. The largest, empty lot makes a good place to park so you can see 360 degrees around. Do not wear your seat belt to allow for a quick exit if needed. Several officers are killed each year from having someone approach and shoot them while they are sitting in their cars. Apply the same precautions while in restaurants or other businesses. How often have you seen the events of a deranged gunman entering a restaurant or other establishment and start shooting everyone? Sadly, it is a common occurrence around the world. Remember that there were three police officers murdered in 2011 as they sat in their cars while not involved in any specific police duty. They were simply in uniform and presented a target.

In *Criminal Interdiction,* I described situational awareness as:

"Be aware of your surroundings at all times. I already know that this not completely possible all of the time. But just like your traffic stops, consider everywhere you stop. As you pull into a parking lot or an abandoned area to work on reports, be aware of the area. When walking into restaurants or convenience stores, do you survey what is going on inside before entering? Do you sit at a restaurant in a place of advantage or disadvantage? Wild Bill Hickok was sitting at a table with his back to a door when killed. Recently in Washington State, four police officers were shot to death while sitting at a table and working on their computers at a coffee shop. Situational awareness is everywhere you go on or off duty. You should park in a well-lit area where you can leave easily. The area where you park should have a clear view all around. This is so you will not be surprised if someone approaches you. Remember, with the technologies that exist today in a patrol car, like in car computers, it causes us to stare at the technology all of the time. Be aware of your surroundings at all times."

Situational awareness is ever changing, fluid and is difficult at best to maintain for very long. At home and in our personal lives, we can relax. Constantly being aware can cause a person to breakdown over time. Our lifestyles have given us a tendency to allow a daily routine to govern our lives. During routines, no or little thought has to occur. Everything just "is," as it flows in and out of our experiences. It becomes easy to allow this calm or routine to flow into our work. Repetition without failure creates a sense of normalcy. As was described in Chapter 5, The Normalization of Deviance begins to overcome the areas, which we know to avoid, yet do not.

Sports psychologist and top Olympic coaches use visualization techniques for their athletes. About 90% of Olympic athletes use some form of visualization and 97% say it helps. Visualization techniques can also reduce stresses and builds confidence. It helps you to focus on doing important things right and is proven to help when the actual task is performed. The mental imaging initiates the repetitive muscle responses that will place the action into your normal motor skills. You can see why this simple mind practice can make a difference in your survival.

When alone, you should practice visualization techniques involving various scenarios. Have them in mind during a traffic stop or other types of encounters. Quickly say in your mind, "If this person does A, I will respond with B. I can follow B with C and D if necessary." These brain games will prepare your mind for various types of threatening events that can occur. Therefore, if they happen, you will automatically respond with planned motor skills. This instant reaction can mean the difference for your survival.

Maintain mental awareness regardless of your agencies actions. What I mean is this is a job of offensive measures despite what your department's political correctness advocates. Job safety depends upon your swift decisions and actions to problems. A good cop is one who is aggressive. They seek out the criminals, not wait for the next call to come in from a civilian. Do not fall into a defensive mindset. Maintain the offensive and take the fight to them.

Agencies bowing down to public opinions based upon political correctness have hurt and killed officers. We do not have to wait for suspects to hit, kick, grab, resist, stab, try to run over, or even shoot before you take action. This entire idea of defensive tactics is ridiculous when you consider that our job is to restrain and arrest which can only be accomplished through offensive tactics. To protect life and property does not mean to sit and wait for them to take the first action. Take the initiative or offense to keep yourself safe.

In 2011, there were four officers, eight in 2012 killed in ambush style attacks by gunfire, and many more ambushed and not killed. You have to remember that this world is a dangerous place. Your destiny will be equivalent to how well you are prepared. Not all evils can be prevented, but situational awareness and visualization techniques can help.

Preparations - 37

Martyrs alert the world to the presence of evil. Warriors do something about it.

- Phil Messina

Once we have directed ourselves towards self-observations of attention understanding, we can now apply it to behaviors. Observation and recognition of behaviors is the difference of survival in a deadly encounter. Advance recognition of their behaviors has taken you through phase 2 of the OODA loop, which can be a second faster than someone else. In a life threatening battle, a few seconds is everything. We also discussed the importance of avoiding distractions. Distractions are intentional acts to draw you away from the focus of the events. This is the reasoning behind the refresher chapter of attention. Simple distractions have led to the deaths and injuries of many police officers over the decades. Understanding how to avoid them is imperative. Recently, I watched a video of an officer who arrests the driver of a car. A female passenger is allowed to roam around on the scene. A second passenger is in the car and a backup officer arrives at the scene. Remember the role of a backup or cover officer. They are only there to cover you. They are not to engage in the activities unless the situation escalates and requires them to take action. Because of the pacing and talkative female, the cover officer engages with her. His role has changed because he allowed it. The rear seat passenger pulls a gun and kills the original officer. Learn how to avoid distractions, recognize behaviors, and control the scenes.

Only through proper preparations can we have the highest expectations of success. Throughout time, soldiers, philosophers, and sports figures have described preparation in various forms.

- "In the fields of observation, chance favors only the prepared mind." – Louis Pasteur
- "We do not rise to the level of our expectations; we fall to the level of our training." – Archilochus
- "Pressure is something that you feel only when you don't know what you're doing." – Chuck Knoll
- "The cerebral part of the game is the most challenging part of the game. The cerebral part is where you can advance yourself and (what you) have to constantly stay on top of. I think sometimes you can get away with the physical part by being a great athlete. I can overcome that, but the cerebral part, you can't get behind in the mental aspect of the game. Everything happens so fast." – Peyton Manning
- "Success depends upon previous preparation, and without such preparation there is sure to be failure." – Confucius
- "Luck is what happens when preparation meets opportunity." - Seneca
- "There are no secrets to success. It is the result of preparation, hard work, and learning from failure." – Colin Powell

Preparations can carry with it a multitude of meaning. We should understand that physical fitness is a process to follow for general health. We also discovered that our appearance can have a significant importance to our safety. The FBI study of interviewed cop killers discovered that many of the murdered officers died because of their appearance. They were sloppy, overweight, and practiced poor safety procedures. The bad guy knew they could overcome them so like any predator, did.

We also learned that stress is the primary cause of many of the ill's that plague law enforcement. Heart attacks are a yearly event that leads to many officers deaths. There were nine in 2011while on duty and countless more off duty. Physical fitness and diet control is necessary law enforcement preparations. It also plays a critical role in a Force Science research study. In their force Fatigue Threshold study, they measure how it takes before the body begins to lose energy to maintain the fight. The study utilized officers who considered themselves fit. The conclusions of the study showed that he body begins to lose strength within 30 seconds, and within 2 minutes, the upper body is fatigued. It takes the body an amazing 15 minutes to recover from the event and more energy is necessary to restrain than resist. Therefore, if you decide to fight someone of equal strengths, the advantage is still theirs as you try to restrain them. Your own physical conditioning, weather, and the amount of equipment you are carrying can reduce these numbers. The FBI found in one of their studies that 12% of the murdered officers who went to the ground in a fight died by one of their own weapons. In my opinion, this study explains this statistic. Within 2 minutes, your upper body has fatigued. No longer capable of defending yourself, the bag guy removes a weapon and kills you. You would not imagine going to work without a service weapon; you should never go to work unfit either mentally or physically.

Of equal importance and in many cases of a far greater importance, are the preparations of the mind. As seen earlier, the mental aspects of the job creates most of the life threatening incidences. We need to fully understand our own focus abilities and strive every day to enhance them. I suggested in *Tactical Survival,* one way to help us maintain control of our attention is through a mental checklist before an actual encounter takes place. By doing this, we can assure ourselves of covering many of the pertinent areas of the event.

According to the Academy of Achievement, a Washington based group designed to bring together the world's most successful people with successful students, there are six keys to success.

1. Passion – A strong feeling or emotion. This career requires passion. You must have a deep passion to overcome evil. Police officers are America's soldiers at home. Without passion in your heart for the job you are simply taking up space. "The inner drive that turns your dreams into a shining reality."

2. Vision – A vivid mental image. "To attain your goal, you must first see it in your mental eye." Just as I have been preaching all along, it is in our mindset that all things are achievable. If you allow distractions to enter your mindset at the critical moments, one day a consequence will befall.

3. Preparation - The cognitive process of thinking about what you will do if something happens. "Success isn't a matter of luck- it requires practice, study, and strategy." We see it in the famous quote mentioned above by Seneca, "Luck is what happens when preparation meets opportunity." Look at the definition itself. You must prepare yourself to overcome adversity. Preparation equates to training. It lies within my own maxim from *Tactical Survival,* Study Train Survive.

4. Courage - A quality of spirit that enables you to face danger. The ability to "prevail despite hardship, pain and mortal danger." I have always proclaimed to all that it takes a special person to become a police officer and an even greater person

to dedicate your life to the profession. Just as most soldiers stay in the services for only a few years, so will most police officers. Then there are those who become "lifers" in both the domestic and foreign services.

5. Perseverance – This stands for not just determination, but for persistent determination. "No great achievement comes without obstacles." Although they were met with failure, they "doggedly persevered until they succeeded against the odds." Regardless of the situation, you represent justice in our society despite what a minority of the population is led to believe. With the correct training and practice you can overcome even the worst of situations.

6. Integrity – An undivided completeness with nothing wanting. A moral soundness. "The road that leads to real success has no short cuts." (Normalization of Deviance) It is an internal awareness that separates you from most others. It establishes trust which without; you become the antithesis of what you stand for.

Imagine a profession founded upon these principles. At the Academy of Achievement, the greatest and most successful people brought together with some of this country's brightest students. These students learn that to reach the level of their mentors, which range from former presidents, military generals, and athletes, these are the six categories of understanding for achievement. They are ours as well. Smile when you understand that these same principles have been our foundation since the first people, afraid of the evil within the populace, hired someone for protection.

Representational Channels - 38

He that has eyes to see and ears to hear may convince himself that no mortal can keep a secret. If his lips are silent, he chatters with his fingertips; betrayal oozes out of him at every pore.

- Sigmund Freud

Communication or informational exchanges pass to and from us via three Representational Channels or modalities by which we communicate. These Channels are Visual, Auditory, and Internalization (feeling or emotional). It is imperative to understand that we can only function within a single channel at any moment. In other words, one will work, but not two or all three at the same time. There is no such thing as multi-tasking. Most people on earth are visual creatures. For the general population the breakdown is:

Visual – 60%
Auditory – 30%
Internal – 10%

As you can see, the general population is 2-times more visual than the other Representational Channels. In earlier times, the 10% Internalization part of the population are victims. This is my opinion. In earlier times, self-preservation was more difficult. If one spent too much time in self-dialogue or pity, they were consumed. The actual communication occurs by one or a combination of channels from these modalities as:

Verbally
Tonality – tone of voice
Non-verbally – body language

Keen sight has always been the primary channel for predators. Acute hearing has always been paramount for prey. This reflects back to our origins as a species. We have all heard of the "fight or flight" syndrome. What most probably has not heard of is the complete and more accurate name of "freeze, flight, fight, or fright" syndrome. These categories are correct in their function and order. There is a phase that occurs at the moment that our senses are heightened called a freeze. It is seen in the animal world by prey animals when they hear or sense something. They will freeze; their ears attentive and pupils expand as they try to determine the cause of the alert. In combat, the same thing occurs. When a soldier encounters an initial sign of threat, the response demanded by his military training and reinforced by other members of his unit, is the "stop, watch, and listen" heightened-alertness response. This is believed to have evolved from the prey trying to avoid detection because predators primarily detect moving objects rather than color.

The second most common reaction is the flight or fleeing from the source of the threat. Thirdly is the well-publicized response of fight. Lastly and even less thought about is a term known as fright. Fright is the body's defense mechanism of total surrender or playing dead. Many animals will play dead when excessively threatened in the wild. This can also play a bearing on why some females when victimized will simply surrender and allow whatever to take place to happen. Many in our society question why someone would just allow such an act to take place without resistance. It is the absolute surrender of yourself due to the threat. Generally, it is because the mind and body has surrendered to the amount of stress applied against it.

Law enforcement training changes their Representational Channel percentages over time to accommodate their function. Police Representational Channels on average are:

87% - Visual
7% - Auditory
6% - Internal

What this has created is an officer who is very astute to the visuals of the job. I am amazed with time and experience, how quickly and easily I could notice the small things that were a part of my job. I recognized the expired tag decal, the tampered temp tag, whether tint was illegal and guess almost dead on what the light transmittance was with a quick glance, the speed of approaching traffic, the driver wearing headsets, etc. They were small essentials of the job that I performed every day and became, like all officers, very efficient with the visuals. I remember once while searching the passenger's compartment of a car, opening a woman's purse on the front seat. I reached in and immediately found a bag with about an ounce of crack cocaine. This woman was standing behind me and to my left with my partner. As I reached into the bag, I saw her start to run in my peripheral vision. I instantly said aloud, "Nothing, there is nothing here." And I closed the purse, turned towards her, and said, "Thanks for cooperating with us today." Nervously she replied, "Your welcome." I grabbed and handcuffed her. She yelled out, "But you said there was nothing there!" My peripheral vision, like that of a predator, attunes to movement.

We are better at noticing many things, yet still miss the most important. They are the simple movements and actions that in some way can be considered "micro expressions." These are not the simple fast twitch movements of the face that we associate with the meaning. I see it as a way to explain the simple things that occur which we commonly miss over the "large expression" items like, running the red light, speeding, observing a fight, or other law breaking violations. What I am discussing are simplistic things related to our survival. The behavior of a person(s) when they first noticed you such as: the way they walk is different with one arm having less movement, the blinker or brakes light of the car are left on after the stop, repetition of questions or statements, the heartbeat in their suprasternal notch, over talkative, dry mouth, wiping hands on their legs, etc. These are some of my noticeable micro expressions.

With this ramped up visual acumen comes other changes as well. One must always remember that we can only operate in a single channel at any one time. Our total abilities within the channels must always equal 100%. Therefore, by increasing our visual abilities, we must also decrease our other channels. As you can "see," our visuals increased to 87%, yet our auditory capacities decreased to a stunning 7% from the general populace percentile of 30. What does all of this mean? Police officers are some of the worse listeners. To improve these listening skills, we have to consciously and deliberately focus on our interviewing skills.

It is our job to conduct interviews with everyone. During a traffic stop, a traffic crash, a domestic intervention, a pedestrian encounter, a burglary report, etc., we are conducting interviews. We conduct them constantly and fail to listen to what they tell us. We over control the interviews because as police officers, we learn to control every situation to maintain an advantage. In interviewing, you have to learn the difference. Ask anyone outside of the profession and they will say that you are not a good listener. You have been programmed not to listen because of the above average visuals to see what others miss. Our attention to understood details makes us effective in an interview

You are roadside with a subject and questioning him and at the same time filling out a form, a ticket, complaint, or field interview. The inflection of their voice and response to your questions are critical. This is certainly a time that requires extra caution. You cannot write and listen at the same time with any proficiency because of the singular Representational Channel rule. You can watch or listen, but not both. Otherwise, you will be asking questions, trying to listen to their response and write their answers down at the same time. While looking at them from several feet away, ask them the question and watch. Observe their behavior and response to the questions. If they provide a satisfactory answer, write the answer down when they are finished. If not, ask a clarifying question. Only write their response in the lull of time, which occurs in between the questions. In other words; watch, listen, wait, and then write.

Because of this transition of channels, new street officers who move to an investigators position will often find it difficult to interview with success. A determined effort is required to slow the process down and pay attention to the person. We also notice that the Internalization channel also reduces, but by only 4 percentage points from 10% to 6% of our totals. Emotional is not one of our strong points. Though sometimes visual, few on earth are more capable of repressing their feelings more than cops. The exception to this statement is in controlling an adrenaline rush from an incident that is almost overwhelming.

Written and recorded statements also fall within these rules. The words of a written statement express only 7% of the meaning that they intend. We can read a book and get a mental picture from the scene by a good writer and their use of punctuation. However, a written statement has ever moved few of us. Each person's interpretation of the statement can misconstrue the words. A written statement can often mean a great deal to the prosecution team, yet mean little to members of the jury. A prosecutor will read the statement aloud with them. Why? It is to add the next means of effective communication to the words; tone of voice.

Tone of voice can change the meaning and the entire theme of the events. It adds an additional 38% of understanding to the words alone. Tone of voice, as we are learning, based on its consistency and use can place in other people's mind an idea whether you are an expert, shy, over-bearing, rude, polite, etc. When the jury reads, "That was when I yelled stop. Then I turned and ran down the street towards my cousin's house." The prosecutor will read it as "That was when I yelled, STOP! Then I turned and RAN, towards my cousin's house!" With the exclamation points and capitalization of the verbs to give them meaning, the sentence takes on more urgency. It is in this urgency that the prosecution tries to make you realize her desperation. As you read the sentences with the exclamation points, you are adding tone in your mind. This tone indicates the severity of the statement. The defense though will read it simply as written as if they had just finished playing and it was time to go home.

We now have the words themselves and the tone of voice, the equivalency of a tape recording. Together, we are receiving 45% of the information they are trying to express. What categories of expression are left to fill in the balance of 55%? There is only one, the visuals or body language that is associated with the words and tones. Our body language or rather the leaking of various clusters, creates the majority of information expressed. Watch a video of the same person who is making the statement and only then do you have the opportunity to grasp the meaning in its entirety.

To help us understand these thoughts, we need to explore our subconscious. It is in the subconscious that our ability to recognize things occurs. It is a built up collection of our experiences, the storage drive if you will. Our brains take in and process so much information; it is natural to conclude there is too much to accept. Nearly every day we experience an event that causes our mind to stop and wonder, "That looks familiar," or "That sounds familiar." As a police officer, we often hear the phrase, "My hair on the back of my neck stood up." This may indicate that you have seen or heard something familiar to your sub conscious, but are unable to at once understand or recognize the trigger of this emotion. Body language exists in the sub conscious. We will see things that cause us to react without hesitation. Our minds, because of the volume of information in the environment, will categorize everything into concepts and miss the details. It is the "I can see the forest, but not the trees" idea.

Where are we going with this and how does it apply to police work? It specifically affects one of the most dangerous occurrences in our profession, complacency. We recognize complacency as the cause of so many officer injuries and deaths. It happens with our subconscious and the training we provide for it. Let's say you average 10 traffic stops a day. Nothing of any significance occurs in 5 days of work. Therefore, you have made about 50 traffic stops where nothing has happened. Your subconscious relaxes and starts to relate these stops to no events. Your own subconscious is lowering your guards. These events are becoming "routine." On the 6th day, something happens which causes an adrenaline spike and you become cautious again. Yet over some time, it will slowly fade again.

To avoid this, place the importance and dangers of the stop in your mind manually. Think about the safety processes and pay attention to the events that are unfolding in front of you. Create a mental checklist as we discussed earlier to use for the events you regularly encounter. This check list has to be followed to the "t" in order to prevent dangerous mistakes and stop the complacencies from happening.

There are many areas of behaviors critical to understand. We must evaluate each person as to the type of personality they have. For instance, are they introverts or extroverts? This will be demonstrated from their behaviors. How do they process information via the three representational channels of visual, auditory, or internal/emotional/Kinesthetic? Determine if they are an optimist or pessimist, narcissistic or altruistic? Questions must appeal to the persons own individual programming or their predisposition toward one or the other at the time of the interview. Let's break these down.

The Representational Channels

1. Visuals – Most people will fall within this category because most of us are visually oriented. In fact 60% of the world's population is visually oriented. I have referred to this group as the primal predators. When speaking to these people they will have some of the following traits:
   - Eyes tend to move up
   - Head and posture is stiff and straight
   - Uses visual phrases (see chart below)
     o Let's look at it differently.
     o See how this works for you.
     o I can't quite picture it.
     o Let's draw a diagram or map.
     o I never forget a face.

- They speak and breathe rapidly
- Have an unrestrained voice tone
- Rapid movements

2. Auditory – These people gather most of their information from sound. They are the students who can tape record a class lecture and comprehend the most by listening to the recording later. I refer to this group as the prey. Only 30% of the population is within this category. These people will have the following traits:
    - Eyes tend to go to the sides
    - A slight head tilt
    - A relaxed posture
    - Some gestures and movements
    - Uses auditory phrases like
        o Clear as a bell.
        o Earful
        o Hold your tongue.
        o To tell the truth
        o Voiced an opinion.
    - Speaks and breathes at a moderate pace

3. Internal/Emotional/Kinesthetic – This involves only 10% of the population. These individuals are what I call "the victims." Always remember that these percentages can change for every individual at any given time based on the circumstances. We all possess some of each of these traits and they expose themselves accordingly in relation to the events we experience. You could be a highly visual subject but when faced with the death of a loved one, switch emotions internally. It is the baseline for each subject under normal circumstances which we are determining. These people will have the following traits:
    - Speaks and moves slowly with a low tone
    - Eyes tend to go down
    - Slumped posture
    - Few if any gestures
    - Slow controlled breathing
    - Uses Kinesthetic phrases
        o All washed up
        o Get in control
        o Hang in there
        o Hold it or hold on
        o Stiff upper lip

NEUROLINGUISTIC EXERCISES

The human brain is divided into two hemispheres; one side is used for storing factual information while the other side is used for creating new information. If you focus closely on an individual's eye movement during the fact gathering portion of the interview, you will be able to determine which hemisphere the person is referencing when gathering factual information and/or creating new information and potentially lying.

If you ask a person a question which they may not expect, it requires them to seek the answer in their stored memory. If the question is not threatening to them, they will look high and to their left to recall the answer if they are right handed. I refer to this as seeking the correct "file in a cabinet" to retrieve. If you ask repetitive questions within the same area, they may not react the same. The file was opened and the information retrieved. There will not be a necessity to seek the information because the "file" was opened at the first question and the brain has reviewed the contents. A better approach is to ask a question followed by another after they answer, but on a different topic. After questioning them through a series of issues, you can now return to the original subject. The file on that information has slowly begun to close, as they were required to open other areas in the "cabinet." Their reaction will be more pronounced and you will be able to observe their response for comparison to the earlier answers.

Below are the question categories that apply to the different Representational Channels. These are standardized for a right handed person. Each person is interviewed to determine their own baseline.

Visual Recall
- What is your social security number?
- What side of the front door is the door knob on?
- What is the seventh letter of the alphabet?
- What did you wear this past Saturday?
- How many windows are in your house?
- What is the first thing you see when you open your front door?
- What was the color of your first bicycle?
- List all of the different colors in your bedroom.

Visual Constructed
- Describe your dream date.

- Imagine yourself as a four foot person playing basketball against the Lakers
- Imagine yourself completely bald wearing a tuxedo.

Auditory Recall
- What are the last six words in the Pledge of Allegiance?
- What was the last song you heard on the radio?
- What sound of nature do you like best?
- What is the fifth word in the national anthem?
- What is the chorus in your favorite song?

Auditory Construct
- If you could ask the President any two questions, what would they be?
- Describe the sound of a vehicle horn becoming a flute and then a drumroll.
- Describe the way you would sound if you tried to talk under water.
- Describe the basic sounds of the Chinese language as you have heard it.

Kinesthetic
- Imagine the feeling of ice cream melting in your hand.
- Describe in detail how you felt this morning immediately after getting out of bed.
- How did you feel the first time you experienced a plane ride?
- If you have ever been sea sick, describe how it came on you and how you felt throughout.

A quick guide to recognizing these automatic, unconscious eye movements, or "eye accessing cues," that often accompany particular thought processes are:

- Eyes Up and Left: Non-dominant hemisphere visualization - i.e., remembered imagery.
- Eyes Up and Right: Dominant hemisphere visualization - i.e., constructed imagery and visual fantasy.
- Eyes Lateral Left: Non-dominant hemisphere auditory processing - i.e., remembered sounds, words, and "tape loops" and tonal discrimination.

- Eyes Lateral Right: Dominant hemisphere auditory processing - i.e., constructed sounds and words
- Eyes Down and Left: Internal dialogue, or inner self-talk.
- Eyes Down and Right: Feelings, both tactile and visceral.
- Eyes Straight Ahead, but Defocused or Dilated: Quick access of almost any sensory information; but usually visual.

PERSONALITY

Next, we want to determine if they are an optimist or pessimist, narcissistic or altruistic. This is established by our initial questioning. It helps to understand what a person's normal mental state is to determine a baseline. We will determine what their standard is so any changes are recognizable. This would include a pessimistic person suddenly becoming an optimist or vice versa. These types of changes indicate an occurrence, which is altering their baseline and may indicate deception. Some sample questioning during an interview would be:

Sample Questions	Optimist vs. Pessimist
How are you today?	Good vs. Not bad
How's the diet?	I'm keeping the weight off vs. I'm not gaining
Still having trouble at work?	I'm still there vs. I haven't quit
How's that car in rain?	It holds the road vs. It doesn't slip
Why did you buy that car?	Good price vs. It wasn't expensive
Why did you move there?	Nice neighborhood vs. Not a lot of crime

Some sample statements once it appears they may confess would be:

Sample Statements	Optimist vs. Pessimist

You will sleep better if you confess vs. No more sleepless nights if you confess
You will have a clear conscious vs. You won't feel so guilty all the time
You'll feel better if you get this off your chest vs. You'll stop feeling stressed
You need to take responsibility vs. You need to stop lying
You need to come forward with the truth vs. You need to stop hiding the truth

Sample Statements	Narcissist vs. Altruist

Look yourself in the mirror vs. Look your wife in the eye (children in the face)

Doing what's best for you vs. Doing what's best for your family

Be the type of person you want to be vs. Be the type of person your parents raised

Take responsibility because you vs. Take responsibility because you know it's the right thing to do

You want to do what's right vs. You want people to know that you did what's right

You want to be honest vs. You want people to know you're an honest person

They can be emotional or reality based personalities in addition to being an introvert or extrovert. All of these areas have to be examined and close attention paid to their behaviors and verbal responses. An emotional based person will react to things in an emotional manner. An introvert may also display behaviors that are perceived as deception when in fact it is their normal display. This will be an important topic later in the book regarding false confessions or interviewing bias. Therefore, they are best dealt with in a sympathetic approach. Look and listen for signals such as:

- Shame
- Embarrassment
- Remorse
- Shyness
- Genuine concern over their problem
- Obviously controlled
- Nervous or worried
- Artistic or sees life as a fairy tail
- Verbalizes frustration, despair, and negative emotions
- Inconsistent behavior

A reality-based personality can be seen as someone who thinks, organizes and plans activities on a logical scale. They are best dealt with on a rational or logical approach. Look and listen for signals such as:

- Lack of genuine emotion
- Lack of remorse
- No shame over the events
- Thinks and talks in facts and figures
- Analyzes

- Thinks in a step by step fashion
- Consistent behavior
- Very aware of all consequences

An introvert personality will show signs of one who prefers to internalize stress. They comprise only 25% of the population.

- They do not make friends easily yet they may have 1 or 2 close friends.

The extrovert personality is the majority of people making up 75% of the populace. They will be:

- Are energized to be around other people
- Fade or get bored when they are left alone
- Is susceptible to confusion
- Doesn't mind their body space being infringed
- Concerned what others may think about them
- Forms quick attachments
- Less likely to show nerves and inhibitions
- Likes bright and flashy clothes
- Loves excitement
- Readily responds to questioning
- Less controlled emotional state

Once you have recognized the person as reality or emotion plus introvert or extrovert, you can exploit the information in an interview.

For an Emotion Based Introvert you can:
- Display total belief in their guilt
- Review the evidence every few minutes
- Compliment them on some personal trait
- Dominate with eye contact and touch
- Rationalize and project constantly
- Be subdued and private
- Point out their mental symptoms of guilt
- Use family, friends and associates against them
- Minimize constantly
- Express your own friendship towards them
- Show empathy to their problems
- Touch them reassuringly

- Wear natural colors

For an Emotion Based Extrovert you can:
- Try to confuse them
- Point to the futility of denying
- Dress should convey status of authority (best suit)
- Appeal constantly to their pride (flatter or challenge pride)
- Be slow and deliberate, emphasize key words and phrases, use lots of silence at key moments
- Use family, friends, and associates against the subject (those who are important)
- For some males who are not strongly extroverted, touching can establish dominance
- The interrogation format should not be tightly controlled

For a Reality Based Introvert you can:
- Gain dominance early
- Dress in natural colors
- Approach should be well organized
- Be subdued and private
- Evaluate carefully before touching this person
- Use props (have photos, evidence, etc. handy)
- Use a matter of fact approach
- Cover facts chronologically or systematically
- Emphasize physical and testimonial evidence
- Approach them with no warmth, be straight forward (niceness is viewed as a weakness by them)

For a Reality Based Extrovert you can:
- point out futility in denying
- Use a matter of fact approach
- Dress forcefully
- Be patient and persistent
- Use questions with "yes" or "no" answer
- Speak slightly louder than normal
- Appeal constantly to their pride (flatter or challenge pride)
- Use a well-organized approach, be chronological or otherwise systematic with case facts
- Approach them with no warmth, be straight forward (niceness is viewed as a weakness by them)

- Have as much evidence as possible readily available (props/bluffs/photo's/charts/anything plausible)
- Interrogation format should not be tightly controlled
- Strictly adhere to one on one interview/interrogation format From the beginning, try to pull the subject into the conversation
- Never show doubt or pause when speaking, be optimistic about the subjects guilt
- Subject will drift if not controlled, keep to the matter at hand
- Once he/she has opened up, be practical and concrete at all times
- If nothing else works, use realistic language

The Interviews - 39

Good detection spares us from unwelcome surprises.

- Barton Whaley

There are numerous areas of an interview that requires examination. This complex process can take years to learn. There have been many studies conducted on what it takes to be a good interviewer. Sadly, people today gather their ideas of reality from television and the internet. Just as a movie may announce, it is "based on a true story," even if the story was about you, after watching we would not recognize the events. This is how most of the ideas surrounding an interview are perceived. Yes, anyone can sit down, ask questions of someone else, and receive an answer. In the world of law enforcement, the business world, and even the military, much more has to be obtained. The stakes can be as high as life threatening to job loss.

There are skills to teach that separate an average from a superior interviewer. In fact, The Department of Defense, Defense Academy for Credibility Assessment group known as DACA conducted a two-year study called: Final Report, May 2007, MIPR#H9C101-G-0051, Assessment of Optimal Interrogation Approaches. The study discovered 17 areas that differentiate superior interrogators from others. These areas are:

1. Preparations for the Interview
2. Develops Themes
3. Builds Rapport
4. Rationalizes and Minimalizes the criminal act

5. Uses Optional Questions
6. Confronts the Subjects
7. Recognizes non-verbal cues
8. Treats the Suspect with respect
9. Shows a Professional Image
10. Separates self from police/authorities
11. Reinforces/rewards/thanks admissions and acts
12. Controls own emotion
13. Maintains a matter of fact approach to questioning
14. Does not allow backtracking
15. Uses hope and fear
16. Allows the suspect to explain what happened in their own words
17. Uses recapping – after confession, has suspect repeat from beginning to end

When conducting an interview, to reasonably evaluate the meaning of the statement made, we must understand the various levels of communication. Verbal, non-verbal, tone, and proxemics of the individual require special attention. With these issues in mind, when a person is telling the truth, the verbal, non-verbal, and tone will complement each other to create the total message. Merely evaluating the spoken word, as most people will, can only be effective if the person interviewed is truthful throughout the interview. When a person is being deceitful, the verbal, non-verbal, tone etc. will contradict each other. If the subject is trying to deceive you, evaluating only the spoken word will miss much of the message and have limited success.

For most people the interview is more like an interrogation. Because of our police trained, dominate attitude, we tend to do the following:

- We allow our police minds to dominate the entire process.
- We talk as much if not more than they do.
- We tend to keep everything non-personal with a "just the facts" attitude.
- We pass by the rapport phase and tend to not pay attention because we already know where we want this to go.

In fact, especially in the beginning of the interview, we need rapport. If I could replace the word interrogation with the words "investigative interview," it could help us relax more and have a better connection to the interview. This is when we need, in addition to rapport, to determine a baseline of their behaviors, detect deceptions, and evaluate themes.

Time is required for this progression to succeed. If you start to take short cuts, you are defeating the entire reasons to initiate the interview. Our position in the beginning is to allow them to do the talking. As police officers, we like to be in control. With two ears and one mouth, we should listen twice as much as we talk. Ask the questions to keep the interview moving. Do not do anything except listen and observe. Remember, there is no such thing as actual multi-tasking. Watch and listen, do not write.

The process begins the moment you enter the room with the subject. Never forget that everything can rest upon the first impression you make. Now is the time to take away your police persona and replace it with that of a "friend." They will not always realize it, but from the time you enter the room they are evaluating you. They will determine "friend or foe" almost instantly.

Proxemics

The distance required from another person to feel comfortable based on the circumstances.

- Intimate- touching to 1.5 feet
- Personal/Business – 1.5 – 4 feet
- Social – 4 – 7 feet
- Public – out as far as 12-25 feet

A little known fact, but on a different scale, is that lion trainers use proxemics to their advantage. Though the whip and gun is exciting and demonstrates falsely their control, distance is maintained with proxemics. The large cats have a natural instinct to back away from someone until they can no more. The trainer will move towards the cats that naturally cause them to move away against the cage wall. Once they cannot move any further, they begin to advance on the trainer always in a straight line. The trainer will monitor their movement, place a stool between them, and immediately back away. The cat will leap onto the stool, but will not advance because the trainer has moved back out of their space.

People will perform a set of actions whenever their personal space is intruded upon without permission. First, they will start to rock, leg swing or tap. This shows that tension is building. Then they will close their eyes, lower their chin and hunch their shoulders. Finally, when nothing else has worked, they will get up and leave. The psychological pressure placed on someone is immense.

In our police academies, stress is added to determine which recruits have the fortitude to withstand the strain. Police work carries with it a tremendous amount of stress. Some people are better adapted to cope with the stress than others are. The military and law enforcement tries to fill their ranks with those personnel capable of withstanding more than most. There will come a day in their lives that the level of stress will exceed anything most people will ever endure. Our goal is to survive this moment with a clear thinking mind. The best example and one of the most recognizable is a drill instructor giving commands.

RAPPORT

Rapport is the condition of mutual trust and understanding between the interviewer and interviewee. Many witnesses and suspects feel uneasy about providing accusatory information. Resistance to the disclosure of information increases if the interviewer is a total stranger.

There are techniques necessary for building rapport. Most people have never considered this topic, and assume it is simply walking in and saying, "Hi." There are utilized and are universal in acceptance, but they will not work on each person. Therefore, it is critical for you understand some rules to building rapport.

- Begin by commenting on a topic of interest to the suspect. Your prior collection of background information should help to provide this information.

- Establish confidence and friendliness by engaging in topics about current events such as: weather; news; TV shows and sports.
- Display pleasant emotional responses and avoid distasteful expressions.
- Don't ask questions in the beginning that lead the suspect to believe that you are suspicious of them.
- Appear interested and sympathetic to his concerns.
- Going through the biographical data will help establish rapport. It also alerts you to information that could be used in the interrogation.
- Don't begin an interrogation until you feel that some form of rapport has been established.

Avoid these areas when attempting to establish rapport:

- Don't sneer or ridicule the suspect.
- Don't bully or try to impress the suspect with your importance.
- Don't make any deliberate false promises.
- Don't belittle the suspect or his position.
- Try not to reveal signs of your own personal beliefs because they may be in contradiction with the suspect's.
- Don't yell, curse or try to alienate the person.

LISTENING

In order to be a successful interviewer, one has to do the single thing that cops do the least; listen. Police officers are some of the worse listeners because we are taught from our entry into the academy to take charge. We have to watch for everything big or small which has increased the visual Representational Channel above the general populace percentages. They changed from 60% visual to 87%, 30% auditory to 7%, and 10% Kinesthetic to 6%. The profession has changed the ways police officers are able to receive the information from those who are trying to communicate. It is pounded into us from day one to watch. However, as one changes so must the others to maintain 100%. Therefore, auditory and kinesthetic have fallen even further, auditory the most. There are several methods we can use for listening; I refer to them as interested continuators. They demonstrate that you are listening to keep the conversation moving forward.

A study from the University of Missouri indicates that many of us spend 70 to 80 percent of our waking hours in some form of communication. Of that time, we spend about 9 percent writing, 16 percent reading, 30 percent speaking, and 45 percent listening. Ironically, we already know that most of us are poor listeners. There are several reasons according to the study.

Even though listening is the communication skill we use the most, it is also the skill in which we have had the least training. We have had much more formal training in other communication skills — writing, reading, and speaking. In fact, very few persons have had any extended formal training in listening.

Another reason for poor listening skills is that we can think faster than someone else can speak. Most of us speak at the rate of about 125 words per minute. However, we have the mental capacity to understand someone speaking at 400 - 500 words per minute. This difference means that when we listen to the average speaker, we're using only 25 percent of our mental capacity. We still have 75 percent to do something else with, so our minds wander. A concentrated effort is necessary to stay focus before our minds begin to tune into other ideas.

Passive Listening – Never express any of your own ideas or judgments. Instead, invite the person to share their feelings and thoughts. Stay with simple verbal responses like:

"Really"
"I see"
"How about that"
"No kidding"

Non-verbal responses like:
Nodding
Smiling/frowning
Raising your eyebrows

More direct responses are:
"I'd like to hear more about that"
"Tell me the whole story"
"This seems pretty important to you"

Active Listening - This type of listening is more effective than passive listening and will assist in building rapport and establishing normative behavior. It identifies what the person is feeling and/or what the message really means. Every message contains two parts:

- The content or factual material
- The speaker's feelings or attitude toward the content

You can put the message into your own words and see if that was what the subject meant. Never be judgmental or act like your giving advice. There are three areas of active listening:

- Paraphrase (rephrasing): repeat mentally and/or out loud to the subject what has been said.
- Clarifying: ask the speaker to repeat, clarify, or simplify
- Summarizing: after the speaker has provided information on one subject, review the information with the speaker

When active listening always:

- make good eye contact
- be patient
- pay close attention
- keep on subject until the thought is complete

Never:

- interrupt
- rush the person
- finish the person's sentence/thought
- look at watch or have wandering eyes
- fidget with pen or pencil
- write things down
- never send back a message of advice or judgment
- never include your opinion unless its expressly asked for or you know it will match the subjects

Robert Montgomery conducted workshops using business executives to learn what they considered effective listening. He surveyed the participating executives on the characteristics of the worst listeners they know. The usual replies are:

- Always interrupts.
- Jumps to conclusions.
- Finishes my sentences.
- Is inattentive; has wandering eyes and poor posture.
- Changes the subject.
- Writes down everything.
- Doesn't give any response.
- Is impatient.
- Loses temper.

- Fidgets with a pen or pencil nervously.

Characteristics of good listeners -
- Looks at me while I'm speaking.
- Questions me to clarify what I'm saying.
- Shows concerns by asking me about my feelings.
- Repeats some of the things I say.
- Doesn't rush me.
- Is poised and emotionally controlled.
- Reacts responsively with a nod of the head, a smile, or a frown.
- Pays close attention.
- Doesn't interrupt me.
- Keeps on the subject till I've finished my thoughts.

In studies, which involve listening, several areas are essential to becoming a good listener. It is considered helping the speaker and can be summed up as the golden rule of listening: a listener should listen to others, as they would like to be listened to themselves. In a criminal investigative interview, you have to appear genuinely interested in what the suspect is saying. This helps to facilitate more information. To accomplish this, everything relies on the listener's outward behaviors and is visual. To help the subject or speaker perform successfully, a listener needs to do four things:

- Avoid distracting verbal comments - This includes not interrupting, changing the subject, finishing sentences for the speaker, or interjecting with "yes, uh-huh" as though on autopilot.
- Avoid distracting nonverbal actions - This includes not fidgeting, slumping, staring blankly, or smiling and nodding in agreement as though on autopilot.
- Offer verbal encouragement and support - This includes everything from a genuine, "Yes, I see," to rescuing a speaker who has been interrupted or lost his or her train of thought with cues like, "You were just saying . . ." or "I think you also wanted to say something about . . . ."
- Offer nonverbal encouragement and support - This includes looking alert and plugged into the conversation by sitting up straight, maintaining eye contact, and responding with facial expressions that are appropriate for the speaker's message.

Distracting behaviors, whether verbal or nonverbal, are avoided for two reasons. First, because they may be considered disrespectful towards the speaker, distracting behaviors may prevent the speaker from sharing their ideas. Secondly, they create a loss in the listener's concentration. Encouraging behaviors help prove to the speaker that the listener is paying attention and they reinforce the listener's efforts to keep paying attention. That is, a listener is more likely to stay mentally tuned in when they are leaning forward and maintaining eye contact with the speaker than when he or she is writing on a note pad or looking out the window.

DECEPTION

Deception is a social norm. Many studies conclude that an individual's success enhances in any task when a certain amount of deceit is implemented at some point. Additionally, it is believed that individuals who are well versed in deception tend to be more successful than those who are not. Because of this social requirement for deception, all humans lie. Human nature is a daily exercise in deceit, yet lying does not come naturally nor is it easy. When a person lies, they undergo a physiological change in an effort to make a lie believable. The untruthful person's physiology:

- The liar will feel threatened by the questions which are part of the specific issue
- If the liar does not convince you of his truthfulness, they are aware of the potential consequences
- Being aware of the consequences is what triggers the fight, flight or freeze response
- In an attempt to mask and contain physiological responses, verbal and non-verbal indicators of deception leak out.

When we perform a conscious action, which changes reality in some way, the following factors apply:

1. The action is not automatic, it's produced
2. The person's cognitive thinking processes involve some degree of rehearsal and consideration of the probable results of the action before it's carried out. Impulsive actions are exception to this process.
3. What may seem to be an impulsive act may have been imagined or fantasized countless times over the person's lifespan. An example would be a pedophile.

4. A combination of incidents may serve as a catalyst in causing one's impulsive behavior

5. Many criminals think about, plan, scheme, and mentally rehearse their crimes prior to putting them into action

For the following signs of a truthful or deceitful person, remember that any single issue may not be indicative of the category. We are always looking at clusters of behavior. A falsehood will result if someone says, "He crossed his leg during the interview therefore he must be lying." This singular act is in the deceitful column but by itself means nothing. It shall be observed and remembered in the event other actions take place.

Signs of a Truthful Person:
- Appears at ease
- Talkative
- Sincere
- Cooperative
- Answers questions directly
- Maintains good eye contact
- Generally appears relaxed
- Lighthearted conversation

Signs of a Deceptive Person:
- Apprehensive
- Worried appearance
- Much sighing or yawning
- Excessive movement
- Dreamy air
- Overly friendly
- Poor eye contact
- Evasive answering
- Aggressive toward the interviewer

Sitting postures can reveal a lot about a person. A Truthful Person will:
- Sits upright
- Relaxed looking
- Faces interviewer
- Does not lean away
- Changes positions smoothly
- Arms open & uncrossed

- Legs open & uncrossed
- Head & shoulders aligned
- Overall appearance casual

A Deceptive Person Will:
- Slouches or sits stiff and rigid
- Shies away from interviewer
- Arms close to side and crossed
- Moves frequently and rapidly
- Faces to the side/leans toward the door
- Head slumped

Facial Expressions

No single facial expression is indicative of guilt or deception. The head, because it is closest to the brain and we are most aware of it, is easiest to control. An example of this is a calm facial expression with a lot of arm and leg movement that indicates high stress.

Facial color changes: Flushing is a good sign that stress is present. Facial color changes usually conform to the following pattern:

- Face becomes white or turns pale = height of "fight or flight"
- Face turns red or reddish = recovery from strong emotion
- Skin turns dark = blood backing up due to constricted veins

Muscle spasms take the form of facial grimaces or muscle constrictions in various parts of the body, especially on the head. These uncontrollable muscle movements will sometimes include the arms and legs, and in a high percentage of the cases, are good indicators of deception. The cheeks or the area around the eyes trembles uncontrollably, which is indicative of stress. This is a reaction I have observed countless of times in my career when interviewing someone. To see it, you have to pay close attention.

The eyes (excluding neurolinguistics):
> a. The most expressive part of the head is the eyes
> b. The following eye movement may indicate a problem
>> 1. Excessive eye shifting
>> 2. Prolonged eye contact
>> 3. Staring at the interviewer

4. Abnormal eye contact

c. It is possible for eye contact to be too good. This is usually an aggressive stare down, which is an attempt to dominate you and/or is the result of the false belief that a truthful person will always look you in the eye.

d. Any break in eye contact, which is timely and not part of the norm, is a sign of stress

f. Breaks in eye contact can be disguised in a number of ways:

> 1. Placing your hand to rub your forehead or other facial area is a form of a break in eye contact
>
> 2. Blinking will increase when a person is under stress

The nose:
- Touching or rubbing the nose indicates stress and/or deception
- Holding the nose between the finger and thumb means "that stinks" or "that smells"
- Sometimes a nose touch is combined with other signs to yield a single movement cluster

The mouth:
- A big smile on the mouth of the subject is not realistic
- Phony smiles are generally upper teeth smiles
- Any obstruction of speech indicates stress and/or deception
- Biting lips
- Squeezing lips together
- Continually licking lips and they remain dry
- Dry mouth making clicking noises
- Strings of thick saliva between teeth and/or lips
- White foam at the corners of the mouth

The hands:
- A change in the activity of the hands
- Grooming, lint picking
- Scratching, rubbing, massaging
- Flipping the hands away indicates the desire to throw away unpleasant subject
- A hand to the throat shows stress, indicates sore spot

- Playing with fingernails
- Drumming fingers, as the tension increases, drumming becomes faster and louder

Crossing of any parts of the body may indicate defensiveness, protectiveness, etc. This emotion can be caused by general fear of the situation or by guilt induced stresses, which may reduce the information intake of the subject.

Meanings of crossed arms:
- Arms crossed tightly in front of chest with fists = uncooperative, cocky
- Arms crossed closely to neck = high level of resistance
- Arms crossed while leaning toward interviewer = very defensive, uncooperative
- A crossing can be, and often is, combined with other gestures

Legs and Feet
- Crossing of the legs has the same general meaning as the crossing of the arms
- Figure 4 leg cross indicates cockiness
- Feet or legs in a V shape indicates confidence
- Putting feet up on chair or desk, moving your chair with their feet, or dragging their chair away from you is an attempt to dominate
- At moments of stress, the legs may:
  1. Cross for the first time
  2. Un-cross for the first time
  3. Change direction of crossing
  4. Legs crossed, upper foot bounces gently (rise in blood pressure)
  5. Legs crossed, upper legs shows fast, forceful swing (impatience or anger)
- Knees wobbling back and forth is a sign of great tension
- Other leg movement indicative of deception:
  1. One leg stretched out in front of the other
  2. Both knees up under chin with feet on chair (rare, generally in females)
  3. Hand placed on inside of leg, trying to comfort self
  4. Toes turn up to point back at self
  5. Feet going under chair/ coming out from under the chair

6. Ankles crossed under chair
7. Feet twitching
8. Toes rising, feet rolling
9. Tapping feet is indicative of agitation

Religious behaviors:
- Praying
- Holding religious items
- Singing gospels
- Raising hands to take oath, "scouts honor"
- Invoking a deity or swearing to God
- Swearing on the souls or life of a loved one

Expressions - 40

The wish to relieve guilt may motivate a confession, but the wish to avoid the humiliation of shame may prevent it.

- Paul Ekman

There are many people in the world that considered an expert on expressions. Typically, we like to think of micro-expressions, which were made popular by television shows like "Lie to Me." In reality, the professional consultant for the show, Paul Ekman, is one of the world's foremost authorities on the subject.

I will, for this examination of the topics include all of the physical expressions made by people in all areas of the body. It is imperative to understand a few simple rules about reading expressions. Some people, who are pathological recognize that others are looking for certain behaviors and they will make efforts to compensate. For instance, we all know that one of the key factors is eye contact. It has been shown that most people have a hard time maintaining eye contact when they are telling a lie. However, some people know this and maintain a strong eye contact.

During a person's interview, everyone should expect pacifying behaviors. The limbic system plays a key role. When someone gets nervous, the stressor will begin to create energy which has to be used. This excess of energy will be displayed as pacifying behaviors. Pacifying behaviors are selective to each individual. Some may twirl their hair, press their lips, rub their neck or thighs, and even their fingers, nose, or bridge of their nose. This can be normal especially at the beginning of an interview as nervousness is natural. The activities should begin to reduce as you build rapport. Watch for an increase in behavior frequency and chatter. If the subject is chewing gum, ask them to spit it out so they to prevent any aid in stress release.

When asking questions, be sure to take your time. Ask the question and wait to watch their reactions. Stress that increases and decreases will often be displayed by how they sit and their pacifying behaviors. An example of this is when they lean back, if they put their feet under the chair they are trying to create distance.

Behavior clues have to be examined in clusters. Just because someone does one thing that we have talked about does not mean they are lying. In fact most of what we have discussed simply demonstrates that a person is nervous. It becomes your job to determine the reasoning behind the nerves. As was said before, you must ask the questions and observe the behaviors which need to appear in clusters or groups. Observe the person as they sit in their chair in the open, not against anything that will give them support. Let's examine the human body:

Feet and legs – They are the furthest from the brain. We first have to look for their normal behavior and then watch for change.

- If they constantly bounce their legs or feet and then suddenly stop or if they sit still and then bounce, ask yourself why?
- If they suddenly turn their toes inward or interlock their feet, they are insecure or feel threatened.
- Foot kicking is a subconscious act of resisting something unpleasant.
- If they have their legs crossed and are jiggling their foot and then start kicking the foot, they are not happy.
- Their feet lock behind the chair legs and they rub their thighs – very stressed
- They move their foot from in front to under the chair is a sign of distancing.
- Happy feet, feet/legs that bounce with joy, are the result of a positive emotion.
- We tend to turn toward things we like and turn away from things that we don't like.
- If a person who is sitting down clasps both hands on his knees then this is a sign he wants to leave.
- Gravity defying behaviors of the feet (pointing a foot upward off the ground, heel to the ground) are positive cues. People with depression rarely exhibit gravity defying behaviors.

- Leg splays, a dominant stance, often communicates that something is wrong.
- Recognizing our leg-splay posture during a heated exchange and adjusting will often lessen the confrontation level and reduce the tension.
- Leg crossing is a display of comfort. If you're standing with your legs crossed you are comfortable with your surroundings (you're not in a "get away fast" position) or with the person you're speaking with. Also, when you cross your legs in company you may subconsciously tilt toward the person you favor most.
- A woman will often play with her shoes and dangle them from her toes when she is comfortable with her companion
- Seated leg crosses when people sit side by side, the direction of their leg crosses become significant. If they are on good terms, the top leg crossed over will point toward the other person.

Torso – This is not a commonly thought of body portion and it is not as recognizable to the person who is affected by it either.

- Trying to lean back or distancing
- Turn slightly away shows a dislike
- Lean into or towards someone or something that interest us
- Crossing our arm or placing something between you at the torso is shielding
- Can be not as noticeable but has the same effect as arm crossing is the playing with a tie, shirt or cufflinks etc.
- Splaying in a chair, sitting with legs spread over chair and facing the back is disrespectful or the dominating of the area
- If you move into their personal space, they sit more straight is a sign of respect or concern
- Chest puffing or jacket removal – fight preparation
- Half shoulder shrugs – they are not committed to their answer
- Slow or weak shoulder rise – lack confidence or uncomfortable
- Full strong shoulder shrug shows confidence

Arms – follows the rules of gravity.

- When they defy gravity like raising of the arms – joy or excitement

- Weight of gravity drags the shoulders down as well – depressed or upset
- Arms at sides or across chest – worried or protective
- Arms behind back – at your mercy or consider myself above you, court or regal stance
- Elbows away from body shows to keep your distance or shows authority while against your waist shows weakness
- Hooding – placing and interlocking fingers behind your head creating a cobra like hood is a show of dominance. Supervisors will often do this at meetings. A sign of dominance.

Think about all of the arm movements that exist in a relationship and their subconscious meanings. Hugs, holding hands, jewelry and tattoos, handshakes, nail biting, hand wringing, steepling (confidence), thumbs up or down and the list continues.

Face – there are so many facets of the face, the eyes, mouth, nose, blushing, tremors, etc.

- Small pupils - do not like what we see
- Large pupils – we like what we see or we see danger
- High eyebrows – confidence
- Low eyebrows – dislike
- Eye blocking – squinting shows concern or dislike
- Closing eyes – block out negatives
- Gaze away during conversation – comfort display or clarity of thought, not rude
- Roving eyes – disinterested or superior
- Rapid eye blinks – inner struggle or stress
- Looking askance – sideways glance or untrusting
- Lip pursing – person rejects what is said
- Thin lips – stress
- Sneer – act of contempt
- Licking the lips – stressed
- Biting the lips – insecure
- Furrowed forehead – frowning – sad
- Nose flare – aroused or intent to do something physical
- Blushing – deep emotional states
- Blanching (turning pale) – shock or high stress
- Crinkle nose – dislike

- Chin down – lacks confidence

A quote from Dr. Birdwhistell, former professor of research in anthropology at Temple University (who initiated basic work in the science of kinesics) warned that "no body position or movement, in and of itself, has a precise meaning." In other words, we cannot always say that crossed arms mean, 'I will not let you in,' or that rubbing the nose with a finger means disapproval or rejection, and steepling the fingers superiority. These are naive interpretations of kinesics. Sometimes they are only true in the context of the entire behavior pattern of a person. Body language and spoken language, Dr. Birdwhistell believes, are dependent on each other. Spoken language alone will not give us the full meaning of what a person is saying, nor can body language alone give us the full meaning. If we listen only to the words when someone is talking, we may get as much of a distortion as we would if we listened only to the body language.

Even though we have looked at many possible meanings for various behaviors, they have to be taken into context with what is said and asked based upon their identified baseline. Take posture as an example. There are many things we can examine that we do every day that are directly linked to posture. There is only so much time that you can observe a person's behavior without making them aware of it as well as being able to consciously focus on everything that is occurring. Most people will have head movements during a conversation. There is usually a specific head movement at the end of a statement which serves as a signal to the other person to start his answer. This activity, not consciously recognized, serves to expedite a conversation so we are not required to say we are finished, your turn.

Often times a rise in voice pitch at the end of a word indicates an asked question and is usually added with a raise in the head position. Ask yourself a question and notice these subtle occurrences. "What time is it?" or "Where are you going?" Control over this inflection shows confidence by the speaker. To allow the voice pitch to rise at the end of a statement indicates doubt or appears that way. Other body parts will rise like the eyelids or even your hands or arms. When we are making a statement, the voice tone and head movement will lower at the end of the last word. These are referred to as linguistic markers. They are the physical aids to the language. If the speaker intends to continue his statement, they will not change their voice pitch, head movement, eyes, or hands as a "marker" to you that they are not yet finished.

Writers and moviemakers have a keen understanding of how these head movements play into our appearance. If they intend to characterize a "cool" or stoic person, one who does not flinch under pressure nor has no emotional attachment, they teach them to talk without head or face movements. Most people will move their heads at least every couple of sentences as well as side-glances, stance adjustments, blinks, touches etc. To contrast this, think of a runway model. They are taught to be emotionless and stoic as they move down the aisle. They hold themselves rigid and unnatural to force everyone to subconsciously recognize the mannequin like exposure.

Body positions are another example. When in a social setting, most persons shift through two to four positions. Rarely does one position last more than twenty minutes. When under stress, people have a tendency to adjust more often. Think about someone listening to a speaker in a specific position of leaning back in their chair. When the speaker reaches a point that the listener disagrees with, they change their position. They lean forward into a position of rebuttal. When he is finished, they generally return to the original position. Again, I stress that a change in posture signifies that something has happened, not what has happened.

Masking emotions is a common process that everyone uses to conceal their true feelings. By masking I mean even though you are mad, you smile. The most common way to mask emotions is with a smile. It is one of our first learned expressions to show happiness or to get a positive response from another.

A husband catches his wife talking low and it sounds like she is talking to another man, he may confront her. She of course denies the affair, but her overall body language in conjunction with word usage will betray her. If you bump into someone accidentally, it is common to smile as a sign of apology. Masking is something we do all day long. It also accounts for many of our behaviors when we are not in public. All day long, we are forced to smile and be courteous even though most of the time we would have preferred to get angry with someone. This built up behavior resistance that occurs all day, releases when we are not in public. In the drive home, you yell and cuss the other drivers. Your behavior at home takes a while to calm and your significant other has learned over time to leave you alone and knows you will get over it all.

Lie Detection from Emotion

The stronger the emotion involved in a lie and the greater the number of different emotions, the more likely it is the lie is betrayed by behavioral leakage. According to Dr. Paul Ekman, guilt is an emotion more problematic for the liar. It causes leakage and the torment of guilt can lead the liar to make mistakes. A lie occurs two ways; conceal and falsify. When given a choice, a person will conceal rather than falsify. It is much easier to do and if caught they can explain it away. "I did not know that" or as we so often hear in court, "I have no recollection."

The best way to conceal an emotion is with a false emotion. I have been in situations that I was genuinely frightened, yet my profession dictated that I was not to show any fear. I disguised the fear with a smile. Another example is how many in the public sector see police officers as calloused because they laugh and tell jokes around horrific crime scenes. Again, this is simply the police officer trying to hide in plain sight the horrific emotions that they are feeling. The smile is the most commonly used mask because the negative expressions or emotions are hard to fake.

There are two clues to deceit: leakage if the liar mistakenly reveals the clues when their behavior suggests they are lying. However, there is no specific sign of deceit. To repeat what we have already discussed, liars conceal and falsify what they expect others are going to watch the most. Liars tend to be careful in their choice of words because they know that they are an expected point of deception. The second most common deception comes from the face and is the primary site to display emotions. It's the first location that everyone looks at first in another and because it's closest to the brain, the easiest to control. Recent research has shown that there is a region of the brain specifically for recognizing faces and we will start our point of attention on the right side of another's face when they are facing you.

Suspicious people should pay more attention to the voice and the body. The voice, like the face, is tied to emotions. Liars are betrayed by their words when they are careless and unprepared to tell a lie. People are also betrayed by their words through slips of the tongue. These Freudian slips occur because the mind processes more words than can be told. The brain can think through almost 500 words per minute while we speak at around 125 words per minute. The third method is during outbursts when emotion overrides their common sense or preparations.

Some people show deception when they have an indirect reply to a question. The most common voice deception clues are pauses. Hesitating at the start of responding to a question or short pauses in a speech or statement can be indicative of deception. Speech errors like "aaa," "uhh," word repetitions like "I, I, I," and partial words like "rea-really" can also be indicative.

The best vocal sign of emotion is pitch. Pitch becomes higher when upset in 70% of people. Pitch will also be louder and faster when upset; slower and lower when sad.

Voice changes are hard to conceal. If you are trying to conceal fear or anger, pitch will be higher and louder and the rate, faster. Guilt can display the same as sadness. Raised pitch is not a sign of deceit, but of fear, anger, or excitement. A person who is stopped roadside by police may display a higher than normal pitch as they become scared of the questions and actions of the officer. An innocent person will generally begin to calm during the encounter.

Emblems are gestures made that have precise meaning within a culture. A shrug or giving a finger is examples. Others are head nods yes or no, hand to ear, which is symbolic for louder, and a hand wave for hello or goodbye.

Emblems deliberately performed. Most occur out front between the waist and neck. They can be leaked or slip. One way is when only a fragment of it is performed. The other is out of the presentation position, like giving a finger when your arms are crossed. Though they slip out, they are very reliable even though neither party is aware of its presentation. They will mean exactly what is performed.

Illustrators illustrate speech as spoken. The hands usually illustrate speech. They help explain ideas that are hard to put into words or when people cannot find a word. An example is to try to explain a zig-zag. This is difficult to accomplish with a verbal explanation, yet with the use of a hand, you can make a letter "z" in the air to demonstrate. Illustrators will increase when furious, horrified, agitated, distressed, or enthused.

If someone uses fewer illustrators, it is because they lack emotional investment. If people fake enthusiasms or concern, it shows in their lack of illustrators with their speech.

They can also decrease when someone is having a difficult time deciding what to say. They also decrease when there is caution with the speech and when someone is lying.

This is the crucial difference between emblems and illustrators. Emblems are specific in meaning and illustrators can involve a wide variety of movements. Interpreting illustrators can require previous acquaintance so a baseline is established.

Manipulators or Pacifiers are when one part of the body grooms, massages, rubs, holds, pinches, picks, scratches, or manipulates another part of the body. An increase in manipulators is a sign of anxiety, not deceit. Typically, it is the hand conducting the activity like twisting hair, finger rubs, or a foot tapped. Common recipients are the hair, ears, nose, or crotch.

Though most people are taught not to do these actions in public most are performed without self-notice. People cannot stop doing them for very long even when they try. People will look away when someone does a manipulator and look back when they are done. Fidgeting and restless movements increase when people are nervous. Body scratching, squeezing, picking, and orifice cleaning and grooming manipulators increase with discomfort.

"Any touching of the face, head, neck, shoulder, arm, hand, or leg in response to a negative stimulus (e.g., a difficult question, an embarrassing situation, or stress as a result of something heard, seen, or thought) is a pacifying behavior," according to Joe Navarro, retired FBI agent and author of numerous books and articles on body language and deception.

Men and women use the neck to pacify differently. Men are more robust, grasping, cupping, rubbing. Women are gentler, playing with a necklace or covering the suprasternal notch (the "neck dimple" below Adam's apple and above chest plate).

Touching or stroking the face, rubbing the forehead, touching, rubbing, or licking lips, pulling or massaging earlobe, stroking face or beard, playing with hair can all serve to pacify when in a stressful situation.

Careful observations are essential in watching body language. This is a system which improves with practice. But just as our systems can improve with practice, so can they atrophy without use. This is why it is so important to study as much as you can and practice what you study. Gather information from as many sources as is possible to collect on the patterns and most current directions of this science.

Autonomic nervous system clues or ANS produces noticeable changes in the body with emotional arousal like; breathing, swallowing, sweating, blushing /blanching, and pupil dilation and are involuntary when aroused. Anger increases heart rate and skin temp, and cold with fear. Raised voice pitch and louder, faster speech equates to fear, anger, and excitement.

The voice moves opposite for sad and guilt. Changes in breathing, sweating, swallowing, and dry mouth indicate strong emotions. When people lie, the "easiest to see" expressions which people pay the most attention to, are usually the false ones. It is the subtle signs that these expressions are not felt which are important and missed. Remember, these are the mask that conceals the facts.

Micro expressions flash by in less than a quarter second. They are actually full-face emotional expressions compress in time. A smile can mask the emotion, but this will not mask the emotions felt in the forehead and upper eyelids.

Crooked expressions are a clue that the feeling is not felt. They are usually stronger on the left side of the face if the person is right handed.

Expressions of long durations, 5-10 seconds, are false. Genuine emotion will not last on the face except for a few seconds. Exception is surprise.

Facial expressions not synchronized with body movements are usually deception. A real smile will raise cheeks, bagged skin below eyes, crow's feet and slight lowering of the eye brow. A fake smile only involves the movement of the mouth. Situations when detecting a lie increases when:

- Does the lie involve emotions felt at the moment? They will have to deal w/ the negative emotions of anger, fear, distress which are hard to conceal
- Is there amnesty if they confess to lying? Increases confession rates.
- High stakes of punishment or reward? Increases stressors
- Does the investigator have info that only the guilty would possess?
- Does the investigator and suspect come from the same culture and background?

Clues to Deceit

Slips of the tongue- May be emotion-specific; may leak information unrelated to emotion

Tirades- May be emotion-specific; may leak information unrelated to emotion

Indirect speech-Verbal line not prepared; or, negative emotions, most likely fear

Pauses and speech errors- Verbal line not prepared; or, negative emotions, most likely fear

Voice pitch raised- Negative emotion, probably anger and/or fear

Voice pitch lowered- Negative emotion, probably sadness

Louder, faster speech- Probably anger, fear and/or excitement

Slower, softer speech- Probably sadness and/or boredom

Emblems- May be emotion-specific; may leak information unrelated to emotion

Illustrator's decrease- Boredom; line not prepared; or, weighing each word

Manipulators increase- Negative emotion

Fast or shallow breathing- Emotion, not specific

Sweating- Emotion, not specific

Frequent swallowing- Emotion, not specific

Micro expressions- Any of the specific emotions

Squelched expressions- Specific emotion; or, may only show that some emotion was interrupted but not which one
Reliable facial muscles- Fear or sadness
Increased blinking- Emotion, not specific
Pupil dilation- Emotion, not specific
Tears- Sadness, distress, uncontrolled laughter
Facial reddening- Embarrassment, shame, or anger; maybe guilt
Facial blanching- Embarrassment, shame, or anger; maybe guilt

With these clues in mind, let's focus on the safety concerns of fear and anger as they are signals of the arousal of emotion. The behavioral clues to these are:

Fear:
- Slips of the tongue
- Tirades
- Indirect speech
- Pauses
- Manipulators increase
- Speech errors
- Voice pitch raised
- Louder and faster speech
- Reliable facial muscles
- Facial blanching or reddening
- Increased illustrators
- Change in breathing
- Sweating
- Frequent swallowing
- Squelched expressions
- Micro expressions
- Increased blinking
- Pupil dilation

Anger:
- Slips of the tongue
- Tirades
- Voice pitch raised
- Louder and faster speech
- Emblems
- Manipulators increase

- Change in breathing
- Sweating
- Frequent swallowing
- Micro expressions
- Squelched expressions
- Increased blinking
- Pupil dilation
- Facial blanching or reddening

If at any time, you are confronting another and you notice more than one of these actions, your awareness of safety should be on high. Fear and anger are two emotions that a person will show at a time of great consequence in their life.

Interviewing Techniques - 41

In theory, there is no difference between theory and practice. But in practice, there is.

- Yogi Berra

Many different styles of interviewing are utilized around the world today. There is also an immense volume of research taking place each day into the various techniques believed to produce the best results. Despite what many believe, the techniques currently taught and deployed are based upon old and outdated information. It is imperative that we continually self-prepare ourselves for the ever-changing world of law enforcement.

As police officers or as socially communicating people, interviewing is a learned skilled which can enhance your abilities to assimilate in society and recognize behavioral changes as they relate to deception. We have reviewed a great deal of non-verbal expressions along with their meanings. After establishing normative behavior or a baseline, evaluate the behavior in clusters or groups. It is a well-proven fact that your chances of recognizing deceptions improve when you focus your attention on both the verbal and non-verbal actions and reactions to a stimulus.

Current research is leading us into the direction of verbal response attention. Numerous studies show how people's verbal response to stress is generally a better indicator than non-verbal. The research into non-verbal communication is much older and far better established and excepted by most of us. It is the path which most of us spend our day's people watching while recognizing certain behaviors and most law enforcement officers possess over confidence in their abilities.

We will examine a variety of techniques which will help build the "pathway" of understanding in the final collaboration of various tried and tested interviewing tactics. To help with this sometimes-confusing subject, we will explore each, where they came from, and how they apply to our learning skills. You will see as we start to conclude how parts of each will become melded together to provide a strategy to improve your skills. The techniques we are going to explore are:

- Probable Lie Comparisons (PLC)
- Statement Validity Assessments (SVA)
- Reality Monitoring (RM)
- Cognitive Interviewing Techniques
- Scan or Statement Analysis
- Assessment Criteria Indicative of Deception (ACID) –
  a combined research effort of the above practices

Behavior Assessment Interview

Behavioral assessment questions, also known as the "suspect elimination questions" are very effective for determining deception during the non-accusatory specific issue interview. Some of the questions are also designed to identify the most effective theme to introduce during the interrogation. They will likewise illicit fear the subject has to overcome in order to confess. These questions are completely non-accusatory and introduced as general or "routine" questions. Establish at the onset of behavioral assessment questioning that "I don't know" and "I have no idea" are unacceptable answers. Explain that everybody has an opinion and surely, the subject has speculated about the topic at hand. You as the investigator are merely trying to get their perspective on the case based upon their observations. Furthermore, explain that their answers are confidential and will not be shared with any other parties involved.

Before we can utilize any of the techniques, we must first be reasonably certain that we have a viable witness or suspect. One way to accomplish this is through the Behavior Assessment Interview. This is a strategy developed to illicit a response from the subject we are interviewing. The strategy includes a series of questions that when asked will bring to the forefront of their mind the topics we suspect or desire them to speak about. If they have reason to fear the topic, their responses should be greater. A guilty thinking person must have a reasonable expectation of punishment for an interview to be successful.

Therefore, these are non-accusatory, structured forensic interview questions designed to elicit verbal, and nonverbal behaviors and attitudinal characteristics of the suspect questioned. The questions asked after behavioral norms are established, are those that attempt to assess the suspect's opportunity, motivation, and propensity for involvement in the issue or, are those used to elicit different verbal and nonverbal behaviors and attitudinal characteristics from truthful and deceptive persons.

In a standard interview, behavioral assessment questions occur during the non-accusatory specific issue discussion. They can be in list form or 'peppered in' throughout the process. In a case where several individuals could have potentially committed the crime under investigation, behavioral assessment questions reduce your pool of suspects. This will be demonstrated later in the section on Statement Analysis.

If being used for suspect elimination, you should pick the ten or so behavioral assessment questions to ask every subject; the same questions used for each subject. You will ask the questions from the list and evaluate the answers. At the end of the questions, separate and leave the opportunity for further contact open. Upon evaluating the answers, you will quickly eliminate the large majority of uninvolved subjects and identify a small group of persons that you will focus on as your core suspects. Usually, behavioral assessment questions can reduce a suspect pool by ninety percent.

Rules for evaluating behavioral assessment/suspect elimination questions:

- A guilty subjects answers will always try to broaden your investigation
- A guilty subjects answers won't logistically make sense
- A guilty subject will suggest inappropriate or mild punishments
- A guilty subject will downplay the significance of the act
- A guilty subject will downplay the impact of the act on the victim
- A guilty subject will introduce and entertain many theories as to what might have taken place, none of them will include him/her
- A guilty subject will refuse to recognize the obvious possibility of involvement
- A guilty subject will not address the question
- A guilty subject will demonstrate significant verbal and non-verbal
  Indicators of deception when answering

Fifteen behavior-provoking questions have been developed for our purposes. From these fifteen, they are reworked to allow for the type of incident involved. You can reword each of these and keep them available to utilize in a specific type of investigation. In other words, develop questions for the most common types of investigation you will regularly encounter. When asking a suspect the questions, you will not want to ask every question, but choose about half to ask that could elicit the best response. The basic 15 questions as well as the reason for asking them and used in a scenario involving a theft are:

1. Purpose: What is your understanding for the purpose of this interview today?
2. You: (Name) If you stole (this money) you should tell me that now. Did you steal that money?
3. Knowledge: Do you know who stole (this money)?

4. Suspicion: Who do you suspect may have stolen (this money)?
5. Vouch: Is there anyone you can vouch for, who you do not think was involved in (this theft of money)?
6. Opportunity: Who would have had the best opportunity to (steal this money) if they wanted to?
7. Think Stolen: Do you think this (money) was actually stolen?
8. Feel: How do you feel about being interviewed regarding this (theft)?
9. Results: How do you think the investigation will come out on you?
10. Think: Have you ever thought about (stealing money)?
11. Punishment: What do you think should happen to the person who stole (this money)?
12. Second Chance: Do you think the person who (stole this money) should be given a second chance?
13. Why Not: Tell me why you wouldn't (steal this money)?
14. Motive: Why do you think someone did (steal this money)?
15. Tell Loved One: Have you told your (mother/spouse/family) about coming in for the interview today?

Another more basic format for the behavior provoking questions is:

1. Tell me whatever you have heard or know about this case?
2. Do you believe this actually happened?
3. Who do you think is responsible?
4. Any reason why somebody would think you're responsible?
5. How do you feel toward people who do these things?
6. How do you think (the victim) feels?
7. What type of person is (the victim)?
8. What should happen to the person who did this?
9. Why do you think a person would do something like this?
10. Why wouldn't you do something like this?
11. What would be your greatest concern if you failed a polygraph?

To illustrate another format for this line of questioning, the following could be used in a suspected drug stop:

1. Tell me what you know about anything illegal in the car
2. Who do you think is responsible for anything illegal in the car?
3. Is there anything illegal?
4. Is there anyone you know who would not have done this?
5. Who do you think had the best opportunity to do this?
6. How do you think this is going to turn out?
7. Have you ever thought about doing this?
8. Is there any reason why someone would have called the police to say you were transporting something illegal?
9. Tell me why you would not be involved with this.
10. How do you feel about people who transport/use?
11. Should people who do this be given a second chance?
12. How do you think the parents of the victims of this feel?
13. What do you think should happen to someone who is caught with this?
14. Why would you think someone would do this?
15. Why wouldn't you do this?

A sample behavioral assessment/suspect elimination questions for determining deception in <u>any criminal matter would be:</u>

Why do you think I am talking to you today?
How do you feel about being interviewed today?
Tell me whatever you have heard or know about the case?
Do you believe this actually happened?
Who do you think is responsible?
Who do you think is the least likely person responsible?
Who had the best opportunity to do this?
Any reason why someone would think you're responsible?
How do you feel toward people who do these things?
Have you ever thought about doing something like this?
How do you think the person that did this feels?
Is it possible that there is any forensic evidence in this case? (BAITING)
Would there be any reason for your (blood, semen, prints) to be found at the scene? (BAITING)
How do you think (victim) feels?
How do you think (victim) feels toward the person who did this?

What should happen to the person who did this when they are caught?
Would you give the person a second chance?
Have you talked with anybody about this case?
Did you lie to any question concerning (issue)?
During your entire life, have you ever told a serious lie to stay out of trouble?
Would you be willing to contribute money to help pay back loss just to make this thing go away?
Regarding (issue)...did you do it?

Again, I should stress that it is not necessary to ask everyone all of these questions. After building some rapport with your baseline biographical questions, ask them at least five of these questions to see how they respond. They will be stimulated and display some type of behavioral change if they are involved in the questioned crime. It is critical to understand that each technique will not work every time. This is why it is so important to have an understanding of a variety of techniques to utilize. Everybody is different in many ways so we need to understand the differences in education, life experiences, and psychological imbalances of the people we interview. Due to their upbringing, some people have been required to lie about almost everything in their life. Often these people will start to believe or confuse the truth with their lies. It can be these individuals that we will have difficulties with, but they are not impossible. The primary causes of failure by police officers to utilize the techniques is to not attempt them completely and/or being lazy in the necessary preparations to the interviews. It is human nature to find the easy way out of a situation. All of the developed programs that follow take a concerted effort, practice, and training by the officer to become efficient.

Steven Varnell

The Probable Lie Comparison (PLC) Test

Polygraph examiners commonly use this type of deceit detection testing. It is accomplished by the use of relevant questions to specific issues as well as comparison questions asked in a certain order or "format." This allows the examiner the opportunity to analyze how someone responds physiologically to questions by the recording of data from changes in blood pressure, heart rate, and perspiration. A relevant question is one that deals with the real issue of the investigation. These questions include asking whether the examinee perpetrated the specific act, knows who did it or is withholding known information concerning the specific issue. It can also include questions about particular pieces of evidence that could incriminate the guilty person. An irrelevant question is one designed not to invoke a response. An easy example of a comparison question would be, "Is today Monday?" Irrelevant questions are typically in the first position of a question list because the physiological responses that follow the appearance of the first question are presumed to have no diagnostic value. They are also at other points in the question sequence. Guilty examinees may show stronger reactions to relevant than to control questions and no reaction to irrelevant questions; innocent examinees could react similarly to both question types.

A Probable Lie Comparison (PLC) question now referred to as "Control" or comparison questions are designed to be a probable lie for the examinee. The PLC question should be similar in nature but unrelated to the specific crime or issue(s) tested. The question should be separated from the relevant issue by time, place, or category. The comparison question should use the same action verb or similar in nature action verb as that of the relevant issue. A comparison question should be broad in scope and time so that it captures as many of the examinees past life experiences as possible. An acceptable example is:

Before 1998, did you ever steal anything of value?

In the PLC format, examiners' compare responses to relevant questions with responses to control. Comparison or control questions ask about generalized acts of the type of event under investigation separated by time, place, or category. In a burglary investigation, you may ask, "Prior to 2013, have you ever stolen anything of value?" In a drug related question you would ask, "Since becoming an adult, have you ever used illegal drugs?" The instructions are designed to induce innocent people to answer in the negative, even though most are lying. Innocent examinees may experience concern about these answers that shows in their physiological responses. Generally, the innocent examinees will react more strongly to the comparison questions, and guilty examinees will react more strongly to relevant questions.

This occurs because an innocent examinee when asked a vague time line question like, "Have you ever used an illegal drug?" has to decide how to answer. There are many people who have never used an illicit drug yet they need to determine in their mind if they have ever used something in a way that could be seen as illicit. This can be as simple as your mother once gave you one of her prescription pills to help with a condition. Still, if you had experimented with marijuana once, 25 years ago, the examinee has to decide if they want to tell this information to the examiner. This internal struggle creates the physiological responses which will show on the testing results. They did not respond to the "Have you used drugs in the past year?" question because it is a present tense question. They are not using now but did use once 25 years ago. This assists the examiner in differentiating between the current deceptions from the past indiscretion.

Before starting a polygraph exam, conduct a physical assessment of the individual. I believe this is always a good idea, polygraph or not, to help show that an individual is of sound mental capacities before an interrogation. It simply helps to eliminate one of the hurdles which will be attempted at a later date by the defense to show their client was not of sound mind at the time of the confession. For instance, you can ask the following:

- What is your general health? Excellent, good, fair or poor. Explain.
- Have you taken any medication in the past 24 hours?
- Ask about effects of medication...You may have to go to PDR or internet.
- Alcohol in the past 24hrs?
- Are you presently being treated by a doctor? If so explain.
- Pregnancy?
- Amount of sleep in past 24 hours? What is the norm?

For the comparison questions, they must be separated from the relevant questions by time, place, or category.

- Time: Before this year...
- Place: Prior to moving to ...
- Category: Did you ever steal any Government Property (Case is theft of Private Property)

Comparison questions must be as broad in scope as possible. "Before this year, did you ever steal anything of value from your current job?"

Once we have developed our line of questioning for the style of interview we are conducting, we will follow a format. This format involves the biographical and medical assessment questions. At the same time, what we are accomplishing is the building of rapport. Rapport is not always necessary to accomplish our goals. All other bias or disdain for the subject must be pushed aside to accomplish rapport. We will seek throughout the entire interview a homeostasis state for the subject. It is required to keep them on topic. When they start to veer off course or start rambling on about insignificant banter, it is your job to return them back to the topic at hand. We need to control every aspect of the interview while not appearing to do so. We can explain to them that at any time, feel free to interject and correct any information that you think is incorrect. Now that we have established a rapport and the biographical/medical assessment, we shall prepare them for the next phase.

We will ask, "I am going to ask you to be 100% truthful with me. Can you do that?" We are now ready to move to the next phase called the free narrative. They are not interrupted or challenged on the facts at this time. "Please describe everything or tell me everything you know about (the topic)?" When finished, ask clarifying questions but do not interrogate. Now we can ask a comparison – "Before today, have you ever used marijuana?" Then relevant questions like "Is there marijuana in the car?" If they become talkative about another subject stop them with a neutral question (Homeostasis) like, "What color is your car?" before asking another comparison question, "Have you ever associated with anyone who used drugs?" Follow this with another relevant question, "If it is not yours than who would have it in the car?" Once all of your questions have been exhausted, you can go into a narrative review. "Let me tell you what I know so far. You are driving this car. I stopped you and smelled marijuana from inside the car. "You told me that …" This allows them to correct anything we say that may be confusing or needs correction. A simplistic example of this would be if you stopped someone for speeding or other violation and suspect them of drug smuggling. Comparison questions can lead you to an assumption one way or the other. Concern for the ticket and not drugs could show a probability of no contraband. Conversely, no concern of paying a fine could indicate contraband possession. A sample questioning may look like this:

- I am going to ask you to be 100% truthful with me. Can you do that?
- Free narrative – Describe everything. Tell me everything you know about this ……
- Comparison – Before today, have you ever used marijuana?
- Relevant – Are there drugs in the car?
- If they become talkative about another subject stop them with a neutral question (Homeostasis) like, "What color is your car?"
- Comparison - Have you ever associated with anyone who used drugs?
- Relevant - If it is not yours than who would have it in the car?
- Narrative Review: You are driving this car. I stopped you and smelled marijuana from inside the car. You told me that ………… Is there anything else you would like to add to prove your innocence in this matter?

If the subject is asked to assess his own level of honesty in the very beginning, the tendency is to over assess his honesty in order to add strength and credibility to his innocence. The discussion can take this direction:

"How about you, in terms of honesty, how would you rate yourself personally on a scale of 1 – 100"? If the estimate is not between 95 – 100 percent continue by saying, "Really? That's kind of low. Most people are higher than that. You know yourself better than I do—give me as accurate an assessment of your honesty as you can." The subjects will then give you a much higher assessment, has now committed themselves to an exceptionally high degree of honesty, and will become vulnerable later on when the comparison questions are established.

Pay close attention to the questioning. Every word that they and you utilize counts in the determination of an answer. If you asked a question such as: "Tell me in as much detail as possible, everything you know about this event?" Look at each word used. You did not ask them for a definitive answer, just what could be possible to tell me now. The word "possible" translates to likely, probable, or potential. You have given them a way out of the question. A better question is: "I need you to tell me everything that you know about this…" or "everything that occurred from the time you arrived at work to the time you left on ………..." Or "Explain everything without leaving out even the smallest detail of your entire day on …….. This type of word analysis will be discussed further in the section on Statement Analysis.

Some examples of irrelevant or comparison would be:
- During the first (DTF) _____ years of your life do you remember (DYR) stealing?
- DTF _____ years of your life DYR cheating?
- DTF _____ years of your life DRY lying?
- DTF _____ years of your life DRY using illegal drugs?

Below is a list of irrelevant or comparison questions you could ask in a drug investigation.
- Did you ever do anything you could be arrested for?
- Did you ever do anything against the law?
- Did you ever lie to anyone about using drugs?
- Did you ever use any drugs illegally?
- Did you ever think of using any illegal drugs?
- Have you used any narcotics since you got out of jail?
- Did you smoke marijuana more than ____ times? (Use the number of times the subject admits.)
- Did you use any narcotics since_____? (Date admitted last used.)
- Did you ever get sick from using drugs?
- Did you ever get "high" from using drugs?
- Did you ever miss work because of using drugs'?
- Did you ever take any medication without a doctor's OK?
- Did you ever smoke anything containing a drug?
- Did you ever inhale anything containing a drug?
- Did you ever smoke marijuana?
- Did you ever use any narcotics?
- Have you used narcotics more than ____ times? (Use the number of times subject admits.)
- Have-you used any drugs since you've been on parole? (probation)
- DYR ever being more involved with drugs than what you told me?
- DYR ever dealing drugs for a profit?

These are some sample comparison questions you could use in a drug investigation. Create a list of the most common types of investigations you conduct each year. Draft a list of comparison and relevant questions that apply to the subject matter. Once completed, you can use the list to effectively inquire about their involvement without the need of creating a new list before each scenario. You have removed much of the needed preparation required to effectively initiate and conduct an interview by streamlining the process and preventing ineffective "off the cuff" questioning.

Statement Validity Assessments

Statement Validity Assessment (SVA) is the technique most widely used for determining the truthfulness of verbal statements. It was developed in Germany in the 1950's for use on minors who were victims of sexual abuse. This was conducted because the testimony of minors could not always be considered dependable. The children were too susceptible to outside influences. This type of testing assist in determining testimony based on a real experience because it differs in quality and content from an imagined event.

SVA consist of three mutually dependent components:

a) A structured interview with the victim.
b) Criteria-Based Content Analysis or CBCA, which assesses the content of the person's testimony.
c) The integration of CBCA with the information obtained through a set of questions called the Validity Checklist.

In order to accomplish the structured interview have the subject talk at least 95% of the time. All too often interviewer's talk, too much which allows the suspect to gather information and tell you information, based around your wording. In other words, we are telling or feeding them what to say. This is one of several types of influences adults can have on children. We learned to be cognizant of our word usage in the Probable Lie Comparison (PLC) section because adults are listening to your words for clues how to best answer the questions. To accomplish this use open-ended questioning styles.

As for the Criteria-Based Content Analysis or CBCA, this is accomplished via a 19-question test analysis of the content of the person's testimony. This question criterion consists of the following questions and categories:

General Characteristics:
    1. Logical structure
    2. Unstructured production
    3. Quantity of details
Specific Content:
    4. Contextual embedding – events are placed in time and location
    5. Description of interactions – I ran left and he approached from the other side.
    6. Reproduction of conversation
    7. Unexpected complications during the incident

Peculiarities of Content:
> 8. Unusual details
> 9. Superfluous details – unrelated, I was watching Family Fued when I heard ....
> 10. Accurately reported details misunderstood
> 11. Related external associations
> 12. Allusions to subjective mental state
> 13. Attribution of the accused's mental state

Motivation-Related Content:
> 14. Spontaneous corrections
> 15. Admitting lack of memory
> 16. Raising doubts about one's own testimony
> 17. Self-Deprecation – humor about something negative
> 18. Pardoning the accused

Specific Elements of the Offence:
> 19. Specific details of the offence

The SVA process begins with the interview. As always, the interviewer must have some preparatory time to develop the theme of questions based upon the criteria. To do this, the interviewer has to be familiar with the content of the case as well as the test criteria. What the subject has or has not experienced will influence the CBCA. Therefore, the interviewer must also take into consideration the biographical background of the subject as well as the person's age, experience and cognitive ability level during rapport building. The analysis of the verbal content of the statement occurs through the application of the 19 criteria, organized in five broad categories, and with the purpose of differentiating between true and fabricated statements. The basic idea is that a true testimony contains a greater n umber of criteria. However, there is no minimal score, yet the higher the score the more valid.

The development and testing of SVA was groundbreaking and found to be highly effective with juvenile victims and witnesses. Researchers then began the testing of these processes with adults. The foundation of the testing was the same except for a reduction of CBCA criteria questions. Research found that the criteria questioning could be reduced. The following are believed to be the 14 most effective questions:

> 1. False statements have few details or an unusually large number of details. True statements have many details or unusual details related to the event.
>   > "The man had a strange odor."
>   > "She screamed real loud before she hit me."
> 2. Superfluous details unrelated to the event.

"I had been watching Americas Funniest Videos that morning so I was in a good mood."

"I had been to McDonalds that morning and they forgot to give me   a straw."

3. Contextual embedding - Events are placed in time and location. Actions are connected with other daily activities.

"I was passing the Publix when I heard the gunshot."

"I was watching the news, which I always do at 6:00 p.m., when I heard a loud scream."

4. Descriptions of Interactions - Action of A - Reaction of B - Reaction of A

"I moved toward the door, he stepped in front of me, I ran the other way."

"He glared at me, I glared back, he started to smile."

"I left him a message, he didn't call back, I called him again."

Deceptive statements are often general

"I ran out the back."

"We stared at each other."

"He never called me back."

5. Reproduction of Conversation

Truthful Statement:

I said. "We should see other people." She replied that, "She would not let that happen."

I asked her why she was lying. She said that she wasn't lying, and I said, "Yes you are."

Deceptive Statements of the same conversation:

"We discussed our relationship."

"She denied that she was lying."

True Statements possess:

6. Unusual details – tattoos, stutters, quirks

7. Spontaneous Corrections

8. Admitting Lack of Memory

9. Raising Doubts about One's Own Testimony

10. Self-Deprecation

11. Pardoning the Perpetrator

12. Subjective Mental State

Describes feelings or thoughts

"I was very scared."

"Her actions made me nervous."

"I felt humiliated."

"He made me so angry."

13. Attribution of Perpetrator's Mental State - Describes the perpetrator's feelings or thoughts experienced at the time of the incident.

> "You could see in his eyes how angry he was."
>
> "The way he held his head let you know that he thought he was in control."
>
> "She seemed confused and perhaps a bit guilty about what she was doing."

14. Clarity

> False statements:
>> Don't make sense
>
> True statements:
>> Have a logical structure
>>
>> Contain details characteristic of the offense
>>
>> Are told with an appropriate affect
>>
>> Are consistent with other statements
>>
>> Are consistent with other evidence

The third component of the process is the integration of CBCA with the information obtained through a set of categories called the Validity Checklist. The Validity Checklist consist of four general categories of information:

a) Psychological characteristics - In this category it is important to assess the appropriateness of language, affect and susceptibility to suggestion.

b) Interview characteristics - Analyze the quality of the interview rating the type of questions asked such as are they suggestive, leading or coactive and their overall appropriateness to the situation.

c) Motivation for making false accusations - The information in this category should help to rule out those aspects that may be influencing the person to provide a false testimony. Additionally, understand that a minor could be under pressure from a third person to make a false statement. An important aspect of this category is the context in which the statement is generated.

d) Aspects related to the investigation - This section is designed with the aim of rating the consistency between previous statements and investigation results.

Steven Varnell

Reality Monitoring

Reality Monitoring identifies memories originating from true experiences and should include more perceptual information (visual details, sounds, smells, tastes and physical feelings related to the event), contextual information (information regarding when and where the event happened), and affective information (details of feelings about thoughts, reasoning, and inferences of events) than memories based on fabrication. This style of interviewing is easier to learn than Statement Validity Analysis or SVA because the questioning is directed towards these specific areas.

The testimony or statement is examined for full sensory representation. Liars tend to talk in the abstract or brief summary rather than complete details. They are likely to make use of audio/visual descriptions that are free of sensory detail. Truth tellers are more likely to add sensory-based detail. Reality monitoring scores the records of interviews along the following dimensions:

- Visual details or descriptions of what the person saw: "I saw that the car was missing."
- Auditory details or descriptions of what was heard: "I heard the screen door slam."
- Spatial details, where the event took place: "I went across the street to Joe's house."
- How objects are arranged in space: "I heard sounds coming from above me."
- Temporal details, how things are arranged in time and how long they lasted: "First, I knocked on the door. Then, I looked in the window. Finally, I let myself in." "I was only there for about five minutes but it seemed like an hour."

Like the CBCA analysis, reality monitoring is usually conducted with a written transcript of the interview. It is scored so that the more the sensory elements appear; the greater the likelihood is that the speaker is telling the truth. Reality monitoring contrasts the characteristics of a full sensory representation of a real event, with the basics of a fabricated story. When lies are presented as truth, the speaker is often unwilling to acknowledge mistakes. Someone trying to deceive will try to stay on a "lie script." This is a prepared idea of how the events took place. It is too difficult to create all of the sensory recognitions to these stories so there are few details and personal narratives included. The lie must be presented as practiced and attempts to access details out of order may increase signs of nervousness.

In contrast, the truth is rich in personal insights and sensory details. A truth teller understands that they may not get it right completely and is willing to adjust the story line. They often ramble and go off track and include details that are irrelevant to the problem at hand. This process is impossible to the deceiver because to change course in their story means leaving the "lie script" and this creates cognitive overload.

The key to lie detection for these methods is to keep track of behavioral details instead of trying to determine whether the speaker was lying. This equates to the need to have the statement in writing. We can then study this statement word for word and keep track of these required details. This will give us the groundwork needed to explain how we understand that the statement is false. Again, the central task is not trying to determine who is lying, but keeping track of the details. These details show us who the truth tellers are. Some of the key details found were:

1. The lag time between the question and the answer (increased for liars)
2. Hand and finger movements without moving the arms (decreased for liars)
3. Speech hesitations: "uhs," "ums," or "aahs" between words (increased for liars)
4. The quantity and specificity of details (decreased for liars)
5. Descriptions of time and location (decreased for liars)
6. The reproduction of conversation (decreased for liars)
7. Descriptions of other people's feelings, thoughts, or motives (decreased for liars);
8. The inclusion of visual and auditory details (decreased for liars)
9. The inclusion of spatial (where) information and temporal (time) details (decreased for liars)

Steven Varnell

Cognitive Interviewing Techniques (CI)

Dr. Edward Geiselman (UCLA) and Dr. Ron Fisher (FIU) developed the Cognitive Interviewing Technique. The standard Cognitive Interviewing (CI) process is a 6-step procedure to enhance memories of witnesses and victims. It has been shown to increase detection of deception by 25-40%.

A common problem which an investigator encounters is when the witnesses or victims "cannot remember" certain events. This is not the result of not witnessing but rather an inability to remember. When we are faced with a situation perceived by the brain as threatening, the brain focuses all of our sensory receptors to the threat in an effort of self-preservation. Because of this focus, we will not remember certain occurrences within an event. The Cognitive Interviewing Technique has been developed to help investigators retrieve this stored information. The steps to this process are as follows:

Step 1 – Introduction / Rapport – Discuss with the subject neutral topics or even topics of shared interest for which they have no reason to lie.
Step 2 - Narrative – Instruct them to tell everything about the event including the smallest of details. As seen, people have a natural habit of editing information. We may not intend to deceive in any way but it takes too long to explain every detail. We want them to return to the scene mentally and relive the before, during, and after events. We should not challenge any statements but extenders are all right. (What happened then?)
Step 3 - Sketch – Ask them to draw a sketch or illustration of the event like the general layout of the area where the incident occurred and then trace the events as they unfolded from start to finish.
Step 4 - Follow-up – Ask open ended questions which will further the clarification w/o confrontation and locks them into the statement.
Steps 5 - Reverse order – When all of the scenes of the narrative are completed with the above steps, ask them to describe the event again but in reverse order; ending to start.
Step 6 - Challenge – Remaining soft spoken and respectful ask them about any inconsistencies or incriminating statements. It is alright to even tell them that you believe they are lying about the entire event.

One of the most important issues in CI is that the interviewer remains silent while the interviewee recalls the experience. However much an interviewee appears to be drifting into irrelevancies, they should remain uninterrupted.

The interviewee must be encouraged to recall the experience without the normal editing of social conversation. Rapport is essential and the interviewer needs to put the interviewee at ease and give them latitude to tell their story in detail. We need to be very attentive to what the interviewee is saying without note taking. This attentiveness and freedom from interruption seems to encourage interviewees to provide numerous details to serve as affirmation the belief that they are taken seriously. They can be placed into such a detailed recall that incidents lasting minutes are recalled in hours.

The main techniques employed to enhance recall is 'context reinstatement'. The purpose is to return the interviewee in their mind to the context in which the experience occurred. Often this entails no more than asking the interviewee to relax, possibly to close their eyes, and recall where and when the incident occurred. They should be encouraged to recall the scene and in their mind to look around it and note who was present, what they could see, hear, touch, and smell. They might be asked to remember what had happened immediately prior to the incident. It can be valuable to ask the interviewee to draw a map of the location and indicate where others were standing, sitting, etc. However achieved, it is important to awaken the interviewee's memory of the context and they should be allowed time to do so. The context cues will then assist recall.

The interviewee is then invited to recount their experience in whatever way they choose. Narrative is the most common structure, but some may begin by recalling the most memorable feature of the experience. Not until they have fully completed this initial recall does the interviewer intervene. There may be elements of the account that fail to connect, e.g. the interviewee has failed to acknowledge that they moved from one location to another, or left unexplained what prompted some specific course of action. The interviewer now invites them to return to each significant moment in turn, reinstating the context each time (paying as much attention to doing so as they did initially) and asks the interviewee to elaborate.

Once the interviewee appears to have recalled as much as possible, it may prove beneficial to use other techniques to unlock their memory. First, we will ask them to reverse the narrative; to ask them to recall what happened immediately prior to some particularly important moment, e.g. what occurred immediately before an eruption of violence. This inhibits interviewees from skipping over steps in the narrative because they are taken for granted. The most important prelude to each exploration of detail must be to reinstate the context and definitely not to rush them into providing an account. The interview may end with the interviewer giving the subject challenge questions to clarify any issues that exist.

An audio recording of the interview is essential because of the large amount of data produced by the recall. A transcript of the interview can be useful in placing the various recalled events of various orders into a useful arrangement of subject matter, e.g. descriptions of people that may be scattered throughout the interview are brought together. It can be useful to the investigator if the transcripts are also collected in an understandable order and scribed in the third person vocabulary. If possible, this investigative composite of the interview can be presented to the interviewee for amendment and endorsement.

When revealing the differences between truthful and deceptive subjects, the following was found.

- Narratives offered were significantly longer by the truthful.
- Drawing task deceptive - Time consuming and failure to include narrative elements, starting over because of inconsistencies, changing or correcting elements of the story and needed the most time to complete.
- Truthful drawing task added new consistent details.
- Truthful follow-ups took longer because of all of the detail.
- Deceptive reverse order stories needed prompts not to significantly leap back in time and reverting to forward recalling details.
- When asked to clarify unresolved inconsistencies, truthful people often explained due to miss communication (let me explain, I wasn't clear before) while deceptive people has a claim of memory (I was mistaken; it was this way)
- When asked if they wanted to add anything, deceptive persons would quickly say no, while truthful persons would elaborate or hesitate before a no.
- When challenged about lying, deceptive persons would look unhappy or uncomfortable, then offer weak denials or deflect the challenge. Truthful people would offer a firm denial of lying and offer additional info to support their position.

There were three major deception indicators prevalent especially during the drawing, reverse order and challenge phase. One is that people trying to deceive tell unnatural stories. These stories have few details, end abruptly, has contradictions, lack chronology, possess vague or an illogical story line, and had awkward use of terms. The second is exaggerated behavior, which includes inappropriate smiling, shrugging, grooming, and rationalizing. The third is unusual eye contact or movements, which included blinking, squinting, exaggerated movements, and looking down or around the room.

As has been the rule of understanding from the beginning and is always worth repeating throughout, examine everything in clusters. Dr. Geiselman was quoted as saying, "Detection of any one indicator should not be taken as sufficient evidence to conclude that the subject is being deceptive. Instead, judgments must be based on the overall pattern of performance through the entire CI protocol."

Statement Analysis (SA) or SCAN Analysis (Scientific Content Analysis)

An entire section is dedicated to this section due to its complexity and begins on page 364.

Assessment Criteria Indicative of Deception (ACID)

Assessment Criteria Indicative of Deception or ACID combines content criteria derived from research in deception and memory along with investigative interviewing to facilitate the detection of deception. Research has found that fictional responses are shorter and have less supporting detail than true responses. This is because a lie is more cognitively demanding than telling the truth and liars must work harder to control their speech

Focus for ACID is placed on two (2) Criteria-Based Content Analysis or CBCA criteria from the Statement Valid Analysis or SVA interviewing process. These criteria are the Unstructured Production (Spontaneous Reproduction) and Quantity of Details (or Sufficient Detail). Like CBCA, Reality Monitoring (RM) decisions often are made from the amount and type of details in a statement. Memories for genuine events should contain more external-sensory details (color, smell, taste, etc.) and more contextual details. Examples:

External details – info gained from the senses. A **tall man** with **black hair** has 2 external details

Contextual details – the relationship between the details. The drugs were **on top** of the bed. I am sure about **the time** because I was **watching Jeopardy** which starts **every night at 7:00pm**.

Internal details – moods and experiences. I saw the man approach and **he frightened** me.

It is understood that a common strategy for deception is to prepare and practice a fictitious account or a "script lie." Therefore, the goal of the investigator is to increase the cognitive load making it difficult for the liar to deceive. They are unable to make changes to their prepared script without making the deception obvious. They will follow their lie script while a truthful subject relives the events.

The ACID system analyzes the length of responses, including potential errors and the details not provided during free recall, but were added in the course of later recall tasks. The process adds detail, requires multiple recall tasks, and includes alternative suggestions to the process, which helps the honest person, but becomes nearly impossible for a deceptive subject to stay on script. This system, a combination of the others discussed, is processed in 8 steps.

1. Baseline and rapport – Not Scored
    a. 'Last meal'
    b. 'First day of work'

2. Free Recall 'Please describe detail, everything that happened.
    a. Free recall

3. Mental reinstatement of context 'Think about and include all sights, sounds, smells, emotions, thoughts, or anything else from time of event.'
    a. Mnemonics (memory aid)

4. Inferential block – Not Scored. This is a question asked so as to take their mind off immediate events.
    a. 'If your spouse had been present, would they have noticed something wrong?'
    b. 'Has a crime been committed?'
    c. 'Did anyone speak about anything illegal?'

5. Recall from other perspective
    a. 'If someone else had been in the room, what would they have seen?' –mnemonics

6. Reverse order recall 'Beginning with last, and ending with first, please describe the entire event in reverse order.'
    a. mnemonics

7. Inferential block 2
    a. 'Did you notice anything unusual about …….?'
    b. 'Would anyone think that you did something you weren't supposed to ……………?'
    c. 'Do you think that you could have been mistaken about anything you have said so far?'

8. Retell entire event
    a. 'Please describe, in as much detail as possible, everything that happened to make sure I have the entire story.

We are watching for issues like; the response length and the number of external, contextual, and internal details reported during free recall. Also the response length and the number of new external, contextual, and internal details reported during the mnemonic section of the interview. Lastly, whether or not the participant admitted that they could have made a mistake.

The mnemonic section of the process or memory aid is used to try and stimulate more information from the subject. The mnemonic section of honest statements consistently contain more details and are longer than the mnemonic section of deceptive statements because it enhances recall. Liars try to stay on script so the memory aid does not assist them because it is not part of the prepared recall. Also, honest people were more likely than deceivers to admit possible error. As we have seen, a liar believes that in order for you to believe their lie, the deception has to be accepted in whole. No part can be false. The free recall portion became a baseline as truth tellers expanded later in mnemonics while liars told the same amount of information. This is similar to measuring the statement for balance as we did with SCAN except now we are balancing the recall with the mnemonic section of the statement.

It all makes sense when you exam the process naturally. You recall events, but we simply are not able to tell a systematic detailed illustration of the event. Our mind will remember yet our ability to write and/or think is substantially slower. Therefore our mind will process the information and explain what it thinks is important. This is true only for the truth tellers. The deceivers have to work their way through what they want to tell you and will generally lock in on a particular script. This script will eventually lead to their demise. If after someone tells all that there is to tell on a subject and then you ask them several mnemonic questions, it should cause them to recall more information and in the context of the last recall, add it to their explanation. This in turn will cause this section of the story to be longer than the first free recall. Script regurgitations are simply that, word vomit. They are unable to add or shorten the context of the story to stay on script.

Handwriting Analysis

I wanted to include this short and simple examination at what some consider important and others compare to a circus act. Either way, I find the thought processes behind the idea intriguing. Though not overly effective, you will find much of the material factual. Handwriting analysis adds value because it can show in some instances the type of person involved in the writing along with their cognitive loads and personalities. Everyone has different handwriting because we all have different structural designs of the hands, fingers, etc. Handwriting is considered by many as brain writing. Our conscious decides what we will write, but the subconscious determines how we will write. Extroverts tend to write with large letters, while introverts with small letters. A much focused mind that seeks perfection will also write very deliberate and small. A good example of focused mind writing is Albert Einstein. His letter expression is small and almost perfect.

The lower case "t" can tell you about how a person feels. This letter has two parts, the vertical line or stem and the horizontal line or T-bar. When a person writes, look for the placement of the T-bar on the stem. The higher the T-bar on the stem, the higher the person's self-esteem while below half way of the stem can indicate they are afraid of failure or lack confidence.

The letter "i" is the same as the "t" except we are looking at the placement of the dot. To the left of the stem, they may procrastinate, while to the right of the stem shows they are driven. The dot placed directly above the stem shows they are careful, or too high above the stem could mean they are unrealistic. If they replace the dot with a circle or happy face, this person may be immature.

The letter "o" is believed to say a lot about a person's feelings. A loop to the left inside the circle shows self-denial; a loop to the right may be deception. A double-looped "o" or an "o" that has two (2) loops inside the circle indicates caution because it shows the writer retracing a letter or placing excessive pressure. The boldness of the letter will stand out signifying that this is at a point of the statement which is causing cognitive load. The brain is trying to work out what to write while the hand sits and waits for the decision, but is unable to sit idle.

The Felons Claw involves the letters g, y, and z. This is an action of placing a sickle or hook at the lower end of the letter. About 80% of the prison population acquires this style, hence its name. The person who utilizes this writing trait could be self-destructive.

It is a fun topic and everyone should explore its foundations thoroughly. The more we understand about writing and sentence structure the more effective investigator you will become. These small inferences can assist you in determining the mindset of the interviewee. As we learned earlier, personality observations are critical to the required interview style.

The Interview Format to Expand the Statement - 42

Understanding the content of a statement and the areas of interest to watch for, we initiate an interview with the persons of interest. The interview gives us witness or suspect viability determinations.

There are numerous areas of an interview to prepare for and everyone has their own list of preparations. They are all essentially the same but here is a list from me. Understand that based on the circumstances, parts of this list can change.

1. Preparing for the Interview:
    a. Room preparations
    b. Audio-video, equipment check
    c. Evidence review to know the case
    d. Witness statement reviews

    e. Plausible evidence themes for bait questions
2. The Introduction including topic confirmation
3. Honesty Check
4. Physical/Mental evaluation

3. Baseline Determinations
4. The Free Narrative
7. Questioning and Clarification
8. Closure

If there are multiple people, interview the least likely suspect or probable witnesses first and continue in order of importance. This way we will have all of the statements before sitting with our prime suspect.

After completing the interview preparations, we will have the introduction. This can be as basic or complex as possible. The investigator must verify that the suspect fully understands why they are there and what is being investigated. Along these lines, Wendell Rudacille presents in his book, "Identifying Lies in Disguise," a fantastic introduction. I have always been a fan of polygraph examiners because of their intensive question development and understanding the importance of each and every word.
An introduction can have the following,

"John, as you know, we are conducting an investigation into these allegations made by ... . The purpose of our investigation is to determine the truth about what happened. The purpose of this interview is so we can take a statement from you and get your information about this. I appreciate your cooperation in this matter and I'm sure you're just as eager to get to the truth of this as we are. It is imperative that you are 100% truthful with me. The truth is like being pregnant; you either are or are not. There is no middle or gray area. Together, we can get past almost anything, but we cannot get past a lie. You must tell only the truth. Do you understand?"

In this introduction, we are covering a lot of territory. In the beginning, they are told why they are there and what is sought. They are told what is expected and that there is many involved in the investigation with the use of the words "we" and "our." We let them know that a bond of trust can be established with the words "Together" and "we." This introduction makes it clear the goals of the interview and can be tweaked to match your own needs.

While we are establishing honesty, we can conduct an honesty check. The subject is asked to assess his own level of honesty and the tendency is to over assess in order to add strength and credibility to his innocence.

Ask them, "Is it your intention today to be completely truthful?" "How about you, John? In terms of honesty, how would you rate yourself personally on a scale of 1 – 100." If estimate is not between 95 – 100 percent continue by saying, "Really? That's kind of low. Most people are higher than that. You know yourself better than I do—give me as accurate an assessment of your honesty as you can." If they go higher, this was your goal. To lock them in on a strong desire to tell the truth.

To reduce the defense's ammunition to use against you, now is a good time for a physical assessment. It is similar to what we would use in a DUI investigation to confirm they are free of mind-altering drugs and are fully understanding of the process.

- What is your general health?...Excellent, good, fair or poor...Explain.
- Have you taken any medication in the past 24 hours?...
- Ask about effects of medication...You may have to go to PDR or internet.
- Alcohol in the past 24hrs?
- Are you presently being treated by a doctor?...Explain...
- Pregnancy?
- Amount of sleep in past 24 hours? What is the norm?

Ask initial personal questions as we establish their baseline. This process was discussed earlier and is involving topics unrelated to the case. Once this process has traveled as far as it can, we are ready to begin the interview. Always initiate as a free narrative. As the interview initiates from the information of the statement, interviewees will often interject questions and comments. You must handle these issues and maintain control over the interview. They will commonly ask,

Q-What exactly do you want me to say?
A-Everything you are aware of.
Q-That'll take me all day! (Known as a procedural complaint)
A-Just put down everything you are aware of.

Your responses are neutral toned and encourage continuing. The less said by you the better. Never give away any facts of the case. Everyone is either emotional or non-emotional. Along these two zones, we will determine the types of questions to develop. An emotional person is a first time offender or someone who appears genuinely upset about the circumstances of the events. These persons are approached calmly while questioning them about their feelings or how the events have affected them. Theme development can be with emotional choices, one indicating the person must be bad to the bone while the other perceives them in a better light.

A non-emotional person is the multi offender who has become more hardened to the process. They show little or no emotion and regret. They are concerned about themselves just as the emotional person is, except in a different manner. Play to their emotion is not effective so we theme develop choices that changes the degree of the crime. "There have been many burglaries in this area recently including several reported rapes. Did you commit all of these burglaries or just this one. If you are involved in all of these others, the implications towards you are severe. It was just this one event, wasn't it."

The interview initiation steps, Step 1e stated plausible evidence themes for bait questions. This is a process to assist the investigator in their question development. We would all like to come directly out of the box and ask or state, "Did you do it?", but this allows them to use their prepared answer. As the suspect thinks about what you are going to ask them, they obtain this information from experiences to television. This allows them to answer your question with their prepared "no" answer. We want to ask questions that they are not prepared to answer but are similar. Along this line, we look at the crime and what evidence exists that is either real or at least plausible. In most cases, these will include some of the following.

Eyewitness
Fingerprints
Footprints
Tire tracks
Timeline issues
Co-conspirators testimony
Cell phone records
Surveillance video
DNA evidence

From these plausible areas of evidence, we can create Bait questions to ask at some point in the interview. After the baseline conversation, we will move to the free narrative. TEDS-PIE can assist us with the phrasing.

TEDS-PIE was created by Dr. Edward Geiselman of Cognitive Interviewing Technique fame, and the London Metropolitan Police, It is another acronym to help you remember and to allow variations to the questioning not as easily recognized by the interviewee. If you found an area of concern within the statement, you will micro-action back with backward reaching reverse questions, which are explained in Chapter 54, starting on page 404. TEDS-PIE was developed to ask questions in a format that does not sound like you are asking the same questions over again.

TEDS stands for:
- "Tell me..."
- "Explain to me..."
- "Describe for me..."
- "Show me...."

PIE stands for:
- "Precisely..."
- "In detail..."
- "Exactly...."

By pairing a term from TEDS with a term from PIE, you have a different way of introducing the same open-ended question as you go through the segments you want the interviewee to expand on. You are still making the same inquiry repeatedly, but it does not appear that way to the subject. This will give you the starting phrase for an open-ended question such as "Tell me what happened" or "Describe for me in complete detail." You can pair them together in any combination such as "Tell me precisely" or "Show me precisely."

Based on the type of investigation we will ask an open-ended question for the start of the free narrative. "Tell me precisely what happened tonight at Bob's house." This assumes you were there and if answered, establishes your presence. Once answered, ask clarifying questions to any story gaps. Based on the themes developed, interject Bait questions. If there was a video surveillance or a possibility of one, ask the bait question. "There was a video surveillance camera that recorded the area at the time of the offense. We are in the process of reviewing the footage. Is there any reason we will see you in the footage? Could you have been mistaken and just forgot to tell us about being there?"

The suspect has no idea if you are telling him the truth, but because of the location of the crime, it is plausible that a camera was recording. In his mind, he has to decide how to answer this question and the strain will be apparent. An innocent person who knows they were not there has no problem.

We must observe them throughout the process and asses their verbal and non-verbal cues. The cues they display must be explored. Once two or more of these occur, we will make note of where in the story they occurred and return there during our clarification stage. Below is a list to observe.

Verbal errors

Failure to answer – 3 strikes rule

Answering the question with superfluous info. The quality/quantity of the answer to question

Verifiable information

No explicit denial – they must give a directed denial

Reluctance to answer – I don't think I can answer that

Hard questions – that's a hard question

Attack response – convincing action to deflect perceived threat back to you

Failure to understand simple questions

Unfinished business – that's about it

Invoking religion

Selective memory – I don't recall

Qualifiers – basically, honestly

I can't statements and any variations

Procedural complaints

Rambling dissertations

Speech errors

Answer delay – must be in context of the degree of difficulty

Behavioral errors

Grooming

Lack of illustrators

Anchor points

Eye assessments

It is the interviewer's job to make sure that you ask questions in a manner which is easily understood. It is the interviewee's job to answer the questions. Along this line, we must keep things simple. Present every word with an even tone and pitch. Do not place any emphasis upon a single word in the questioning. Be direct and ask in a simple non-discreet manner, people are less likely to take offense. Remember the three strikes rule – once you have asked a subject a question three times and have not received an appropriate answer, do not get aggressive. This only builds a wall. Determine if there is something about the question, they do not understand and ask the question again. If you are still unable to get an answer, move on.

Once the free narrative is complete, you can ask open and closed ended questions to answer any questions you may have. It is all right to exit the room to review the statement thus far. Have someone else watching the interview either in the room or outside who is taking note of areas of concern or areas of the statement that requires understanding. All gaps are closed and this is accomplished through Backward Reaching Questions. Once the process is completed, a closure is given.

The closure ends the process and tries to keep it open for future options. "I want to thank you for your time today. If I have any other questions, you would agree to talk to me again, wouldn't you?" Later if they do not we can ask, "I don't understand. When we spoke before, you agreed that you would talk with me again. Why are you now unable to do so? What's changed?" Again, it is an opportunity to see how they respond and why.

Common Errors by Lie Detectors - 43

Once you eliminate the impossible, whatever remains, no matter how improbable, must be the truth.
- Sherlock Holmes by Sir Arthur Conan Doyle

Examining the wrong cues

Despite being common examples, gaze aversion and grooming are not reliable indicators of deception. The only reliable singular observation to deceptive behaviors is a decrease of illustrators. Many observers who believed someone was lying overestimated nonverbal cues and sought out information to confirm their bias. They will also downplay information to prove the innocence of the suspects.

Overemphasis on nonverbal cues

Dependent on the circumstances, too much attention can be applied to nonverbal cues because we are accustomed to people watching. The nonverbal cues observed can cause a predetermination of guilt for the viewers. Don't judge a book by its cover. It takes time and effort to formulate and ask the best questions.

An example of this over-emphasis in non-verbal behaviors occurred in Chapter 5, the fifth Fatal Error was Recognizing Danger. In addition, one of the deceptive traits of murdered officers also from

Chapter 5 is; Feels they can "read" others/situations and will drop guard as a result.

Speech content is more accurate than nonverbal cues

There are a number of explanations that lead us to place too much information on the verbal cues and not enough on the verbal indications. These are some of the most common:

- The Othello Effect - We must always remember that a truth teller can be as nervous as a liar out of fear of being wrongly accused or fear of us thinking of them as liars. These behaviors will lead us to say someone is guilty by their nonverbal characteristics alone without taking into account all of the other circumstances or evidence.

- Heuristics - These are general decision rules. The overall population believes everyone is innocent causing them to make insufficient decisions while cops feel the opposite causing guilt biased decisions. The letter of the law is that everyone is innocent until proven guilty. We all know that this can sometimes be reversed.

- Neglect of interpersonal differences - The tendency to interpret nervous behaviors as suspicious without taking individual differences into account. An example would be the social clumsiness of introverts and the impression created of tension, nervousness, or fear that is naturally given off by socially anxious individuals.

- Neglect of intrapersonal variations - This happens in the rapport stage. Engaging in small talk and discussing the crime itself are fundamentally different situations. Small talk is low stress while talk of the crime is high stress. The observable behaviors and responses have to be in the company of stress. Without it, no one has the fear of lying.

- Existing Interview Techniques - Law enforcement are sometimes advised to confront suspects at the beginning of the interview with the evidence they have. Disclosing evidence early provides liars with the opportunity to change their stories and provides an innocent explanation for the evidence. Be careful about accusing someone of lying because it can cause them to shut down (Why talk you're not going to believe me anyways).

- Overconfidence in lie detecting skills - Many in our profession are overconfident in their abilities in believing they can catch a liar. Again it falls to us to enter the scenario and try to not only show proof of the person's guilt but to equally try and show their innocence. Our truth finding efforts will pay off as long as we have placed the necessary efforts and examined all of the evidence.

Avoiding the Errors

We must pay attention to both verbal and nonverbal cues. Police often refuse to believe much of the information presented because it may contradict what they consider occurred. Avoid relying only on nonverbal cues alone. Countless studies showed that in order to detect lies, listening carefully to what is said is necessary and paying attention only to behavior impairs lie detection.

The best classifications of truths and lies are made when both sets of cues are taken into account. There are three (3) ways to help you pay attention to both verbal and nonverbal cues:

- We can take into account both nonverbal and verbal cues without looking at the relation between the two sets of cues. In other words, examine each set of cues in their single context. What are the verbal cues saying and then what are the nonverbal cues demonstrating.
- Examine nonverbal behavior in relation to speech content watching for any mismatches between the two. Are their nonverbal cues matching what would be expected of their verbal cues? At a point of the narrative, the subject is telling a very excited portion of the events, yet their nonverbal show a lack of illustrators.
- Avoid the Othello effect of misidentifying signs of nervousness. Establish a specific baseline of behavior and personality type of the subject to help you determine their nervous behavior as simply normal or indicative of deceit.

There are two (2) interview styles; informational-gathering and accusatory. We must try to stay with the informational-gathering style to keep them talking. Accusatorial questions can cause them to shut down. The longer they talk the longer you have to catch them in a lie and the informational-gathering style also projects less stress to help prevent a false confession.

Exploit the different psychological states of truth tellers and liars via two different approaches; Strategic questioning and cognitive loading. Either way requires the person to talk. Ask unanticipated questions to break a lie script through cognitive loading.

> "Where were you between 4-5pm?"
> "I was at the gym."
> "How many others were there?"
> "Who was working the desk?"
> "Who else saw you there?"

These are questions which could cause the subject to fall out of the prepared script because they are areas which they may not have considered during their script prep.

Compared with liars, truth tellers should be able to recall the event through various approaches to the story. "How old are you?" followed by the question, "what is your date of birth?" is more difficult to answer for liars resulting in longer delays than for truth tellers.

Lying is already difficult but by loading more thought processes, it becomes harder. One way is the reverse order retell of the events and the other is having them maintain eye contact with you at all times during the explanation. This adds stress because when people have to concentrate, they are inclined to look away occasionally to a motionless point. Maintaining eye contact is distracting. A truth teller will still be able to express the recall truths but a liar will have a difficult time.

Specific or strategic questions or the Devil's Advocate's questioning approach. This line of questioning can be important in many security settings like border security or risk assessments of informants. They are asked for their opinion for and against their specific area of information. ("What are your reasons for supporting the Americans in the war in Afghanistan?" vs. Playing devil's advocate, "Is there anything you can say against the involvement of the Americans in Afghanistan?")

People normally think more deeply about and are able to generate reasons that support rather than oppose their beliefs and opinions. Truth tellers are likely to provide more information in their responses to the opinion-eliciting question than to the devil's advocate question. Truth tellers' answers are longer than their devil's advocate answers. Also, the truth tellers' answers sounded more direct and believable while revealing more emotional involvement than did their devil's advocate answers.

This line of questioning could have been used December 30, 2009 in Afghanistan. The CIA had used a polygraph to determine the truthful intentions of an informant who wanted to give them information on Taliban and Al Qaeda members. They were aware of his extremist views against the Americans but decided after the polygraph that he was using it as a cover. The subject came to a CIA building where he blew himself up killing seven CIA agents.

The strategic use of evidence: Guilty suspects are inclined to use avoidance strategies or denial strategies. A man has his wallet stolen from his office drawer. You have fingerprints that indicate who opened the drawer but you do not disclose this to the suspect. Have them describe their activities in the office. They will deny being around the drawer. Then you can ask questions about the area where the wallet had been and see how they respond. Again, the subject has denial of any knowledge. The final phase is to reveal the fingerprints and ask them to explain the contradictions.

Preventing False Confessions

A false confession is an admission of guilt in a crime in which the confessor is not responsible for the crime. Even though false confessions might appear to be the exception, they occur on a regular basis and false confessions are becoming a greater reality. Care has to be taken by the investigator to ensure the validity of the confession. Many of us believe that no one would confess to a crime they had not committed. Yet it is believed that about 5% of confessions could be false based on 25% of the DNA overturned cases.

According to a study out of Northwestern University, in Illinois, of 55 wrongfully convicted defendants who confessed or the conviction was based upon a codefendants confession:

83.6% police misconduct
27.3% prosecutorial misconduct
25.5% false or misleading forensic evidence
30.9% incorrect eyewitness testimony
70.9% testimony by informants

Adult false confessions occur when:

- Evidence is so stacked against the subject; they begin to believe that they are the only one who could have committed the crime.
- They become exhausted after extremely long interrogations.
- Authorities misconstrue suspect's innocent statements as guilty admissions.

- Suspects are duped into believing all will be alright by admitting to the crime.

Presumptions during the interview can lead to "bias" or tunnel vision. This can lead to a condition known as confirmation bias, which is only the information that gives credence to your expectations are valid and discounts all other information.

Offers of leniency and minimization tactics showed an increase in guilty confessions of 72% over false confessions of 20%. This verifies the practice of offering leniency in exchange for a confession. Juveniles and mentally impaired subjects are the most vulnerable to a false confession and require extreme caution when being interviewed.

Statement Validity Analysis was developed for and is showing great promise in interviewing these groups. Most proven false confessions occur with murder and rape cases. The primary causes are:

- Overly long interrogations
- Presentations of false evidence
- Investigator tunnel vision
- Prolonged isolation
- Lack of sleep

One corrective measure is to videotape the entire process. Once the video process begins, do not allow any other interviews to occur once the taping has stopped. This not only protects the accused but also protects your agency from any accusations of abuse. Our normal process is to develop theories and prove them correct. It is equally important to try to disprove them.

- Have another investigator view the interview process.
- Independently verify the information given is case specific and not gathered from officer's statements and media.
- Verify the evidence to the statements provided.

Assassinations and Serial Killings - 44

Come as you are. Bring what cha got.

Comment from a U.S. Special Forces Operator when asked about sending in SOF to try and rescue our personnel from the Benghazi, Libya U.S. Embassy attack where 4 Americans were killed and help never arrived.

Exceptional Case Study Project (ECSP)

The ECSP is a joint study by the United States Secret Service (USSS) and several psychiatrists in an effort to determine if there are patterns to an attacker or if a line of questioning could be developed to separate legitimate threats from hoaxes. From 1949 to 1996, it was discovered that 83 subjects participated in 73 incidents and were identified and known to have attacked or came close to an attacking a prominent public official or figure just in the United States. There were a variety of motives listed in the study that included: notoriety, revenge, idiosyncratic thinking, hopes to be killed, interest in bringing about political change, and money. Idiosyncratic beliefs, like a wish to save the world, bring attention to a perceived wrong, or desire for a special relationship with the target, filled 40% of the incidents. These subjects were more likely to attack a public figure like a celebrity than a protected official was. Subjects with motives like notoriety or a wish to be killed by law enforcement were more likely to attack the President. These subjects were at the time of the incident:

Ages 16-73
Half received at least some college
Near lethal attackers were likely to be single and never married rather than attackers

Study Results

- Women were more likely to be attackers rather than approachers. Subjects who targeted the President were more likely to be full-time employed. Both had a history of transience.
- Most were social isolates, but one third was not.
- Many had a history of harassing other persons.
- Most had a history of explosive, angry behavior and half had a history of violent behavior.
- Few had histories of arrest for violent crimes or weapons.
- Few had ever been incarcerated.
- Most had a history of weapons use but no formal training.
- Most had an interest in militant ideas and groups but were not active members of any.
- Many had a history of depression.
- Many were known to have attempted suicide.
- Many had had contact with a Mental Health Facility but did not reveal their considerations.
- Attackers were less likely to have delusional ideas or be delusional than were near lethal approachers.
- Few had histories of command hallucinations.
- Few had a history of substance abuse.
- Almost all American assassins, attackers, or would-be attackers believed they had difficulties coping with problems in their life.
- All, at some point, came to see an attack as a solution for their problems.
- Fewer than a quarter of the subjects are known to have developed an escape plan.
- One third of the subjects expected to be killed.
- None lived an exemplary life and had difficulties maintaining a consistent relationship, job performance and achievements.
- Not "losers," half college, two fifths had been married, one third were parents, completed military service, one attended

law school, another medical school, another was a retired police officer, another a firefighter, postal worker, and several engineers.

- One truth was that the events began after a period of downward spiral in their lives in the 12 months prior to the event.
- Most are preventable because always follow a path to the attack.
- There may be interest in previous attacks.
- They are likely to communicate their intentions to others or keep a journal.
- This is also true for stalkers and certain types of workplace violence.
- Very few made threats to their targets or police.
- If a threat is made it should be taken serious because the lack of concern can be perceived as permission to proceed.
- They will practice and carry out visits to the targets office, home, or visiting places.
- They will often choose several targets choosing the target after knowing the opportunity exist and it will fulfill their goals.
- Few have much cunning and lack the bravado that many perceive them as having.

"Threat assessment" is the term used to describe the set of investigative and operational techniques used by law enforcement professionals to identify, assess, and manage the risks of targeted violence and its potential perpetrators. Violence is a process, as well as an act. Careful analysis of violent incidents shows that violent acts often are the culmination of long-developing, identifiable trails of problems, conflicts, disputes, and failures. A key to investigation and resolution of threat assessment cases is identification of the subject's "attack-related" behaviors. Violence is the product of an interaction among three factors:

a) The individual who takes violent action.
b) Stimulus or triggering conditions that lead the subject to see violence as an option, "way out," or solution to problems or life situation.
c) A setting that facilitates or permits the violence, or at least does not stop it from occurring.

Perpetrators of targeted acts of violence engage in discrete behaviors that precede and are linked to their attacks; they consider, plan, and prepare before engaging. The threat assessment approach is a fact-based method of evaluation developed by the USSS. Although it was developed based on data used to attack or attempt to attack public officials, with modification it can evaluate other forms of targeted violence. This approach is innovative in two ways:

(1) it does not rely on descriptive, demographic, or psychological profiles and (2) it does not rely on verbal or written threats as a threshold for risk. It moves away from classic profiles and looks at ideas and behaviors that may lead to violent behavior.

Profiles are useful for eliminating the field of suspects after the crime. Instead of looking at demographic and psychological characteristics, the threat assessment approach focuses on a subject's thinking and behaviors. The question is not what does the person look like, but has the subject engaged in recent behavior that suggests that they are moving on a path toward violence. Investigators make a distinction between people who make threats and those who pose a threat.

Persons who appear to pose a threat provoke the greatest level of concern. Very few of these threatener's have ever attempted to harm someone. None of the people who attacked a public figure in the last 50 years ever directly communicated the threat. Attack-related behaviors may move along a continuum. Preparatory behaviors including selection and location of the target, securing a weapon, subverting security measures, etc. Behaviors of concern include:

(1) An unusual interest in instances of targeted violence
(2) Evidence of ideas or plans to attack a specific target (e.g., diary notes, recent acquisition of a weapon),
(3) Communications of inappropriate interest or plans to attack a target to family, friends, co-workers, etc.
(4) Following a target or visiting a possible location of an attack
(5) Approaching a target or protected setting

The U.S. Secret Service, based on experience and assassination research, has identified 10 key questions to guide a protective intelligence or threat assessment investigation:

1: What motivated the subject to make the statements, or take the action, that caused him/her to come to attention?

2: What has the subject communicated to anyone concerning his/her intentions?

3: Has the subject shown an interest in targeted violence, perpetrators of targeted violence, weapons, extremist groups, or murder?

4: Has the subject engaged in attack-related behavior, including any menacing, harassing, and/or stalking-type behavior?

5: Does the subject have a history of mental illness involving command hallucinations, delusional ideas, feelings of persecution, etc. with indications that the subject has acted on those beliefs?

6: How organized is the subject? Is he/she capable of developing and carry out a plan?

7: Has the subject experienced a recent loss and or loss of status, and has this led to feelings of desperation and despair?

8: Corroboration - What is the subject saying and is it consistent with his/her actions?

9: Is there concern among those that know the subject that he/she might take action based on inappropriate ideas?

10: What factors in the subject's life and/or environment might increase/decrease the likelihood of the subject attempting to attack a target?

These threat assessments can also be utilized in common stalker cases. Collecting intelligence and gathering information from sources can enhance your interdiction of this person from carrying out the threats. If someone is contemplating these actions, the more matches that they possess within this threat assessment, the greater the likelihood the threat is credible.

Serial Killings

There are many, both in law enforcement and academia, who study serial killers extensively. I wanted to include serial killers because they are examined, profiled and identified based on behaviors. A serial killer is separated in category from spree killers and mass killers by their actions as demonstrated by the chart below.

	Mass	Spree	Serial
# victims	4+	2+	2+
# events	1	1	2+
# locations	1	2+	2+
Cooling-off	no	no	yes

Note: The number of victims for serial killers was revised from 3 to 2 at the 2005 by the FBI.

As shown, a serial killer must have 2 or more killings from 2 or more separate events which occur in different locations and have a cooling off period or a time frame that they stop killing. 88% of all serial killers will be male and average 29 years of age at the time of their first killing.

A Modus Operandi or MO is the actions taken by the offender to perpetrate the offense. It relates to the degree of criminal sophistication on the part of the offender. The MO is a learned behavior that evolves as the offender becomes more sophisticated and confident. It may change or be improved upon as he gains in experience, learning from previous mistakes relating to issues of the crime. Change can also occur for the protection of the offender's identity as well as their escape from the scene.

In a serial killers pattern of behavior can exist a signature. It is related to the motivation of the offender and is a significant pattern of behavior that is personal to the offender to conduct in the scene.

A third event, commonly espoused in the public's mind as common is staging. Staging occurs when someone purposely alters the scene prior to the arrival of the police. It is normally performed to direct the investigation away from the suspect, be a part of a ritual, or add to the shock value.

We have all heard of MO, signatures and staging with respect to a serial killer, but they are not the norm. A MO will change, as will the events of a crime. The killer will learn from experience and try to make adjustments in the next incident to correct issues they did not like in the previous event. Therefore, with an ever-changing set of rules, the

MO also changes. A signature to a crime scene is actually a rarity. It makes for exciting writing and story lines, yet is not as common as the public believes. A signature is actually a subset of a ritual behavior. A study by the Journal of the American Academy of Psychiatry and the Law was conducted in 2010 of 38 sexually motivated serial homicide offenders and their 162 victims involving cases supplied by the FBI's Behavioral Science Unit. The average number of murders committed by the offenders was 4.2.

A ritual was defined as crime scene acts by the offenders that were "unnecessary for the perpetration of the homicide, involved activity that exceeded that which could cause death, and occurred with at least two victims. Examples include body posing, foreign object insertions, torture, or overkill that occurred with two or more victims in a series."

A signature was defined as a ritualistic act that was a distinct or unique behavior, not seen at any other crime scene (e.g., eye removal); a ritualistic act that was a unique or distinctive way to carry out a familiar act (e.g., posing victims, but with legs spread and propped up on pillows); or a combination of acts that, when taken together, were distinctive and unique (e.g., inserting vegetables into victims and photographing them).

There were thirty-seven (97.4%) of the 38 offenders engaged in ritualistic behaviors with at least two victims in their homicide series. Of the 162 homicides studied, 147 (90.7%) involved ritualistic acts. Of the 37 offenders who engaged in some type of ritualistic behavior, 33 (89.2%) did so with all their victims. Of the four offenders who did not engage in ritualistic behavior at every crime scene, one engaged in ritualistic behavior with 29 percent of his victims, one with 40 percent, one with 60 percent, and one with 80 percent.

The most common ritualistic acts were:

Act		No	%
Penis penetration		20	39.2
Binding	18	31.6	
Overkill	17	25.3	
Beating	11	21.5	
Posing	13	17.7	
Mutilation		10	13.3
Trophies and souvenirs	6	12.0	
Photographs and documentation	4	11.4	
Dismemberment		5	9.5
Foreign object insertion	9	8.9	
Torture	4	7.6	

Biting		4	7.0
Gagging	7	6.3
Necrophilia		3	1.9

Of the 37 offenders who engaged in ritualistic behavior, only 5 (13.5%) used exactly the same ritual with every victim in the series. 31 (83.8%) of the 37 offenders engaged in ritual behaviors which were behaviorally similar with at least two of their victims. However, an offender engaged in recognizable and repetitive signature behaviors in only 18 percent of his homicides.

The notion that offenders leave unique signatures at every scene is not supported by any data. Although most of the offenders engaged in some form of ritualistic behavior, they rarely engaged in exactly the same behavior at every murder.

Almost half of the subjects experimented at one or sometimes more crime scenes which created unique behaviors to that scene. This type of crime scene behavior could easily lead an investigator who is inexperienced with serial sexual murder cases to conclude incorrectly that such different behavior indicates the work of another offender.

Contrary to popular belief, only two offenders evidenced any type of psychosis, and in both cases, the offender's psychotic symptoms were not at all connected to any of their homicides or to their ritualistic or signature behaviors. Most events were the result of carrying out fantasies.

Another important fact to understand is that serial killers are perceived to be of higher intellect. The fact is the opposite. Rarely do we see, even the notorious Ted Bundy, someone who exhibits above average intellect. Most are not caught because of their intellect; in fact, most are caught by the idiotic mistakes they make. It is also important to recognize that these profiles can carry over to arson and rape investigations

What is some of the obtainable information with a criminal profile? With a properly trained and experienced investigator with a good eye for the crime scene, assisted by careful crime scene technicians, we may be able to deduct some of the following:

Age
Sex
Race
Marital Status
Intelligence Scholastic Achievement
Life-Style
Rearing Environment

Social Adjustment
Personality Style/Characteristics
Appearance/grooming
Residence in relation to Crime Scene
Vehicle
Socio-economic Status
Sexual Adjustment
Type of Sexual perversion
Prior Criminal Record
Motive

There are two types of crime scene, Organized and Disorganized. Some differences between the two include but are not limited to:

Disorganized Offenders:
- behavior is unpredictable
- lacks criminal sophistication
- all ages
- different races
- alcohol or drug use
- prior institutionalization
- futile attempt to disguise handwriting
- lower to middle class
- poor communication skills
- unemployed, sloppy
- older car, if at all

Organized Offenders:
- average intelligence
- criminal sophistication
- criminal history may include financial or property crimes
- good communication skills
- middle class
- sporadic employment
- neat appearance/well-maintained vehicle
- owns a well maintained late model vehicle

Any one crime may reveal characteristics of both the organized and disorganized personalities. A crime may transform from organized to disorganized, however the reverse is rare. A shift from organized to disorganized can occur as a result of drug or alcohol use, lack of criminal experience, or the youth of the offender.

In domestic homicides, where a family member kills another family member, one or several cues can be indicative. The victim, usually the female, will rarely be found nude. Though he killed her, she is still his wife and he does not want others to view her nude. If suicide is suspected, the suicide note will be typed. This occurred post mortem and the suspect knows they will not be able to duplicate the handwriting. Another sign of domestic homicide is the deceased spouse was the least threat to an intruder. Often times the killer will try to cover the events of the crime with the excuse that someone broke into the home and murdered their wife. An armed intruder will usually have the most to fear from the husband. If a threat is to be eliminated, they will not kill the least threat (wife) and leave the husband. Another determination of domestic homicide is by interviewing neighbors, friends and family to determine if the deceased was scared of their significant other. Violence will follow a path and has a tendency to escalate.

There is much more involved in this topic though I have left much out to prevent someone from possibly adjusting their activities to avoid detection. It is still an area which requires a lot more study and more investigators should be trained in the techniques. Not so they can become mind readers, but to help them in thoroughly exploring homicide, rape and arson scenes.

Below is a list of serial killings by decade. As with much in society, changes are occurring with serial killers as well.

Decade	White	Black	Hispanic	Asian	Native
1900	62.5	37.5	0.0	0.0	0.0
1910	45.7	54.3	0.0	0.0	0.0
1920	72.4	27.6	0.0	0.0	0.0
1930	53.6	46.4	0.0	0.0	0.0
1940	63.0	29.6	3.7	0.0	3.7
1950	79.5	20.5	0.0	0.0	0.0
1960	68.7	29.8	0.0	0.0	1.5
1970	62.0	33.6	3.3	0.6	0.6
1980	54.3	37.0	6.6	0.6	1.5
1990	41.8	52.3	4.6	1.3	0.0
2000	28.4	68.6	1.5	1.0	0.5
2010	12.5	75.0	12.5	0.0	0.0
TOTAL	52.0	42.8	3.8	0.7	0.8

Steven Varnell

Statement Analysis -
An ISS Course Workbook

Prologue

This book was created to accompany my course on Statement Analysis. It is also helpful for anyone to understand the importance of analyzing statements made in both the forensic and non-forensic fields. There are countless studies and published reports of new and developing research in analyzing statements. The field is very exciting with continual advancements. Few other lie detection methods are as effective because Statement Analysis explores our use of language, which follows specific rules. It is the unconscious violation of these rules which we shall examine.

Today people can use a variety of techniques to enhance their ability to recognize deceit. Most people do not lie about an entire statement, but will "gloss" over the sensitive part that they intend to disguise. This can make recognition of the deception difficult because once completed, they will continue with the truth. We have to determine if they are conveying or convincing. A truthful person will convey the truth. A deceitful person will try to convince you that they are telling the truth.

There is so much material to understand that it requires you to become a regular student of Discourse Analysis. Discourse Analysis is a term for various approaches to analyzing written or verbal communications. I am excited about the possibilities in the field because not only do we study language use, but explore beyond syntax and analyze the natural use of language from different individuals. As with everything, you must study, practice, and use it to stay proficient.

It has been proven that even police officers, are rarely better than chance at detecting deception. My advice is to take as many courses that are available to you and read as many books as possible on these topics. As I always "yell from the rooftop," if you can learn just one thing from any book or class, it was a great book or class. You have been able to add another tool to your toolbox. The more tools in the toolbox, the better prepared you become for any task.

2 Maccabees 2:32

"At this point, therefore, let us begin our narrative, without adding any more to what has already been said, for it would be foolish to lengthen the preface while cutting short the history itself."

-104 to 63 B.C. in one of the Apocryphal books, which relates the history of Judas Maccabeus

"Society cannot afford investigative interviewing to be poor. This affects people's perceptions of the criminal justice system. The convicted, justice for children and vulnerable adults is inadequate. Poor interviewing is of no value to anyone; it is a waste of time, resources and money. No one wins.

People will not come forward if they have no confidence in the quality of investigators' interviewing techniques".

From: Rebecca Milne & Ray Bull.
Investigative Interviewing: psychology and practice.
John Wiley and Sons Ltd: Chichester, 1999, p191.

Statement Analysis - 45

Statement Analysis (SA) is the practice of analyzing a person's words to determine if the subject is being truthful or deceptive via a written statement. Written communication is the preferred examination method of any investigator. It should be attempted before any significant information exchange to commit them into a story. The best analysis comes from the written statement. If unavailable, record the statement for later transcription. Another method prevalent in Europe is for the officer to write it out and the suspect to approve and sign. However, this prevents the very purpose of the process; to allow the person to choose the starting point, what, and how to write, and where to stop.

Lying by omission is the preferred method to lie. Liars will tell the truth up to the point where they want to conceal information, skip over the withheld information, and tell the truth again. Successful liars construct sentences that allow them to skip over withheld information to make the story appear truthful. Lies, omissions, half-truths, false leads, and the truth may occur in any given statement.

Everyone has a truth bias that they must navigate around when deceit is attempted. By combining truthful parts with lies in a statement, it is difficult for us to recognize. To listen to a statement from a subject, we can easily overlook key elements. Their speech prevents us from recognizing certain characteristics. Placed in written format and we can analyze the document word for word.

In written narratives, grammar structures are the only mechanisms liars have to link. This is called the truth gap. Since words create sentences and sentence construction follows a pre-determined set of grammar rules, a careful examination of these structures may identify specific sections that signify deception. We use words to define our reality. When we lie, we're trying to adjust two things in our minds at the same time: the real events and the invented or disguised version of them. The language we use reflects that tension and does not follow our normal patterns.

This technique was created by Avinoam Sapir, a former Israeli police lieutenant, based on years of experience interrogating subjects and is only now becoming theoretically based. Sapir calls it Scientific Content Analysis or SCAN, which examines open-ended written accounts where the writers choose where to begin and what to include in the statements. The goal is to highlight areas of a text that require clarification as part of an interview strategy. People will always word their statement based on all of their knowledge of the incident. Therefore, their statement may include information they did not intend to share.

It is nearly impossible to give a lengthy deceptive statement without revealing it a lie. These techniques are very accurate because they are based on the English language, specifically word definitions and the rules of grammar. Many deceptive stories will push the main issue of the statement to the end and does not continue the narrative afterward. They end abruptly or not at all, as if they didn't want to tell the big lie and waited as long as possible to do it. We will see this in Chapter 12 under balancing a statement.

We tend to talk about what is important to us or fresh in our memory. We relive our experiences sequentially in our mind and tend to be consistent and fluid. The most common deceptions are lying by omission and misdirection. This requires someone to think which affects fluidity, consistency, and sequence.

To initiate the analysis, have them verbalize why they are there with you! If they are not sure, tell them. It starts them thinking about what to say. It does not mean they are lying, but people have a tendency to just say part of the entire story. No person relates every detail of anything they have experienced. It takes too long. We all "edit" by telling condensed versions deemed important to include in a statement. We also do this in conversation. SA takes into consideration only the words used by the person.

SA can be applied anywhere there is an "open statement," in which the answer is anything the writer chooses. SA deals only with activities and not with intentions and does not deal with what people did, but with what people said that they did.

"I would not do that" while often taken as a denial, is not a denial of past activity. It is a statement of future intent, telling us what the subject would not do. This is not the same as "I have not done …." or "I did not do …."

SA is a tool to help you obtain and evaluate information. To assist in this endeavor, do not use a computer for a written statement. The grammar/spell checker will alter the statement and we want the subject's own words, not those that are grammatically correct. Also, a pen is preferred so corrections can be identified.

A written statement is a narrative relating to an event by the author. Narratives are not unbiased retellings of events, but the reconstruction of the reality based on the authors memory to create meaning to them. They manipulate by selecting or omitting events and changes to get across their point. Therefore, each narrative is evaluated for its clarity and word usage.

After we have confirmed with the subject that they understand the purpose of the interview, explain to them how important it is for them to be completely truthful. There is no gray area. The truth is like being pregnant, you either are or you are not. Let them know that we can work through anything, but we cannot work through a lie. This is the shot across the bow and places pressure against resisting their instinctual truth bias.

Now is the time to have them give you a written statement. Stop everything and let's get the statement in writing. Whether they are a witness, complainant or suspect, get it in writing. This one simple act locks them into their statement. We have already explained to them how important it is to tell the complete truth, now confirm it in writing. Listening to the topic we have the disadvantage of missing critical information. Our ability to listen and analyze every word is very limited. When they are writing, they will concentrate on the exact wording they believe will allow their story to be accepted. We can then analyze this written statement word for word to see where it fails.

We are always seeking discrepancies in specific word use, syntax, tense, verb and pronoun use, adverb and adjective use, clarity, contextual information, reproduction of conversation, perceptual and affective information, balance, negations, segmentation markers, and transitional wording. The remaining sections of this book will cover these areas of concern.

Statement Dissections - 46

It always starts with the statement. Read it sentence for sentence, word for word. Examine their word usages for normality's. When you see the abnormal word usages, they will stand out like a beacon. Read the following statement and analyze for discrepancies.

"Around 5:00am / 5:30am I was in the process of giving my son his scheduled feeding. During this feeding he bucked & fell approx. 2ft. to the floor, hitting his head on the floor. His body landed head first; I attempted to catch him but was unsuccessful. When I picked him up he cried for about 90 sec. then started to gag. His eyes were glazed. I immediately called 911."

What catches my eye with this statement is the fathers' use of the noun "body" to name his son before he hits his head. This demonstrates that the son is already dead and falsifies the statement.

"Around 5:00am / 5:30am I was in the process of giving my son his scheduled feeding. During this feeding he bucked & fell approx. 2ft. to the floor, hitting his head on the floor. His **_body_** landed head first; I attempted to catch him but was unsuccessful. When I picked him up he cried for about 90 sec. then started to gag. His eyes were glazed. I immediately called 911."

Now examine the following statement from a traffic crash.

Steven Varnell

"I saw the stop sign. Before I entered the intersection, I looked both ways, drove into the intersection and was struck in the right passenger door by the other vehicle."

I prefer to break a statement down to episodic markers of time, place, and punctuation markers. These will be explained later as transitional words and episode markers.

1. I saw the stop sign.
2. Before I entered the intersection,
3. I looked both ways,
4. Drove into the intersection and
5. was struck in the right passenger door by the other vehicle.

The writer has explained each action taken except one. Do you see it? We are not told if the driver stopped at the stop sign.

A witness said that the motorist did look both ways at the intersection, but he did not stop at the stop sign. In reality, the motorist did see the stop sign. He did look both ways before entering the intersection, and the other vehicle did strike the motorist's passenger side door; however, the motorist failed to write that he did not stop at the stop sign. The motorist used the Text Bridge "before" to bridge the withheld information with the truth. We will discuss Text Bridge's in Chapter 6.

People always mean exactly what they said. "I am trying to be honest." The speaker is telling us that they are not being honest. The word "tried" means to only attempt to be truthful. When a rape victim uses the pronoun "we" in her statement regarding her attacker, this shows plurality and a partnership was formed. This is not an expected word usage. We can think of many expletives, but not a union. Vice versa, we shall also see where an accused rapist will use the phrase "she and I" instead of "we" when trying to convince that it was consensual.

President Obama said to the small business owners of the country:

"Somebody invested in roads and bridges. If you've got a business — you did not build that."

There are two subject matters in this statement based upon the sentence closing;

1- roads and bridges,
2- a business.

We were told that he was referring to the roads and bridges. If true, then he would be required to use "those" instead of "that." "That" is singular specific and can only refer to "a business," the only singular object in the sentence.

Sometimes, the writer will complete the statement with admission's that there is more information concerning a certain topic or issue which has not yet been divulged. These are called unfinished business statements. In SA, we can recognize these occasions with the word usages of:

"That's about it."

"That's about the size of it."

"That's about all."

There are admissions that certain information cannot be given at the moment for whatever reason. Deception exists concerning the topic which precipitated the response. They are demonstrated by the use of the words:

"I can't say."

"I can't think of anything."

"I can't tell you anything about that."

"I can say this ……."

"I can only tell you this ……"

When a speaker uses the conditional verbal's of could, would, should or ought to preface a verbal response, remember that these are indicative of future intent. They are often used in hypotheticals. However, if something is hypothetical then it is not occurring in the present and cannot have occurred in the past. Most people referring to past events confuse these words. "I could have done…" is not saying what has happened, but what may happen next time.

Rambling chatter is often used as a smokescreen. Keep them on topic. The answer that does not equate to what was specifically asked is the most common tactic used by politicians. They will espouse many long sentences and never answer the question.

But - Behold the Underlying Truth; whenever you see the word or a synonym of "but" - however, then, nonetheless, then again, yet, still, although, though, anyway. These words withdraw the previous assertions. Pay attention to what follows.

The word "this" indicates closeness while the word "that" shows distance. However, people will use the wrong word such as:
"I walked into the room and saw this gun and immediately ran out."
The "this" gun referred to in the statement was on the other side of the room. The phrase should have been "that gun" to indicate they saw the gun and ran out. "This gun" says they were close to the gun and had entered further than stated.

SA examines language based deception; therefore we should take each statement or sentence into account. (Lies, omissions, half-truths, false leads and the truth may occur) Remember, they will tell you what they want and much of what they say will be true, but true of what? This is known as Millers Law. Miller's law is part of a theory of communication formulated by George Miller, Princeton Professor and psychologist. It instructs us to suspend judgment about what someone is saying so we can first understand them without instilling their message with our own personal interpretations. We can accept that what they tell us is true, but determine what is it true of? The law states:

"To understand what another person is saying, you must assume that it is true and try to imagine what it could be true of."

The point is not to blindly accept what people say, but to do a better job of listening for understanding. It helps to prevent bias. "Imagining what it could be true of" is another way of saying to consider the consequences of the truth, but to also think about what must be true for the speaker's "truth" to make sense. This initial acceptance of the truth is essential to help prevent false interpretations. When we initiate the interview with the belief they are lying, this bias can cause us to falsely read between the lines.

Understanding Syntax - 47

A statement must have:

- structure and length
- text coherence
- factual and sensory detail
- word or phrase structure choice
- verbal immediacy - refers to the degree of separation created between the speaker and the object of their communication as a result of the particular words used by the speaker. "you and I" is considered non-immediate because it uses two symbols ("you" and "I") to designate two separate entities when ("we") could have been used.

Statement Analysis has been enhanced with the understanding that truthful statements include sensory information. Deceptive statements will often lack contextual (time and location), perceptual (sensory), and affective (feelings or thoughts) information. We must examine each word within every sentence to see how it correlates with the topic. Clarity is a must. When we are telling a story from memory, we can explain so it flows naturally. There should not be continual episodic segmentations or short sentences which are steadily changing.

Analyze the verb tenses in a statement. When a person is telling us what happened, they are required to speak in the past tense

"I **_am_** sitting in my car when a man opened my door, pointed a gun at me and **_tells_** me to get out of the car."

The words "am" and "tells" are present tense. We cannot recount a past activity in present tense. It can <u>only</u> be in the tense that we remember it for it to be real.

Indefinite articles, "a" or "an" are used when something or someone is first introduced. Once used, it change's to "the."

"**_A man_** approached me and pointed **_a gun_** at me. He stuck **_the gun_** in my ribs and forced me into **_the car_**."

"The gun" was already introduced and is correct with "the". "The car" is the first time it is mentioned. Either it did not happen or "the car" was recognized, therefore using "the" correctly.

"I went shopping with my wife."

"With" in a statement can mean distance. "I" in the beginning and "wife" at the end, then add in the "with" means I was not happy about shopping. There is separation in the statement.

"My wife and I went shopping."

The word "and" attaches us together. We say what we mean because we do not think about everything we say.

President Bill Clinton said, "I was bound to be truthful and I tried to be." "Tried" means attempted or he attempted to be honest, but was not.

"Never" cannot be used to replace the word "no". It is only appropriate on its own to advise the issue has not ever occurred.

Example: "Are you transporting drugs?"

"I would never do that!"

They are not saying no because they mentally cannot. They also included the futuristic word "would" which tells us; "In the future I will not transport drugs."

A yes or no question demands a yes or no answer. If not, some type of deception has occurred.

Q- Are there drugs in the car?

A- "I would never have drugs."

How many problems exist in this brief sentence?

1 - This is a question that asked for a yes or no answer.

2 - They used the word "never" which is not a substitute for no.

3 – "Would" shows future intentions; present tense is "I do not have any drugs."

Connie Chung interview of Congressman Gary Condit in regards to his missing intern, Chandra Levy.

1. Chung: Do you know what happened to Chandra Levy?
2. Condit: No, I do not.
3. Chung: Did you have anything to do with her disappearance?
4. Condit: No, I didn't
5. Chung: Did you say anything or do anything that could have caused her to drop out of sight?
6. Condit: You know, Chandra and I never had a cross word.
7. Chung: Did you kill Chandra Levy?
8. Condit: I did not

In this exchange, we can see how Condit's answers are initiated and completed based on the question asked except once. In line 6, the answer to line 5 changes pattern and indicates concern. We later learned that they had had an affair which he broke off causing her to run away. She was murdered by another person, but Condit felt guilty over their argument.

Joran Van der Sloot on the murder of Stephany Flores in Peru:

"Yes, I want to plead guilty. I wanted from the first moment to confess sincerely. I truly am sorry for this act. I feel very bad."

1. "Yes, I want to plead guilty." (I want to but cannot. Different from I am guilty)
2. "I wanted from the first moment to confess sincerely." (Again he is not saying he confesses he just says he wanted to)
3. "I truly am sorry for this act." (This act but not others. He got caught this time)

4.   "I feel very bad. "

The entire statement is narcissistic or about himself, not the crimes he committed or the victims he left behind

Current Research shows there are 12 linguistic indicators of deception cited in the psychological and criminal justice literature to be considered for each sentence in a statement. We are always watching for a lack of commitment to a statement. This occurs when they use linguistic devices to avoid making a direct statement of fact.

- Linguistic hedges - whose meaning implicitly involves fuzziness, e.g., maybe, I guess, and sort of. Hedging shows a lack of commitment.
- Qualified assertions, which leave open whether an act was performed, e.g. I needed to get my inhaler (Was it used?), I wanted to find a weapon. (Did you?) (Uncompleted action verbs)
- Unexplained lapses of time, e.g. later that day
- Overzealous expressions, e.g. I swear to God
- Rationalization of an action, e.g. I was unfamiliar with the road.

Preference for negative expressions in word choice, syntactic structure (rules of combining words to create sentences) and semantics (word meanings).

- Negative forms, either complete words such as "never" or negative meanings as in "inconceivable."
- Negative emotions, e.g. I was a nervous wreck.
- Memory loss, e.g. I forget.

Inconsistencies with respect to verb and noun forms

- Verb tense changes
- Thematic role changes, e.g. changing the theme role from specific name (Cindy) in one sentence to patient or she in another.
- Noun phrase changes – person, place or thing.
- Pronoun changes – they, he, she, we

The following is a transcript of an oral statement from a college student who reported that a man broke into her apartment at 3:30 am and raped her.

"He grabbed me and held a knife to my throat. And when I woke up and I was, I mean I was really asleep and I didn't know what was going on, and I kind of you know I was scared and I kind of startled when I woke up, you know, you know I was startled and he, he told, he kept telling me to shut up and he asked me if I could feel the knife."

Watch for anything that stands out or is odd. As you can see, it is easier if we break the statement in separate items.

1. He grabbed me and
2. held a knife to my throat.
3. And when I woke up and
4. I was, I mean I was really asleep and
5. I didn't know what was going on,
6. and I kind of you know I was scared and
7. I kind of startled when I woke up,
8. you know, you know I was startled and
9. he, he told, he kept telling me to shut up and
10. he asked me if I could feel the knife.

What stands out in this statement is the word usage for the situation. Line 7 shows us that she was "kinda of startled?" Imagine yourself, male or female, waking up at 3:30 am and seeing a man at your bedside holding a knife at your throat. Would you be startled or scared sh..less!

Changes in Tense - 48

The questions asked needs to be in the proper past or present tense. In this example, we are able to guide them to the correct answer by recognizing their improper use of present tense wording.

Q – "Have you ever smoked marijuana?" Past tense

A – "I don't use drugs." Present tense

Q – "That was not the question, have you ever?"

A - "I have tried it once."

"It happened Saturday night. I went out on my back deck to water the plants. It was almost dark. A man <u>runs</u> out of the bushes. He <u>comes</u> onto the deck, <u>grabs</u> me and <u>knocks</u> me down."

Past tense narratives are the norm for truthful accounts of past events. However, it is deviations from the past tense that often correlate with deception. These changes in tense can be more indicative of deception than the overall choice of tense, even though each can demonstrate error.

Investigating an accident, both drivers claim it is the others fault. Each is asked to give written statements.

D1 – began by describing activities using past tense. "I was driving... looking at the scenery. I didn't think much of it...I was not blocking traffic. She had plenty of room...she moved alongside of me and stayed there.... When I glanced in her direction, she looked at me like I was dirt. We drive like this for some time and then she cuts right in front of me. I don't see her coming until it's too late. We pulled off the road and she started screaming that I ran into her."

Notice the tense change at the critical point of the statement, "she looked at me like I was dirt." It is at this moment that the reason for the accident has occurred and his use of tense moves to present. This is indicative that he told the truth up to this point and lied at the critical point and then reverts back to past tense.

"We ***drive*** like this for some time and then she **cuts** right in front of me. I ***don't*** see her coming until ***it's*** too late. We pulled off the road and she started screaming that I ran into her."

Look at the statement by Susan Smith who left her little boys strapped into her car and rolled it into a lake. She claimed that she was carjacked and the kids kidnapped.

"I just feel hopeless, I can't do enough. My children wanted me. They needed me. And now I can't help them. I just feel like such a failure."

Break the statement into individual sentences for better recognition of deceptions.

"I just **feel** hopeless,

I **can't** do enough.

My children **wanted** me.

They **needed** me.

And now I **can't** help them.

I just **feel** like such a failure."

When speaking about herself, she phrases the sentences in present tense. When speaking of her children, she phrases them in past tense and returns to present tense for herself. She knows her children are dead.

Self-Referencing Pronouns, Adverbs and Adjectives - 49

Studies of deception have found that deceivers tend to use fewer self-referencing expressions (I, my, mine) than truth-tellers and fewer references to others. When someone is relating a story that they are involved in, their commitment is usually expressed with the pronoun "I."

"I got up at 7:00 when my alarm went off. I took a shower and got dressed. I decided to go out for breakfast. I went to the McDonald's on the corner. I finished breakfast and drove to work."

Now look at the same statement again to see the area of concern.

"I got up at 7:00 when my alarm went off. I took a shower and got dressed. I decided to go out for breakfast. I went to the McDonald's on the corner. Met a man who lives nearby. Talked with him for a few minutes. I finished breakfast and drove to work."

Scott Peterson's initial police interview is characterized by a high number of omitted first person references:

BROCCHINI: You drive straight home?

PETERSON: To the warehouse, dropped off the boat.

So was Levi Aron murder confession of a missing NY City boy.

382

"A boy approached me on where the Judaica book store was. He was still there when went out from the dentist's office. He asked me for a ride to the Judaica book store."

Possession Pronouns requires: my, his, hers.

Responsibility is indicated by: I, he, and she. We, us, and they, shows plural involvement. "I" is a necessity for a person's statement to be believable. It shows commitment in the statement.

Contrary to the first statement, that deception can be indicated with a lack of self-referencing pronouns, too many can be as bad. This will be shown in Chapter 11.

We have already seen how the self-referencing pronoun "I" is important to the commitment of the story. When and how it is used versus the plural first person referencing pronoun "we" also tells variations to a story.

A young woman who reported that she had been abducted at a shopping center provided the following written statement:

"I parked and started getting out of my car when a white male about 200 pounds 6 feet tall approached me and told me to get in the car or he would hurt me. He then got in   the back. I got in the front and began to drive. He told me to drive west on the highway. He asked me if I had any money. I told him no. We drove for about an hour. During that hour, he hit me repeatedly on the right side of my face. When we got to the exit, I told him I had no gas. He got mad and told me to get off the exit. We went straight off the exit for about 4-5 miles. He told me to turn down the first street on my left. We went down it about 1/4 of a mile. He told me to stop. He opened the door, put both feet out, hit me, and took off walking quickly. He took off to the east of where I was parked. After that, I took off and lost sight of him."

Examine this statement and make a determination if there are any issues.

A true abduction statement includes phrases like "He forced me to drive..." or "He made me get off at the exit...." Traumatized victims who are telling the truth do not use the pronoun "we" to describe assailants and themselves. Identify other errors in the statement.

Any time you see an 'ly or y" adverbs connected to a statement (examples-basically, very etc.) Try to recognize this as a potential area of sensitivity and explore. Always watch for the words "actually," "really" and "basically" in a statement. They are synonymous with each other and used to indicate a summation of the most important aspects of a more complex situation have been undertaken. They are used to bolster a sentence, but it usually weakens it. In writing, less is more. Consider the following statement from Casey Anthony's 911 call:

CA: My daughter has been missing for the last 31 days.

911: And you know who has her?

CA: I know who has her. I've tried to contact her.

CA: I actually received a phone call today. Now from a number that is no longer in service.

We see in the last statement that she uses "actually" to say she had received a call today. People are always trying to either convince or convey. Actually is synonymous with really and basically. They are 'ly adverbs that are unnecessary and therefore used to try and convince someone that what is being said is the truth. The truth needs only to be conveyed.

Every study indicates that an excessive use of adverbs and/or adjectives is symptomatic of deception.

Text Bridges - 50

When a person uses phrases such as "later on" or "afterwards" they have withheld some information by skipping over something in the story. This is considered hedging or a text bridge and is non-committal to the statement. Text bridges allow people to transition from one topic to another without tedious details. For example, in the sentence "I got up, and then I took a shower, and then I ate breakfast," the text bridge "then" signals withheld information. The withheld information does not have to constitute deception. The writer did not want to bore the listener with all of the extraneous information and "jumped" over it. However, text bridges used at critical times during interviews may signal deception.

The most commonly used text bridges are: **then, so, after, when, as, while, and next.** The second most used are: **once, finally, afterwards, eventually.** Memorize this list of text bridges and you will have a powerful tool to identify where people withhold information during interviews or conversations.

Adverbial conjunctions, transitional and subordinating words are all text bridges. Adverbial conjunctions transition from one idea to the next. A transitional word connects themes and ideas or establishes relationships. Subordinating words connect independent and dependent clauses. They also connect unequal but related ideas and create time gaps.

For a complete list of Text Bridge words, refer to Chapter 57.

"It rained on Saturday; therefore, the picnic was canceled."

The idea that it rained was connected to the idea of the canceled picnic with the transitional word "therefore." They can both separate and connect ideas.

"During the break I drank a soda."

"During" brings the ideas of a break and drinking a soda together.

"We went bowling instead of going to the movies."

The transitional word "instead" contrasts the act of going bowling and the act of going to the movies.

What is the text bridge in the following sentence?

"Mary went to the store and then she went home."

The adverbial conjunctive "then" connects the first complete idea, "Mary went to the store," with the second complete idea," she went home."

A husband suspected of killing his wife arrived home at 5:00 p.m. and made the following statement to the investigating detective,

"After I came home, I found my wife dead."

Is there a text bridge in this sentence to require further examination?

The subordinating word "after" creates an information gap from the time the man came home until the time he found his wife dead. The murder suspect wanted to give the impression that he arrived home and immediately found his wife dead. The murder suspect arrived home at 5:00 p.m. but did not indicate what time he found his wife dead. A time gap exists from 5:00 p.m. until the suspect found his wife dead. During this information gap, the murder suspect got into an altercation with his wife and killed her. The murder suspect hid the physical altercation with his wife by using the text bridge" after."

The following illustration demonstrates how text bridges function. A student wrote a statement in response to allegations that' she took $20 from her instructor's office during the first class break. Pursuant to an informal investigation, the student wrote a narrative account of her activities from the time she entered the building until the end of the first break. The following is a copy of her statement:

"I arrived at 7:45 a.m. with Jenna. I came into the room, put my bag at my desk and Jenna and I went to the little snack area to get some coffee. I returned to the classroom and sat at my desk. At 8:50 we went on a break. Jenna and I went to the bathroom. After that I came back to the classroom and Jenna stayed in the bathroom. She came back to the classroom soon after. We sat at our desk and waited for our class to continue."

Identify the truth gap.

"After" is the text bridge used to give the statement a temporal lacuna or time gap. This is the point where she disguised her actions of going to the office and stealing the money.

Text bridges used at critical junctures during interviews or written narratives signals that the interviewee intentionally or unintentionally withheld information. Text bridges indicate missing information. If the withheld information is of no value, then we can ignore the text bridge. For example, if the crime occurred at 8:00p.m., the suspect may be directed to write a narrative relating his activities from the time he woke up until the time he went to sleep.

"At about 7 o'clock that night, I went to a friend's house for a while and then I went directly home."

The text bridge "then" is significant because the writer created a temporal lacuna (time gap) between 7 o'clock and the time the writer arrived at home. In this case, the suspect probably committed the crime after he left his friend's house but before he arrived home. By using a text bridge, the suspect avoided telling a lie. The suspect did go to his friend's house at 7 o'clock and the suspect did go home. The suspect failed to mention the fact that he committed the crime between the time he left his friend's house and the time he went home.

It has already been shown that liars use fewer words in a statement. In addition, the number of text bridges is also indicative of deception. To determine the number of text bridges in a statement, you can divide the total number of text bridges in a statement by the total number of words to produce a text bridge ratio. This can be helpful when there is no truthful narrative to use as a comparison.

Negations and Opposites - 51

Negations and spontaneous negations are similar to a text bridge and can be recognized by the variations of the word "no." Examples are, no, no one, none, nothing, contractions with the word no, isn't, can't, hasn't, haven't, etc. It also includes the word "never." They fail to state what specific actions the suspect took.

Did you rob the store?

No, I did not rob the store.

This is a negative answer to a direct question and appropriate when used directly in response to a yes or no question.

Spontaneous negations are used when people are presented with open-ended questions. They should relate the actions they took versus the actions they did not take.

(Statement from a rape/murder case)

"Did you want to kiss her?"

"I...I...I didn't feel...I didn't remember feeling any attraction to her. "
(The exact opposite is usually true)

Negations are words that negate part or all of a sentences meaning. We have to also watch for their excessive usage with words like, no, never, no one, nothing, not.

Negators or negative words have prefixed verbs by adding "un-" such as unsuccessful. Other negators are – a-, de-, dis-, in-, mis-, and –less. These produce passive language to help separate the speaker from the action.

Words with equivalent opposites require two or more words to complete their definitions. The word "upstairs," cannot be defined without the word "downstairs." The word "hot" cannot be defined without the word "cold." Some words need more than two words to complete their meanings. The word "medium" cannot be defined without the words "large" and "small." The word "warm" cannot be defined without the words "hot" and "cold."

If someone says, "I don't remember," the listener can presume that in order for the speaker to not remember something, he must have had to remember it first. The same logic applies to the responses, "I don't recall" and "I forgot. "

Dad: What did you do last night?

Daughter: I went to the library and then I came straight home.

The text bridge "then" signals missing information, which does not necessarily mean the daughter, is lying. You should inquire further to verify. Look at the opposite of the word "straight." It is conjoined with the word "crooked." After further talking, the daughter admitted going to the library, but for only a few minutes. A temporal lacuna was exposed with the word "then" and was intensified with the word straight. After leaving the library, she admitted to going to a party.

In the last Chapter we saw the statement:

"At about 7 o'clock that night, I went to a friend's house for a while and then I went directly home."

We know that the text bridge is the word "then." We also see in this sentence the opposition word "directly" which like "straight," has an opposite, "indirectly."

Steven Varnell

Passive Language and Uncompleted Action Verbs - 52

Passive voice or language is when we try to place blame elsewhere or to someone to distance themselves. The husband of a woman who had disappeared wrote in his narrative about the incident that "it was determined that I would drop her off to run." Instead of writing, "I determined" or "we determined," the husband used passive voice or an unknown of "it was determined."

Good follow-up questions to this situation are:

- You wrote that "it was determined that I would drop her off to run." Can you explain this to me?
- Who exactly "determined" that you would drop her off?
- Where was Michelle when "it was determined"?
- Did Michelle participate in the decision to drop her off?

Other examples of a passive voice are using the words someone, somebody, anyone etc.

In an effort to camouflage their deeds, people occasionally use "uncompleted" action verbs or words that denote reference to activity on the part of speakers or writers without any indication that this action was completed. Some of the more common words that fall into this category include ***started***, ***commenced***, ***initiated***, and ***proceeded***. These words reveal the possibility that something or someone interrupted the action and, therefore, warrant scrutiny.

The husband from the last case was asked to write what he knew about his wife's disappearance. He responded,

"Michelle put a workout tape in the VCR and started her workout. I was in the bathroom for a while getting ready for the day."

The word "started" should capture your attention. It shows that something may have interrupted the workout and required some follow-up questions.

- You wrote that "Michelle put a workout tape in the VCR and started her workout." Can you tell me more about this?
- How long did the workout last?
- Where were you when she started her workout?
- You stated that you were "in the bathroom for a while." How long was "a while"?
- What did you do in the bathroom?
- Did Michelle finish her workout?
- Did something interrupt her workout?

The husband eventually admitted strangling her after an argument and dumped her body.

Another example of an uncompleted action verb:

The following is a portion of a statement from a deputy who reported that he was assaulted by an inmate in a court lock-up facility. This is a partial statement surrounding the description of the assault.

Was the deputy actually punched?

"...I then held his shoulders and began to direct him to a seating position, while continuing to try to talk him into compliance. He shifted his body laterally to avoid being directed into the seating posture, arching his back & struggling against me. While I continued to push on him, he was able to punch the right side of my face in the vicinity of my nose and eye..."

He did not say "he punched the right side of my face." He said the inmate "was able to." Clarity through additional questioning is required.

As we have seen, people may hide their actions by using passive voice, or include uncompleted action verbs. With our recognition of these actions we can focus our questions appropriately.

"The pistol was fired by someone."

- Tell me about the pistol being fired. Did you fire it?

"I started to pack my bags."

- Who or what interrupted?
- You said you "started to pack your bag." Did you finish packing?
- Did something interrupt you?

Words That Convey Conversation - 53

We must pay attention to words that convey dialogue. Once recognized, we will want to direct our questions to fill in the conversation. Examples, Talked, spoke, chatted, discussed, and e-mailed.

- What was the conversation about?
- When did the conversation occur in relation to the crime?
- Who did the conversing?
- Were different words used to describe any conversation and, if so, why?
- Were different words used to describe any conversation with the same person or with another person?

Specific Questions regarding conversation

- Tell me what you talked about.
- Was this talk cordial, emotional, angry?
- When did you two talk? What time was it?
- Who else was present when you talked?
- Who might have overheard you?
- What happened after you talked?
- Who initiated the talk?

- Who said what to whom?
- You said, "He and I talked." Tell me about this.
- You said, "We chatted." Tell me more about this chat.

Some words are used that act as a camouflage that a communication occurred. Some examples are; met for coffee, ate lunch, and watched TV. People typically engage in verbal interaction during social activities. Once recognized, specify your questions for clarity.

- What was discussed during the activity?
- Tell me about your meeting for coffee. What did you talk about?
- When did you meet?
- Who else was there?

Backward Reaching Questions or Micro-Action Interviewing - 54

"I went to the bedroom. After leaving the bedroom, I left for work. After arriving at work, I met with my boss."

Guilty persons will often practice deception by omitting information they believe will incriminate them. Leaving out these details is a common way to mislead investigators because technically, it is not lying. It also does not produce as much stress as telling an outright falsehood. Once these text bridges are recognized, you must force closed the time gap. With each question you can close it further until it is fulfilled.

Get a written statement and examine each sentence in the initial narrative for indicators of missing information.

The opening scenario contains four potential areas of omitted details:

1) What happened in the bedroom?

2) What the suspect did after leaving the bedroom before departing for work;

3) What occurred on the way to work; and

4) What transpired after arriving at the office before meeting with the boss?

Although these details may not be important, you should not take the chance.

Once a temporal lacuna is recognized it should be addressed. Also, note the areas of the statement which caused a pause. There may be numerous words marked out, letters written over and show as much darker, or maybe a period which is too dark.

First, return them to the exact point in the narrative where a possible omission of information began. Have them restate word-for-word the information directly preceding the omission; it is important to use the exact language used by the subject. Then, have the suspect expand on the previous information, ensuring that they identify any additional gaps in time and missing details.

Some interviewers make the mistake of going directly to the areas of greatest interest. Instead, they should proceed chronologically, beginning with and closing the first area of omission and patiently moving on to the subsequent areas. By doing so, interviewers avoid alerting the subject to specific areas of interest. In interviews, at least two people are seeking information—the investigator and the interviewee.

From the earlier statement, "I went to the bedroom. After leaving the bedroom, I left for work. After arriving at work, I met with my boss." we can follow up by asking:

- "Earlier you said that you went to the bedroom. What did you do next?"

"Next" would force the subject to discuss the subsequent period of time with either the truth or a descriptive lie. Interviewers also could close the same omission by asking,

- "You said you went to the bedroom and that later you left. Tell me everything you did while in the bedroom."

If a subject says, "That is basically what happened" or "That is about it," you should consider that the interviewee has more to say.

Follow up by reaching back and restating the exact words used to compose the original statement:

"Mr. Jones, a few moments ago, you said that is about all you can remember. What else happened at the meeting, or what else do you remember?"

The same technique can effectively address qualifiers. With the statement "I have no specific recollection," ask, "Earlier, you said you had no specific recollection. What recollection do you have?"

These are backward-reaching questions and can address a noncommittal phrase, such as "I cannot remember." The interviewer could ask,

"Mr. Jones, earlier, you said that you do not remember who was present at the meeting. Take a moment and think hard about the meeting again and tell me everyone who was present."

Example:

"Tell me about the last time you saw your wife."

"I recall that, ah, it was one evening, probably 11 o'clock. We were both in bed and we had not gone to sleep yet and she got out of bed. I, ah, thought she was probably going to the bathroom and then I hear the, ah, front door close and I waited for a minute to see what she was doing and then I hear the car start and I look out the window and see the car disappearing around the corner and that's the last time I ever saw her."

Using the backward reaching questions or micro-action interviewing in which we back our line of questioning to the point just prior a text bridge and fill in the gap. Use as many questions as is necessary to satisfy the time period. As they talk use verbal continuators to keep them moving; "What happened next?" If they skip over another part, you have to move the questioning back to prior of the bridge and continue.

Truthful people may find the process tedious, but will continue to answer and add info. Liars will struggle as the time gap is reduced. They will struggle to find words to fill in the gap. This is a good location to ask other questions such as.

- "You were pretty mad at her at the time weren't you?
- I don't think it was all your fault. We all have a point of no return and she caused you to enter yours. True?"

Arson Investigation

"I turned off the hard-top road, got out of the car and left it running. I reached in and dropped it in gear, steering it over the hill. The car went way over an embankment. I walked down and shut the car off. I removed the keys and soaked the whole car in gasoline. I took a cigarette lighter and lit it. I took off back up the steep hill."

"I caught a ride with someone on the hard-top road, but I'm not sure who it was. I'm not sure where I went right after that, but I ended up at my house. I really don't remember much more than what I've told you."

What did you notice?

He became vague using fewer perceptual phrases, included negations, and passive voice.

I turned off the hard-top road, got out of the car and left it running (touch). I reached in and dropped it in gear, steering it over the hill (touch). The car went way over an embankment (sight). I walked down and shut the car off (touch). I removed the keys and soaked the whole car in gasoline (touch). I took a cigarette lighter and lit it (touch). I took off back up the steep hill (touch).

I caught a ride with someone (vague or passive voice) on the hard-top road, but I'm not sure (negation, lack of knowledge) who it was. I'm not sure (negation, lack of knowledge) where I went right after that, but I ended up at my house. I really don't remember (negation, lack of memory) much more than what I've told you.

Statement of man accused of rape

"I put her clothes on and, um, and she and I walked outside and said our good-byes. I gave her a hug and told her I had a good time and she talked for a minute and then I left. I walked home."

The suspect did not use the pronoun "we" to describe the two, but, instead, he said, "she and I." In sexual assault cases, especially those where the subject alleges that the sexual contact was consensual, you should listen for the absence of the pronoun "we." This lack of a word suggests that a healthy relationship did not exist between the two individuals and increases the likelihood that the sexual contact was less then consensual. This is the exact opposite situation we saw in the beginning.

The suspect did not state that the woman said that she had a good time; instead, he said, "she and I said our goodbyes," a vague and imprecise comment. In addition, he stated that "she talked." The statement suggests that a lot of conversation occurred, thus you should focus your line of questioning there. Some follow up questions could be:

• You said that "she and I said our good-byes." What did you mean by this? What exactly was said by her and then by you?

• You told her that you had a good time. What precisely did you tell her? Tell me exactly what you said.

• Did she ever state that she also had a good time? What did she have to say about the sexual relations? How did she feel about it?

• You said that "she talked for a minute and then I left." What exactly did she talk about? What words did she use? After she talked, you then left. What happened before you left? Why did you leave? Why did you go home? What did you do when you got home?

Following the rape, the suspect attempted to apologize to her for what he had done and even tried to give her a hug, which she rejected. The victim had advised investigators that she told the assailant that she was going to report the rape to the police and that he tried to get her to reconsider before he left in tears.

Look at the last part of his statement, "she talked for a minute and then I left. I walked home." He used a text bridge "then" which creates a time loss which we later learn. She was going to report the rape to the police and that he tried to get her to reconsider before he left in tears. He could not retell that part because it shows her feelings of rape and calling the police and his pleading with her not to.

A woman's open ended question to what she did today

"I got up around 6 a.m. while he stayed in bed. He came down about 8 a.m., and he and I talked. I then left to pick up my partner, Stan, about

8:20. Met Stan and we chatted the whole way. We got to our rooms at 2 p.m., and I started to get cleaned up. That's about it."

Tell me what you see in this statement?

She never introduces the first person she spoke to. She said "he and I talked" but she "chatted" with Stan. We later discover that the first person was her husband whom she was having arguments and having an affair with Stan. "That's about it" in closing tells us there is certainly more.

"While Darin was gone, the boys brought down their blankets and pillows and asked if they could watch TV. I said yes. Darin came home and sat down with us while we watched TV. Soon after that, the boys both fell asleep. We talked about a few problems that we were having with the car and the boat and had a few words between us. I told Darin that I was desperate because I had not been able to take the boys anywhere because we only had one car."

Tell me what you see in this statement?

"Darin came home and sat down with us while we watched TV. " She never indicated that her husband actively participated with them in watching television, a social encounter often used to conceal verbal interaction.

You could ask,

• "Tell me about your husband sitting down "with us while we watched TV."

• What were you watching?

• Who was the "we" that watched TV?

• Did your husband watch TV with you? What did the two of you talk about while the boys watched TV?

Parents often wait until their children cannot hear them before engaging in a serious conversation. In fact, after her sons fell asleep, her words suggested that the exchange with her husband became tense.

• What were the "few problems" you talked about?

• What did you mean by "We...had a few words between us"?

"I was at home with my girlfriend and ate dinner around 6:00pm. We watched TV for a while then she left. I then watched TV until midnight."

- What did you eat and did you both eat together?

- Can you remember the exact time that you ate?

- What time did you start and finish watching TV?

- What time did she leave?

- What time did you start watching TV again?

All of the time gaps must be filled in in order to see the entire picture of the statement.

Episode Markers - 55

Researchers Isabel Picornell and Jack Schafer have independently developed different approaches to SA. They study linguistic patterns in people to help identify fraud. At a minimum, a narrative contains 2 clauses, the reportable events (what happened) and temporal separation (the time separating the earlier from the later events). Fully formed narratives have a beginning, middle, and an end. Narrators use segmentation markers as signals to manage the flow and understanding of information. They are deliberate and divide narratives into separate episodes to draw attention to change and to areas considered important. Deviation from the standard sentence construction of main clause + subordinate clause to that of subordinate clause + main clause can be significant.

Examples:

The ambulance arrived moments later.

Moments later, the ambulance arrived.

We met with a group of friends once we got to the movie theatre.

Once we got to the movie theatre, we met with a group of friends.

Language is influenced by the author's focus, and that focus is in turn managed by the author's intentions. The finished product (the deception) is a compilation of the deceiver's intention (to tell the truth or to lie) and choice of communication strategy to achieve that intent.

Episode markers are important as they are subconscious markers of the narrator to break the continuity of the statement. Excessive fragmentation is associated with artificial timelines. When a sequence of events is imagined or gaps in time occur, the continuity of the narrative breaks down. Narratives fragment into multiple short episodes because the events described are not anchored in real time. They are created with punctuations and words like: ***and, when, then, but.***

We can use episode markers in a statement to break it down from before, during and after, but further with each episode. (Changes in time, place or markers) The shorter or more plentiful are episode markers, the greater the likelihood of their non-commit to the statement.

He grabbed me and held a knife to my throat. And when I woke up and I was, I mean I was really asleep and I didn't know what was going on, and I kind of you know I was scared and I kind of startled when I woke up, you know, you know I was startled and he, he told, he kept telling me to shut up and he asked me if I could feel the knife.

{He grabbed me} and {held a knife to my throat.} And {when I woke up} and {I was}, {I mean I was really asleep} and {I didn't know what was going on,} and {I kind of you know I was scared} and {I kind of startled when I woke up,} {you know,} {you know I was startled} and {he,} {he told,} {he kept telling me to shut up} and {he asked me if I could feel the knife.}

There are two types of strategies which have been identified in narratives; 1) wordy and personal 2) impersonal.

1) Wordy and personal use of a lot of words and can appear important, yet are vague and utilize an excessive number of pronouns like ***I, me,*** and ***my.*** Me and my represent passive pronouns and should be watched.

Verb strings are also indicative of deceptive issues. Verb strings are 2 or more verbs that function as a verb (went to call, started yelling, tried to open).

Cognitive verbs or cognitive functions like ***think***, ***appear***, and ***seem*** are short cuts and not based in emotion.

Indefinite pronouns which refer to something or someone unspecified are also known as passive voice words. ***something***, ***someone***,

Watch for conjunctions that join a negation to an assertion: "I was in the vehicle, but I was ***not*** aware of what was going on."

Watch for excessive adverb/adjective use.

In the sentence "I do not remember seeing someone behind me" contains a Negation (not), a Cognitive Verb (remember), a Verb String (remember seeing), and a passive voice (someone).

Analyze the next paragraph:

He grabbed me and held a knife to my throat. And when I woke up and I was, I mean I was really asleep and I didn't know what was going on, and I kind of you know I was scared and I kind of startled when I woke up, you know, you know I was startled and he, he told, he kept telling me to shut up and he asked me if I could feel the knife.

2) impersonal strategies are when deceivers become increasingly other oriented resulting in a high use of third person (he, she, they, we, us) and prefer to be absent by replacing I with me or my.

Then **he** told **me** to stop crying. **He** told **me** to stop the car. **He** took tape out and put it on **my** wrists.

People remember what they said, not how they said it. Memory is not stored in verbal form. We do not remember:

- Slang & non-standard grammar forms: gonna, gimme, buddy
- Acknowledgements: yeah, okay, sure
- Fillers: like, you know what I mean, sort of
- Adverbial modifiers: just, really, very

When two texts are very similar, it is more likely that one has been "borrowed" from another text rather than the same speaker creating them independently. They still have to decide how to convey the false account in a way that will appear balanced and consistent with the known truths; without feedback, deceivers have to guess as to how best to structure their deception so as to appear truthful and convincing.

Mental Dictionary, Balance, and Emotions - 56

The exact size of the mental dictionary is not known, although it is estimated that there are about 30,000 words in our vocabulary. Research calculates that with an average rate of speech of 150 words per minute, peaking at approximately 300 words per minute, the average speaker has 200—400 milliseconds to select the words they wish to use. Expressed another way:

2 to 5 times a second we have to make the right choice from those 30,000 words. It is estimated that the probability of making the wrong choice is one in a thousand. Formulae make the business of speaking (and that of hearing) easier. When a speaker uses a formula they need to retrieve it from the dictionary instead of building it up from its basic parts. In other words, such expressions exist as whole or partial statements within the speaker's dictionary and need not be built up from scratch on every new occasion.

A story, like most things in life, requires balance. It has been found that a balanced story is suggestive of truth. This balance is shown as:

- Prologue (introduction) 20%
- Event (incident) 50%
- Epilogue (conclusion) 30%

To assist in this determination, draw a border around the criminal incident section and glance at the entire statement to see the lengths of each section. For a more accurate balance, calculate the word count percentage of each section by dividing the total number of words in the statement into the number of words in each section. Examine the word-count percentages of the three sections to determine the lengths of each section. A relatively long prologue may indicate deception. This occurs when the subject is trying to explain why (convince) something happened instead of telling us what (convey) happened.

Significant variations from average sentence length require explanation. A way to do this is to calculate the average sentence length and look for sentences with a large change from the average. Look for excessive descriptors, and change in pronouns and tense. Breaks in logic are indicators of deception. Watch for information balance such as is there too much or too little information. Everything in the statement needs relevance. Everything in the narrative must be relevant to something else in the narrative and the narrative must, overall, be relevant to the episode. The categories of this relevance include time, place, and so forth.

Truthful statements will have more affective statements involved or statements about feelings. In a traumatic event, these emotions will spill out in the epilogue or conclusion of the statement. It is not until a traumatic event concludes that we will see the inclusion of emotion because this is when they occur.

A victim of a quickly occurring traumatic event may not be aware of emotions until the trauma ends. Truthful victims may include specific descriptions of fear, anger, embarrassment, or shock in their conclusions. Because emotions in the conclusion reveal the crime's effect on the writer, the presence of emotions may provide a clue that the event actually was experienced, not fabricated.

A bank robbery getaway driver wrote that she "was nervous and scared" and "heard a gunshot and jumped because it scared me." The descriptions of fear in her written statement indicated that the incident described likely did happen and it did not traumatize her..

A rape victim concluded her statement with: "I was hysterical and locked all the doors." The location of the emotion inclusion is important. During a traumatic event, we will not experience emotion until it is over. This is all part of our autonomic nervous system. In these examples, the trauma of the rape victim was properly in the end while the scared driver included it within.

I am often asked how we can use these strategies in court. Dr Picornell said it best with her advice that reports gathered and constructed using forensic linguistics should not be used as principal evidence in court — for now — but only as supporting evidence.

Transitional Words & Phrases - 57

Using transitional words and phrases helps papers read more smoothly, and at the same time allows the reader to flow more smoothly from one point to the next. Transitions enhance logical organization and understandability and improve the connections between thoughts. They indicate relations, whether within a sentence, paragraph, or paper.

A Comprehensive List of Adverbial Conjunctions and Their Functions

Addition - again, also, then, besides, equally important, finally, first, further, furthermore, in addition, in the first place, last, moreover, next, second, still, as well as, coupled with, in addition, likewise, similarly

Comparison - also, in the same way, likewise, similarly

Concession - granted, naturally, of course

Contrast - although, yet, at the same time, despite that, even so, even though, for all that, however, in contrast, in spite of, instead, nevertheless, though, notwithstanding, on the contrary, on the other hand, otherwise, regardless, still, but, contrast

Emphasis - certainly, indeed, in fact, of course

Example or Illustration - after all, as an illustration, even, for example, for instance, in conclusion, indeed, in fact, in other words, in short, of course, namely, specifically, that is, to illustrate, thus, truly

Summary - altogether, finally, in brief, in conclusion, in other words, in short, in simpler terms, in summary, on the whole, therefore, to put it differently, to summarize

Consequence - accordingly, as a result, consequently, for this reason, for this purpose, hence, otherwise, so then, subsequently, therefore, thus, thereupon, wherefore

Time Sequence – after a while, afterward, again, also, then, as long as, at last, at length, at that time, before, besides, earlier, eventually, finally, formerly, further, furthermore, in addition, in the first place, in the past, last, lately, meanwhile, moreover, next, now, presently, second, shortly, simultaneously, since, so far, soon, still, subsequently, thereafter, too, until, when, for now, later on, simultaneously.

Transitional Words

Time - after, afterward, before, during, earlier, final, first, later, since, meanwhile, then, until

Contrast - however, in contrast, indeed, instead, nevertheless, on the contrary, on the other hand, yet

Result - As a result, because, consequently, on account of, so, then, therefore, thus, chiefly

Addition or Example - also, besides, for example, furthermore, in addition, moreover

It rained on Saturday; therefore, the picnic was canceled

The idea of it rained was connected to the idea of the canceled picnic with the transitional word, therefore

They can both separate and connect ideas

During the break I drank a soda.

During brings the ideas of a break and drinking a soda together.

We went bowling instead of going to the movies.

The transitional word instead contrasts the act of going bowling and the act of going to the movies.

Subordinating Words

Subordinating words connect unequal but related ideas and create time gaps.

Subordinating words include after, although, as if, as long as, because, before, even though, if, in order that, since, so, that, than, though, unless, until, when, whenever, where, wherever, where, whenever, and while.

Examples:

When there is a trusting relationship <u>coupled with</u> positive reinforcement, the partners will be able to overcome difficult situations.

Highway traffic came to a stop <u>as a result</u> of an accident that morning.

The children were very happy. <u>On the other hand</u>, and perhaps more importantly, their parents were very proactive in providing good care.

She scanned the horizon for any sign <u>though</u> in the distance she could not see the surprise coming her way.

Consensus was arrived at by all of the members <u>then</u> we decided to hold off on the vote.

Some friends and I drove up the beautiful coast <u>chiefly</u> to avoid the heat island of the city.

There were a few very talented artists in the class, <u>but</u> for the most part the students only wanted to avoid the alternative course.

The research was presented in a very dry style <u>though</u> was coupled with examples that made the audience tear up.

In their advertising business, saying things directly was not the rule. <u>That is to say</u>, they tried to convey the message subtly though with creativity.

The music had a very retro sound <u>but</u> at the same time incorporated a complex modern rhythm.

She didn't seem willing to sell the car this week, <u>but</u> in any case I don't get paid until the end of the month.

Example 1

"Did you strike Frank?"

Which of the following sentences are more truthful?

- "Me? Hit someone? Really?"
- "Hitting is not something in my nature."
- "No, I didn't hit him. I wasn't even in town."

Note: In the first two statements: neither uses "I" nor denies the act. If the person responding doesn't deny something expressly, don't supply the express denial for them. The first two statements also are referencing in present tense.

Example 2

"Did you steal $150.00 from the register on Monday?"

- "That missing money isn't my fault."
- "Look, drawers are constantly short, this sort of thing happens all the time."
- "No, I didn't steal anything."

In the first 2 statements, the writer has removed the primary verb steal and replaced it with softer verbs; missing and short. In addition, we do not see the confirming pronoun "I."

Statement made by Steven Avery about his meeting with Teresa Halbach, a photographer for an Auto Trader magazine. She was never seen again after the shoot. Her body was found buried on his property.

"Took a picture, collect the money, and say hi. That's about it."

He does not use any pronouns such as "I", "she", or "we" indicating a lack of commitment. He uses present tense verbs describing a past event; "collect the money" and "say hi". He concludes the statement with the phrase "That's about it" which tells us there is more.

Statement Reviews - 58

I mentioned earlier that I find it easier to break a statement down into separate sentences. This can be broken down even further by chances in time, place or segmentation markers. You can number each separate line for identification purposes to assist in the statement dissection. You will see examples of each in the upcoming section of "Some Well Known Cases."

There is another practice used by UK police forces known as SE3R. SE3R is a mnemonic (memory aid) specifying five steps that help get the most from a particular interview statement. SE3R stands for Survey, Extract, Read, Review, and Recall. The process is as follows:

• Survey - the document is skimmed i.e. read through once at a faster than normal pace

• Extract - the document is gone through systematically, with fine-grain detail (using symbols, abbreviations, etc) being extracted and entered on an 'event line' (which becomes known as the 'SE3R' for ease of purpose)

• Read - document is read at normal speed checking the text against the event line information and making any necessary corrections

• Review - document is set aside and the event line and accompanying information is examined thoroughly for completeness, consistency, clarity and so on

• Recall - the processes involved in producing the SE3R will have ensured much of the material entered the long-term memory, thus making it both familiar and easily recalled. If necessary, specific efforts can be made to ensure all of it is memorized.

The SE3R is designed to:

• Help officers collate witness and suspect accounts for evaluation as part of the investigation process

• Act as an aide to planning further investigation and interviews

• To be used as a reference in further interviews

• Help compare one interviewee's account with that of another

• Help identify gaps, contradictions and so on

• Help evaluate the validity and reliability of the reported information

• Help an investigator communicate the results of interviews or statements to key parties like supervisors and prosecutors.

As we can see, this is an interesting process to assist you in developing a time line with the listed facts. If you utilized this method on each statement that has multiple statements, you can determine if each statement is the same. You could utilize SE3R on one side and our syntax breakdown arraignment of time, place, and segmentation markers. I can see how this could be a very effective combined method of keeping everything straight and understanding both who needs to be re-interviewed and what parts of the statements should be readdressed.

In addition to the Statement Analysis process, a set of ten questions (Behavior Analysis) was developed to assist in determining the truthful persons when multiple suspects existed. It is called the VIEW or Statement Questionnaire. These sets of questions are in written format, issued to the subjects under investigation, and designed to focus the investigation based solely on the analysis of what they write. It has also been called the SCAN questionnaire. They follow along four types of questions. Open questions to obtain information, specific questions to force the guilty to lie, projective questions to assess verbal clues, and post interview questions to help identify the truthful persons.

Instructions:
Every word is important and may be checked later on
There is only one chance to write your answers so be sure to think about how you are going to phrase the answers.
Please write your answers as detailed as you can to enable us to understand your answers.
Use pen only, no pencils or typing is allowed.
Write in clear handwriting in order for us to understand them.
You are not to make any corrections. If you feel you need to make a correction, circle the words you would like to change and then write in your correction which will be taken into consideration.

Page 2 – We have reached the conclusion that something has taken place (theft of money, property, etc.). How would you explain this? Please write in detail your ideas that would account for this.

Page 3 – If you were going to conduct the investigation, how would you do it?

Page 4 – List the five most important causes that have created this situation.

Page 5 – Describe in detail your work day on (date), covering the time you came into work until the time you ended your day or your entire day from waking to sleep.

Page 6 – A) It does not mean you are right and whatever you say is confidential, if you had to suspect someone of doing this, who would you suspect and why?
B) Who would you least suspect and why?
C) What do you think should happen to the person that did this when they are caught?
D) Would you give them a second chance?
E) Do you believe this was deliberate or an accident?

Page 7 – Do you know for sure who did this?
A) Did you do this?
B) How do you think the investigation will turn out concerning you, and whether you did this?

Page 8 – Would you like to change any of the information that you gave us?
A) Is there anything we did not ask you about this that you think is important for us to know?

Page 9 – Post Interview – How do you feel now that you have completed the form?
A) Should we believe your answers?
B) If your answer to the last question is yes, give us one reason why?
C) What would you say if it was later determined you lied on this form?
D) What were your emotions while filling out the form?
E) Were you afraid?
F) If you were asked to pay for _____ how much would you be willing to pay?

To evaluate the questionnaire, the last page, post-interview is reviewed first. If the subject answered "yes" to question A (Should we believe your answers?) and then answered any other question with:
I told the truth.
I did not lie
I did not do the crime
Place the suspect in the truthful group. Attach all others to the problem group.
For the problem group, the questionnaire is reissued except with a change to question 2 – We have reached the conclusion you have not told us everything you know about the (crime). How would you explain this? Please write in detail your ideas that would account for this.
Having to answer the questionnaire is irritating to truthful persons, and they are more likely to answer question A part 9 on the last page that we should believe their answers and allow themselves elimination by answering at least one of the other questions with:
I told the truth.
I did not lie
I did not do the crime
It is also important to see if there is a strong focus of the group to blame someone for the crime and eliminate a person.

Scenario –
Page 2 – Miscount or misplaced, I can see missing one day and find the next.
3 – More attention downstairs, people watching the door more closely.
4 – Watching the door, check for alarms, check in and out.

5 – Do you know who took – no
Did you – No, of course no
Who do you suspect – no one
Who would you least suspect – everyone the same
What should happen to them – the boss's job
Second chance – bosses job
Any reason evidence turn up against you – I don't think so
Stolen or misplaced – misplaced or stolen by customers
How do you feel – sad
Should we believe you - it depends on you, your opinion
If yes why – because this is my answer
What if it turned out it was you – no reason to believe this

Epilogue

I understand that much of this material can be confusing. There is a lot to cover in a short amount of time. Your comprehension of the techniques will fade a little each day without review and use. There is a forgetting curve. The forgetting curve works on the principle that we forget remembered topics continually. It occurs faster in the beginning as our brains make room for ideas introduced. In fact, by the end of the first day after learning new information, we will lose 50-80 percent of that information unless reviewed. However, by reviewing the learned information within 24 hours, you have told your brain that the material is important and needs remembering. Your brain responds by not allowing this memory from being pushed out too quickly. One week later, if you will review the material again, you are sealing it within your own mental computer. Afterwards, a review every 30 days should suffice for you to remember the information well.

As with everything in our toolbox, we must use them or they begin to oxidize and rust. None of these techniques will work 100% of the time, on 100% of the people, in 100% of the situations. Therefore, to become an effective interviewer, you must be able to recognize when one technique is failing and be prepared to attempt another with the same confidence. This requires study and use. Some people excel at lying and you must be just as good at their detection.

As I said in the beginning, take as many courses that are available to you and read as many books as possible on these topics. If you can learn just one thing from any book or class, it was a great book or class. You have been able to add another tool to your toolbox. The more tools in the toolbox, the better prepared you become for any task.

If you did not notice, I intentionally made my Prologue (introduction) and Epilogue (conclusion) about the same size to give this book balance. It is a reminder to not forget that every story must have a beginning, a body, and an end.

The End of the Shift

I always finish my books with a chapter called, "The End of the Shift." This is the pentacle of each day. This is the time each day, either after your shift has concluded or your career ends. It is the most important day for the rest of your life. Both measure success mentally and physically when our shift is over. I truly believe that this outcome rest squarely on our own shoulders. There will be events that will happen by the grace of God; however, we do control the outcome of most. The best we can do each day is plan, prepare, pay attention, and react.

Stress is the root cause of most of our physical and mental ailments. Confrontation is the leading cause of stress. Ours is a profession of confrontation that can rarely last more than a few decades. It is in the street where conflict occurs and it is through asshole confrontation that most of our greatest stressors originate.

Society is at war with itself. America is embroiled in a war, not in the Middle East, but here on our streets. As law enforcement officers, you are the front line troops. The difference is in how the war is fought. There are few winners and many losers. The best we can achieve is the maintenance of basic order. There will always be bad guys and a need for police officers. The differences are occurring in the upcoming generations whose belief systems are formed by a media and leaders who continue to meld distorted ideas of truths and freedoms.

With all that troubles our society today, I watch in amazement the topics that have become critical to the sheep of society like drug legalization and gun control. It is an interesting dichotomy of people

419

and their generations who actually believe these are the pressing topics of the day. The one that bothers me the most is the belief that drug legalization will make any positive changes to our country or society. It is just as sad that the majority, who could stand up and say "enough is enough" and put an end to all of these ridiculous topics, choose to sit idle. Yet as we have seen over and over, the mainstream fails to stand up for itself and avoids that great stressor; confrontation. As Col. David Grossman likes to put it, there are the sheep, the wolves, and the sheepdogs. The sheep make up for about 98% of the total population while the other 2% is divided between the sheepdogs and the wolves. The sheep do not like the sheepdogs, but they have a clear understanding that when the wolves are around, the sheep want the sheepdogs close by. The sheep ultimately become victims twice; once when they are attacked by the wolves and again while living in the constant fear of another attack.

If you have decided upon a career in law enforcement, you must learn to deal with confrontation from both the sheep and the wolves. A strain exist that will wear you down over time. Stand true to your principles which brought you here to begin with and help teach others how to stand again. Only collectively shall we ever become the majority that we have always been.

In the end, when you are tired and ready to give it all up, it will be your family who is there waiting for you. The day after you leave, the job has already forgotten you. Life goes on no matter how important you think you were. Did you make a difference? All of the things you accomplished throughout your career did make a difference to people you will never know. Your actions saved someone somewhere. No one may ever know this, but you. I said it at the beginning and will say it again in the end. The job entails more than most realize and produces a brotherhood that few understand. We will all feel that self-satisfaction, at the end of the shift.

Bibliography

Adams, Susan (April 2003). COMMUNICATION UNDER STRESS: INDICATORS OF VERACITY AND DECEPTION IN WRITTEN NARRATIVES.

Assessment of Optimal Interrogation Approaches.

Assessment Criteria Indicative of Deception (ACID): An Integrated System of Investigative Interviewing and Detecting Deception; KEVIN COLWELL, CHERYL K. HISCOCK-ANISMAN, AMINA MEMON, LAURA TAYLOR and JESSICA PREWETT; Journal of Investigative Psychology and Offender Profiling, J. Investig. Psych. Offender Profi l. 4: 167–180 (2007).

Blandon-Gitlin, Iris; Pezdek, Kathy; Lindsay, D. Stephen; Hagen, Lisa; Criteria-based Content Analysis of True and Suggested Accounts of Events; APPLIED COGNITIVE PSYCHOLOGY Appl. Cognit. Psychol. 23: 901–917 (2009) Published online 11 August 2008 in Wiley InterScience

Buckley, Wendy; Adult ESOL Instructor; November 2010; Overview of "What Every Body Is Saying by Joe Navarro, 2008.

Colwell, Kevin, Hiscock-Anisman, Memon, Amina, Taylor, Laura, Prewett, Jessica; Assessment Criteria Indicative of Deception (ACID): An Integrated System of Investigative Interviewing and Detecting Deception; Journal of Investigative Psychology and Offender Profiling

J. Investig. Psych. Offender Profi l. 4: 167–180 (2007)

Conducting Effective Interviews; AICPA Forensic and Valuation Services Section

Coram, Robert (2002). Boyd, The Fighter Pilot Who Changed the Art of War, Little, Brown and Company.

Criteria-based Content Analysis of True and Suggested Accounts of Events; IRIS BLANDO´ N-GITLIN, KATHY PEZDEK2,

D. STEPHEN LINDSAY and LISA HAGEN; Published online 11 August 2008 in Wiley InterScience.

CRITERIA-BASED CONTENT ANALYSIS (CBCA) IN STATEMENT CREDIBILITY ASSESSMENT; Verónica Godoy-Cervera and Lorenzo Higueras, Papeles del Psicólogo, 2005. Vol. 26, pp. 92-98.

Dennis, Andrew. Officer Down! A practical Tactical Guide to Surviving Injury in the Street. Kendall Hunt. 2013. Print

Detecting Deception; Dr. Mike Aamodt, Radford University, presentation

DOD Defense Academy for Credibility Assessment; Final Report May 2007,

DOD Polygraph Department, Seeking the Truth, June 1991

Ekman, Paul, Telling Lies, Berkley Books 1987.

F. Borelli, "Twenty-one Feet Is Way Too Close," Law Enforcement Trainer, July/August 2001, 12-15

False Confessions: Causes, Consequences, and Implications; Richard A. Leo, PhD, JD; The Journal of the American Academy of Psychiatry and the Law, 2009.

Fast, Julius (1973). The Body Language of Sex, Power, and Aggression. M Evans and Company Inc.

FBI Law Enforcement Bulletin; January 2008, Volume 77, Number 1; Interview Clues by Vincent A. Sandoval

FBI Law Enforcement Bulletin; October 2004, Volume 73, Number 10: Are You Telling Me the Truth? Indicators of Veracity in Written Statements By Susan H. Adams, Ph.D., and John P. Jarvis, Ph.D

FBI Law Enforcement Bulletin; January 2008, Volume 77, Number 1; Text Bridges and the Micro-Action Interview by John R. Schafer

Final Report, May 2007, Assessment of Optimal Interrogation Approaches, MIPR#H9C101-G-0051. The Department of Defense, Defense Academy for Credibility Assessment

Givens, David G. 2009. The Nonverbal Dictionary of Gestures, Signs & Body Language Cues. Spokane: Center for Nonverbal Studies (http://www.center-for-nonverbal-studies.org/6101.html)

Horvath, E, Jayne, B., and Buckley, J., "Differentiation of Truthful and Deceptive Criminal Suspects in Behavior Analysis Interviews,"Journal of Forensic Sciences, JFSCA, Vol. 39, No. 3, May 1994, pp. 793-807

H. Stefan Bracha, M.D., Tyler C. Ralston, M.A., Jennifer M. Matsukawa, M.A., National Center for PTSD, Department of Veterans Affairs, Pacific Islands Health Care System, Spark M. Matsunaga Medical Center, Honolulu, Hawaii, Andrew E. Williams, M.A., Department of Psychology, University of Hawaii at Manoa, Honolulu, Hawaii, and Adam S. Bracha, B.A., Biomedical-Research Consultant, Honolulu, Hawaii, Does "Fight or Flight" Need Updating?

Jaume Masip , Siegfried L. Sporer , Eugenio Garrido & Carmen Herrero (2005):
The detection of deception with the reality monitoring approach: a review of the empirical evidence, Psychology, Crime & Law, 11:1, 99-122

Knapp, M.L., Hart, R.P., and Dennis, H.S. 1974. An exploration of deception as a communication construct. Human Communication Research, 1, 15-29.

Lakoff, G. 1972. Hedges: A study in meaning criteria and the logic of fuzzy concepts. In 4 7 Papers from the 8th Regional Meeting, Chicago Linguistic Society

Learning To Listen, Facilitator Guide; Second Edition;by HRDQ

Leo, Richard A., False Confessions: Causes, Consequences, and Implications, J Am Acad Psychiatry Law 37:332–43, 2009

Lying Words: Predicting Deception From Linguistic Styles; Matthew L. Newman, James W. Pennebaker,; Diane S. Berry; Jane M. Richards

Madden, Timothy J, Sgt CSP (2006). Investigative Interview Techniques.

Matsumoto, David; Sung Hwang; Hyi; Skinner, Lisa; and Frank, Mark. Evaluating Truthfulness and Detecting Deception

McClish, Mark (2011). 10 Easy Ways To Spot A Liar: The best techniques of Statement Analysis, Nonverbal Communication and Handwriting Analysis.

Miller, Laurence, Personality-guided interview and interrogation, Practical psychology for law enforcement investigators

National Research Council. The Polygraph and Lie Detection . Washington, DC: The National Academies Press, 2003.

Navarro, Joe (2008). What Every BODY is Saying: An Ex-FBI Agent's Guide to Speed-Reading People, William Morrow Paperbacks

Newman, M. L., Pennebaker, J. W., Berry, D. S. and J. M. Richards. 2003. Lying words: predicting deception from linguistic styles. Personality and Social Psychology Bulletin. 29, 665-675.

Ost, James, Aldert Vrij, Alan Costall & Ray Bull. Crashing memories and reality monitoring: Distinguishing between perceptions, imaginations and 'false memories.' Department of Psychology, University of Portsmouth, Portsmouth, Hampshire.

Patrick, Urey W. and Hall, John C. In Defense of Self and Others—Issues, Facts and Fallacies; The Realities of Law Enforcement's Use of Force. Carolina Academic Press. 2005, 2010. Print

Personality-guided interview and interrogation; Practical psychology for law enforcement investigators By Laurence Miller, PhD.

Picornell, Isabell, 2013. THE FLEXIBLE LIAR: A STRATEGY FOR DECEPTION DETECTION IN WRITTEN WITNESS STATEMENTS

Picornell, Isabell, 2013. Cues to Deception in a Textual Narrative Context

Pitfalls and Opportunities in Nonverbal and Verbal Lie Detection, Aldert Vrij, Pär Anders Granhag, and Stephen Porter; Psychological Science in the Public Interest; 11(3) 89–121.

Porter, Wayne. Serial Killer presentation.

Protective Intelligence and Threat Assessment: A Guide for State and Local Law Enforcement Officials, by Robert A. Fein and Bryan Vossekuil, May 1998, USDOJ

Reading Between the Lies; Dr. Paul Ekman; September, October, November, December, 2009 Volume 2, number4.

Renaud, Ray, COMPARISON! COMPARISON! COMPARISON!

Ritual and Signature in Serial Sexual Homicide, Louis B. Schlesinger, PhD, Martin Kassen, MA, V. Blair Mesa, MA and Anthony J. Pinizzotto, PhD. J Am Acad Psychiatry Law 38:2:239-246 (June 2010), Copyright © 2013 by the American Academy of Psychiatry and the Law.

Sapir, A. 1987. *Scientific Content Analysis(SCAN)*. Laboratory of Scientific Interrogation. Phoenix, AZ.

Sapir, A. 1995. *The View Guidebook: Verbal Inquiry – the Effective Witness*. Laboratory of Scientific Interrogation. Phoenix, AZ.

Serial Killers; Dr. Mike Aamodt, Radford University. Presentation.

Schafer, John A. 2007. Content Analysis of Written Statements

Schollum, Mary. September 2005, Investigative interviewing: THE LITERATURE, Office of the Commissioner of Police, PO Box 3017 Wellington NZ

Serial Killer Statistics; Aamodt, M. G. (2012, September 9). Serial killer statistics..

Sheppard, Peter (March 2009). Transforming the Mind.

Statement Analysis Presentation, Patrick J Kelly.

Techniques and Controversies in the Interrogation of Suspects: The Artful Practice versus the Scientific Study; Allison D. Redlich, Christian Meissner; J. L. Skeem, K. Douglas, & S. Lilienfeld (Eds.), Psychological science in the courtroom: Controversies and consensus.

The FBI Law Enforcement Bulletin, March 2006, Volume 75 Number 3.

Van Horne, Patrick and Riley, Jason A. Left of Bang. Black Irish Entertainment LLC. 2014. Print

Varnell, Steven (2010). "Criminal Interdiction", Dog Ear Publishing.

Varnell, Steven (2012). "Tactical Survival", Steven Varnell Publishing.

Verification and Implementation of Language Based Deception Indicators in Civil and Criminal Narrative; Bachenko, , Joan; Fitzpatrick, Eileen; Schonwetter, Michael; Proceedings of the 22nd International Conference Linguistics, 2008.

Verónica Godoy-Cervera and Lorenzo Higueras, CRITERIA-BASED CONTENT ANALYSIS (CBCA) IN STATEMENT, Papeles del Psicólogo, 2005. Vol. 26, pp. 92-98 CREDIBILITY ASSESSMENT

Vrij, Aldert (2007). Interviewing to Detect Deception: Full Research Report.
ESRC End of Award Report, RES-000-23-0292. Swindon: ESRC

Vrij, Aldert (2006). Statement Validity Assessment

Willis, Gordon (1994). "Cognitive Interviewing and Questionnaire Design: A
Training Manual," (Working Paper #7, National Center for Health Statistics,
Cognitive Interviewing

U.S. Department of Justice, Federal Bureau of Investigation, Firearms Training Unit, Handgun Wounding Factors and Effectiveness (Quantico, VA, July 14, 1989).

Web Sites

1 - http://www.fbi.gov/ucr/ucr.htm. 01Aug. 2010

2 - http://en.wikipedia.org/wiki/Police. 28 July 2010

3 - http://www.mattbraun.com/published.htm. 01 June 2009

4 - http://bjs.ojp.usdoj.gov/index.cfm?ty=tp&tid=702. 26 June 2010

5 - http://www.script-o-rama.com/movie_scripts/u/untouchables-script-transcript-david-   mamet.html. 01 Aug. 2010

6 - http://www-fars.nhtsa.dot.gov/Main/index.aspx. 26 July 2010

7 - http://www.odmp.org/. 02 Aug 2010

8 - http://www.fbi.gov/ucr/ucr.htm. 01Aug. 2010

9 - http://www.fbi.gov/ucr/ucr.htm. 01Aug. 2010

10 - http://www.forcescience.org/. 28 July 2010

13   - http://caselaw.lp.findlaw.com/scripts/getcase.pl?court=us&vol=000&invol=U20005. 04 Aug. 2010

14 - http://www.fbi.gov/ucr/ucr.htm. 01Aug. 2010

15 - http://smokingwithstyle.com/blunt_rolling.htm. 02 Aug 2010

16 - http://www.forcescience.org/. 28 July 2010

17 - http://www.batonrougetoday.com/2010/07/03/state-trooper-shot-during-traffic-stop-on-i-10/ , 10 July 2010

18 - http://www.fbi.gov/ucr/ucr.htm. 01Aug. 2010

19 - http://www.fbi.gov/ucr/ucr.htm. 01Aug. 2010

20 - http://www.justice.gov/dea/index.htm. 03 Aug 2010

21 - http://www.portlandonline.com/police/index.cfm?c=38594. 02 June 2010

22 - http://articles.sun-sentinel.com/2009-10-30/news/sfl-florida-cuban-pot2-103109_1_cuban-drug-trafficking-organizations-growhouses-arrests. 20 July 2010

23 - http://articles.sun-sentinel.com/2009-10-30/news/sfl-florida-cuban-pot2-103109_1_cuban-drug-trafficking-organizations-growhouses-arrests . 20 July 2010

24 - http://sparkreport.net/2009/07/5-good-places-to-hide-marijuana-in-a-vehicle/. 28 June 2010

25 - http://www.heroinhelper.com/user/acquire/hiding_drugs.shtml. 28 June 2010

26 - http://www.drugsandbooze.com/showthread.php?p=325189. 28 June 2010

27 - http://www.fmcsa.dot.gov/rules-regulations/truck/driver/hos/fmcsa-guide-to-hos.PDF. 30 July 2010

28 - http://www.truckinfo.net/trucking/stats.htm. 30 July 2010

29 - Broward County Commission on Substance Abuse, United Way, 2008.

30 - http://www.deadiversion.usdoj.gov/pubs/brochures/pharmguide.htm. 11Aug. 2010

31 - http://www.nlm.nih.gov/medlineplus/prescriptiondrugabuse.html. 11 Aug. 2010

32 - http://www.globalsecurity.org/military/ops/iraq_casualties.htm. 28 Aug. 2010

33 - http://www.odmp.org/. 28 Aug 2010

34 - http://www.tearsofacop.com/police/articles/constant.html 22 Aug. 2010

35 – http://www.heavybadge.com/efstress.html 22 Aug. 2010

http://www.nlm.nih.gov/medlineplus/ency/article/000039.htm

http://www.spyingforlying.com/2012/08/research-lyings-telltale-cluster.html

http://www.blifaloo.com/info/microexpressions.php

http://www.statementanalysis.com/cases/

http://www.lsiscan.com/reports.htm

http://content.yudu.com/Library/A17lly/BodyLanguageJULIUS FA/resources/124.htm

http://www.k-state.edu/actr/2010/12/20/suspect-interrogation-communication-strategies-and-key-personality-constructs-jessica-heuback/default.htm

http://www.footjax.com/Prop.html

http://crimeandclues.com/2013/03/02/statement-analysis-what-do-suspects-words-really-reveal/5/

http://en.wikipedia.org/wiki/False_confession

http://i-sight.com/investigation/7-ways-to-get-at-truth-in-workplace-investigation/

http://blog.al.com/birmingham-news-stories/2009/12/pelham_officers_slaying_baffle.html

http://www.tuscaloosanews.com/article/20091215/NEWS/912 149930?p=1&tc=pg

http://officerphilipdavis.com/

http://en.wikipedia.org/wiki/Peripheral_vision

http://www.psychologytoday.com/experts/joe-navarro-ma

http://www.psychologytoday.com/blog/beyond-words/201110/space-invaders-the-republican-debate

http://www.nlpu.com/Articles/artic14.htm

http://www.lsiscan.com/reports.htm

http://crimeandclues.com/2013/03/02/statement-analysis-what-do-suspects-words-really-reveal/5/

http://seamusoriley.blogspot.com/

http://www.hwprosandcons.com/Statement_Analysis.html

http://www.psychologytoday.com/blog/let-their-words-do-the-talking/201103/text-bridges

http://www2.fbi.gov/publications/leb/1996/oct964.txt

http://www.forcescience.org/fsnews/245.html

http://www.forcescience.org/fsnews/260.html

http://www.forcescience.org/fsnews/258.html

http://www.forcescience.org/fsnews/267.html

http://www.forcescience.org/fsnews/262.html

http://www.forcescience.org/fsnews/243.html

http://www.forcescience.org/fsnews/239.html

http://www.forcescience.org/fsnews/224.html

http://www.jhsph.edu/news/news-releases/2013/pollack-swedler-police-homicides.html

http://www.statementanalysis.com/cases/

Acknowledgements

The very first I need to thank are the readers themselves. Most are the professionals who keep our society safe from evil. The sheepdogs! Everywhere I have lectured has been a delight and the feedback on the books and classes, fantastic. Thank You All!

I have to give thanks to my wonderful and patient wife. She has learned this patience from the years I was on the job and now with my passion to continue to learn and teach. For my son who is among the many standing the wall and daughter who has found her passion in teaching and now, writing as well.

To the many friends who had to listen without complaint to my ideas for this book and for providing their insights. On a more positive note, after all they have endured they are still my friends. Thanks. All of the information and ideas contained here are my own, but was collected off the backs of those who walked the walk before and after me.

Thanks to all of my former partners from law enforcement, mostly retired and hopefully enjoying this ride as much as I am.

Thank you, God, for all these days and may you all be blessed.

About the Author

Steven Varnell is a law enforcement-training specialist who retired after serving over 29 years with the Florida Highway Patrol. During his career, he worked Patrol, Field Training, Criminal Interdiction, SRT, and K9. He instructed Firearms, Baton, Felony Stops, and Criminal Interdiction Courses. As an adjunct instructor for the MCTFT Program at St. Petersburg College, he taught Highway Interdiction, Officer Safety, Patrol, and Interviews and Interrogation classes for law enforcement agencies throughout the country. He was a part of FHP's criminal interdiction pilot program, which began in 1983, where he served in interdiction and K9 duties for 27 year making him one of the most experienced interdiction officers in the country.

Steve is the author of *Criminal Interdiction, Tactical Survival, and Behavior Analysis and Interviewing Techniques (BAIT), and Statement Analysis, An ISS Workbook,* four widely acclaimed books available through bookstores everywhere. He is a widely sought instructor and speaker in the fields of Interviewing, Interrogations, and Officer Safety. Steve developed a lecture company called Interdiction and Survival Strategies (ISS), where with a former partner; together they have established a new approach to criminal based training for all levels of officers. You can reach Steve at criminalinterdiction@live.com. For more information and training information on the ISS group, go to isspolicetraining.com.